The Twelfth-Century Renewal
of Latin Metaphysics

Medieval metaphysics is usually bound up with Scholasticism and its influential exemplars, such as Aquinas and Duns Scotus. However, the foundations of the new discipline, which would reshape the entire edifice of Western philosophy, were established well before the rise of Scholasticism through an encounter with the Arabic philosophical tradition. *The Twelfth-Century Renewal of Latin Metaphysics* uncovers what rightly should be considered the first attempt to construct a metaphysical system in the Latin Middle Ages in the work of Dominicus Gundissalinus.

A philosopher and translator who worked in Toledo in the second half of the twelfth century, Gundissalinus elaborated a fascinating metaphysics grounded on a substantive revision of the Latin tradition through the work of Avicenna, Ibn Gabirol, and al-Farabi. Based on a series of structural dualities of being that express the ontological difference between the caused universe and the uncaused creator who lies beyond any duality, it was to prove original and far-reaching. With Gundissalinus we witness the first Latin appropriation of crucial doctrines, like the modal distinction between necessary and possible existence, formal pluralism, and universal hylomorphism. This study thoroughly analyses Gundissalinus's revisionary interpretation of his Latin and Arabic sources, paying particular attention to the "unlikely blending" of Ibn Gabirol's universal hylomorphism and Avicenna's modal ontology which became the cornerstone of his metaphysics.

Institute of Medieval
and Early Modern Studies

DURHAM PUBLICATIONS
IN MEDIEVAL AND RENAISSANCE STUDIES
General Editor Professor Nicole Reinhardt
Deputy Editor Professor Giles Gasper

DURHAM MEDIEVAL AND RENAISSANCE TEXTS AND TRANSLATIONS
Series Editors Professor John McKinnell, Dr David Ashurst,
and Professor Neil Cartlidge

DURHAM MEDIEVAL AND RENAISSANCE
MONOGRAPHS AND ESSAYS
Series Editors Professor Luke Sunderland and Professor Stefano Cracolici

GENERAL EDITORIAL BOARD
Dr Paul Bibire
Professor James Carley
Dr Robert Carver
Professor Richard Gameson
Professor Andy Orchard
Dr Toby Osborne
Professor Michael Prestwich
Professor Corinne Saunders
Professor Sarah Semple
Professor Jane H. Taylor

DURHAM MEDIEVAL AND RENAISSANCE
MONOGRAPHS AND ESSAYS 6

The Twelfth-Century Renewal of Latin Metaphysics
Gundissalinus's Ontology of Matter and Form

NICOLA POLLONI

Institute of Medieval and Early Modern Studies
Durham University

Pontifical Institute of Mediaeval Studies
Toronto

Library and Archives Canada Cataloguing in Publication

Title: The twelfth-century renewal of Latin metaphysics : Gundissalinus's ontology of matter and form / Nicola Polloni.
Other titles: Gundissalinus's ontology of matter and form
Names: Polloni, Nicola, author. | Pontifical Institute of Mediaeval Studies, publisher. | University of Durham. Institute of Medieval and Early Modern Studies, publisher.
Series: Durham medieval and Renaissance monographs and essays ; 6.
Description: Series statement: Durham medieval and Renaissance monographs and essays ; 6 | Includes bibliographical references and index.
Identifiers: Canadiana 20200151398 | ISBN 9780888448651 (hardcover)
Subjects: LCSH: Gundissalinus, Dominicus, active 12th century. | LCSH: Philosophy, Medieval.
Classification: LCC B765.G984 P65 2020 | DDC 189–dc23

© 2020
Institute of Medieval and Early Modern Studies,
Durham University

Pontifical Institute of Mediaeval Studies
59 Queen's Park Crescent East
Toronto, Ontario M5S 2C4
Canada
www.pims.ca

PRINTED IN CANADA

Contents

Preface   viii

Seeding Transitions: A Historical Introduction   1

CHAPTER ONE
Pioneering Transformations: Gundissalinus's Philosophical Reflection   20
    Problems of Attribution   *20*
    Unities   *30*
    Souls   *37*
    Sciences   *47*
    Cosmogenesis   *54*

CHAPTER TWO
Reshaping Frameworks: Gundissalinus and the Latin Tradition   77
    Aetas Boethiana   *78*
    Decoding *Timaeus*   *88*
    God and Numbers   *100*
    Disordered Universes   *110*
    Furnaces of Being   *128*

CHAPTER THREE
Rooting Reality: Gundissalinus and Ibn Gabirol   144
    A Hylomorphic and Hypostatic Universe   *147*
    Hylomorphism Without Act and Potency   *165*
    Psychological Hylomorphism   *177*
    Structures of Functional Dualities   *190*

vi | *Contents*

CHAPTER FOUR

Appraising Existence: Gundissalinus, Avicenna, and Ibn Daud   210
    Modalities of Existence   *210*
    Theoretical Crossroads   *225*
    Gundissalinus's Ontology of Possible Being   *232*
    Contrasting Hylomorphisms   *244*
    Matter for Bodies   *253*

CONCLUSION

Unity into Duality   263

Bibliography   272
Index   313

We are characters in plots, without the compression and numinous sheen. Our lives, examined carefully in all their affinities and links, abound with suggestive meaning, with themes and involute turnings we have not allowed ourselves to see completely. He would show the secret symmetries in a nondescript life.

Don DeLillo, *Libra* (1988)

Preface

This book is about a curious philosopher who was active in Toledo in the second half of the twelfth century. Although he was one of the most important figures of that century, his name—like that of the main character of a famous British television drama—usually prompts a simple yet surprising question: "Gundissalinus Who?" Outside the boundaries of specialised knowledge and research, this intriguing thinker is unknown. Within those boundaries, scholars have sometimes underestimated both the relevance and originality of Gundissalinus's production. Recent scholarship has contributed to a profound shift in outlook, pointing out many relevant doctrines which were elaborated by Gundissalinus. This study contributes to this process of Gundissalinus's re-discovery, with a philosophical and historical analysis of his metaphysical reflection in order to display its profound originality and pioneering contribution to the course of medieval philosophy.

Dominicus Gundissalinus may be rightly considered as an inaugural figure in a paradigm shift that would characterise the passage from the twelfth to the thirteenth century. A first peculiarity of Gundissalinus is his twofold activity. He was a philosopher, but also and crucially a translator from Arabic into Latin, and was active in the unique context which was Toledo in the second half of the twelfth century. Geographically located at the centre of the Iberian Peninsula, Toledo was a cultural melting pot of Muslims, Jews, and Christians, both before and after its taking by the Castilian army in 1085. As former capital of the Visigoths, one of the most influential cities under the Omayyad caliphate, and see of the primate of Spain, Toledo benefitted in terms of wealth, importance, and relative social peace. As a consequence of the Almohad invasion of al-Andalus, thousands of migrants had no choice but to flee from southern Spain up north, finding a haven in Toledo. These refugees were often learned people, and their presence in Castile had a most fortunate outcome. It could even be said that the migratory crisis in al-Andalus laid the bases for the establishment of relevant clusters of translators and translations in Toledo. These clusters contributed to impressive advancements of knowledge in medieval Europe.

As for Gundissalinus, the migratory crisis also had personal repercussions. Among the people fleeing from al-Andalus was a Jewish philosopher and historian, Abraham ibn Daud. His decision to move north from al-Andalus – rather than south, as Maimonides did – was to be crucial for what later happened in Gundissalinus's life. Ibn Daud's aim to make the works of Avicenna available to the Latins, and Archbishop John II's acceptance of this goal, indeed required Gundissalinus to move from Segovia to Toledo in order to collaborate with Ibn Daud on this revolutionary project. This fact is of the utmost importance. Together with a third member of the group, Johannes Hispanus, Ibn Daud and Gundissalinus would constitute something more than a simple translating team. As Charles Burnett has remarked, they would create a sort of *philosophical circle* where the Arabic texts were not only translated but also discussed, interpreted, assimilated, and criticised. Crucially, they wrote philosophical treatises in which Arabic sources are used and developed in different and often divergent ways. They pollinated each other's reflections with their own perspectives, in an intriguing, fascinating, and unique kind of collaboration.

Gundissalinus's philosophical production was nourished by the translations made by his team, and his activity as translator was inseparable from his philosophical reflection. His philosophical thought is bound to two different worlds. On the one hand, Gundissalinus was philosophically trained in the Latin tradition. On the other hand, Gundissalinus found answers to the philosophical problems originating from that Latin training in the Arabic tradition of authors and texts which he himself translated.

This study is articulated into a series of encounters and contrasts. Rather than focusing on a thematic approach privileging the most relevant features with which Gundissalinus engaged, this book examines Gundissalinus's appropriation and rejection of (or, more often, tactical silence regarding) influential doctrines author by author. However, not every author or every source used by Gundissalinus will be considered, for the reason of one main consideration. The main theoretical synthesis Gundissalinus proposed (or attempted) was a fusion between universal hylomorphism and modal ontology. Accordingly, the main focus of this study is Gundissalinus's recourse to Ibn Gabirol and Avicenna as eminent metaphysical sources. It is my conviction – a conviction that will hopefully be shared by the reader once she arrives at the end of this book – that this process of amalgamation was influenced by Gundissalinus's colleague, Abraham ibn Daud. In addition, the originality of Gundissalinus's thought cannot be fully understood without a consideration of some main aspects which he inherited from the Latin philosophical tradition – Boethius, Calcidius, and Chartres. The organisation of this study follows this branching of problems and concerns.

The historical introduction, "Seeding Transitions," explores the available data concerning Gundissalinus, sketching his biography and examining the cultural environment of the Toledan translation activities in the second half of the twelfth century. The biographical context of Gundissalinus's reflection is of primary importance to correctly understand not only the originality, but also the historical reasons for and dimension of his philosophical thought.

The first chapter, "Pioneering Transformations," thoroughly examines the treatises authored by Gundissalinus. After a short analysis of doubtfully attributed works, the chapter discusses Gundissalinus's first work, *De unitate et uno*. This is a rather short treatise, focused on the metaphysical concept of unity and oneness, and based almost exclusively on Ibn Gabirol's *Fons vitae*. Gundissalinus assimilates and exposits some main features of Gabirolian ontology and cosmology, doctrines that he would later problematise, starting with his *De anima*, his psychological treatise. Through constant recourse to three main sources – Ibn Gabirol, Avicenna, and Qusta ibn Luqa – Gundissalinus's *De anima* addresses some central problems concerning the philosophical consideration of the soul, from the question of its origin to its cognitive and intellectual powers. In *De divisione philosophiae*, Gundissalinus aimed at proposing a hierarchical theory of the division of science able to facilitate the insertion of the new sciences made available by the translation movement. Finally, *De processione mundi* is Gundissalinus's most important metaphysical treatise. The explicit purpose of the treatise is the analysis of the *invisibilia Dei*, the secret and invisible aspects of God, which can be known only through the examination of their effects. The ontology therein examined is grounded on two main doctrines: universal hylomorphism and modal ontology. Gundissalinus describes the origin of the universe through the progressive stratification of forms into matter as the actualisation of ontological possibilities.

The second chapter, "Reshaping Frameworks," is centred on Gundissalinus's Latin philosophical groundwork, examining some of the main influences he received from authors working in the twelfth century and the main *auctoritates* of the time. In particular, a first part of the chapter engages with Boethius's ontology and Calcidius's development of the theory of the three principles, with some references to his speculative method of *compositio* and *resolutio*. A second part of the chapter is focused on Thierry of Chartres and William of Conches, examining in particular their theories of the Holy Trinity and the impact their reflections appear to have had on Gundissalinus. This examination is followed by a discussion of a highly controversial doctrine: the theory of primordial chaos. Gundissalinus criticises this cosmogonic account using a text by Hugh of St Victor, possibly under the influence of William of Conches. Finally, a third part of the chapter analyses the indebtedness of Gundissalinus to Hermann of Carinthia. Gundissalinus used Hermann's *De essentiis* throughout *De processione mundi*, reelaborating Hermann's doctrine of cosmogonic causality and linking it to doctrines of Ibn Gabirol and Avicenna. At the same time, though, Hermann's perspective is perhaps the farthest away from Gundissalinus's. While the former is still based on twelfth-century reflections grounded on the *Timaeus*, the latter is already approaching thirteenth-century Aristotelianism, even though it is without a substantial contribution from Aristotle.

The third chapter, "Rooting Reality," examines the pivotal influence *Fons vitae* had on Gundissalinus's reflection. Ibn Gabirol is the first *auctoritas* Gundissalinus relied upon while writing his first work, *De unitate et uno*. An examination of Ibn Gabirol's complex and intricate ontology shows how the perspective presented by the *Fons vitae* has some problematic implications. These problems are inherited by Gundissalinus, who first accepted Ibn Gabirol's hylomorphic theory and cosmology. Progressively, though, Gundissalinus detaches himself from these problematic features, introducing some important developments to his hylomorphism in the *De anima*, before abandoning Gabirolian cosmology altogether and reshaping his ontology in *De processione mundi*.

Gundissalinus's detachment from Ibn Gabirol appears to be a meaningful consequence of his encounter with Avicenna. The fourth and final chapter, "Appraising Existence," is focused on this crucial philosophical connection between these two authors, and the influence played by Abraham ibn Daud. Gundissalinus developed Avicenna's philosophy to amend many cosmological, ontological, and even psychological outcomes derived from Ibn Gabirol's reflection. The outcome of this attitude is the formulation of a quite peculiar set of philosophical positions. While Gundissalinus abandoned some of the doctrines espoused in the *Fons vitae*, he restructured his thought without forsaking universal hylomorphism, which is inadmissible from an Avicennian point of view. The comparative analysis of Avicenna's and Gundissalinus's perspectives shows also the limits of Gundissalinus's recourse to Avicenna, with whom he never established a real philosophical *dialogue*, nor properly problematised his doctrines while using them. Finally, an epilogue traces the main lines of my enquiry and engages with some aspects of the problematic impact Gundissalinus's works had in the following decades.

In this study, I try to avoid as much as possible any de-contextualisation of Gundissalinus's doctrinal stances. While the truth and falsity of premises and outcomes is evidently transcultural and atemporal, this acknowledgement should not lead scholarship to underestimate the pre-eminent contextual horizon of either Gundissalinus's, or even our own, historical conditions. The reader will find in this book different methods applied to different circumstances. Some chapters present a systematic and analytical approach, especially while dealing with Gundissalinus's interpretation of Ibn Gabirol and my interpretation of Gundissalinus's functional duality. Other chapters display a more historical and descriptive approach, especially when I address Gundissalinus's contextual use of

Latin sources or introduce his biography. Accordingly, this study comprises an analysis of the sources used by the author; an evaluation of doctrinal consistency within the systematic unity of the theories; an assessment of coherences, criticisms, detachments, and alterations made in contrast with the theoretical contents of the used sources; and a thorough analysis of spoken or unspoken outcomes and assumptions of those philosophical stances.

I am persuaded that only a plurality of approaches can cope with the plurality of problems arising from any encounter with a philosophical text which is historically determined, at least in part, by its temporal distance from us. Therefore, I shall ask the reader to consider this study as an opening of interpretations and problems rather than a closure. It is my hope that this opening will be pursued by future scholarship, conceivably through substantive criticism of Gundissalinus's stances – and mine as well. There is nothing worse for research than being exhaustively closed to the continuous stream of interpretations and discussions which is the course of human knowledge.

Another preliminary remark to the reader. After some reticence, I decided to refer to the divine with the masculine singular pronoun. This choice follows purely philological acknowledgments: *Deus* is a masculine noun. My choice does not entail any strong claim concerning the gender of the divine. Curiously, one could even extend Gundissalinus's consideration of the ontological duality of created being to gender studies and possibly affirm that, lying beyond any duality, God cannot be considered as male or female, as the divine cannot be considered either as act or potency or as matter or form – all dualities proper only to created beings. Such an assertion would evidently lead Gundissalinus's readers astray – although it could possibly open his ontology to modern interpretations that surely and plainly lie outside the scope of this study.

The following pages are the result of many years of passionate dialogue and discussions with Gundissalinus. I do hope this study offers the reader some glimpses of Gundissalinus's reflection and his attempt at capturing something of the mystery by which the universe came to be.

There are many people I should mention with immense gratitude for their help with the research grounding this book. I will only mention some of them, without imputing to them any responsibility concerning possible mistakes or misinterpretations. I shall start with Michela Pereira, who guided me in my first encounter with Gundissalinus during my MA at the University of Siena. And Cristina D'Ancona who, during a meeting in Pisa, valorously suggested that I engage with Gundissalinus (in what was my personal "doctor who?" moment with him). After this first encounter, Gundissalinus accompanied me during my years as a doctoral student in Pavia and Barcelona. Without the constant support and guidance of my mentors, Alexander Fidora and Chiara Crisciani, many of the problematic issues I have tried to resolve in this study would still be unsolved. I owe a most considerable debt to Charles Burnett, for his expert help and constant support during my research and for the many engrossing conversations on so many aspects of this study. Further special thanks are owed to Maria Jesús Soto-Bruna, for her many insights concerning Gundissalinus's philosophical reflection and her never-ending encouragement, and to Carla Casagrande, for her constant help and support.

Some conspicuous aspects of the present study are a result of a research seminar organised by the *Aquinas and "the Arabs" International Working Group* in 2017. I am deeply grateful to Richard Taylor for having been so audacious as to invite me to lead that seminar and for the constant and enthusiastic support he has given to me since the very first moment I had the luck to meet him on a sunny day in Dijon. A special thanks also goes to Giles Gasper and the Institute for Medieval and Early Modern Studies of Durham University, for so many things I could not possibly mention. And also to Dominik Perler for his invaluable help in decoding the theoretical coordinates and unspoken implications of this study. Finally, I want to thank Rachel Lott for her careful editing of the manuscript, and express my immense gratitude to Fred Unwalla, Megan Jones, and the Pontifical Institute of Mediaeval Studies for having believed in this project since the very beginning and for their splendid work.

There are more people to thank than fit into these pages. I just want to quickly thank my friends Cecilia Panti, Pedro Mantas, Katja Krause, Therese Cory, David Cory, Lucas Oro, Celia López, Dragos Calma, Luca De Giovanni, Filippo Cristini, Marco Persichina, and, above all, Vincenzo and my family, for the patience, resilience, and never-ending support during these past years. Without even one of them, this book would not be in front of you now. And while authorship and responsibilities are mine alone, it is always important to remember that any human contribution always reflects the complex phenomenon that is a human life. This, per se, is always a collaboration of molecules, cells, and people.

Nicola Polloni
Berlin, June 2019

Seeding Transitions:
A Historical Introduction

During the first centuries of the Middle Ages, only a few Latin translations of works by Plato and Aristotle were available. Access to the former was limited to a part of the *Timaeus* translated by Calcidius.[1] Only a partial translation of the *Organon*, realised by Boethius, was available from the latter.[2] Plato's and Aristotle's philosophies, however, were indirectly disseminated through pivotal Latin works like Macrobius's *Commentarius in somnium Scipionis*, Martianus Capella's *De nuptiis Philologiae et Mercurii*, a commentary on Plato's *Timaeus* by Calcidius, and the overall philosophical work of Boethius and, *mutatis mutandis*, Augustine. Over time, Latin thinkers became increasingly dissatisfied with the limited sources at their disposal, especially in comparison to the accelerating scientific and philosophical developments in the Muslim world. At the borders of Christian Europe – namely, southern Italy and the Iberian peninsula – cultural and trade contacts with "the Arabs" (and, crucially, the Byzantines, who still had access to the original Greek version of the works by Aristotle and his commentators) promoted and spread a social perception of the "cultural backwardness" of Latin science and philosophy in comparison to Greek and Arabic scholarship. Evidence of this feeling – sometimes rhetor-

---

1 See Monika Asztalos, "Boethius as a Transmitter of Greek Logic to the Latin West: The Categories," *Harvard Studies in Classical Philology* 95 (1993): 367–407; and Sten Ebbesen, "Boethius as an Aristotelian Commentator," in *Aristotle Transformed: The Ancient Commentators and Their Influence*, ed. Richard Sorabji (Ithaca, 1990), 373–91.

2 See Stephen Gersh, *Middle Platonism and Neoplatonism: The Latin Tradition* (Notre Dame, 1986); and Anna Somfai, "Calcidius's 'Commentary' on Plato's 'Timaeus' and Its Place in the Commentary Tradition: The Concept of 'Analogia' in Text and Diagrams," *Bulletin of the Institute of Classical Studies* Supplement 83.1 (2004): 203–20. Cicero, too, made a translation of Plato's *Timaeus*, which had practically no influence on the Middle Ages. See Francesco Aronadio, "L'orientamento filosofico di Cicerone e la sua traduzione del *Timeo*," *Méthexis* 21 (2008): 111–29.

2 | *Seeding Transitions: A Historical Introduction*

ically exaggerated – can be found in many prologues to Latin translations realised during the twelfth century.[3]

This emerging awareness regarding the unavailability of books and sources was a consequence of an overall reorganisation of clerical and lay education which took place at the beginning of the twelfth century. The so-called Gregorian reform – a series of ecclesiastical reforms put in place from 1046 to 1122 and aimed at reshaping the Church in a more centralised fashion, with increased clerical presence and influence in the dioceses – urged the dioceses to provide a sufficient ecclesiastical education to the clergy.[4] One of its main effects was the progressive establishment of cathedral schools in almost every diocese. Here, the clergy could receive a basic education. The phenomenon of the cathedral schools would be accompanied very soon by the establishment of similar institutions in towns. And it is this institutional landscape from which the universities would rise a few decades later.

The intersection of these tendencies – an increasing self-consciousness and a new educational framework – laid the basis for the complex phenomenon of the cross-cultural exchange of knowledge in the Middle Ages and the production of Latin translations from Greek and Arabic. Translations never ceased to be made during the Middle Ages. Between the eleventh and the thirteenth century, though, an impressively high number of translations appeared in a relatively short time. The twelfth-century translations can be preliminarily divided into two main linguistic groups – the Greek-into-Latin and the Arabic-into-Latin translation movements – which, with only few exceptions, took place in southern Italy and the Iberian peninsula, respectively.[5]

In southern Italy at the end of the eleventh century, translators like Constantine the African and Alphanus of Salerno translated pivotal scientific (and predominantly medical) works into Latin, an activity structurally bound, on the one hand, to the library resources of the Byzantine territories, and on the other

---

3 See, for instance, Plato of Tivoli's prologue to his translation of al-Battani's *De scientia stellarum* in Marie-Thérèse D'Alverny, "Translations and Translators," in *Renaissance and Renewal in the Twelfth Century*, ed. Robert Benson and Giles Constable, 421–62 (Cambridge, MA, 1982), at 451. Also, another good example of this attitude can be found in the prologue of Gundissalinus's *De scientiis*. See Gundissalinus, *De scientiis*, ed. Manuel Alonso Alonso (Madrid, 1954), 55.2–56.1.

4 See José Orlandis, *La Iglesia antigua y medieval* (Madrid, 1974), 277–98.

5 For historical reasons, the Greek-into-Latin translations were realised predominantly in the Mediterranean area between Byzantium and Sicily, on the border of southern Italy (and Sicily, in particular), where Arab dominion left the region in the hands of the Normans, whose political activity was crucially bound to the Byzantine Empire. For similar reasons, the Arabic-into-Latin translations were mainly based in the Iberian Peninsula, with some incursion beyond the Pyrenees, and later, with Michael Scot, in Sicily.

to the specificities of the rapidly blossoming medical school of Salerno.[6] These pioneering works were soon followed by the rise of Greek-into-Latin clusters of translations based in Sicily, southern Italy, and the Byzantine territories that, thanks to James of Venice, produced the crucial Latin translations of many works by Aristotle.[7]

The Greek-into-Latin translations were soon joined by similar activity focused on Arabic writings in the Iberian peninsula. The rise of the first Iberian clusters of translations is associated with an evocative and often overinterpreted event that took place in 1085: the taking of Toledo, the city which would become the most important centre of Arabic-into-Latin translations in the Middle Ages. On 25 May 1085, Alfonso VI of Castile entered Toledo and proclaimed himself *imperator totius Hispaniae*. Through the acquisition of the former capital of the Visigoth kingdom, the territory of Castile was massively expanded into southern Iberia, gaining some tactical and commercial advantage throughout an area of central geographical importance. The taking of Toledo also put an end to the *reinos de taifa*, as the Almoravids invaded Iberia and by 1111 assimilated all Islamic city-states into their kingdom.[8]

After the taking of Toledo, the borders of the main geopolitical entities (Castile, Aragon, Navarra, and al-Andalus) remained stable for decades, until the battle of Las Navas de Tolosa (1212). This situation of relative peace was crucial in order for translators to move to Iberia and start their activities during the first half of the twelfth century. A first stage of this phenomenon was marked by two fundamental characteristics. First, translators were distributed throughout the whole Peninsula, from the Ebro valley to Seville, Barcelona, and southern France. Second, this stage saw translators working almost exclusively on scientific texts, predominantly on astronomy. Over a few decades, more than a hundred treatises and works were made available to Latin scholars thanks to the

6 See Charles Burnett and Danielle Jacquart, *Constantine the African and 'Alī Ibn al-'Abbās al-Maǧūsī: The Pantegni and Related Texts* (Leiden, 1994); and Paul Kristeller, "The School of Salerno," *Bulletin of the History of Medicine* 17 (1945): 138–92.

7 See Lorenzo Minio-Paluello, "Iacobus Veneticus Grecus: Canonist and Translator of Aristotle," *Traditio* 8 (1952): 265–304. See also Ezio Franceschini, "Ricerche e studi su Aristotele nel Medioevo Latino," in *Aristotele nella critica e negli studi contemporanei* (Milan, 1956), 144–66.

8 Almoravid power, though, was not strong enough to stabilise the political situation of al-Andalus, and between 1143 and 1147, Almoravid dominion floundered and a second period of *reinos de taifa* began. See Muhammad Inan, *The Andalusian Petty Kingdoms: From Their Rise to the Almoravide Conquest* (Cairo, 1970); Humphrey Fisher, "What's in a Name? The Almoravids of the Eleventh Century in Western Sahara," *Journal of Religion in Africa* 22 (1992): 290–317; and María Cobaleda, *Los almorávides: arquitectura de un imperio* (Granada, 2015).

4 | *Seeding Transitions: A Historical Introduction*

work of translators like Hermann of Carinthia, Robert of Ketton, John of Seville, Robert of Chester, Hugh of Santalla, and Plato of Tivoli.[9]

Excluding some rare exceptions, like Ibn Luqa's *De differentia spiritus et animae*, there are no purely philosophical writings among the translations in this first stage of the Arabic-into-Latin "translation movement." The translations were usually scientific works, mainly astronomical and astrological, but also included writings dealing with "new" doctrines like alchemy, geomancy, or the Hermetic tradition.[10] This focus on science and astronomy was a typical feature of the first generation of Arabic-into-Latin translators and would be slowly abandoned by the second generation of translators, who began translating philosophical writings into Latin.

The second half of the century was marked by a new phase. A second generation of translators emerged which was distinguished by a few peculiarities and, pivotally, a much more philosophical interest. The geographical dispersion of translators throughout the peninsula, typical of the first generation, foundered in this new phase, which is instead characterised by the centrality of Toledo.

9 See the following works by Charles Burnett: "Literal Translation and Intelligent Adaptation amongst the Arabic-Latin Translators of the First Half of the Twelfth Century," in *La diffusione delle scienze islamiche nel Medio Evo Europeo*, ed. Biancamaria Scarcia Amoretti (Rome, 1987), 9–28; "The Translating Activity in Medieval Spain," *The Legacy of Muslim Spain*, ed. Salma Jayyusi (Leiden, 1992), 1036–58; "Robert of Ketton," in *Oxford Dictionary of National Biography* (Oxford, 2004); "Arabic into Latin: The Reception of Arabic Philosophy into Western Europe," *The Cambridge Companion to Arabic Philosophy*, ed. Peter Adamson and Richard Taylor (Cambridge, 2005), 370–404. See also Richard Lemay, "L'authenticité de la préface de Robert de Chester à sa traduction du Morienus (1144)," *Chrysopoeia* 4 (1991): 3–32; Adeline Rucquoi, "Littérature scientifique aux frontières du Moyen Âge hispanique: Textes en traduction," *Euphrosyne* 27 (2009): 193–210, at 197–98; James Kritzeck, *Peter the Venerable and Islam* (Princeton, 1964); and Barnabas Hughues, *Robert of Chester's Latin Translation of Al-Khwarizmi's* Al-Jabr (Stuttgart, 1989).

10 See Claudio Moreschini, *Storia dell'ermetismo cristiano* (Brescia, 2000); Charles Burnett, "The Establishment of Medieval Hermeticism," in *The Medieval World*, ed. Peter Linehan and Janet Nelson (London, 2001), 111–30; and Charles Burnett, "Hermann of Carinthia and the *Kitab al-Istamatis*: Further Evidence for the Transmission of Hermetic Magic," *Journal of the Warburg and Courtauld Institutes* 44 (1981): 167–69. Alchemy entered the Latin world through the translation of Morienus Latinus's *Liber de compositione alchemiae* made by Robert of Chester in the 1140s. A few decades after this pioneering translation, many further works were translated and diffused throughout Europe, grounding a new discipline upon vast bibliographical references to accounts and recipes, cosmologies and practices. See Robert Halleaux, "The Reception of Arabic Alchemy in the West," in *Encyclopedia of the History of Arabic Sciences*, ed. Roshdi Rashed (London, 1996), 3: 886–902. See also Michela Pereira, "Cosmologie alchemiche," in *Cosmogonie e cosmologie nel medioevo: Atti del convegno della Società Italiana per lo Studio del Pensiero Medievale (SISPM), Catania, 22–24 settembre 2006*, ed. Concetto Martello, Chiara Militello, and Andrea Vella (Turnhout, 2008), 363–410.

Seeding Transitions: A Historical Introduction | 5

The fast collapse of the Almoravid kingdom left space for a new dynasty, with a very different political and cultural approach: the Almohads.[11] The rise of the Almohad empire is structurally bound to the fascinating history of the founder and inspirer of the Almohad movement, Ibn Tumart. A peculiar fusion of Ash'ari elements with tendencies and doctrines from al-Ghazali's writings, Ibn Tumart's teaching was founded upon the doctrine of God's unicity and oneness (*tawhid*) and aimed at re-establishing the genuineness of the first *Ummah* of believers.[12] Interweaving of religious and social reform soon acquired the traits of a political revolution. The Almohad troops, led by al-Mu'min, took Marrakesh in 1147, and his army proceeded to conquer the Iberian peninsula, displacing the Almoravids. In 1148 the Almohads took Cordoba, and by 1171 al-Andalus was entirely annexed. The arrival of the Almohads and their radical policies produced a shock within the Iberian Peninsula. Many Christians and Jews, but also many Muslims, fled. A migratory flow – famously exemplified by the biography of Moses ben Maimon (Maimonides) – occurred outward from al-Andalus toward the Maghreb and even the Mashreq in the south, and toward the Iberian Christian kingdoms in the north. The first important city to be encountered on the northern route was Toledo, the Castilian capital and the main population centre receiving this migratory flow from al-Andalus. Toledo, indeed, was in a privileged geopolitical position. It lay not far from the border of al-Andalus, was well protected, and served as the hub of the commercial routes on the Peninsula.

Crucially, Toledo also had a tradition of religious tolerance and a prodigious cultural heritage.[13] Under Arabic rule, Toledan Christians were protected by their *Dhimmi* status as *Ahl al-Kitab*, or "People of the Book," although they were separated from the Roman Church and its developments. These Arabic-speaking Christians, whose liturgy autonomously developed from an ancient Visigoth rite, are the *mozárabes*; they played a pivotal role in the first decades after 1085,

11 See Ambrosio Huici Miranda, *Historia política del imperio almohade* (Tetuán, 1956); and Allen Fromherz, *The Almohads: The Rise of an Islamic Empire* (London, 2010).

12 On Ibn Tumart's thought, see Robert Brunschvig, "Sur la doctrine du Mahdi Ibn Tumart," *Arabica* 2 (1955): 137–49; Robert Brunschvig, "Encore sur la doctrine du Mahdi Ibn Tumart," *Folia Orientalia* 12 (1970): 33–40; Tilman Nagel, "Le Mahdisme d'Ibn Tûmart et d'Ibn Qasî: Une analyse phénoménologique," *Revue des mondes Musulmans et de la Méditerranée* 91–94 (2000): 125–36; Madeleine Fletcher, "Ibn Tumart's Teachers: The Relationship with al-Ghazali," *Al-Qantara* 18 (1997): 305–30; and Maribel Fierro, "Le mahdi Ibn Tûmart et al-Andalus: L'élaboration de la légitimité almohade," *Revue des mondes Musulmans et de la Méditerranée* 91–94 (2000): 107–24.

13 Nonetheless, a celebration of Toledo as the city of medieval tolerance would be rather simplistic and exaggerated. See José Jerez Riesco, "Tolerancia e intolerancia en el Toledo medieval," *Revista del Instituto Egipcio de Estudios Islámicos en Madrid* 26 (1993): 91–101.

6 | Seeding Transitions: A Historical Introduction

as they had knowledge of the Arabic language and were familiar with the customs of Muslims, who still populated large parts of the city.[14] Toledo also hosted one of the wealthiest Jewish communities of the Peninsula and was the destination of Castilian migration from the north of the Iberian Peninsula. In addition, the establishment of a French community in Toledo reflected a direct link between the Castilian capital and the French *milieu*.[15] Besides this, it should be recalled that Toledo was the venue of the "circle of Sa'id Andalusi," a group of scientists and scholars who resided in the Castilian town before its taking by the Christian troops. In addition to Sa'id Andalusi, the noted astronomer al-Zarqali was also counted among the members of this circle.[16] As a multicultural town with a prestigious scientific heritage, Toledo must have seemed, to many learned people from al-Andalus, like a valuable refuge during the Almohad revolution.

Material effects of this migratory flow are attested by documentary sources. From the end of the eleventh century to the middle of the twelfth century, a gradual "Latinisation" of the Toledan culture occurred, documented within the extant writings of the period. Until 1125, most of the extant documents are in Arabic, the language used by the three traditional communities of Toledo: *mozárabes*, Jews, and Muslims. Around 1150, with the apex of the Castilian migration to Toledo, a balance between Latin and Arabic as the primary language was struck. But soon

14 While the Mozarabic population was safeguarded by the Castilian crown, their liturgy was a problem for the Catholic Church. The "Romanisation" of the Iberian Christian tradition was pursued by a series of French archbishops of Toledo, directly bound to Cluny, who held the Toledan archbishopric for almost a century beginning with Bernard of Sedirac. See Ángel González Palencia, *Los mozárabes de Toledo en los siglos XII y XIII* (Madrid, 1930); Diego Olstein, *La era mozárabe: Los mozárabes de Toledo (siglos XII y XIII) en la historiografía, las fuentes y la historia* (Salamanca, 2006); Juan Francisco Rivera Recio, *Los arzobispos de Toledo en la baja Edad Media (s. XII–XV)* (Toledo, 1969); and Juan Francisco Rivera Recio, *La Iglesia de Toledo en el siglo XII (1086–1208)* (Rome, 1966). Concerning the term "mozárabe," see Yasmine Beale-Rivaya, "The History and Evolution of the Term 'Mozarab,'" *Imago Temporis* 4 (2010): 51–72.

15 See Charles Burnett, "Communities of Learning in the Twelfth-Century Toledo," in *Communities of Learning: Networks and the Shaping of Intellectual Identity in Europe, 1110–1500*, ed. Constant Mews and John Crossley (Turnhout, 2011), 9–18.

16 See Eloísa Llavero Ruiz, "Panorama cultural de Al'Andalus según Abū l-Qāsim Ṣāʿid b. Aḥmad, cadí de Toledo," *Boletín de la Asociación Española de Orientalistas* 23 (1987): 79–100; Gabriel Martinez-Gros, "La clôture du temps chez le cadi Ṣāʿid, une conception implicite de l'histoire," *Revue de l'Occident musulman et de la Méditerranée* 40 (1985): 147–53; and Lutz Richter-Bernburg, "Ṣāʿid, the Toledan Tables, and Andalusī Science," *From Deferent to Equant: A Volume of Studies in the History of Science in the Ancient and Medieval Near East in Honor of E. S. Kennedy*, ed. David King and George Saliba (New York, 1987), 373–401. For a general perspective, see Julio Samsó, *Islamic Astronomy and Medieval Spain* (Aldershot, 1994).

after, a predominance of Arabic documents returned, as a consequence of the migration of the Arabic-speaking population from al-Andalus after the arrival of the Almohads.[17] The peak of migration from al-Andalus coincided with the apex of the number of translations in Toledo. The contribution of these Arabic-speaking peoples – with their distinctive books, skills, cultures, and experience – was the main condition which nurtured the Toledan clusters of translations. Abraham Ibn Daud, a pivotal figure in the development of medieval philosophy, is also likely to have arrived in Toledo from Cordoba at this time. Charles Burnett[18] emphasises a further fundamental factor in explaining why Toledo became the main centre of Arabic-into-Latin translations: the transfer of the Banu Hud's library from Zaragoza to Toledo around 1140. The wide collection of scientific writings owned by the Banu Hud seems to correspond to Gerard of Cremona's translations, as Burnett points out, and its presence in Toledo surely helped establish the city as a hub for translation and for the study of scientific texts. Finally, a third main factor was the wealth of the Toledan cathedral chapter. Gundissalinus, along with Gerard of Cremona, another of the most important translators of the time, held ecclesiastical roles in the chapter, Gundissalinus as *archidiaconus*, Gerard as *magister*.[19] The Toledan chapter had vast economic resources.[20] All the members of the chapter received substantial prebends and *raciones*, corroborating Francisco Fernández Conde[21] when he describes this advanced system of economic benefices as one of the main financial factors contributing to the viability of the Toledan translations.

During the second half of the twelfth century, Toledo was, thus, the place where a series of scientific and philosophical translations could best be pursued. And indeed, the most famous translator of that time, Gerard of Cremona, worked

17 See Miguel Ladero Quesada, *La formación medieval de España: Territorios, regiones, reinos* (Madrid, 2004), 257–64. See also Yasmine Beale-Rivaya, "The Written Record as Witness: Language Shift from Arabic to Romance in the Documents of the Mozarabs of Toledo in the Twelfth and Thirteenth Centuries," *La Corónica* 40/2 (2012): 27–50.

18 See Charles Burnett, "The Coherence of the Arabic-Latin Translation Programme in Toledo in the Twelfth Century," *Science in Context* 14 (2001): 249–88.

19 See Alfonso García Gallo, *El Concilio de Coyanza: Contribución al estudio del derecho canónico español en la Alta Edad Media* (Madrid, 1951); and Burnett, "Communities of Learning," 9–18.

20 See Francisco Fernández Conde, *La religiosidad medieval en España: Plena Edad Media (siglos XI–XIII)* (Oviedo, 2005), 198–234; and Francisco Pérez Rodríguez, *La Iglesia de Santiago de Compostela en la Edad Media: El cabildo catredalicio (1100–1400)* (Santiago de Compostela, 1996), 37. See also Enrique Torija Rodríguez, "La Iglesia de Toledo en la Edad Media: Organización institucional y formas de vida religiosa. Estado de la cuestión: Archivos y descripción de manuscritos," *Hispania Sacra* 69 (2017): 31–47.

21 See Fernández Conde, *La religiosidad medieval en España*, 266.

8 | *Seeding Transitions: A Historical Introduction*

in Toledo from at least 1157,[22] having arrived with the aim of finding and translating Ptolemy's *Almagest*.[23] Over his thirty-odd years of activity in Toledo, Gerard translated more than sixty works into Latin. An extant eulogy prepared by his students offers a catalogue of the translations by Gerard – an impressive list considering the breadth of the works, authors, and topics that Gerard dealt with. Many of the translated works are scientific writings dealing with astronomy, medicine, and mathematics (but also astrology and geomancy), by authors such as al-Farghani, Geminus of Rhodes, Theodosius, Galen, Euclid. At the same time, the list presents many important works on philosophy by Islamic, Jewish, and Greek authors: al-Kindi, al-Farabi, Isaac Israeli, and, significantly, Aristotle. Gerard translated five Aristotelian writings from Arabic into Latin: *Posterior Analytics, Physics, On the Heavens, On Generation and Corruption,* and *Meteorology*. To these five, one could add two pseudo-Aristotelian treatises: *De causis et proprietatum elementorum* and *De expositione bonitatis purae,* i.e., *Liber de causis*.[24] In the realisation of these translations, Gerard worked in tandem with Galippus, a *mozárabe*, following a biphasic translating method utilised by many authors. The first collaborator translated Arabic into Spanish vernacular, while the second translated the vernacular into Latin.

Gerard's activity was directly connected to his presence in the Toledan chapter; indeed, the capitulary archives identify Gerard as a *magister*, a position that would have covered and funded his work as translator. It is probable that the Toledan chapter provided a kind of scholastic institution for the clergy, serving as a cathedral school. The references to Gerard as *magister* seem to corroborate this hypothesis: indeed, after the council of Coyanza in 1050, cathedral schools were established throughout the Iberian Peninsula, enacting the Gregorian Reform.[25] This fact, nonetheless, does not prove that the cathedral school of Toledo was a "translation school" – a hypothesis proposed decades ago by Valentin Rose but denied by many scholars.[26] Still, a Toledan cathedral school focusing on translation would help explain the infamous medieval legend about a Toledan "school of necromancy."[27]

22 See Francisco Hernández, *Los Cartularios de Toledo: Catálogo Documental* (Madrid, 1985), 117 n119.

23 See Burnett, "The Coherence of the Arabic-Latin Translation Programme," 275.

24 Ibid.

25 See García Gallo, *El Concilio de Coyanza*.

26 See Valentin Rose, "Ptolemaeus und die Schule von Toledo," *Hermes* 8 (1874), 327–49; and Charles Burnett, "The Institutional Context of Arabic-Latin Translations of the Middle Ages: A Reassessment of the 'School of Toledo,'" in *Vocabulary of Teaching and Research Between Middle Ages and Renaissance: Proceedings of the Colloquium London, Warburg Institute, 11–12 March 1994*, ed. Olga Weijers (Turnhout, 1995), 214–35.

27 See Jaime Ferreiro Alemparte, "La escuela de nigromancia de Toledo," *Anuario de Estudios Medievales* 13 (1983): 205–68.

Gerard of Cremona died in Toledo in 1187 after completing a vast number of Latin translations in the Castilian capital over more than thirty years. For the majority of this period, another team of translators was active in Toledo, spearheaded by its most famous figure, Dominicus Gundissalinus.

Even the name of Dominicus Gundissalinus poses a problem for historians, due to divergences in documents and manuscripts. The manuscript witnesses provide a plurality of spellings, which can be quite baffling. The reading "Dominicus Gundisalvi" appears in some manuscripts, such as the translation of Avicenna's *Philosophia prima*, conserved in Paris, Bibliothèque nationale de France, lat. 6443.[28] Other manuscripts present the reading "Dominicus Gundisalvus." See, for example, the translation of Avicenna's self-same text in Oxford, Bodleian Library, Digby 217.[29] Further manuscripts provide an entirely different rendering of the author's name. This is the case within Gundissalinus's *De immortalitate animae* in Paris, Bibliothèque nationale de France, lat. 16613,[30] where the author is named "Gondissalinus." Other witnesses significantly alter the name's stem, as in "Gundipsalmi," author of the *De processione mundi* in Oxford, Oriel College, 7,[31] or "Gimdrisalinus" in Città del Vaticano, Biblioteca Apostolica Vaticana, Ottob. lat. 1870.[32]

That said, a manuscript survey provides some important data. Notably, the manuscript tradition consistently names the author "Dominicus."[33] The main differences among the witnesses arise in regard to the second part of the name. Given the cultural conventions of the time, the various appellations following the name "Dominicus" must refer to the patronymic of the author and should therefore be in the genitive case. The name "Gundisalvus" was very common in medieval Castile and, given its resemblance to the names recorded by the witnesses, is the most likely root of Dominicus's patronymic. Therefore, the

---

28 See Paris, Bibliothèque nationale de France, lat. 6443, fol. 44r: "Completus est liber quem transtulit Dominicus Gundisalvi archidiaconus Tholeti de arabico in latinum."

29 See Oxford, Bodleian Library, Digby 217, fol. 176v: "Completus est liber – laudetur Deus super omnia quemadmodum decet et oportet – quem transtulit Dnus Gundisalvus archidyaconus Toleti de arabico in latinum."

30 See Paris, Bibliothèque nationale de France, lat. 16613, fol. 43r: "Gondissalinus de immortalitate anime."

31 See Oxford, Oriel College, 7, fol. 187v: "Incipit liber Gundipsalmi."

32 See Città del Vaticano, Biblioteca Apostolica Vaticana, Ottob. lat. 1870, fol. 135v: "Incipit liber de invisibilibus dei sive de materia et forma quem composuit Gimdrisalinus."

33 For instance, Cambridge, Gonville and Caius College, 504, which reads (fol. 169v): "Incipit liber secundum philosophos de creatione celi et mundi a Domi.o Gundissalino Tholeti archid. translatus de arabico in latinum"; or Paris, Bibliothèque nationale de France, lat. 6443, reading (fol. 44r): "Completus est liber quem transtulit Dominicus Gundisalvi archidiaconus Tholeti de arabico in latinum."

10 | *Seeding Transitions: A Historical Introduction*

patronymic of Dominicus is most correctly rendered as "Gundisalvi" and the actual name of the Toledan philosopher should be "Dominicus Gundisalvi." The use of "Gundissalinus" seems to involve the adjectivisation of the patronymic, subsequently rendered as a substantive[34] and now commonly used to refer to the author. In order to remain consistent with other recent scholarship, the conventional "Gundissalinus" is used below.

Through an examination of the manuscript tradition, it is also possible to cast some light on the actual duties performed by Gundissalinus. Many witnesses consistently describe the Toledan philosopher as "archidiaconus Toleti,"[35] while others present a more precise description of his role as "archidiaconus Segobiensis apud Toletum,"[36] archdeacon of Segovia in Toledo. The capitulary archives of Segovia and Toledo, as well as those of the archive of Burgos, contain some important documents, dated from 1148 until 1181, which refer to a "Dominicus archidiaconus," who must be identified with Dominicus Gundisalvi.

The first document attesting to the presence of Gundissalinus in Castile is dated 6 May 1148[37] and notes the presence of a "Dominicus archidiaconus" in Segovia. A second document[38] clarifies his duty in the Segovian chapter, referring to him as "Dominicus archidiaconus Collarensis," i.e., archdeacon of Cuéllar,[39] a small town not far from Segovia. From these documents, one can infer that Gundissalinus spent thirteen years in Segovia; the last document witnessing his presence there dates to February 1161.[40] After this point, Gundissalinus presumably moved to Toledo, where he appears for the first time in the capitulary archive in 1162.[41] Unfortunately, neither the town archive in Cuéllar nor the Segovian chapter gives further information on Gundissalinus's activity during these years. Although some preliminary

34 I thank Charles Burnett for the crucial help he gave me in solving this point, as well as many others.

35 See, for example, Paris, Bibliothèque nationale de France, lat. 6443, fol. 44r; Città del Vaticano, Biblioteca Apostolica Vaticana, Vat. lat. 4428, fol. 78r; Città del Vaticano, Biblioteca Apostolica Vaticana, Ottob. lat. 2186, fol. 1r; and Cambridge, Gonville and Caius College, 504, fol. 169v.

36 For instance, Paris, Bibliothèque nationale de France, lat. 6552, fol. 55r.

37 See Luís Villar García, *Documentación medieval de la Catedral de Segovia (1115–1300)* (Salamanca, 1990), 91 n41.

38 Ibid., 93 n42.

39 See Balbino Velazco Bayón, *Colección documental de Cuéllar (943–1492)* (Cuéllar, 2010), 149–50.

40 See Villar García, *Documentación medieval de la Catedral de Segovia*, 109 n61: "Ego Dominicus Colar dictus archidiachonus."

41 See Hernández, *Los Cartularios de Toledo*, 130 n134.

Seeding Transitions: A Historical Introduction | 11

hypotheses have been fashioned, any definitive answers must wait upon the discovery of new evidence.[42]

Some scholars have proposed that, before moving to Cuéllar or Segovia, Gundissalinus received his education in Chartres, perhaps studying under William of Conches and/or Thierry of Chartres. It is evident from both his use of technical parlance and the discussions he pursues in his writings that Gundissalinus had a good knowledge of the cultural debates of his time. Gundissalinus's arguments are similar to the philosophical approaches of the twelfth-century schools in Île-de-France, particularly those of the Chartrean masters.[43]

Nikolaus Häring has pointed out an initial link between Gundissalinus and Chartres relating to Thierry of Chartres's *accessus* to Cicero's *De inventione*.[44] A comparison between Thierry's commentary and Gundissalinus's *De divisione philosophiae* shows a contiguity that indicates Gundissalinus's direct use of Thierry's text.[45] Moreover, one should notice, as previously noted by Häring, that Gundissalinus split Thierry's text and disseminated it in his discussion of both *grammatica* and *rhetorica*.[46] Gundissalinus detached a number of textual passages from their original context (a rhetorical one), and reproposed them in a new context (the analysis of grammar), a style distinctly attributable to Gundissalinus, who used sources through their fragmentation and re-contextualisation.[47]

---

42 See Nicola Polloni, "The Toledan Translation Movement and Gundissalinus: Some Remarks on His Activity and Presence in Castile," in *A Companion to Medieval Toledo: Reconsidering the Canons*, ed. Yasmine Beale-Rivaya and Jason Busic (Leiden, 2018), 263–80.

43 Marie-Thérèse D'Alverny, "Les traductions à deux interprètes, d'arabe en langue vernaculaire et de langue vernaculaire en latin," in *Traduction et traducteurs au Moyen Âge: Actes du colloque international du CNRS organisée à Paris, Institut de recherche et d'histoire des textes, les 26–28 mai 1986, Paris 1989*, ed. Geneviève Contamine (Paris, 1989), 193–206, at 197: "d'après ses œuvres connues, en particulier le *De processione mundi* et le *De divisione philosophiae*, il connaît des ouvrages écrits en France par des contemporains, soit qu'il ait étudié en France, soit que des clercs français aient apporté les livres à Tolède; d'après son vocabulaire il a une bonne culture philosophique; ce n'est pas un latiniste indifférent qu'a désigné l'archevêque pour traduire un grand philosophe arabe. Même si, ayant étudié d'abord en France, il n'avait pas su l'arabe, il aurait été rapidement initié en arrivant à Tolède, vivant parmi des mozarabes dans une cité bilingue."

44 See Nikolaus Häring, "Thierry of Chartres and Dominicus Gundissalinus," *Mediaeval Studies* 26 (1964): 271–86.

45 See Thierry of Chartres, *Super Rhetoricam Ciceronis*, ed. Karin M. Fredborg, *The Latin Rhetorical Commentaries by Thierry of Chartres* (Toronto, 1988), 49.1–55.32; and Gundissalinus, *De divisione philosophiae*, ed. Ludwig Baur (Münster, 1903), 63.21–69.7.

46 Häring, "Thierry of Chartres and Dominicus Gundissalinus."

47 See Nicola Polloni, "Gundissalinus on Necessary Being: Textual and Doctrinal Alterations in the Exposition of Avicenna's Metaphysics," *Arabic Sciences and Philosophy* 26 (2016): 129–60.

12 | *Seeding Transitions: A Historical Introduction*

This also reveals Gundissalinus's high degree of confidence in the Chartrean author.

Karin Fredborg confirms and extends Häring's remarks, showing that Thierry's commentary was used by both Gundissalinus and Petrus Helias.[48] In addition, while Richard Hunt underlines the proximities between Gundissalinus's *De divisione* and Helias's *Summa super Priscianum*, Fredborg points out that another fundamental source of the latter is William of Conches's *Glosae super Priscianum*.[49] In this manner, Helias shared his approach with Gundissalinus, as Alexander Fidora has recently suggested by demonstrating the dependence of Gundissalinus's *De divisione* on the second version of William's *Glosae super Priscianum*.[50] The relation between Gundissalinus and William seems to extend beyond *De divisione*: Fidora underscores the parallels which can be drawn between William's refutation of primordial chaos and Gundissalinus's arguments against it.[51]

Burnett has established that Gundissalinus made use of the *Ars artium* – a text whose origins can be traced back to Chartres – and he has emphasised the overt relation between Gundissalinus and Hermann of Carinthia. Hermann was a pupil of Thierry, a translator of Arabic into Latin, and the author of *De essentiis,* one of the most important sources of Gundissalinus's *De processione mundi*.[52]

These amassed data testify in favour of a link between Gundissalinus and Chartres. Nevertheless, this link only indicates that Gundissalinus had access to a wide range of Chartrean sources, not that he was *personally* connected to Chartres. Establishing a direct connection between Gundissalinus and Chartres would require a further step, that is, a demonstration that those texts were not

48 See Fredborg, *The Latin Rhetorical Commentaries by Thierry of Chartres*, 14–20.

49 See Richard Hunt, "The Introduction to the 'Artes' in the Twelfth Century," in *Studia mediaevalia in honorem admodum Reverendi Patris Raymundi Josephi Martin*, ed. Raymond Martin (Bruges, 1948), 85–112; Karin M. Fredborg, "The Dependence of Petrus Helias's *Summa super Priscianum* on William of Conches's *Glosae super Priscianum*," *Cahiers de l'Institut du Moyen Âge grec et latin* 11 (1973): 1–57; and Fredborg, "Petrus Helias on Rhetoric," *Cahiers de l'Institut du Moyen Âge grec et latin* 13 (1974): 31–41.

50 See Alexander Fidora, "Le débat sur la création: Guillaume de Conches, maître de Dominique Gundisalvi?" in *Guillaume de Conches: Philosophie et science au XII siècle*, ed. Barbara Obrist and Irene Caiazzo (Florence, 2011), 271–88. See also Édouard Jeauneau, "Deux rédactions des gloses de Guillaume de Conches sur Priscien," *Recherches de théologie ancienne et médiévale* 27 (1960): 243–47.

51 See Fidora, "Le débat sur la création"; and Dorothy Elford, "William of Conches," in *A History of Twelfth-Century Western Philosophy*, ed. Peter Dronke (Cambridge, 1988), 308–27.

52 See Charles Burnett, "A New Source for Dominicus Gundissalinus's Account of the Science of the Stars?" *Annals of Science* 47 (1990): 361–74.

available or in use in Toledo other than through Gundissalinus himself. This is a thorny problem. As I have had occasion to point out, alternative hypotheses (namely, a Cluniac or Cistercian Castilian mediation) seem insufficient to explain Gundissalinus's in-depth knowledge of the Chartrean writings.[53] However, deep theoretical differences between Gundissalinus and thinkers associated with Chartres undermine the notion that he received his training there. While some doctrinal connections can be established between Gundissalinus's and Thierry of Chartres's ontological theories,[54] the former are often in open contradiction with Chartrean speculation. Even accepting that Fidora is right in supposing that Gundissalinus was aware of the debate between William of Conches and Hugh of St Victor about primordial chaos, the solution the Toledan philosopher proposed does not prove much about Gundissalinus's presence in Chartres. Gundissalinus's thought, indeed, aimed at a global renovation of Latin philosophy through Arabic sources, a renovation which entailed the superseding of Chartrean philosophy. Moreover, recent studies have noted that Gundissalinus knew many French sources in addition to the Chartrean authors (or Hugh of St Victor), as is made clear by his use of Peter Lombard's *Sentences*.[55]

The connection with Chartres, as a hypothesis, is drastically weakened by Daniel of Morley's *Philosophia*. In this work, which was reportedly written after his return from Toledo (where Daniel studied during the same years Gundissalinus was there), Daniel of Morley made wide and profound use of texts by William of Conches, elaborating a philosophical perspective which, in contrast with Gundissalinus's, is fundamentally in accord with the Chartrean tradition. Yet many of the insights of Daniel's account have been questioned by Burnett.[56] Still, given that there are no traces of contact between Daniel and Gundissalinus or his works, this text offers some crucial evidence that many texts of Chartrean masters were available in Toledo independently of Gundissalinus's presence there. Available evidence, therefore, is insufficient to establish a consistent hypothesis on Gundissalinus's pre-Segovian activities.[57]

---

53 See Nicola Polloni, "Elementi per una biografia di Dominicus Gundisalvi," *Archives d'histoire doctrinale et littéraire du Moyen Âge* 82 (2015): 7–22.

54 See Nicola Polloni, "Thierry of Chartres and Gundissalinus on Spiritual Substance: The Problem of Hylomorphic Composition," *Bulletin de Philosophie Médiévale* 57 (2015): 35–57.

55 See Nicola Polloni, "Gundissalinus on the Angelic Creation of the Human Soul: A Peculiar Example of Philosophical Appropriation," *Oriens* 47 (2019): 313–47.

56 See Burnett, "The Institutional Context of Arabic-Latin Translations of the Middle Ages."

57 In sum, while the supposition of a Chartrean education appears to be a consequence of the analysis of Gundissalinus's sources, other possibilities should be considered. Never-

14 | *Seeding Transitions: A Historical Introduction*

Proceeding from Chartres or not, Gundissalinus spent a few years in Segovia before moving to Toledo. When he arrived in Toledo, Gerard of Cremona was already there, as evidenced by documentation from 1157.[58] Gundissalinus spent more than twenty years in Toledo, and the Segovian chapter does not refer to him again during this period. Instead, the Toledan archive registers his presence throughout this period[59] and up to 1178,[60] although Gundissalinus remained in Toledo longer, without participating in the chapter. One last document regarding the sale of land, written in Arabic and dated to 1181, testifies to his presence in Toledo.[61] After this, Gundissalinus probably went back to Segovia, since the last extant document witnessing him alive is an account of a meeting between the chapters of Segovia and Burgos, held in Segovia in 1190,[62] in which Gundissalinus participated.[63] After 1190, there are no further sources naming

---

theless, although it does not seem to be sufficiently corroborated, supposition of a period spent by Gundissalinus in Chartres still remains a valuable and likely hypothesis. Were it demonstrated, it should be supposed that Gundissalinus spent a few years in Chartres, sometime between 1135 and 1148.

58 See Hernández, *Los Cartularios de Toledo*, 117 n119. In that same document, Gerard's name is followed by two further *magistri* – Domenicus and Ricardus – and a "Gundisalvus archidiaconus." At first glance, one might think this is a reference to Gundissalinus. Nonetheless, the capitulary archives of Toledo and Segovia show an otherwise remarkable consistency, and these are what must be used to verify a member's presence, as official statements of name and office. All further references to Gundissalinus consistently mention him as "Dominicus, archidiaconus Collarensis" or "D. archidiaconus Collarensis," not "Gundisalvus archidiaconus," as appears in the 1157 document. Moreover, it should be recalled that "Gundisalvus" is a first name, while "Gundisalvi" is a patronymic. Therefore, "Gundisalvus" cannot be identified with Gundissalinus, who indeed arrived in Toledo in 1162.

59 Gundissalinus is witnessed by the Toledan capitulary archive in the following dates: 11 March 1162: "Dominicus Colarensis archidiaconus"; December 1164: "D(ominicus) Colarensis archidiaconus"; January 1170: "D. archidiaconus Colarensis"; March 1174: "D. Colarensis archidiaconus"; May 1174: "Dominicus Colarensis archidiaconus"; 1 March 1176: "D. Colarensis archidiaconus"; 1176: "[Dominicus] archidiacunus C(olarensis)"; 20 December 1177: "D(ominicus) Colarensis archidiaconus"; 1 December 1178: "D. archidiacono [Colarensis]." See Hernández, *Los Cartularios de Toledo*, 130–85, nn134, 144, 155, 165, 167, 174, 178, 182, and 185.

60 Ibid., 185 n185.

61 See Manuel Alonso Alonso, "Notas sobre los traductores toledanos Domingo Gundisalvo y Juan Hispano," *Al-Andalus* 8 (1943): 155–88; and González Palencia, *Los mozárabes de Toledo en los siglos XII y XIII*.

62 See Villar García, *Documentación medieval de la Catedral de Segovia*, 135 n81.

63 The document is conserved in the capitulary archive of both Segovia and Burgos. See Demetrio Mansilla, "La documentación pontificia del archivo de la catedral de Burgos," *Hispania Sacra* 1 (1948): 427–38, entry 161; and Mansilla, *Catálogo documental del archivo catedral de Burgos (804–1416)* (Madrid, 1971), 279 n40.

Gundissalinus. Therefore, it is impossible to establish an exact date for his death. A *terminus ante quem* can be fixed to 1193, when a new archdeacon of Cuéllar is mentioned by the capitulary archive of Toledo.[64] This new archdeacon, John, has been identified by Burnett and Juan Francisco Rivera Recio as one of Gundissalinus's collaborators, Johannes Hispanus.[65]

An examination of documentary sources and of the manuscript tradition provides a valuable but meagre picture of Gundissalinus's biography. It can be stated with a good degree of certainty that he spent at least thirteen years in Segovia (1148–1161/2) before moving to Toledo, where he remained almost twenty years (1162–1181) until he presumably returned to Segovia. Certainly still alive in 1190, Gundissalinus likely died between 1190 and 1193. Considering these data, one could surmise that he was born between 1115 and 1125, with all probability on the Iberian Peninsula. Aside from the details of Gundissalinus's education, another pivotal aspect of this chronology remains obscure: the circumstances of his moving to Toledo in 1161/2.

It should be noted that, in 1149, John of Castelmoron was elected bishop of Segovia.[66] While very little is known about his life before his election to the bishopric, the Toledan archives clearly state that the same John would, in 1152 and with the name of John II, become archbishop of Toledo, an office he would hold until 1166.[67] John, thus, was the bishop of Segovia while Gundissalinus was there, and the very same John was the archbishop of Toledo during Gundissalinus's transfer.

Another important event occurred in 1160/61: Abraham ibn Daud is attested in Toledo. Ibn Daud, or Avendauth, was Gundissalinus's main collaborator for the translation of Avicenna, but he was also an important Jewish philosopher in his own right within the Aristotelian and Avicennian tradition. As Amos Bertolacci has noted, even the decision to translate Avicenna's corpus can be

---

64 See Hernández, *Los Cartularios de Toledo*, 229 n249.

65 See Charles Burnett, "Magister Iohannes Hispanus: Towards the Identity of a Toledan Translator," in *Comprendre et maîtriser la nature au Moyen Âge, Mélanges d'histoire des sciences offerts à Guy Beaujouan*, ed. Georges Comet (Geneva, 1994), 425–36; Charles Burnett, "John of Seville and John of Spain: A Mise au Point," *Bulletin de philosophie médiévale* 44 (2002): 59–78; and Juan Francisco Rivera Recio, "Nuevos datos sobre los traductores Gundisalvo y Juan Hispano," *Al-Andalus* 31 (1966): 267–80.

66 Among the documents preserved in the capitulary archives there is also the oath taken by John II. See Rivera Recio, *La Iglesia de Toledo en el siglo XII*, 280 n75.

67 See Rivera Recio, *Los arzobispos de Toledo en la baja Edad Media*, at 21–26.

16 | *Seeding Transitions: A Historical Introduction*

ascribed to Ibn Daud.[68] Indeed, the first translation of Avicenna in Toledo was the prologue to the *Liber sufficientiae,* completed by Ibn Daud. As Bertolacci has pointed out,[69] the dedicatory letter to the archbishop of Toledo accompanying the translation of the prologue displays some pivotal peculiarities.[70] Ibn Daud aims to persuade the recipient, i.e., the archbishop of Toledo, to sponsor a series of translations of the whole Avicennian corpus of the *Kitab aš-Šifa.*[71] As Ibn Daud arrived in Toledo in 1160/61, the recipient must have been John II, whose archbishopric lasted between 1152 and 1166. And in fact, another dedicatory letter was addressed to John II, this time accompanying the translation of Avicenna's *De anima.*[72] This second letter is intimately bound to the first. Bertolacci has remarked that the execution of the Latin translation of the *De anima* indicates with certainty that Ibn Daud successfully convinced John II to sponsor a translation of Avicenna's works.[73] That said, there is an important distinction between the ways in which the two translations were realised: while the first was completed by Ibn Daud alone, the second translation was a collaboration between Ibn Daud and Dominicus Gundissalinus. In the letter accompanying this translation, Gundissalinus's position remains ancillary; the sender – and thus the main translator – is Ibn Daud, while Gundissalinus appears only in the final part, in which Ibn Daud describes the biphasic method adopted.[74]

68 See Amos Bertolacci, "A Community of Translators: The Latin Medieval Versions of Avicenna's Book of the Cure," in *Communities of Learning: Networks and the Shaping of Intellectual Identity in Europe, 1100–1500,* ed. Constant Mews and John Crossley (Turnhout, 2011), 37–54.

69 Bertolacci, "A Community of Translators."

70 Avicenna, *Prologus discipuli et capitula,* ed. Aleksander Birkenmajer, in "Avicennas Vorrede zum 'Liber Sufficientiae' und Roger Bacon," *Revue néoscolastique de philosophie* 36 (1934): 308–20, at 314.

71 Bertolacci, "A Community of Translators." It should be recalled that this was a common practice amongst the medieval Jewish philosophers. See Gad Freudenthal, "Abraham Ibn Daud, Avendauth, Dominicus Gundissalinus and Practical Mathematics in Mid-Twelfth Century Toledo," *Aleph* 16 (2016): 60–106; Gad Freudenthal, "Abraham Ibn Ezra and Judah Ibn Tibbon as Cultural Intermediaries: Early Stages in the Introduction of Non-Rabbinic Learning into Provence in the Mid-Twelfth Century," in *Exchange and Transmission Across Cultural Boundaries: Philosophy, Mysticism and Science in the Mediterranean World,* ed. Haggai Ben-Shammai et al. (Jerusalem, 2013), 58–81.

72 Avicenna, *Liber de anima seu Sextus de naturalibus, prologus,* ed. Simone Van Riet (Louvain, 1968–72), 1: 3.1–4.26.

73 Bertolacci, "A Community of Translators."

74 See Avicenna, *Liber de anima seu Sextus de naturalibus, prologus,* ed. Van Riet, 1: 4.21–23: "Here you have the book translated from Arabic, as I have first uttered the [meaning of its Arabic] words in vernacular, one by one, while Dominicus, the archdeacon, has translated them into Latin, one by one." ("Habetis ergo librum, nobis praecipiente et singula verba vulgariter proferente, et Dominico Archidiacono singula in latinum convertente, ex arabico translatum.")

Three fundamental things are made clear by these remarks:

1. The translation of Avicenna's *De anima* occurred later than the prologue of the *Liber sufficientiae*;
2. Both translations were completed before 1166, since the *De anima* is dedicated to John II;
3. The *De anima* must have been completed after 1162, the year in which sources first attest to Gundissalinus's presence in Toledo.

These three implications suggest that Gundissalinus's arrival in Toledo was no accident. On the contrary, he seems to have left Segovia in response to the Avicennian translation project, proposed by Ibn Daud and advocated for in his first letter to John II. John II's sponsorship of the project provided Ibn Daud the economic and practical means to draw a learned Latinist with philosophical skills who could allow him to correctly translate the dense texts of Avicenna into Latin. Gundissalinus was well suited to the job. It is undisputed that John II already knew Gundissalinus, as he was the bishop of Segovia while Gundissalinus was a member of its chapter. Knowing him, John was surely aware of both his philosophical education and his vast knowledge of Latin, characteristics that made Gundissalinus the best candidate for the position required by Ibn Daud. Therefore, Gundissalinus likely arrived in Toledo in 1162, under the appointment of John II, in order to take part in Ibn Daud's translation project. This helps clarify why Gundissalinus is presented as an ancillary within the second dedicatory letter, as it was his first translation of Avicenna and he was a mere participant within a project developed by Ibn Daud. Gundissalinus's role would progressively broaden and deepen, although the origins of the translations of Avicenna into Latin are most accurately credited to Ibn Daud, not Gundissalinus. For this reason, framing this impressive cluster of translations as the singular effort of Gundissalinus would be disingenuous; the best appellation for this Toledan endeavour is the one proposed by Burnett, the "Gundissalinus Circle."[75] This achievement was accomplished within a speculative milieu where scientific and philosophical works were translated, studied, and elaborated by Gundissalinus, Ibn Daud, and probably Johannes Hispanus.[76]

During his twenty years of activity, Gundissalinus participated in the translation of approximately twenty philosophical works from Arabic into

75 Charles Burnett proposed this appellation in his paper "The Gundissalinus Circle" given at the conference "Idee, testi e autori arabi ed ebraici e la loro ricezione latina" held in Pavia on 3–4 December 2014.

76 See Burnett, "John of Seville and John of Spain"; and Freudenthal, "Abraham Ibn Daud, Avendauth, Dominicus Gundissalinus and Practical Mathematics."

Latin.[77] The authors selected for translation by Gundissalinus and his circle were all Muslim or Jewish philosophers, apart from Alexander of Aphrodisias, whose *De intellectu et intellecto* is the only originally Greek text translated from Arabic by Gundissalinus. These translations share a stylistic quirk, namely literalism in their Latin, due to the *de verbo ad verbum* method, which occasionally rendered problematic Arabic words into calques and neologisms.[78] Together with the works translated by his colleagues, the translations made by Gundissalinus would provide the seeds of a philosophical and scientific transition from a Latin-inherited to a much more Mediterranean tradition. The era germinating from this shift would be mostly grounded on Aristotle and the Arabic Aristotelian tradition, from Avicenna and al-Ghazali to Maimonides and Averroes and, during the final centuries of the Middle Ages, would grow into the scholastic philosophy of European universities. Before the rise of scholasticism, the first Latin thinker to pioneer the new philosophical framework which was opened by and grounded upon those recently translated works was one of their translators – Dominicus Gundissalinus. His philosophical innovations, developed through a series of treatises, are deeply indebted to the translations he made and, in particular, to the works of two Arabic-writing authors: Ibn Gabirol and Avicenna. Engaging with psychological, epistemological, and metaphysical problems inherited from the Latin tradition, Gundissalinus aimed to renovate Latin philosophy through the advancements of the Arabs. Implicitly, his work was also an attempt to display how these two cultures, the Latin and the

77 Here is a comprehensive list of all the known translations ascribed to Gundissalinus: Alexander of Aphrodisias, *De intellectu et intellecto*; al-Farabi, *De intellectu et intellecto*; al-Farabi, *Expositio libri quinti Elementorum Euclidis*; al-Farabi (ps.), *De ortu scientiarum*; al-Ghazali, *Summa theoricae philosophiae* (*Metaphysica* and *Logica*); al-Kindi, *De intellectu*; al-Kindi, *De mutatione temporum*; Ibn Gabirol, *Fons vitae*; Avicenna, *De anima*; Avicenna, *De convenientia et differentia scientiarum*; Avicenna, *De universalibus*; Avicenna, *Liber de philosophia prima*; Avicenna, *Physica* I–III; Avicenna, *De diluviis*; Avicenna, *De viribus cordis*; Avicenna (ps.), *Liber celi et mundi*; Ikhwan as-Safa, *In artem logicae demonstrationis*; Isaac Israeli, *De definitionibus*. This list will probably be reshaped in the near future, thanks to the brilliant work by Dag Nikolaus Hasse and his team, reassessing the authorship of many anonymous medieval translations. See Alexander Fidora, *Domingo Gundisalvo y la teoría de la ciencia arábigo-aristotélica* (Pamplona, 2009), 246–47; and the crucial study by Hasse and Andreas Büttner, "Notes on Anonymous Twelfth-Century Translations of Philosophical Texts from Arabic into Latin on the Iberian Peninsula," in *The Arabic, Hebrew, and Latin Reception of Avicenna's Physics and Cosmology*, ed. Dag N. Hasse and Amos Bertolacci (Berlin, 2018), 313–69.

78 See Charles Burnett, "Translating from Arabic into Latin in the Middle Ages: Theory, Practice, and Criticism," in *Éditer, traduire, interpreter: essais de méthodologie philosophique*, ed. Steve Lofts and Philipp Rosemann (Louvain, 1997), 55–78; and Manuel Alonso Alonso, "Coincidencias verbales típicas en las obras y traducciones de Gundisalvo," *Al-Andalus* 20 (1955): 129–52 and 345–79.

Arabic, even if politically and religiously at odds, still shared a common philosophical and scientific ground.

The following chapters will examine the philosophical thought of Dominicus Gundissalinus, a presumably unwitting protagonist of an often-forgotten cultural revolution. Indeed, while Gundissalinus's translations and philosophical treatises were intended to renovate the Latin tradition, the overall effects of the doctrines he directly or indirectly inserted into that tradition were ultimately groundbreaking. From the separateness of the agent intellect to a radical universal hylomorphism founded upon modal ontology, many of the theories Gundissalinus accepted and developed had an explosive effect on the philosophical debate. Over a few decades, Latin reflection would be almost completely reshaped through a new speculative paradigm that would endure for centuries to come.

CHAPTER ONE

Pioneering Transformations: Gundissalinus's Philosophical Reflection

Gundissalinus has a peculiar position in the history of European thought. With first-hand access to many new Arabic sources and a remarkable philosophical education, Gundissalinus grounds his work simultaneously in both Latin and Arabic traditions. Through processes of cutting and pasting, cherry-picking, and re-contextualizing his sources, Gundissalinus's treatises are grounded on blind and often altered quotations.[1] These works disclose a unique philosophical approach, one which resists traditional attitudes toward the philosophical problems of that time. Gundissalinus helped open a new speculative horizon, the coordinates of which were plotted by newly translated Arabic texts, in a process of progressive assimilation and criticism that would find its full extension in the thirteenth century.

Problems of Attribution

The exact number of the treatises authored by Gundissalinus remains a point of contention. Traditionally, six works have been ascribed to him: *On Unity and the One* (*De unitate et uno*), *On the Immortality of the Soul* (*De immortalitate animae*), *On the Sciences* (*De scientiis*), *On the Soul* (*De anima*), *On the Division of Philosophy* (*De divisione philosophiae*), and *On the Procession of the World* (*De processione mundi*). Four of these works clearly originate with Gundissalinus: *De anima*, *De*

---

1 Cf. Nicola Polloni, "Gundissalinus on Necessary Being: Textual and Doctrinal Alterations in the Exposition of Avicenna's *Metaphysics*," *Arabic Sciences and Philosophy* 26 (2016): 129–60; and Dag Nikolaus Hasse, *Avicenna's* De anima *in the Latin West: The Formation of a Peripatetic Philosophy of the Soul 1160–1300* (London, 2000), 13–18. Notwithstanding his indebtedness, Gundissalinus's writings are far from being correctly defined as mere *collactiones*. The voluntary changes regarding the semantic context, the introduction or elimination of parts of the quoted text, and the lexical and morpho-syntactical alterations upon which Gundissalinus's alteration strategy is based make the use of his sources idiosyncratic. His is a peculiar and fascinating speculative approach one can detect in all his writings.

divisione philosophiae, De unitate et uno, and *De processione mundi.*[2] Nonetheless, questions of authorship remain unsettled for further works supposedly connected to Gundissalinus.

The aims of the treatise *On the Immortality of the Soul* are to address and correct the mistakes of those claiming that the human soul is mortal, as the title suggests. Its sources are mainly Ibn Gabirol's *Fons vitae* and Avicenna's *De anima* – both translated by Gundissalinus. According to the text, belief in the mortality of the soul is an error, the falsity of which can be displayed through four types of demonstration: sensible experience, divine law, philosophical argumentation, and authority.[3] The treatise uses the third kind of proof, i.e., a philosophical demonstrative approach. Specifically, the treatise focuses on consequences that an admission of the soul's mortality would have in consideration of divine justice, psychological faculties, and the ontological composition of the soul. If the soul were mortal, God could not mete out justice through retribution or recompenses through reward. As divine justice cannot be found in this world, it must be given to souls after the death of the body. Divine justice, therefore, requires the immortality of the soul as a necessary condition for the very eschatology which it presupposes.[4] At the same time, the soul is "other" and separated from the body. This is clearly demonstrated by simple reflection, as intellectual activity is not dependent on the body. Intellect and body are indeed characterised by opposite qualities. Through aging, the body deteriorates while the intellect gains force, reaching its utmost power when separated from the body, as in the state of mystical ecstasy.[5]

Among the numerous proofs in *De immortalitate*, the discussion of the ontological composition of the soul is most relevant to the question of its authorship.[6] The author claims that every substance whose form is incorruptible is so in virtue of itself. Therefore, as the soul and the intelligible substances have no material form, they must be incorruptible and immortal. Substantial corruption, indeed, can only happen in four ways: through the separation of the

2 *De unitate et uno* spread throughout Europe during the thirteenth century as a work by Boethius. Even though Thomas Aquinas finally refuted its Boethian authorship, Gundissalinus was not commonly identified as the author until Correns's critical edition. See Aquinas, *Quaestiones de quolibet*, ed. René-Antoine Gauthier (Rome, 1996), 9.4.1.2 ad 2; and Aquinas, *Quaestio disputata de spiritualibus creaturis*, ed. Joseph Cos (Rome, 2000), 1.21 ad 21.

3 Gundissalinus, *De immortalitate animae*, ed. Georg Bülow, *Des Dominicus Gundissalinus Schrift Von der Unsterblichkeit der Seele* (Münster, 1897), 1–38, at 1.1–2.19.

4 The author presents further arguments following the same line of reasoning. See ibid., 3.16–4.24.

5 Ibid., 5.1–26.19.

6 Ibid., 26.20–39.13.

22 | CHAPTER ONE

form from its matter; through the division of its integral parts; through the destruction of what sustains the substance itself; or through the removal of its efficient cause.[7] Since the soul cannot be subject to any of them, the soul must be immortal.

The author is candid in affirming that the soul is a pure form, simple and not joined to any matter. The soul is a spiritual form.[8] If someone were to erroneously suppose that the soul is composed of matter and form, the error of this supposition would easily be shown by considering the intelligible power of the soul. The soul implies its own spirituality, because intellection can be pursued only by similar substances.[9] Accordingly, if the soul had a contrary through which it might be corrupted, the soul would not have a complete and natural intellection – an inadmissible position.[10]

The series of ontological proofs for the immortality of the soul establishes a fundamental obstacle for any attempt at ascribing *De immortalitate animae* to Gundissalinus. The theoretical base on which these arguments are grounded is the formal existence of the soul. As a spiritual substance, the soul is a form that subsists beyond and despite matter. In contrast, the most characteristic metaphysical position developed by Gundissalinus states exactly the opposite. One of his most characteristic doctrines, i.e., universal hylomorphism, claims indeed that all created beings, be they spiritual or corporeal, are composed of both matter and form – a hylomorphism therefore common to bodies and souls, brute animals and angels. *De immortalitate animae* not only opposes Gundissalinus's ontological position but serves as a kind of refutation of universal hylomorphism. As a consequence, it seems rather unlikely that Gundissalinus is the author of this treatise.

The theoretical inconsistency between Gundissalinus's writings and the *De immortalitate* was first pointed out by Antonio Masnovo.[11] In addition to this discrepancy, another pivotal problem concerns the history of the text. *De immortalitate animae* has a divergent manuscript tradition, which presents two different versions of the work and two different authors, Dominicus Gundissalinus and William of Auvergne. The two versions circulated as two different treatises until Abraham Loewenthal pointed out that they are, in fact, the same work.[12] This observation was accepted a few years later by Georg Bülow,

---

7 See ibid., 26.20–27.13.

8 See ibid., 28.14–16.

9 See ibid., 28.17–29.8.

10 Ibid., 29.8–10.

11 See Amato Masnovo, *Da Guglielmo d'Auvergne a san Tommaso d'Aquino* (Milan, 1945–1946), at 119–123.

12 See Abraham Loewenthal, *Pseudo-Aristoteles über die Seele* (Berlin, 1891), at 59.

the critical editor of *De immortalitate animae*, who opined that the author of the treatise was Gundissalinus.[13] In the mid-twentieth century, this hypothesis was refuted by Masnovo, who noted several inconsistencies in Bülow's palaeographic analysis. In Masnovo's opinion, the treatise must be ascribed to William of Auvergne since the Parisian archbishop ascribes to himself a text on the immortality of the soul.[14] A few years later, Baudoin Allard discovered six more manuscript witnesses of the treatise which supposedly corroborated the hypothesis of William as the author.[15] As a consequence, Roland Teske published an English translation of Bülow's edition which attributed the work to William of Auvergne. This editorial choice contributed to a provisional resolution of the question of the authorship of the *De immortalitate animae*, and the problem disappeared almost entirely from scholarly discussion without having been definitively resolved.[16]

Alessandra Ingarao revisited this problem in 2002, opposing the treatise's *de facto* attribution to William and highlighting the *status quaestionis* of its authorship.[17] Regarding the history of the text and its intra-textual relations, Ingarao raised two aspects that are often unconsidered. First, she noted that one of the most important manuscripts on Bülow's *stemma codicum* (i.e., Paris, Bibliothèque nationale de France, lat. 16613) was composed during the first half of the thirteenth century and owned by Gerard de Abbatis, a gift he received from the famous library of Richard de Fournival.[18] Both Gerard and William were masters in Paris, but the version of the *De immortalitate* owned by Gerard identifies Gundissalinus as the author of the treatise. Ingarao stressed the oddity

13 See Bülow, *Des Dominicus Gundissalinus Schrift von der Unsterblichkeit der Seele*, at 63–143. Accordingly, Bülow points out that one should avoid any accusation of plagiarism against William of Auvergne, who supposedly revised Gundissalinus's authentic work, adapting it for his own purposes, while lacking awareness of a modern sense of authorship and intellectual property.

14 Masnovo, *Da Guglielmo d'Auvergne a san Tommaso d'Aquino*, 119–23.

15 Baudoin Allard, "Nouvelles additions et corrections au *Répertoire* de Glorieux: À propos de Guillaume d'Auvergne," *Bulletin de philosophie médiévale* 10–12 (1968–70): 212–24; and Allard, "Note sur le *De immortalitate animae* de Guillaume d'Auvergne," *Bulletin de philosophie médiévale* 18 (1976): 68–72.

16 See William of Auvergne, *The Immortality of the Soul*, trans. Roland Teske (Milwaukee, 1991), especially at 4.

17 Alessandra Ingarao, "Lo status quaestionis sulla paternità del 'De immortalitate animae' attribuito a Domingo Gundisalvi (Toledo 1170 ca. – Parigi 1228 ca.)," in *Enosis kai filia: Unione e amicizia*, ed. Maria Barbanti, Giovanna Giardina, and Paolo Manganaro (Catania, 2002), 557–68.

18 See Richard Rouse, "Manuscripts Belonging to Richard de Fournival," *Revue d'histoire des textes* 3 (1973): 253–69.

24 | CHAPTER ONE

of Gerard ascribing a text written by someone he knew to another author without amending it. Second, the manuscript was part of Fournival's collection, a collection which contained other works and translations completed by Gundissalinus in Toledo.[19] This fact could be an important clue that part of Fournival's collection, acquired in 1230, was an acquisition of manuscripts translated and written in Toledo. This ought to be considered when contemplating the authorship of the *De immortalitate animae*.[20] Third, Ingarao analysed the textual relations between Jean de la Rochelle, Robert of Melun, and the *De immortalitate*. The chronological relation among these texts, and Jean de la Rochelle's and Robert of Melun's reliance upon the treatise, made Ingarao conclude that the author cannot be William of Auvergne.[21]

The analysis provided by Ingarao seems consistent with Bülow's initial hypothesis. Nonetheless, without further evidence, and in light of the scant knowledge available on the fifty years separating Gundissalinus and William of Auvergne, neither can be definitively named as the author of the *De immortalitate animae*.

A different set of problems arises from the consideration of the *Liber mahameleth* (*Book of Transactions*), an anonymous work which has been ascribed to Gundissalinus's circle by Charles Burnett and Anne-Marie Vlasschaert.[22] The nature of this work is quite peculiar; the *Liber mahameleth* is a mathematical and commercial treatise – as expressed by its title – and, following the tradition of the Arabic mathematical sciences, deals with several problems of applied mathematics and algebra.[23] The first part of the treatise is dedicated to the analysis of mathematical principles and their reciprocal operations, while the second part focuses on the application of mathematical operations to practical problems related to everyday life and trade (like consumption of lamp-oil or bread, cost of grinding, or wages of paid workers). This is odd considering that all other extant writings ascribed to Gundissalinus are philosophical treatises. Gundissalinus broaches epistemological,

19 See Marie-Thérèse D'Alverny, "L'introduction d'Avicenne en Occident," *Revue du Caire* 14/141 (1951): 130–39.

20 See Ingarao, "Lo status quaestionis," 564–65.

21 See Joseph A. Enders, "Die Nachwirkung von Gundissalinus 'De immortalitate animae,'" *Philosophische Jahrbuch* 12 (1899): 382–92; and Raymond Martin, "L'immortalité de l'âme d'après Robert de Melun," *Revue néo-scolastique de philosophie* 41 (1934): 128–45.

22 See Anne-Marie Vlasschaert's introduction to her edition of this work: *Le Liber mahameleth*, ed. Vlasschaert (Stuttgart, 2010), 7–32.

23 See Charles Burnett, "John of Seville and John of Spain: A Mise au Point," *Bulletin de philosophie médiévale* 44 (2002): 59–78, at 67.

psychological, and metaphysical questions with sharp philosophical skill, a skill only tangential to the cultivated scientific skills demonstrated by the author of the *Liber mahameleth*.

In short, the treatise seems unrelated to Gundissalinus's interests. One way to reconcile this discrepancy is provided by the stylistic nature of the treatise. As the critical editor of the text underlines, the author has access to many Arabic texts on mathematics and trade, and diffusely quotes them in the text. In truth, the *Liber mahameleth* itself could be a worked-up version of an Arabic text, profoundly revised and adapted by a Latin translator – traits that also characterise Gundissalinus's *De scientiis*.[24] At the same time, it is possible to detect a quite philosophically learned approach to the topic of mathematics within the opening lines of the treatise, where the author presents the study of numbers through an epistemological application of the Porphyrian tree and mirrors Boethius's division of sciences.[25]

Thanks to the practical part of the *Liber mahameleth*, Burnett and Vlasschaert have dated and geographically circumscribed the production of the treatise.[26] The author names different currencies, among which are the *baetis* of Baeza and the *malequinus* of Malaga. These two circulated only between 1143 and 1153, revealing the work was written between these two dates. Likewise, the author ostensibly discloses his provenence when he refers to the currencies of Segovia and Toledo, towns where Gundissalinus surely lived. These specific indicators aside, the most important thread which ties Gundissalinus to the *Liber mahameleth* is Gundissalinus himself. He quotes excerpts from the anonymous text both in his *De divisione philosophiae* and *De scientiis* while dealing with mathematics.[27] This fact displays Gundissalinus's knowledge of the *Liber mahameleth*, and the high value he bestowed upon it. Excerpts from the mathematical work, though, are also contained within the *Liber alchorismi de pratica arismetice*, ascribed to Johannes Hispanus – one of Gundissalinus's collaborators – and supposedly written between 1156 and 1159.[28] These connections between the *Liber mahameleth* and Gundissalinus led Burnett and Vlasschaert to suppose that Gundissalinus was the actual author of the treatise,

---

24 See Vlasschaert, *Le Liber mahameleth*, 8–11.

25 See ibid., 7.2–9.

26 See Burnett, "John of Seville and John of Spain," 67; and Vlasschaert, *Le Liber mahameleth*, 11–13.

27 See Burnett, "John of Seville and John of Spain," 68–70; and Vlasschaert, *Le Liber mahameleth*, 28–30.

28 See Burnett, "John of Seville and John of Spain," 66–67; and Vlasschaert, *Le Liber mahameleth*, 27–28.

26 | CHAPTER ONE

while the other critical editor, Jacques Sesiano, focused on the hypothesis that Johannes Hispanus was the translator or author.[29]

In sum, Gundissalinus directly quoted the *Liber mahameleth* in his epistemological works, while another direct quotation can be found in Johannes Hispanus's *Liber alchorismi de pratica arismetice*. Since the *Liber mahameleth* makes explicit reference to two currencies that were in circulation only between 1143 and 1153, it could not have been written much later than 1153, as the author seems to have knowledge of the existence of *baetis* and *malequinus* but not of the cessation of their utilisation. Meanwhile, the *Liber alchorismi* has its *terminus post quem* in 1156. If this is true, as it seems to be, the author of the *Liber alchorismi*, Johannes Hispanus, had access to the *Liber mahameleth* in the second half of the 1150s, while he was already working on his *Liber alchorismi*. Nonetheless, one should remember that Gundissalinus was in Segovia between 1148 and 1161. As a consequence, if Gundissalinus is the author of the *Liber mahameleth*, then this treatise must have been written or translated in Segovia rather than Toledo, and perhaps the translation movement and the collaboration between Gundissalinus and Johannes Hispanus began before Gundissalinus's transfer to Toledo in 1162.

There is some data that seems to support this hypothesis, starting with the references to currencies in the *Liber mahameleth*. The treatise mentions different currencies from many cities of the Iberian Peninsula, but its author makes specific reference to the currencies of Segovia and Toledo,[30] claiming that they are the most familiar to him.[31] Since Toledo was the most prominent city of the kingdom of Castile, it is patent that the author used this currency, while the reference to Segovia is less obvious. In this latter reference, one likely sees a clue regarding the author's link to Segovia. There, in the first half of 1140s, Robert of Chester was working on the translation of one of the most important Arabic treatises on mathematics, al-Khwarizmi's *al-Jabr*. Robert's choice to work in Segovia must not have been incidental. On the contrary, it implies that Arabic scientific works were available in Segovia at the time. The authors of both the *Liber mahameleth* and the *Liber alchorismi* could have found a perfect environment in Segovia, where they could easily find the Arabic mathematical sources they would need and, moreover, Latin translations by Robert of Chester.

---

29 See Burnett, "John of Seville and John of Spain," 71–72; Vlasschaert, *Le Liber mahameleth*, 30–32; and Jacques Sesiano, "Un recueil du XIIIème siècle de problèmes mathématiques," *Sciamus: Sources and Commentaries in Exact Sciences* 1 (2000): 71–132. See also *The Liber mahameleth*, ed. Jacques Sesiano (Berlin, 2014).

30 *Le Liber mahameleth*, ed. Vlasschaert, 369.21–22.

31 See ibid., 369.20, and Vlasschaert's remarks at 12.

One further clue in favour of Gundissalinus's authorship of the *Liber mahameleth* has been recently presented by Gad Freudenthal.[32] In a recent study, Freudenthal presents an excerpt by Abraham ibn Daud, Gundissalinus's collaborator, in which he attacks those people who spend their time in useless activities like mathematical games. This criticism seems to be directed to the author of a treatise that actually deals with mathematical exercises that could be easily and disdainfully defined as "games," i.e., the author of the *Liber mahameleth*. This would not be the only place where Ibn Daud directly or indirectly criticises his colleague, as will later be made clear. Accordingly, the supposition that Gundissalinus is the author of this treatise, while plausible, still needs further corroboration through textual analysis of the many unidentified or unexplored sources used by Gundissalinus and the author of the *Liber mahameleth*.

The third problematic treatise ascribed to Gundissalinus, *De scientiis*, proposes a new division of the sciences, integrating the traditional *trivium* and *quadrivium* with sciences traditionally held as extending beyond the domain of the liberal arts.[33] Ultimately, the treatise catalogues, enumerates, and establishes the pre-eminence of the sciences treated therein, subsuming the lesser sciences under the authority of the greater disciplines, a project that Gundissalinus would only fully complete in his *De divisione philosophiae*. This specific interest in the division of sciences is probably due to the fact that the Latin *curriculum studiorum*, comprised of the seven liberal arts, displayed intrinsic limits in the face of the "new" sciences cultivated by the Arabs. When these arrived in Europe, the constraints of Latin science and philosophy were made manifest.[34] Both required reforms not only through the insertion of new sources and authorities, but also in the form of a new epistemological system – a system which allowed the integration of these "new" sciences into Latin thought.

De scientiis addresses these needs. The scientific model it presented reflects on the place of grammar, followed by that of logic and of the *scientiae doctrinales*. Then, the text treats physics and the divine science, before ending with a short discussion on civic and juridical sciences. Each science is subdivided into a number of sub-disciplines. Grammar, for example, is composed of seven parts, while logic is composed of eight parts, each one named after a logical work by

---

32 See Gad Freudenthal, "Abraham Ibn Daud, Avendauth, Dominicus Gundissalinus and Practical Mathematics in Mid-Twelfth Century Toledo," *Aleph* 16 (2016): 60–106.

33 Gundissalinus, *De scientiis*, ed. Manuel Alonso Alonso (Madrid, 1954); and Gundissalinus, *De scientiis secundum versionem Dominici Gundisalvi*, trans. Jakob Schneider (Freiburg im Breisgau, 2006).

34 For example: Gundissalinus, *De scientiis*, ed. Alonso Alonso, 55.5–56.1.

28 | CHAPTER ONE

Aristotle.[35] Logic by itself is merely instrumental in this work, its purpose being to clarify and ensure the rectitude of reasoning, specifically of syllogisms.

Mathematics is divided into seven sciences, themselves divided even further. Arithmetic, for instance, is divided into its theoretical and practical applications.[36] In the same fashion, geometry, music and astronomy are divided into theoretical and practical parts. As noted earlier, the four traditional disciplines of the *quadrivium* are paired with three disciplines (a partnership originally found in the Arabic division of the sciences): the *scientia de aspectibus*, i.e., optics; the *scientia de ponderibus*, the sciences of weights and measures; and the *scientia de ingeniis*, the discipline which deals with the application of mathematics to physical bodies.[37] Continuing this classification of the sciences, the author moves on to natural science, which studies natural bodies and the accidents whose being derives from these bodies, and to divine science, which studies essences and the principles of being.[38] The treatise ends with a brief examination of civil science and juridical science which is itself divided into two sub-disciplines.[39]

The structure of the treatise mirrors its main and almost exclusive source, al-Farabi's *Kitab Ihsa al-'Ulum*.[40] However, Gundissalinus modifies, develops, and cuts long portions of the original text, using only those sections that seem to satisfy his own endorsed epistemology.[41] For this reason, classifying the *De scientiis* is problematic. Some scholars prefer not to consider this treatise as one of Gundissalinus's original productions.[42] Nonetheless, a textual comparison with a distinct Latin translation of al-Farabi's *Ihsa al-'Ulum*, realised by Gerard of Cremona, displays how much the translations differ both in length and content. Gerard's version is effectively a word-for-word translation of al-Farabi's text, while Gundissalinus's shows an undeniably high degree of original reworking.[43]

35 Ibid., 77.14–80.3.

36 Ibid., 86.1–10.

37 See ibid., 93.9–99.4 (*de aspectibus*); 108.1–8 (*de ponderibus*); and 108.9–112.6 (*de ingeniis*).

38 Ibid., 127.7–128.13.

39 Ibid., 128.7–131.15.

40 Al-Farabi, *Ihsa' al-'Ulum li-al-Farabi*, ed. 'Uthman Amin (al-Qahirah, 1949).

41 See *De scientiis*, ed. Alonso Alonso, at 17.

42 For instance, Noburu Kinoshita. See Kinoshita, *El pensamento filosófico de Domingo Gundisalvo* (Salamanca, 1988), 47–90.

43 See al-Farabi, *Über die Wissenschaften / De scientiis: Nach der lateinischen Übersetzung Gerhards von Cremona*, trans. Franz Schupp (Hamburg, 2005); and Jakob Hans Josef Schneider, "Philosophy and Theology in the Islamic Culture: Al-Farabi's *De scientiis*," *Philosophy Study* 1 (2011): 41–51, at 42; and *De scientiis*, ed. Alonso Alonso, at 13–32. See also Alain Galonnier, *Le "De scientiis Alfarabii" de Gérard de Crémone: Contribution aux problèmes*

Beyond the aforementioned direct quotation from the *Liber mahameleth*, Manuel Alonso Alonso and Jean Jolivet have pointed out that some of the references presented in the *De scientiis* are also not part of the original Arabic text by al-Farabi, for instance the quotations from pseudo-al-Farabi's *De ortu scientiarum*. As is usual with Gundissalinus, these excerpts appear to aim at clarifying or improving the line of reasoning developed in the text.[44] Thus, Gundissalinus's *De scientiis* can be considered both a "creative translation" and a "scarcely original work." In either case, the *De scientiis* stands as one of the first philosophical contributions by Gundissalinus beyond mere translation, escaping the modern boundaries between originality and translation.

The four treatises undeniably by Gundissalinus cover three philosophical disciplines: metaphysics (*De unitate et uno* and *De processione mundi*), psychology (*De anima*), and epistemology (*De divisione philosophiae*). These three main aspects of Gundissalinus's reflection are bound together by consistency of approach and continuity of questions and answers. Such a consistency, though, does not imply that Gundissalinus did not change his mind on some significant issues.

Regarding the chronological order of Gundissalinus's writings, an analysis of the sources he used in his treatises and the recognition of a progressive problematisation of some key doctrines (especially his cosmology and ontology) allows an acknowledgement of *De unitate et uno* as the first treatise written by Gundissalinus and of *De processione mundi* as his last. In the middle, *De anima* might have been written before the translation of Avicenna's *Liber de philosophia prima* and certainly after that of his *De anima*, while the large quotation from Avicenna's *Kitab al-Burhan* (a work which had not been translated into Latin) presented in the *De divisione philosophiae* seems to point to a later stage of production, after the translation of *Philosophia prima*.

---

de l'acculturation au XIIe siècle (Turnhout, 2016); and Alain Galonnier, "Dominicus Gundissalinus et Gérard de Crémone, deux possibles stratégies de traduction: Le cas de l'encyclopédie farabienne du *De scientiis*," in *Une lumière venue d'ailleurs: Héritages et ouvertures dans les encyclopédies d'Orient et d'Occident au Moyen Âge*, ed. Godefroid de Callataÿ and Baudouin Van den Abeele, 103–17.

44 See *De scientiis*, ed. Alonso Alonso, 7–51; and Jean Jolivet, "The Arabic Inheritance," in *A History of Twelfth-Century Western Philosophy*, ed. Peter Dronke (Cambridge, 1988), 113–48.

30 | CHAPTER ONE

Unities

De unitate et uno is a short treatise dealing with the metaphysical concept of oneness.[45] Its main source is Ibn Gabirol's *Fons vitae*. For almost a century, *De unitate* was believed to be a treatise by Boethius, a fact that, until Thomas Aquinas declared it spurious, crucially contributed to the diffusion of the work.[46] At the heart of the treatise is the assertion that "whatever exists, therefore, exists because it is one" ("quidquid est, ideo est, quia unum est.")[47] By this fundamental principle, Gundissalinus establishes a precise bond between unity and existence, or even more ambitiously, between oneness and being, claiming that

> Unity is that whereby each thing is said to be one. Whether it is simple or composite, spiritual or corporeal, a thing is one by unity, and can be one only by unity, just as it can be white only by whiteness, or be so much only by quantity. Besides, [a thing] not only is one by unity, but as long as it is something, it is what it is as long as unity is in it, and when it ceases to be one, it ceases to be what it is.[48]

Be it simple or composed, spiritual or corporeal, everything exists because it has some unity, and it exists only as long as it is one. Unity, indeed, is a metaphysical principle directly related to existence, since only what participates in it can be said to be "one," i.e., to have an actual and singular existence. Gundissalinus also underlines a fundamental relation between existence and form. Gundissalinus claims, accordingly, that "all being is from the form."[49] This causal bond is only valid for created substances, as it implies a compositional aspect – a duality which

45 On Gundissalinus's use of the Neoplatonic concept of Oneness, see María Jesús Soto Bruna, "La 'causalidad del uno' en Domingo Gundisalvo," *Revista española de filosofía medieval* 21 (2014): 53–68; María Jesús Soto Bruna, "El concepto de naturaleza como unidad causal en D. Gundissalinus," *De Natura: La naturaleza en la Edad Media*, ed. José Luis Fuertes Herreros and Ángel Poncela González (Ribeirão, 2015), 2: 851–58; and Rafael Ramón Guerrero, "Sobre el uno y la unidad en la filosofía árabe: apunte historiográfico," in *Metafísica y antropología en el siglo XII*, ed. María Jesús Soto Bruna (Pamplona, 2005), 69–80.

46 See footnote 79 below.

47 See Gundissalinus, *De unitate et uno*, ed. María Jesús Soto Bruna and Concepción Alonso Del Real (Pamplona, 2015), 104.3.

48 Ibid., 102.2–104.1: "Unitas est qua unaquaeque res dicitur esse una. Sive enim sit simplex sive composita, sive sit spiritualis sive corporea, res unitate una est. Nec potest esse una nisi unitate, sicut nec alba nisi albedine, nec quanta nisi quantitate. Non solum autem unitate una est, sed etiam tamdiu est, quicquid est id quod est quamdiu in se unitas est. Cum autem desinit esse unum, desinit esse id quod est."

49 Ibid., 104.4: "Omne enim esse ex forma est, in creatis scilicet."

is absent in the existence of the divine. Since form cannot exist without being joined to matter, the "philosophers" have stated that "being is the existence of form into matter."[50] The being of any substance, then, is caused by the union of matter and form, as,

> When the form is made one with matter, however, from their conjunction something which is one is constituted necessarily, and that one, in its constitution, only persists as long as unity holds the form together with matter. Consequently, the destruction of a thing is nothing else but the separation of form from matter.[51]

For Gundissalinus, the destruction of a thing – the process in virtue of which a substance ceases to be "one" and to be what it is – coincides with the separation of matter and form, a separation that corresponds to the dissolution of the essence of that substance.[52] Accordingly, a participation in the metaphysical unity which makes possible the existence of the created thing is equivalent to the concrete compositional unity of matter and form in virtue of which "being and one are inseparable partners and appear to be together by nature."[53]

Being and unity are *concomites in existentia* but cannot be identified with one and the same principle – they are not convertible. Nevertheless, created being and derived unity are always the consequence of an act of union and, for this reason, they can subsist only as the result of two different things "made one" in a compound, which is the actual created being. In contrast to creation, the absolute Being and Unity giver of unity, is radically simple. His unity is utterly different from the derived unity of created beings, since it is the simple and absolute subsistence of being. A significant implication of this theory is that universal hylomorphism among creatures provides the main characteristic distinguishing created and divine beings. Created beings have a unity made of different principles – a multiplicity composed into unity which marks their difference from God's absolute ontological simplicity. The principles which are made "one" in the ontological composition of created being are matter and form. Therefore, it is necessary that the being of every creature – spiritual or corporeal, simple or composed

---

50 Ibid., 106.1: "esse est existentia formae cum materia."

51 Ibid., 106.2–5: "Cum autem forma materiae unitur, ex coniunctione utriusque necessario aliquid unum constituitur. In qua constitutione illud unum non permanet nisi quamdiu unitas formam cum materia tenet. Igitur destructio rei non est aliud quam separatio formae a materia."

52 See ibid., 108.1–4.

53 Ibid., 108.4–5: "esse et unum inseparabiliter concomitantur se et videntur esse simul natura."

32 | CHAPTER ONE

– is a compound of both matter and form. As a consequence, created unity can exist only as a unity of matter and form, whose union corresponds to the existential causation of whatever creature is operated on by God's unity. Every creature, therefore, moves toward the One, as its desire for being corresponds to its desire of being "one" through the One.[54]

The modalities through which unity causes created being are referred by Gundissalinus to the peculiarities of matter's ontology. Unity fulfils matter, which is what *per se* lacks unity. In itself, indeed, matter tends towards dispersion and division. Without being held together by unity, matter could not be joined to its form and then exist within the created compound.[55] Unity, therefore, appears to perform two main ontological functions in relation to the caused being:

1. It preliminarily holds together matter, making it suitable to be joined to its form.
2. It holds together both matter and form originating their compound.

Nevertheless, Gundissalinus is redundant in claiming that matter can be joined only to form. The unifying factor must be performed as a formal function – unity must be a form.[56] Accordingly, unity is the first form which joins matter, making it one and able to be joined by further forms specifying that substance. In this ordered series of forms, the form of unity must be the first to join matter and the last to disappear when the substance is destroyed. The identification of derived unity and form – only assumed as such in *De unitate*, and later discussed in *De processione* – does not imply that the absolute One is a pure form. Following the Neoplatonic tendencies he found in *Fons vitae*, Gundissalinus stresses the tension between diversity and the similarity of cause and caused, by which every caused thing is similar to its cause, but different from it in various respects. Indeed,

> since every created thing must be completely different from what has created it, therefore, the created unity must be completely different and almost opposite to the creating Unity. Because the creating Unity has neither beginning nor end, neither change nor diversity. Therefore, multiplicity, diversity, and mutability accrue to the created unity. In some matter, then, [unity] has a beginning and an end, while in another [matter] it has a beginning, but not

54 See ibid., 110.1–112.2.
55 See ibid., 112.3–114.6.
56 See ibid., 114.8–9.

Pioneering Transformations: Gundissalinus's Philosophical Reflection | 33

an end, because in some it is subject to change and corruption, and in others [unity is subject to] change, but not to corruption.[57]

The radical difference between creator and creature is displayed by the different ways in which caused unity is instantiated into creatures. There are many different species of substances, each one of which is characterised by peculiarities. As a result, some beings are perpetual while others are subject to generation and corruption. Differences in the outcomes of hylomorphic union are the result of matter's precarious ontological status. When form is joined to a subtle and simple matter, the resulting being is indivisible and perpetual – like angels and celestial spheres. When form is joined to a thicker and feebler matter, the result is a weaker unity, characteristic of those substances suffering generation and corruption – the sensible world.[58] The closer a form is to the One, the stronger is the power it enacts upon matter: "For the more any unity is closer to the first and true unity, the more one and simple the matter it informs will be; and to the opposite, the further unity is from the first unity, the more multiplied and composed [its matter will be]."[59]

The ontological degradation of beings down to the final layer of reality, therefore, is caused by the progressive thickening of matter, which is accompanied – if not tacitly caused – by the gradual weakening of form/unity. The latter appears to be implied by the description of the former. Being dense and thick, matter cannot be acted upon by form, whose power is weaker due to its distance from the origin of unity. Notwithstanding this obvious implication, Gundissalinus is adamant in affirming that "all this does not happen on account of the diversity of the power (*virtus*) of the agent, but on account of the aptitude of the matter receiving [it]."[60] As a consequence of this process, different degrees of matter (subtler/thicker) and the form's effectiveness (stronger/weaker) give origin to

---

57 Ibid., 116.1–9: "quia omne creatum omnino diversum est a quo creatum est, profecto creata unitas a creante unitate omnino diversa esse debuit et quasi opposita. Sed quia creatrix unitas non habet principium neque finem nec permutationem nec diversitatem, ideo creatae unitati accidit multiplicitas et diversitas et mutabilitas; ita ut in quadam materia sit habens principium et finem, in quadam vero principium et non finem, quia in quibusdam subiacet permutationi et corruptioni, in quibusdam permutationi sed non corruptioni."

58 See ibid., 118.1–8.

59 Ibid., 118.9–120.2: "Quanto enim unaquaeque unitas fuerit propinquior primae et verae unitati, tanto materia formata per illam erit magis una et simplicior; et e contrario, quanto remotior fuerit a prima unitate, tanto erit multiplicior et compositior."

60 Ibid., 128.4–5: "hoc non accidit ex diversitate virtutis agentis, sed ex aptitudine materiae suscipientis."

34 | CHAPTER ONE

the different hypostatic layers of which reality is constituted. The first cosmic hypostasis is the Intelligence, whose simplicity and unity are the highest possible for a created being. Intelligence is followed by the Soul, which is characterised by a weaker unity and a greater degree of complexity. The Soul is cosmologically articulated into Rational, Sensible, and Vegetative Souls in a progressive corporealisation that finally produces the sensible world, through Nature, the last psychological layer. The sensible world is characterised by an extreme remoteness of the form/unity from its origin and, correspondingly, by an exceedingly thick sort of matter. Consequently, no further layer of reality can be established below this final bulky and precarious instantiation.[61]

Different degrees of proximity of each hypostasis to the first Cause also justify the diversity of ontological qualities between the strata. The Intelligence is essentially, but not incidentally, indivisible and is caused by the One without any mediation, while the Soul suffers change and diversity and is instantiated in three hierarchically disposed sub-hypostases. Finally, the sensible world has the greatest degree of multiplicity and is borne by "matter sustaining quantity." Following another *topos* of the Neoplatonic tradition, Gundissalinus explains the origin of the universe through the metaphor of light, claiming that,

> Form, indeed, is like light: for just as a thing is seen on account of light, so too cognition and knowledge of the things are provided by the form, and not by matter. This light, though, is brighter in some things and darker in others, depending on whether the matter in which it is infused comes to be brighter or darker. The more sublime matter is, the subtler it will be, and completely penetrated by light: consequently, that substance will be wiser and more perfect, such as the Intelligence and the Rational Soul. And on the contrary, the lower matter is, the thicker and darker it will be, not completely penetrated by light. As it has been said already, the more matter descends, [the more] it is made compact, thick, and corpulent, and its middle parts block the last ones from being perfectly penetrated by light. It is impossible, indeed, for light to penetrate the second part as much as [it does] the first; nor does as much light reach the third part as reaches the middle part, and so on, little by little, down to the lowest part, in which the light is weakened for it is furthest away from the source of light. Nonetheless, as it has been said, this does not happen on account of the light in itself, but on account of the great density and obscurity of matter in itself. Similarly, when the sun-

61 See ibid., 120.3–122.10.

Pioneering Transformations: Gundissalinus's Philosophical Reflection | 35

light is mixed with the dark air, it lacks the power (virtus) [that it has] when is mixed with bright air ...[62]

The twofold interaction between the progression of matter and form, masterfully rendered by the example of light, would be further developed and problematised by Gundissalinus in his later works.

The final part of *De unitate* deals with two problems apparently far away from the metaphysical discussion exposited above: the different meanings of the term "unitas" and the question of continuous and discrete quantities.[63] It is interesting to note that the problem of the different meanings of "unity" is traced back by Gundissalinus to the very ontological degradation of the form in its progression toward the edges of reality – a process causing the internal differentiation of the form, which in itself is one.[64] This gradual distinction of form/unity implies different varieties of participation and, through this, a manifold meaning of what can be said to be one. Gundissalinus lists fourteen senses of "unity" and gives some clarifying examples. Unfortunately, however, Gundissalinus does not explain in detail what he means with this description. One could certainly interpret his scheme as a direct consequence of the diversification of the form/unity in the cosmogonic progression. Accordingly, the fundamental distinction would be between the essential unity of God, who is in himself one for the simplicity of his essence, and the accidental unity/oneness of all created things, which are incidentally one in themselves and which, in various ways, participate in the unity that derives from the absolute unity of God.

---

62 Ibid., 128.8–134.1: "Forma enim est quasi lumen, eo quod sicut per lumen res videtur, sic per formam cognitio et scientia rei habetur, non per materiam; sed hoc lumen in quibusdam est clarius, in quibusdam vero obscurius, prout materia, cui infunditur, fuerit clarior vel obscurior. Quo enim materia fuerit sublimior, fit subtilior et penetratur tota a lumine; et ideo substantia ipsa fit sapientior et perfectior sicut intelligentia et rationalis anima. Et e contrario, quo materia fuerit inferior, fit spissior et obscurior et non ita tota penetratur a lumine. Quo magis enim materia descendit, sicut iam dictum est, constringitur et spissatur et corpulentatur et partes eius mediae prohibent ultimas perfecte penetrari a lumine. Non enim est possibile ut tantum luminis penetret partem secundam, quantum primam, nec ad tertiam tantum luminis pervenit, quantum ad mediam. Et sic paulatim donec perveniatur usque ad partem infimam. Quae, quia remotissima est a fonte luminis, lumen debilitatur in illa. Nec tamen hoc fit sicut praedictum est propter lumen in se, sed propter multam densitatem et obscuritatem materiae in se. Quemadmodum lumen solis, cum admiscetur tenebroso aeri, non est illius virtutis, cuius est admixtum claro aeri ... ."

63 See, respectively, ibid., 136.1–140.6 and 140.7–146.6.

64 See ibid., 136.1–2.

36 | CHAPTER ONE

Nevertheless, Gundissalinus mentions accidental unity only as one of the many possible meanings of unity. Furthermore, the conjecture that all these different kinds of unity are caused by the same form seems to be unjustified, since a reference to the differentiating process of the form/unity in its encounter with matter does not provide a sufficient justification for how one and the same form can provide different effects in a single being. Gundissalinus's scheme, therefore, does not resolve the implicit problem of how a single form can produce different effects in the same being. Besides the intentions of its author, it only gives a description of the verbal ambiguities of the term "unity," and has a metaphysical value only if related to the difference between the substantial and accidental predication of unity.

Similar tensions are in place within the closing paragraph of the treatise, where Gundissalinus engages with the problem of continuous and discrete quantities. The basis of his analysis is the desire for unity common to all existing things.[65] Every being desires to be one, and therefore it endeavours to be a unity. This is Gundissalinus's key to explaining the difference between continuous and discrete quantities. Plurality is always a heap of unities. When these unities are aggregated, they become a continuous quantity, and while they remain separated they constitute a discrete quantity. Thus, the difference between continuous and discrete unity is only apparent, since "it is true that the continuous quantity comes into substance only on account of the unity joining and flowing in it."[66]

From a general point of view, it can be said that *De unitate et uno* is a first attempt by Gundissalinus at understanding the implications of two theories he eagerly accepts: the grounding role of God's absolute oneness and unity, and universal hylomorphism as a key justification of the ontological difference between creator and creature. Noticeably, the horizon on which these doctrines are presented is utterly Neoplatonic. Nevertheless, *De unitate* does not show any real thematisation of the causal relation between God and creatures, nor any problematisation of the cosmogonic process. Both features are described but not analysed. Their implications and any problematic outcomes, such as atomism, are left unconsidered.

65 See ibid., 140.7–142.2.

66 Ibid., 146.5–6: "continua quantitas non venit in substantiam nisi ex coniunctione et constrictione unitatum in illa." Gundissalinus actually goes a step further, proposing a sort of reduction of continuity to discrete quantity. A continuous quantity is an aggregate of discrete unities held together, unities that, when scattered, are said to be discrete and, once gathered, are called a continuous quantity. It is a position very close to atomism, and Gundissalinus calls these basic unities from which dimensionality arises the "roots" of quantity. See Nicola Polloni, "Dominicus Gundissalinus's *On Unity and the One*," in *Medieval Philosophy and the Jewish, Islamic, and Christian Traditions: Essays in Honor of Richard Taylor*, ed. Luis Xavier López Farjeat, Katja Krause, and Nicholas Oschman, forthcoming.

Some of the theories Gundissalinus sketched in *De unitate et uno* would find further development in *De anima* and *De processione mundi*. Especially in the latter, his perspective would be changed and rooted in a different framework, requiring him to detach himself from positions he previously accepted.

Souls

Gundissalinus's *De anima* aims at addressing four main problems concerning the soul: its existence and definition, its ontological composition and number, its origin and immortality, and finally, the powers of the soul.[67] A thorough examination of the soul was urgent, as expressed by Gundissalinus at the beginning of his treatise, where he observes that some people, absorbed by their senses, fell into such madness as to even affirm that God himself does not exist.[68] Luckily for Gundissalinus, the "philosophers" have elaborated many arguments to demonstrate that the soul exists. He proposes four sets of "proofs," arguing that a consideration of both movement and parts of a body sufficiently demonstrate that there must be a soul governing it.[69]

The soul is the principle of movement of a body, a principle which moves without being moved and impels corporeal movement through desire, hate, fear,

67 See Hasse, *Avicenna's* De anima *in the Latin West*, in particular 14.

68 Gundissalinus, *De anima*, ed. María Jesús Soto Bruna and Concepción Alonso Del Real (Pamplona, 2009), 68.3–9. It should be noticed that Gundissalinus seems willing to establish a precise and clear bond with Avicenna's *De anima*. Even if the Persian philosopher is never mentioned by name in the *De anima*, Gundissalinus's prologue directly recalls the dedicatory letter accompanying the Latin translation of Avicenna's *De anima*. A comparison between the two excerpts makes clear that Gundissalinus wants to present his work in direct continuity with Avicenna's *De anima*; that is, indeed, the main and primary source on which Gundissalinus's psychological discussion relies. Compare ibid., 64.5–16 and Avicenna, *Liber de anima seu Sextus de naturalibus, prologus*, ed. Simone Van Riet (Louvain, 1968–72), 1: 3.4–4.20.

69 Concisely, Gundissalinus's sets of arguments are developed as follows. (1) A body cannot be the principle of its own movement. If that were the case, the body would never cease to move. That being false, it is clear that the body needs an external agent of its movement, and that cause is the soul. (2) All bodies are composed of parts, and these parts need to be united in some way. Nevertheless, as they cannot be made one in virtue of themselves, the existence of an external cause of the corporeal unity must be admitted. (3) Consideration of movement as a passage from potency to act leads to similar results. Moved and mover must always be different and, therefore, the soul must be the mover of the body, which cannot be moved to act by itself. (4) Finally, what is animated, before being so, was necessarily unanimated. If this is true, one must admit a cause of its animation, which is the soul. See Gundissalinus, *De anima*, ed. Soto Bruna and Alonso Del Real, 68.10–72.21.

38 | CHAPTER ONE

and natural tendency.[70] From Gundissalinus's perspective, his position is consistent with both Plato's and Aristotle's definitions of the soul.[71] Neither Plato nor Aristotle, however, serves as his direct source. While Plato's definition of the soul is conveyed through Qusta ibn Luqa's *De differentia animae et spiritus*,[72] the main source of Gundissalinus's discussion is the fifth book of Avicenna's *De anima* – with Gundissalinus copying and pasting passages and demonstrations from that work. In *De anima*, Gundissalinus's indebtedness to Avicenna is profound and enveloping. He expands on many arguments on the difference between soul and body, and the irreducible difference between them. Among these proofs, we can find the famous argument of the "flying man," the mental experiment proposed by Avicenna in his *De anima* and attested here for the first time in the Latin tradition.[73]

A similar scenario is offered by the discussion of Aristotle's definition of the soul as the first perfection of a natural, organic, and potentially living body.[74] This definition, found in another quotation from Qusta ibn Luqa, is thoroughly discussed by Gundissalinus. He examines the function of the soul as first perfection of the body (a function which is pursued through the soul's powers), as soul of an organic body (the organs are finalised to life, that is to say, to the soul), and as soul of a potentially living body (since the soul is the act of the body and the cause of its life). Soon after, though, the discussion returns to Avicenna's *De anima*. Gundissalinus finally claims that the soul is "something like a form" for the body, *quasi forma*, which actualises the body by animating it and giving it its complexion as its *forma complexionali*.[75] Therefore, once the soul is removed, the subject of the animated body becomes a subject of something else. Unanimated, the body changes completely as it has lost what was qualifying its substantiality as such.

Gundissalinus's reliance on Avicenna's *De anima* on this point should not be regarded as signifying an uncritical adherence to the Avicennian framework in its entirety. To the contrary, a peculiar trait of Gundissalinus's speculation is a sort of synthesis of Avicenna's and Ibn Gabirol's perspectives. In *De anima*, this synthesizing tendency is firstly and mostly instantiated in a fusion of Avicenna's

70 See ibid., 82.14–22.

71 See ibid., 11–12.

72 Qusta ibn Luqa, *De differentia animae et spiritus*, ed. Carl Sigmund Barach, Bibliotheca Philosophorum Mediae Aetatis (Innsbruck: 1878), 3: 120–39, at 130–37. See also José Martínez Gázquez and Anna Maranini, "La *recensio* única del *De differentia inter spiritum et animam* de Costa Ben Luca," *Faventia* 19/2 (1997): 115–29.

73 See Gundissalinus, *De anima*, ed. Soto Bruna and Alonso Del Real, 86.1–17.

74 See ibid., 96.6–7.

75 See ibid., 100.6–10.

psychology and Ibn Gabirol's ontology – specifically his most famous ontological doctrine, universal hylomorphism. Bearing in his mind the discussion on unity and substantiality he had expounded in his earlier *De unitate et uno*, Gundissalinus states that even if the soul performs a form-like function, the soul cannot be considered to be a form *per se*. It is instead a rational spirit.[76]

The soul is not a simple substance, like matter and form. It is a composed substance which is said to be simple only by comparison with much more composite substances (bodies). The human soul is a relatively simple rational spirit which is made of matter and form. The presence of matter in its substance does not, however, imply that the soul is corporeal. Matter, as an overarching term, can have three significations. It can connote first matter, simple but able to receive any form. It can also refer to corporeal or spiritual matter, once they have received, respectively, the forms of corporeity and spirituality. Finally, the term "matter" might signify the matter of tangible bodies, i.e., elements and elemental aggregates (*elementata*).[77] The soul has matter in its second meaning, i.e., a spiritual matter, joined to its form (or better, forms).[78]

This claim is the foundation of Gundissalinus's psychological hylomorphism. Justification of this crucial doctrine is developed in chapter seven of *De anima*. This chapter can be considered a sort of cherry-picked agglomerate of quotations from Ibn Gabirol's *Fons vitae*. Gundissalinus expounds a set of twenty-three arguments aimed at demonstrating psychological hylomorphism, all derived from book four of *Fons vitae*. Often redundant, these demonstrations share the following common demonstration strategies:

1. The primary function of a form is to specify, that is, divide the genus into species. Accordingly, it is necessary to posit something in which everything convenes before being specified by the form: that common substrate is matter. If that were not the case, there would be neither commonality nor diversity among creatures. As a consequence, a form always requires matter and also the soul must be composed of both form and matter.[79]

2. Created existence is a consequence of hylomorphic union. If spiritual substances, like souls, were form only, they would not exist.[80]

---

76 See ibid., 102.18–103.3.

77 See ibid., 142.13–20.

78 Even though Gundissalinus does not clarify this point, it should be assumed, based on the overall discussion of this topic (explicitly in *De processione* and implicitly in *De anima*), that the matter of the soul is joined to at least four forms: unity, substantiality, spirituality, and rationality.

79 An application of this strategy is provided in ibid., 148.9–13.

80 See ibid., 152.3–5.

3. The human intellect primarily comprehends through abstraction. Abstraction, though, only happens when a form is abstracted from its matter. Therefore, only what is composed of matter and form and is limited by form can be abstracted and understood. As a consequence, the soul is composed of matter and form, otherwise it would be incomprehensible.[81]

4. The hylomorphic composition of the soul is an ontological manifestation of the difference between creator and creature. God being simply and absolutely one, the effect of his causation cannot be something completely one, but must be intrinsically dual. This ontological duality, specific to created being, corresponds to the composition of matter and form, which is shared by every creature, including the soul.[82]

Matter has a grounding position in the chain of being depicted by Gundissalinus. Every creature, spiritual or corporeal, is composed of matter. Therefore, the creation of the common substrate must precede – at least logically, if not chronologically – that of the human souls. This being the case, the souls must not be created *ex nihilo*, but from first matter. Gundissalinus was well aware of this implication and eagerly accepts it, claiming that

> Consequently, although it is said that new human souls are created every day, nonetheless, they appear to be created not from nothing but from first matter. If all being comes forth by form, therefore, the rational soul has being only by the form, but the form has being only when it is in matter. As a result, the form by which the rational soul comes forth into being, is enmattered, and therefore, the soul appears to consist of matter and form.[83]

The souls cannot be co-eternal with God. Consideration of the soul's progressive acquisition of perfection through knowledge proves that it has a beginning and that its imperfection derives from something perfect. So, when is the soul created? Some affirm that all souls were created together at the beginning of time, but this position has been refuted by the "philosophers." Without mentioning who these "philosophers" are (almost certainly Avicenna), Gundissalinus points out that alterity and distinction among the souls derive from their being

81 See ibid., 152.11–19.

82 For instance, ibid., 156.4–7.

83 Ibid., 158.20–160.2: "Quamvis ergo humanae animae cotidie novae creari dicantur, non tamen de nihilo, sed de materia prima creari videntur. Si enim omne esse ex forma est, profecto rationalis anima non habet esse nisi per formam; sed forma non habet esse nisi in materia; forma igitur qua anima rationalis est non est nisi in materia; ac per hoc anima videtur constare ex materia et forma."

united to their bodies. Accordingly, the souls cannot have been created before their corporeal union. Otherwise, they would have been one and the same soul. Moreover, if the soul were created before its union to the body, the soul itself would be useless in its own being. However, since nothing in nature is superfluous and a non-embodied soul would be superfluous, it must be admitted that new souls are created on daily basis.[84]

As a consequence, new souls are created from matter every day. In one of the most original points of his discussion, Gundissalinus engages with the problem of the causal origin of souls to plainly deny that God is their efficient cause. This point, too, has been demonstrated by the "philosophers" (here, Ibn Gabirol), as Gundissalinus reports:

> The philosophers, though, demonstrate that the souls are created not by God, but rather by the angels, in the following way. If the first Maker is the maker of the souls by himself, then the soul would always have existed with him. But the soul did not always exist with God since new souls are created every day. Therefore, the soul is not made by the first Maker, and the first Maker is not the maker of the soul by himself. Consequently, between God and the soul, an intermediary is necessary and it is the maker of the soul.[85]

If God were the direct cause of souls, there would be no justification for why the souls would leave his complete perfection to be embodied. In other words, the souls would never leave God's beatitude. Nonetheless, new souls are created every day in their corporeal bodies. As a consequence, God cannot be considered the direct cause of the souls, and there must be a mediating cause between God and the created soul. The latter is the central point of Gundissalinus's arguments. Without a mediator, inadmissible consequences would be implied, like mutability in God's being or the coeternity of God and souls. In addition, Gundissalinus points out that God creates from nothing, while the souls are made from matter and form. Accordingly, God cannot be their cause. With a similar approach, Gundissalinus also claims that God, being neither act nor potency, cannot actualise a potency such as the potential being of a soul.[86]

84 See ibid., 124.3–136.14.

85 Ibid., 128.17–22: "Probant autem philosophi animas non a Deo sed ab angelis creari hoc modo: si factor primus est factor animae per se, tunc anima semper fuit apud eum; sed anima non semper fuit apud Deum quoniam cotidie creantur novae; igitur anima non est facta a primo factore, nec primus factor est factor eius per se. Igitur necesse est ut aliquid sit medium inter Deum et animam, quod sit factor animae."

86 See ibid., 128.22–134.18.

42 | CHAPTER ONE

God therefore cannot be the maker of souls. As a result, the "philosophers" (in this case, Avicenna *and* Ibn Gabirol)[87] have demonstrated that souls are created by the angels. Gundissalinus adds that the causation of the soul is analogous to baptism. As a priest baptises by his ministry and through the authority of Christ, so too the angels make souls as part of their ministry and through the authority of God. Gundissalinus expounds that

> For what the philosophers demonstrate – namely, that the souls are not created by God, but by the angels – can be easily understood in this way, that they are created by the angel's ministry rather than God's. Nonetheless, when it is said that "God creates the soul," this sentence must be understood as referring to divine authority, not to his service, as when it is said of Christ that "He is the one who baptises," while [it is] the priest [who] baptises. Christ does so through his authority, not his ministry, and the priest does so through his ministry, not his authority.[88]

Gundissalinus's discussion of the origins of human souls touches further aspects, starting with the number of existing original souls (one or many) and the correlated doctrine of traducianism.[89] Regarding the latter, Gundissalinus presents the famous metaphor of the candle proposed by Augustine, describing the *tradux animae* from father to son in terms of the passage of light from one candle to another.[90] Augustine's account of the traducianist heresy, though, is oddly combined with a quotation from Ibn Gabirol's metaphors of the heat of fire and sunlight.[91] In *Fons vitae*, these metaphors are used to exposit the doctrine of the derivation and irradiation of spiritual substances. Curiously, Gundissalinus appears to use Ibn Gabirol's excerpts as examples of the "traducianist mistake" – perhaps with some implicit criticism of his doctrine of the causation of spiritual

87 See Nicola Polloni, "Gundissalinus on the Angelic Creation of the Human Soul: A Peculiar Example of Philosophical Appropriation," *Oriens* 47 (2019): 313–47.

88 Gundissalinus, *De anima*, ed. Soto Bruna and Alonso Del Real, 134.19–136.4: "Hoc autem quod philosophi probant, animas non a Deo sed ab angelis creari, sane quidem potest intelligi, scilicet non Dei ministerio sed angelorum. Et tamen cum dicitur 'Deus creat animas,' intelligendum est auctoritate non ministerio, sicut cum dicitur de Christo: 'hic est qui baptizat,' cum sacerdos baptiset. Sed Christus auctoritate non ministerio; sacerdos vero ministerio tantum, non auctoritate; sic et angeli creant animas ministerio tantum, non auctoritate."

89 Gundissalinus's discussion of the existence of a plurality of souls, one for each living being, is grounded upon Avicenna. See ibid., 108.3–14.

90 See Augustine, *Epistula* 190.4, PL 33.

91 See Ibn Gabirol, *Fons vitae* 3, ed. Clemens Baeumker (Münster, 1892–95), 200.2–11; ed. Marienza Benedetto (Milan, 2007), 294.

substances. Gundissalinus, though, easily supersedes the traducianist problem, stating tongue-in-cheek that "everyone already knows that the soul does not derive through transmission."[92]

Concerning the immortality of the soul, Gundissalinus argues that the substance of the soul is separated from the body, because the body is not the efficient but the accidental cause of the soul. Accordingly, being temporal and essential prior to the body, the soul is not destroyed by the death of the body. Indeed, the destruction of what is posterior (the body) cannot affect what is prior to it (the soul).[93]

The second part of De anima – chapters nine and ten – are dedicated to a detailed discussion of human psychological powers, a discussion almost completely based on Avicenna. Human knowledge is produced through a plurality of faculties which, nonetheless, are all related to one and the same subject: the rational soul. At the same time, these faculties correspond to three main powers that are the vegetative, sensitive, and rational powers.[94]

The vegetative power is articulated into three faculties: the nutritive power (vis nutritiva), the power of growth (vis augmentativa), and the generative power (vis generativa). The nutritive power converts a foreign body from its previous bodily kind into something similar to the body of the subject on which it performs, restoring what has been consumed and lost in waste. Similarly, power of growth assimilates the substance which has been received from the nutritive power and proportionally increases the corporeal dimensions of its body, leading it to its perfection. Finally, the generative power receives from its body something similar to the potency of that body and converts it into something similar to that body in act, through corporeal assimilation, generation, and bodily complexion.[95] Pursued through the four natural faculties of the body (vires attractiva, retentiva, digestiva, and expulsiva), the vegetative soul

---

92 Gundissalinus, De anima, ed. Soto Bruna and Alonso Del Real, 138.11–140.3. (" … iam tamen omnes tenent animam non esse ex traduce … ." Ibid., 140.6–7.)

93 See ibid., 166.3–176.4. Further arguments are aimed at demonstrating that the very substance of the soul cannot be destroyed in any way. It should be noted that the lines along which Gundissalinus argues that the substance of the soul cannot be divided into matter and form are very dense and complex. At first glance, it would even seem that Gundissalinus is denying a hylomorphic composition of the soul to consider it as a simple form. Convoluted language and scarcity of details may be the result of Gundissalinus's unwillingness to deal again with a topic he had already engaged with in a much wider and detailed fashion. Unfortunately, the problem of the authorship of the De immortalitate animae and the links to De anima escape the present discussion.

94 See ibid., 186.3–6.

95 See ibid., 186.9–20.

44 | CHAPTER ONE

uses its three powers to nourish and increase the body and to generate new bodies.[96]

The sensitive soul performs two operations – perception and voluntary movement – through the two faculties of the *vis motiva* and *vis apprehensiva*.[97] The *vis motiva* is composed of two powers: the appetitive or desiderative power, which imposes movement on the muscles of the body when it imagines something it desires or rejects. The "faculty infused into the body" performs the movement commanded by the appetitive power, contracting or relaxing muscles and nerves. Similarly, the *vis apprehensiva* is divided into two main faculties, which preside over two different kinds of sensible experience, i.e., internal and external apprehensions. External apprehension is pursued through the five senses – taste, sight, touch, smell, and hearing – each of which has eight species of perception.[98] In turn, internal apprehension is twofold. The first part of the cognitive process apprehends sensible forms, while the second part of the process apprehends sensible intentions. In this context, Gundissalinus clarifies that intentions and forms are two different mental elements. A form is the knowable content of the sensible body/event, while an intention is an assessable – or actually assessed – consideration of that content.[99] Following Avicenna, Gundissalinus presents this doctrine with the famous example of the difference between a sheep seeing the figure and colour of a wolf and assessing it as something dangerous, in fear of which the sheep runs away.[100]

There are five internal apprehensive faculties: phantasy, imagination, imaginative/cogitative faculty (which works on the sensible forms), estimative faculty, and memory, the latter two of which work on the sensible intentions. All sensible perceptions impressed into the five external senses are transferred to the phantasy, or common sense, in which these perceptions are united. This process is strictly connected with the subsequent two faculties, imagination and

---

96 See ibid., 186.21–188.3. This dynamic is further discussed by Gundissalinus, pointing out the specificity of each of the three powers and underlining that those who believe that the vegetative power operates in the human body as the nature operates in the plants are wrong. Operations of nature are indeed different from those of the soul, for the former is always performed in the same way, while the psychological operations are performed in different ways, because the action of the soul is stronger than that of nature.

97 Ibid., 190.18–192.3.

98 See ibid., 192.21–202.10.

99 See ibid., 212.3–19.

100 See ibid., 228.17–20, and Avicenna, *Liber de anima seu Sextus de naturalibus* 1.5, ed. Van Riet, 1: 86.93–6. See also Dominik Perler, "Why is the Sheep Afraid of the Wolf? Medieval Debates of Animal Passions," in *Emotion and Cognitive Life in Medieval and Early Modern Philosophy*, ed. Martin Pickavé and Lisa Shapiro (Oxford, 2012), 32–52.

Pioneering Transformations: Gundissalinus's Philosophical Reflection | 45

the cogitative faculty. Imagination receives and conserves the formal contents of phantasy, which are then elaborated by the cogitative faculty.

The first intentional faculty is the estimative power, which apprehends non-perceived intentions of sensible beings and acts on the imaginative contents. The estimative power, therefore, assesses the sensible event with a non-predetermined judgment, from which derives the majority of the animal's actions. For animals, as well as for unlearned men, the estimative is "the best judge" (*excellentior iudex*). The estimative power, continues Gundissalinus, can be produced in different ways: either as a natural caution (*cautela naturalis*), as when a child learns to walk and fears to fall; or "through experience" (*per experientiam*), that is to say, when the animal suffers pain or pleasure, and that impression is conserved in the memory. Finally, estimation can be given "through similarities" (*ad modum similitudinis*), when an intention has been repeatedly acquired together with some sensible forms, and then when these forms are perceived, the intention also is apprehended thanks to memory and senses.[101]

The last apprehensive power to be discussed is memory.[102] The *vis memorativa* holds all the intentional contents elaborated by the estimative faculty, while the formal contents are conserved by the imaginative faculty. Gundissalinus describes the process of converting the intentional and formal contents, and distinguishes memory from *recordatio*, the ability to recall memories proper to the human being. With memory, Gundissalinus's discussion of the sensitive soul is complete. He then passes to the analysis of the intellective process of the rational soul, the characteristic feature of human knowledge. The rational soul has two main faculties, the active and contemplative faculties, both equivocally called *intellectus*. The active faculty (*virtus activa*) is the principle moving the body in relation to the action the subject decides to perform, following the sensitive powers (appetitive and estimative) or the *virtus activa* itself. In contrast, the contemplative faculty (*virtus contemplativa*) is the faculty which is informed by the universal forms deprived of matter. The active and contemplative powers, thus, have two different cognitive processes and are finalised into two different kinds of judgments. The contemplative intellect assesses whether a universal is true or false (and necessary, possible, or impossible), while the active intellect assesses whether a particular is (ethically) just or unjust.[103]

From an epistemological point of view, both active and contemplative intellects have three degrees of statement – *dubitatio*, *opinio*, and *sententia* – but while the contemplative intellect has knowledge of the principles *per se*, the active intel-

---

101 See Gundissalinus, *De anima*, ed. Soto Bruna and Alonso Del Real, 226.10–230.16.
102 See ibid., 230.19–234.10.
103 Ibid., 252.5–8.

46 | CHAPTER ONE

lect does so only through what is probable or generally accepted, through the authorities, and through experience (*ex experimentis*). Therefore, different kinds of knowledge are provided by these powers: the active faculty gives science and knowledge of the habits, while the contemplative faculty gives wisdom.[104]

Having the capacity for knowledge, both intellects have a potential status which is progressively actualised. And since the term "potency" has three meanings – material potency, possible potency, and perfection – both intellects are progressively actualised through these three ontological statuses. This is Avicenna's doctrine of intellection, interpreted and discussed for the first time in Latin Europe. By itself, the intellect is in a potential state deprived of any perfection, called the material intellect (*intellectus materialis*), as it is similar to first matter which has no form. When the intellect receives the principles through which it can acquire its perfection, the intellect is called *intellectus in habitu*, and is actual in comparison to the material intellect. The contemplative intellect *in habitu*, therefore, has the intelligible forms and, when it considers them in act, it knows them. Nonetheless, the *intellectus in habitu* is still potential in comparison to what follows, the intellect when it has in itself the form and performs its intellection, which is called *intellectus adeptus ab alio*: the intellect which is absolutely in act and whose potency is actualised. As every potency, though, must be actualised by something external which is already in act, the potency of the intellect must be actualised by an intellect which is already in act.[105]

This intellect is an intelligence which provides human intellects with the principles of intelligible abstracted forms and joins the potential intellect, impressing in it some species of the forms. The dynamic through which the active intellect acts upon the potential intellect is immediately compared by Gundissalinus with the relation between sight and light. As it is impossible to have any sight without light, so too it is impossible to comprehend the truth without the agent intellect. As a consequence, when the light of the agent intellect is absent, there is ignorance, but when this light appears, then there is science.[106]

The final pages of *De anima* are marked by an abrupt thematic and stylistic shift. The previously constant references to Arabic sources suddenly disappear, replaced by a new web of quotations and allusions to biblical authority.[107] Reasons for this change of style and approach are unclear, but it can be supposed that Gundissalinus had some "consistency worries" in relation to the Arabic sources he was using. As a result, Gundissalinus's prose becomes rather bulky in

104 See ibid., 252.12–258.3.
105 See ibid., 262.1–9.
106 See ibid., 262.11–264.5.
107 In just a few pages, we find eighteen explicit references to the Bible, in a total of twenty-one references to the Scriptures throughout the entire *De anima*.

Pioneering Transformations: Gundissalinus's Philosophical Reflection | 47

discussing the human intellect: he uses the term *intelligentia* in a new and different sense, as the highest faculty of the human being, through which human beings have *sapientia* – therefore, an immanent faculty rather than a separate principle.[108] This identification seems to contradict what the Toledan philosopher presented only a few pages before, identifying the active intellect with an angelic creature, and even proposing the doctrine of the union of the soul with the active intelligence in the afterlife.[109] Notwithstanding this somewhat bizarre conclusion, the contribution of Gundissalinus's *De anima* is invaluable. Gundissalinus was the first Latin thinker to engage with new pivotal psychological doctrines derived mainly from Avicenna's *De anima*. The peculiarities of his interpretations in relation to Latin- and Christian-based problems, together with the odd merging of Avicenna's doctrines with Ibn Gabirol's, are indispensable witnesses of the first insertion of Arabic psychology within the Latin tradition.

Sciences

It is difficult to overestimate the importance of Gundissalinus's *De divisione philosophiae*. Directly linked to the looming "Aristotelian shift" which would characterise the thirteenth century, *De divisione* discusses, for the first time in Latin Europe, disciplines that were until then unknown or lacking reliable epistemological justification. It therefore constitutes a central contribution to the history of medieval thought, as Henri Hugonnard-Roche and Jean Jolivet have pointed out.[110] The treatise organises these "new" and "old" sciences into a hierarchical order grounded on the definition of their subject of study and

108 For instance, ibid., 304.1–4. It is worth noting that Themistius, in his *Paraphrase of Aristotle's De anima*, claimed that humans are provided with an individual active intellect in order to receive the power of the separated Agent Intellect, thus allowing human minds to have abstraction.

109 See ibid., 136.9–12.

110 See Henri Hugonnard-Roche, "La classification des sciences de Gundissalinus et l'influence d'Avicenne," in *Études sur Avicenne*, ed. Jean Jolivet and Roshdi Rashed (Paris, 1984), 41; and Jolivet, "The Arabic Inheritance," 137. On the influence of Gundissalinus's epistemological writing, see Anton-Hermann Chroust, "The Definitions of Philosophy in the *De Divisione Philosophiae* of Dominicus Gundissalinus," *The New Scholasticism* 25 (1951), 253–81; Gundissalinus, *Über die Einteilung der Philosophie*, trans. Alexander Fidora and Dorothée Werner (Freiburg, 2007), 40–49; M. Grignaschi, "Le *De divisione philosophiae* de Dominicus Gundissalinus et les *Questiones II–V in Sextum Metaphysicorum* de Jean de Jandun," in *Knowledge and the Sciences in Medieval Philosophy: Proceedings of the Eighth International Congress of Medieval Philosophy*, ed. Simo Knuuttila et al. (Helsinki, 1990), 53–61; and, in the same volume, Charles Burnett, "Innovations in the Classification of the Sciences in the Twelfth Century," 25–42.

48 | CHAPTER ONE

theoretical relations – a task fulfilled, again, thanks to Avicenna. From a broad perspective, *De divisione* aims at a global renewal of the Latin organisation of sciences through a meta-encyclopedic analysis of human knowledge. Accordingly, *De divisione* is rooted in a wide array of sources, both Latin (Cicero, Bede, Isidore of Seville, Boethius, William of Conches, Thierry of Chartres) and Arabic (Avicenna, al-Farabi, pseudo-al-Farabi, al-Ghazali, Isaac Israeli, al-Kindi, the Brethren of Purity).[111]

The incipit of the *De divisione philosophiae* makes clear its purpose – to provide an overall examination of what wisdom and philosophy are, through the analysis of the disciplines which compose them.[112] Implicitly, Gundissalinus's aim is also to justify the integration of new disciplines among the recognised Latin sciences, disciplines which were seeing rapid and substantial development thanks to the new works translated from Greek and Arabic into Latin throughout the twelfth century. Discussion of the seventeen main sciences to which Gundissalinus reserves specific treatment is preceded by a large prologue in which the author preliminarily describes the meanings of knowledge and wisdom.

Composed of both body and soul, human beings tend to desire only what is related to flesh or spirit. Flesh and spirit, though, have different and contrasting aspects. Flesh is subject to necessity, desire, and curiosity, but only "necessity" (i.e., what is necessary to the body to be conserved) provides the human being

111   This dense web of sources has been analysed in detail by Alexander Fidora, whose studies have shown that Gundissalinus's use of his Latin sources, and of Isidore and Boethius in particular, aims at simplifying an acceptance of the new doctrinal elements derived by the Arabs, as Gundissalinus's expositions of astronomy and medicine clearly display. From this point of view, Fidora states that the role played by the Latin sources in the *De divisione philosophiae* can be correctly understood as the "hermeneutical condition" for the comprehension of the Arabic doctrines therein presented. Fidora, *Domingo Gundisalvo y la teoría* (Pamplona, 2009), 103–25. See also Fidora, "La recepción de San Isidoro de Sevilla por Domingo Gundisalvo," *Estudios eclesiásticos* 75 (2000): 663–77; Fidora, "La metodología de las ciencias según Boecio," *Revista Española de Filosofía Medieval* 7 (2000): 127–36; Giulio D'Onofrio, "La scala ricamata: La *Philosophiae divisio* di Severino Boezio tra essere e conoscere," in *La divisione della filosofia e le sue ragioni*, ed. Giulio D'Onofrio (Cava de' Tirreni, 2001), 11–63; Henry G. Farmer, "Who Was the Author of the *Liber introductorius in artem logicae demonstrationis?*" *Journal of the Royal Asiatic Society* 3 (1934): 553–56; and Carmela Baffioni, "Il *Liber introductorius in artem logicae demonstrationis*: Problemi storici e filologici," *Studi filosofici* 17 (1994): 69–90.

112   Gundissalinus, *De divisione philosophiae*, ed. Ludwig Baur (Münster, 1903), 3–142, at 3.4–17. For the *De divisione philosophiae* I will also use, when necessary, the critical revision of the text made by Fidora and and Werner in Gudissalinus, *Über die Einteilung der Philosophie*, quoting the relative passages in Baur's critical edition.

with actual knowledge. Similarly, the spirit is subject to culpable, vain, and useful things, but only the latter produces virtues and knowledge.[113] Accordingly, true knowledge must be limited to two grounding fields. These are the knowledge of how to preserve the body and the righteous knowledge (*honesta scientia*) of what is actually useful for the spirit. The latter is further divided into two kinds: divine science and human science.[114] Divine science is the knowledge that God had provided to human beings through revelation, while human science is knowledge that is traditionally structured in the so-called liberal arts. Some of these arts lead the human being toward eloquence, which is formed by those sciences which concern the right and elegant speech, such as grammar, poetics, rhetoric, and law. Other liberal sciences lead toward wisdom, which counts all those sciences enlightening the human soul to the cognition of the truth and joining the love of that which is good. These disciplines are called "philosophy." Its aim is the comprehension of the truth of every existing thing as far as it is possible for human beings.[115]

As some things exist by nature while others are produced by human actions, so too philosophy is primarily divided into two main branches. One of them is related to the knowledge of human actions, the other is directed to the knowledge of that which is independent from human actions. Respectively, these are practical and theoretical philosophy. The former is the knowledge of how to act or behave, while the latter is the knowledge of what must be the object of intellection through mental cognition.[116] Both theoretical and practical philosophy are divided into three main disciplines. As Hugonnard-Roche and Alexander Fidora have pointed out, Gundissalinus uses and combines different perspectives – basically Avicenna's and Boethius's – to ground the intrinsic correlations between the theoretical and the practical.[117] Differences between physics, mathematics, and metaphysics are due to the ontological differences among their subject. Indeed,

> Physics (*philosophia naturalis*) deals with objects that are in movement and in matter, and which are studied in their movement and matter.
> Mathematics (*scientia disciplinalis*) treats objects in movement and matter, which are studied regardless of their movement and matter.

113 See Gundissalinus, *De divisione philosophiae*, ed. Baur, 4.6–5.3.
114 Ibid., 5.4–11.
115 See ibid., 5.11–18 and 9.21–22.
116 Ibid., 11.14–18.
117 See Hugonnard-Roche, "La classification des sciences," and Fidora, *Domingo Gundisalvo y la teoría*, 53–78.

Metaphysics (*philosophia prima*) deals with immaterial and immobile objects, studied in their immobility and immateriality.[118]

Practical philosophy, too, is composed of three sciences, namely, politics, economics, and ethics. As with theoretical philosophy, Gundissalinus follows the Aristotelian tradition, although he does not show any independent interest in practical philosophy. The prologue dedicates only a few lines to this topic, and just a few pages at the end of the treatise engage with the disciplines of practical philosophy.[119]

It should be recalled that Gundissalinus had already written (or translated) a work on the classification of sciences, *De scientiis*. A comparison with this earlier and scarcely original treatise demonstrates the originality and relevance of *De divisione philosophiae*. A most important contribution to Latin medieval speculation is Gundissalinus's application of Avicenna's theory of subalternation, presented in the section named *Summa Avicennae de convenientia et differentia scientiarum praedictarum*.[120] Located in the final pages of the treatise, this section provides the very theoretical pillars upon which the work's articulation of knowledge is built.

118 A problem of consistency seems to arise from Gundissalinus's discussion of the subject of theoretical sciences. In fact, Gundissalinus further mentions the angels among those things without matter that constitute the object of metaphysics (Gundissalinus, *De divisione philosophiae*, ed. Baur, 14.2–6), in patent contradiction with Gundissalinus's universal hylomorphism. It should be noted, though, that Gundissalinus's prologue is a presentation of a program of study that proceeds from the sciences of eloquence to first philosophy. In such a presentation, universal hylomorphism is *not* a preliminary assumption, but the outcome of metaphysical analysis, as Gundissalinus himself claims in the closing sentences of his prologue (ibid., 18.1–6). The preliminary position of angels among those creatures without matter, then, seems to be instrumental to Gundissalinus's program.

119 It should be appreciated that the closure of *De divisione philosophiae* is dedicated to logic. This discipline suffered a certain degree of oscillation between being considered as an autonomous philosophical discipline and as being of mere instrumental value to philosophy. Gundissalinus points out the fundamental usefulness of logic, specifically regarding the distinction between known and unknown truths. Logic indeed is the only science to teach how to pass from what it is already known to what is yet unknown. Because of this particular relevance displayed by logic, it can be said to be an instrument, but also a part of philosophy. See ibid., 18.7–19.2. It is also worth noting that the last paragraph of this rich prologue expounds the famous method of *didaskaliká* that Gundissalinus would use in its description and analysis of the sciences. See ibid., 19.5–10. See Fidora, "The Arabic Influence on the Classification of Philosophy in the Latin West: The Case of the Introductions to Philosophy," *Micrologus* 28 (2020), forthcoming.

120 See Jules Janssens, "Le *De divisione philosophiae* de Gundissalinus: quelques remarques préliminaires à une édition critique," in *De l'antiquité tardive au Moyen Âge: études de logique aristotélicienne et de philosophie grecque, syriaque, arabe et latine offertes à Henri Hugonnard-Roche*, ed. Elisa Coda and Cecilia Martini Bonadeo (Paris, 2014), 559–70.

It corresponds to chapter seven of the only extant Latin translation of the second part of Avicenna's *Kitab al-Burhan*.[121] Probably Gundissalinus translated this passage with the purpose of quoting it in *De divisione philosophiae* – a hypothesis which would also explain why Gundissalinus presents this section explicitly as a long quotation, whereas he usually tends to blind-quote authors and texts without explicitly mentioning the author's name or the title of the work he is referring to.

Quoting this long passage from Avicenna's *al-Burhan*, Gundissalinus introduces the famous distinction between parts (*partes*) of a science and disciplines subordinated to that science – which in *De divisione* are called "species."[122] This distinction is of the utmost importance. It lays the basis for an organic structure of knowledge in which every science is connected to the science hierarchically superior to it as its *pars* or *species*, up to first philosophy, or metaphysics. Moreover, this doctrine allows Gundissalinus to place, within the Latin system of science, new disciplines that were finally available to the Latins but that could not be considered as parts of the theoretical sciences.

While the science which is part of the superior science provides a kind of internal development of that science, the subordinated science is a separated discipline that shares something with the science to which is subordinated.[123] The distinction between *partes* and *species* allows the construction of an organic, hierarchically ordered system of knowledge. The peak of this system is metaphysics. This science deals with being and oneness, which are common to the objects of every other science. No other science treats being and oneness through a discussion of their essence, an examination which is proper to metaphysics only. As a result, every science is subordinated to metaphysics, while metaphysics is not subordinated to anything else.

As Fidora has recently pointed out, Gundissalinus is the first Latin thinker to refer to "metaphysics" as a discipline rather than an Aristotelian work.[124] Being

---

121 On this fascinating translation by Gundissalinus, see Riccardo Strobino, "Avicenna's *Kitab al-Burhan*, II.7 and Its Latin Translation by Gundissalinus: Content and Text," *Documenti e Studi sulla Tradizione Filosofica Medievale* 28 (2017): 105–47. See also Françoise Hudry, "La traduction latine de la *Logica Avicennae* et son auteur," *Documenti e Studi sulla Tradizione Filosofica Medievale* 28 (2017): 1–28.

122 See Pedro Mantas-España, "Interpreting the New Sciences: Beyond the Completion of the Traditional Liberal Arts Curriculum," in *Appropriation, Interpretation and Criticism: Philosophical and Theological Exchanges between the Arabic, Hebrew and Latin Intellectual Traditions*, ed. Alexander Fidora and Nicola Polloni (Barcelona, 2017), 51–91.

123 Gundissalinus discusses four kinds of this subordination. See Gundissalinus, *De divisione philosophiae*, ed. Baur, 126.18–20.

124 See Alexander Fidora, "Dominicus Gundissalinus and the Introduction of Metaphysics into the Latin West," *The Review of Metaphysics* 66 (2013): 691–712.

52 | CHAPTER ONE

the highest point of human science, this discipline has various names, as it deals with different aspects of the highest philosophical importance. Metaphysics corresponds to wisdom (*sapientia*), since both metaphysics and wisdom are the noblest of all sciences in terms of their certitude and their object of study, which is the first cause of existence. All the same, divine science also certifies the principles of the subsequent sciences in the hierarchical epistemological order, making their principles certain since it deals with what is most evident and common, i.e., being.[125]

A fascinating aspect of Gundissalinus's discussion of metaphysical science is his description of its *ordo inquirendi* through a large passage from al-Farabi's *Kitab Ihsa al-'Ulum* – presented also in *De scientiis*.[126] Gundissalinus claims that metaphysics follows, in order, physics and mathematics, using their results in its own study of the essences, their ontological correlates, and the principles of demonstration. Metaphysics must demonstrate the finite plurality in the number of the essences, their mutual differences, and their hierarchical order up to the first cause that precedes everything. The first cause provides every existent with being, unity, and truth, as the first cause is the absolute being, one, and trueness. Once metaphysics has dealt with the examination of God's causality and existence, metaphysics descends back to created beings, analysing how every essence proceeds from God in a causal and mutually connected order. Finally, metaphysics has to demonstrate that the cosmic establishment operated by God is complete, without any kind of superfluity or deficiency, refuting every possible error concerning God and creation. Gundissalinus's description of this detailed procedure of metaphysical research, almost completely derived from al-Farabi, plays a peculiar role in his own philosophical reflection. Gundissalinus, indeed, abstracts from this description a "metaphysical procedure" structured into an ascending and a descending moment. And he applies it in his own metaphysical treatise *De processione mundi*, as I recently had the occasion to underline.[127]

Another discipline on which Gundissalinus's contribution can be effectively appreciated is physics. Natural philosophy, or natural science, is the part of the-

---

125 Gundissalinus, *De divisione philosophiae*, ed. Baur, 38.7–18. The passage is evidently derived from Avicenna, *Liber de philosophia prima* 1.2, ed. Simone Van Riet (Louvain, 1977–83), 15.86–16.1.

126 Gundissalinus, *De divisione philosophiae*, ed. Baur, 39.15–41.16.

127 See Nicola Polloni, "Gundissalinus's Application of al-Fārābi's Metaphysical Programme: A Case of Epistemological Transfer," *Mediterranea* 1 (2016): 69–106. It should be appreciated that Gundissalinus's speculation appears to be even more consistent through a consideration of this metaphysical program. Gundissalinus's mature writings – *De anima, De divisione philosophiae*, and *De processione mundi* – appear to be characterised by a profound degree of consistency in both approach and outcomes, although they are also accompanied by problematic cores whose resolution seems at least difficult.

oretical philosophy closer to us, and considers its object as unabstracted and in motion.[128] Indeed, its *genus* is the first part of theoretical philosophy, and its object (*materia*) is the body not as it is a being, a substance, or a hylomorphic compound, but just as it is subject to movement, rest, and change.[129] Having presented natural philosophy in general, Gundissalinus distinguishes between eight parts and eight subordinated sciences as follows:

Articulation of Natural Philosophy

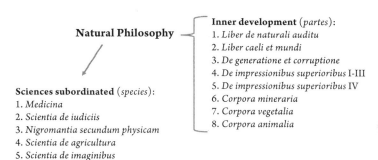

Natural philosophy is composed of eight parts, which are connected to one specific work or part of a work written by Aristotle (or pseudo-Aristotle).[130] The first part of physics deals with what is common to every natural body – its principle and necessary consequents – as presented by *De naturali auditu* (Aristotle's *Physics*). The second part of physics deals with simple bodies, studying their existence and number as expounded in *Liber celi et mundi*. The third part corresponds to an examination of the mixture and corruption of natural bodies and elements, as Aristotle exposited in *De generatione et corruptione*. The fourth part examines the principles of action and passion proper to the elements and their compounds (as in *De impressionibus superioribus*), while the fifth part treats composite bodies considering their similar and dissimilar parts (again, *De impressionibus superioribus*). The sixth part of physics studies the commonalities of composite bodies with similar parts, and specifically minerals, as taught in the *De mineris*. Finally, the seventh part deals with what is common and proper to the vegetable species (*De vegetabilibus*), and

---

128 See Gundissalinus, *De divisione philosophiae*, ed. Baur, 19.12–16.
129 See ibid., 20.3–7.
130 See ibid., 20.20–23.15.

54 | CHAPTER ONE

the eighth and last part studies the animals, as expounded by *De animalibus, De anima,* and the last book of *De naturalibus.*

Beside its internal division into parts, natural philosophy provides eight subordinated sciences with their objects. These are medicine, the science of astrological judgement, necromancy according to nature, agriculture, the science of images, navigation, the science of mirrors, and alchemy. These eight sciences – among which alchemy is mentioned as a discipline for the first time by a Latin thinker – are derived from pseudo-al-Farabi's *De ortu scientiarum.*[131] Gundissalinus uses this text but roots its list of disciplines in the epistemological distinction between *partes* and *species* he developed from Avicenna. His aim probably was to count among the physical sciences some new disciplines that had just entered Europe thanks to the translation movement. In other words, he was probably trying to further open the "epistemic field" on which some new disciplines could be effectively grounded and justified.

The case of natural philosophy is a good example of Gundissalinus's aims and approach. With *De divisione philosophiae,* he provided Latin thinkers with a wide epistemological frame in which to insert and justify some new disciplines derived from the translation movement. He also, and crucially, provided them with a hierarchical and organic structure of knowledge and a procedure for the study of metaphysics and of theoretical sciences in general. The treatise would have a wide reception, even if it would be superseded by different systems, more Aristotelian and suitable for the exigencies of Latin scholastic philosophy. Moreover, some of the sciences Gundissalinus tried to include in his system of knowledge would not have a shared positive reception by Latin scholars, as with the cases of alchemy and astrology.

Cosmogenesis

Gundissalinus's *De processione mundi* is a complex onto-cosmological examination of the universe, grounded on recently translated Arabic sources.[132] With a

131 See ibid., 20.11–19 and pseudo-al-Farabi, *De ortu scientiarum,* ed. Clemens Baeumker, *Über den Ursprung der Wissenschaften* (Münster, 1916), 20.23–28.

132 Beside Marcelino Menéndez y Pelayo's transcription (see *La historia de los heterodoxos españoles* [Madrid, 1880–82]), two critical editions of this work have been completed: Gundissalinus, *De processione mundi,* ed. Georg Bülow, *Des Dominicus Gundissalinus Schrift Von dem Hervorgange der Welt* (Münster, 1925), 1–56; and Gundissalinus, *De processione mundi,* ed. María Jesús Soto Bruna and Concepción Alonso del Real, *De processione mundi: Estudio y edición crítica del tratado de D. Gundisalvo* (Pamplona, 1999). I will refer in the notes to both editions, using my own critical revision of the text when necessary.

much more mature approach than *De unitate*, *De processione* poses a difficult discussion of the origin of the world based on a radical ontological difference between creator and creature. In turn, this ontology is rooted in two divergent doctrines: universal hylomorphism and modal ontology. Intersections and tensions between these two theories and the systems Ibn Gabirol and Avicenna proposed in their works provide both ground and limits to Gundissalinus's reflection on cosmology and metaphysics. *De processione mundi* is based on a wider set of sources, both Arabic and Latin. Noticeably, Gundissalinus makes abundant use of authors who were implicitly or explicitly connected to the Aristotelian tradition, but does not make such use of Aristotle himself. Traces of Aristotle's works can be found in Gundissalinus's treatises, but they play a rather secondary role in comparison to Arabic authors like Avicenna.[133]

The opening of Gundissalinus's *De processione mundi* grounds the feasibility of a metaphysical study of God's creation. Knowledge of the "secret aspects" of God's existence, or *invisibilia Dei* (Rom. 1:20), is possible and desirable. Indeed,

the invisible things of God are seen, having been understood from the creation of the world by means of the things that have been made. For, if we vigilantly observe these visible things, we will ascend by means of these same things to the contemplation of the invisible things of God. After all, the wonderful works of this visible creation are traces of the creator, and for this reason we come to him by following through these works, which are from him. Hence, in the Book of Wisdom it is written: "Through the greatness and beauty of creation, the creator can be seen by means of the intellect." For, since greatness, beauty, and usefulness are set forth to be admired so much, the power, wisdom, and goodness of the creator, which are the invisible things of God, are certainly revealed. After all, he would not make such great things unless he were powerful, nor such beautiful things unless he were wise, nor such useful things unless he were good. Hence, it is written

133 That many works by Aristotle (*Physics, On the Heavens, On Generation and Corruption*, and *Meteorology*) were translated by Gerard of Cremona in Toledo during the decades Gundissalinus was active there appears to imply that Gundissalinus had no specific interest in Aristotle. As I have had occasion to underline, there is some ground to affirm that, at least in Gundissalinus's circle, Avicenna was considered not only to be in explicit coherence with Aristotle, but also to offer a "theoretical surplus" which made his works more attractive than Aristotle's. See Nicola Polloni, "Aristotle in Toledo: Gundissalinus, the Arabs, and Gerard of Cremona's Translations," in *"Ex Oriente Lux": Translating Words, Scripts and Styles in the Medieval Mediterranean World*, ed. Charles Burnett and Pedro Mantas España (Córdoba, 2016), 147–85.

56 | CHAPTER ONE

about Wisdom: "In the ways she reveals herself cheerfully, and in every thought she meets them." For the ways to the creator are his works. Provided we observe them diligently, we attain knowledge of his hidden things in some way or another.[134]

With this opening, Gundissalinus bases the entirety of his examination of the universe upon a religious (but not necessarily theological) justification. The opening is grounded upon three biblical quotations stating the rightfulness of an inquiry into the creation – an inquiry through which the human being can grasp the "secret aspects" of God, his most intimate and secret attributes.[135] Indeed, "if we vigilantly observe these visible things, we will ascend by means of these same things to the contemplation of the invisible things of God." What is invisible is seen through the visible effects of God's power.

This position implies a fundamental methodological choice. A metaphysical analysis must be preliminarily centred on creation, rather than God or the principles. It is only through the examination of the creatures that an ascent towards the origin of existence is possible, since "the wonderful works of this visible creation are traces of the creator, and for this reason we come to him by following through these works, which are from him," and "the ways to the Creator are his works." As a consequence, the course followed by *De processione mundi* is to inquire *a posteriori* into the knowledge of God, a course that coincides with an application of the metaphysical procedure presented by Gundissalinus in *De divisione philosophiae*. Its "ascending moment" corresponds to the rising of the intellect from the created universe up to its cause. Before undertaking this examination, Gundissalinus expounds the method he applies in his analysis, as well as the secondary tracks of the main path which leads to the acquisition of that

---

134 Gundissalinus, *De processione mundi*, ed. Bülow, 1.3–2.3; ed. Soto Bruna and Alonso Del Real, 120.3–16: "Invisibilia dei per ea, quae facta sunt, a creatura mundi intellecta conspiciuntur. Si enim vigilanter haec visibilia conspicimus, per ipsa eadem ad invisibilia dei contemplanda conscendimus. Vestigia enim creatoris sunt mira opera visibilis creaturae et ideo per haec, quae ab ipso sunt, sequendo pervenimus ad ipsum. Unde in libro sapientiae scriptum est: per magnitudinem creaturae et speciem potest intelligibiliter creator videri. Cum enim magnitudo, pulchritudo et utilitas tantum miranda proponitur: profecto potentia creatoris, sapientia et bonitas, quae invisibilia dei sunt, revelantur. Non enim tam magna faceret, nisi potens esset, tam pulchra, nisi sapiens, tam utilia, nisi bonus. Unde de sapientia scriptum est: in viis ostendit se hilariter et in omni providentia occurrit illis. Viae quippe ad creatorem sunt opera ipsius; quae dum diligenter attendimus, ad cognoscenda occulta eius utcunque attingimus." English translation by John Laumakis, *The Procession of the World* (Milwaukee, 2002), 33.

135 See Rom. 1:20; Sap. 13:15; and Sap. 6:16.

Pioneering Transformations: Gundissalinus's Philosophical Reflection | 57

desired knowledge. Contemplation of the created universe implies a consideration of three main aspects, whose discussion is necessary as,

> to understand the invisible things of God, a threefold matter of investigation is proposed for us: namely, in the composition and disposition of things and the efficient cause of each of them. Composition is the principle from which some union is brought about. Disposition is the ordered relation of the united elements. But one efficient cause is primary, another secondary, another is of the third rank, and so forth.[136]

An examination of the universe entails an analysis of how creatures are made (their composition, *compositio*), how they are ordered (their disposition, *dispositio*), and what their efficient cause is (*causa movente*). Gundissalinus's discussion shows how these three aspects are profoundly interconnected. Their analysis corresponds to the same description of God's institution of the universe, which is enacted both directly and through the mediation of secondary causes. Gundissalinus's mention of the three cosmological aspects, however, is instrumental to the general epistemological discussion at the beginning of the treatise. Composition, disposition, and efficient cause are the object of specific psychological faculties: reason (*ratio*) grasps composition, demonstrative power (*demonstratio*) comprehends disposition, and intelligence (*intelligentia*) understands the efficient cause.[137] These faculties and objects are finally connected to the three theoretical sciences (physics, mathematics, and metaphysics), as "it is said that it is necessary to conduct oneself with natural things in a rational way, with mathematical things in an instructive way, and with theological things in an intelligent way."[138] The process leading to an understanding of the intimate nature of God, therefore, appears to correspond to a joint venture of the three theoretical sciences: the study of how creatures are made belongs to natural phi-

---

136 Gundissalinus, *De processione mundi*, ed. Bülow, 2.4–6; ed. Soto Bruna and Alonso Del Real, 120.17–19: "Unde ad intelligendum invisibilia dei speculationis materia nobis tripertita proponitur: scilicet in rerum compositione et dispositione et causa utrumque movente. Compositio est principium, ex quibus aliqua fit coniunctio; dispositio est coniunctorum ordinata habitudo; causa vero movens alia est primaria, alia secundaria, alia est tertiae dignitatis, et deinceps." English translation by Laumakis, *The Procession of the World*, 33.

137 See Gundissalinus, *De processione mundi*, ed. Bülow, 2.9–11; ed. Soto Bruna and Alonso Del Real, 120.22–23.

138 Ibid., ed. Bülow, 2.13–14; ed. Soto Bruna and Alonso Del Real, 122.1–3: "dicitur, quod in naturalibus rationaliter, in mathematicis disciplinaliter, in theologicis intelligentialiter versari oportet." English translation by Laumakis, *The Procession of the World*, 34. The passage is evidently derived from Boethius, *De Trinitate* 2, 5.21.

58 | CHAPTER ONE

losophy, that of how they are ordered to mathematics, and the examination of the efficient cause of everything to metaphysics.[139] The peculiarities of the proposed task also require a specific method, which is the twofold procedure of composition and resolution (*compositio et resolutio*). This method is directly related to the aims of Gundissalinus's examination:

> Reason investigates by composing and resolving. By resolving, it ascends; by composing, it descends. For, in resolution, it begins from the last things; in composition, it begins from the first things. Hence, the creature of the world sees the invisible things of God that have been understood by means of the things that were made, since reason deals with composition in this way.[140]

Reason proceeds through composition and resolution. The former starts from the first things (*a primis*) and descends to the last, while resolution starts from the last things (*ab ultimis*) and ascends to the first principles.[141] Curiously, the relevance Gundissalinus bestows upon composition and resolution seems to have a direct, yet unspoken, implication for the entire examination he is going to undertake. If *compositio* and *resolutio* are the "ways" through which reason knows, and if reason knows primarily the composition of things which, in turn, is treated by natural philosophy, then the point of departure of Gundissalinus's examination, and a vast part of its development as well, should be pursued by physics. It

139 The interconnections among the three theoretical sciences are further stated by the examination of the cognitive process, where the faculties presiding over them constitute the act of understanding. Gundissalinus claims that the cognitive process starts with the sense experiencing the sensible forms in matter, proceeds to the imagination, thanks to which one has cognition of the sensible forms even when their matter is not experienced, and then it is developed by reason, which deals with the sensible forms finally abstracted from – and known independently of – matter. The intellectual track of the cognitive process is performed by the intellect, whose objects are the intelligible forms, while intelligence knows one simple form. See Gundissalinus, *De processione mundi*, ed. Bülow, 2.16–3.5; ed. Soto Bruna and Alonso Del Real, 122.4–13. See also Fidora, "La metodología de las ciencias según Boecio."

140 Gundissalinus, *De processione mundi*, ed. Bülow, 3.6–10; ed. Soto Bruna and Alonso Del Real, 122.13–17: "Ratio inquirit componendo et resolvendo; resolvendo ascendit, componendo descendit. In resolvendo enim ab ultimis incipit, in componendo a primis incipit. Unde per ea, quae facta sunt, invisibilia dei intellecta creatura mundi conspicit, cum ratio ad compositionem accedit hoc modo." English translation by Laumakis, *The Procession of the World*, 34.

141 Although at first glance Gundissalinus's mention of *compositio* and *resolutio* could be supposed to be a reference to Aristotle's *Posterior Analytics*, the actual source is Calcidius, as will be shown in chapter 2.

is the first Latin instantiation of a specific problem within the Aristotelian framework. Examination of the physical composition of natural things corresponds to the analysis of their constituents, matter and form, whose theoretical bases, as principles, are exquisitely metaphysical. The outcome of this twofold theoretical belonging to both physics and metaphysics would originate tensions between these two branches of theoretical philosophy within the Latin tradition.

As for Gundissalinus, these tensions are only in place when he has to define, implicitly or explicitly, the branch to which an examination of matter and form (the composition of created beings) pertains, as he never engages with a genuinely physical examination of the universe. Indeed, the analysis pursued by Gundissalinus is focused on three main themes: the simplicity of God, the ontological constituents of the universe, and the modalities through which the universe was established. These themes are connected to the *invisibilia Dei* mentioned at the beginning of the treatise, and are later identified by Gundissalinus with God's power, wisdom, and goodness.[142]

Al-Farabi's metaphysical procedure requires two different moments: an examination of the universe which allows an inference about God's existence and attributes (ascending moment) and an analysis of the universe following the knowledge gained by the discussion of God (descending moment). Gundissalinus's application of this procedure is quite accurate and, after having expounded the modalities of his research, he presents four arguments for God's existence – the first step of al-Farabi's ascending moment. In coherence with what he has previously stated, all arguments are *a posteriori*. Only from a consideration of the sensible world is possible to grasp the first basic notion we can have of God, i.e., that he exists.

Gundissalinus's first argument considers the opposition among the elements. Everything placed between the earth and the sphere of the moon is composed of heavy and light things (i.e., the elements). Heavy elements move downward, light elements upward. Their opposed movement shows that they are contrary to each other, and yet they compose every corporeal thing. Accordingly, a cause which composes them, resolving their contrariety, must be supposed, and this is the first cause.[143] Gundissalinus's second proof discusses the hylomorphic composition of the bodies. Every corporeal being is composed of matter and form. As with the elements, matter and form have opposed properties which impede them from converging into a compound without an external cause joining them and resolving their opposition. This composing cause of the bod-

---

142 See Gundissalinus, *De processione mundi*, ed. Bülow, 1.10–12; ed. Soto Bruna and Alonso Del Real, 120.10–11.

143 See ibid., ed. Bülow, 3.10–17; ed. Soto Bruna and Alonso Del Real, 122.18–124.1.

60 | CHAPTER ONE

ies is, again, identified as the first cause.[144] A third proof of the existence of God is developed through a consideration of corruption as a ubiquitous characteristic of natural beings. Observation of the world shows that every existing thing, once destroyed, dissolves into its components. Anything which can be corrupted, though, must previously have been generated. Only a generated thing can be corrupted – *sed non convertitur*. As no creature can be supposed to be the efficient cause of itself, generation must be the result of an external cause that realises the possibility of existence for that thing. Therefore, Gundissalinus reasons, there must be a first cause of the universe.[145] A fourth and last demonstration is grounded by Gundissalinus upon the doctrine of potency and act. The coming to be of any being corresponds to the actualisation of its potency – actualisation which is a kind of movement. Accordingly, there must be a mover whose movement causes the actualisation of this potentiality. As nothing can be the efficient cause of itself, that mover must be an external efficient cause of that particular being and of every caused being in general.[146]

The four proofs expounded by Gundissalinus argue that a first cause is necessary to explain the existence of the universe. That first cause is identified with God. Gundissalinus's proofs echo Aristotle's theories, even though these Aristotelian shades seem to be mediated by at least two main sources: Avicenna and Boethius. This fact is particularly evident within the discussion of God as prime mover, an immobile cause that, staying at rest, moves everything.[147] God's essence is perfect and does not require any actualisation. If that were not the case, God would be subject to movement and change (because the actualisation of a potency is a kind of motion). This is impossible; if change were possible in God, he would be lacking something, as every movement is always aimed at receiving a perfection which the mobile thing lacks. No imperfection, insufficiency, or potentiality can be found in God, who is the immobile cause of every

---

144 See ibid., ed. Bülow, 3.17–4.7; ed. Soto Bruna and Alonso Del Real, 124.1–11. It should be noticed that here the preliminary "restriction" of matter and form to the corporeal beings only is due to the very gradualness of the examination Gundissalinus proposes. No one would doubt that matter and form are the ontological constituents of bodies. The *De processione mundi* has to demonstrate that they are *also* the constituents of the spiritual substances and every created being in general: a demonstration that follows the proofs of God's existence in Gundissalinus's application of al-Farabi's metaphysical procedure. A case similar to this has already been stressed regarding the prologue to Gundissalinus's *De divisione philosophiae*, where universal hylomorphism is counted among the things to be demonstrated, and thus it is not used for the general taxonomy presented by Gundissalinus.

145 See ibid., ed. Bülow, 4.8–22; ed. Soto Bruna and Alonso Del Real, 124.12–25.
146 See ibid., ed. Bülow, 4.23–5.14; ed. Soto Bruna and Alonso Del Real, 126.1–10.
147 See ibid., ed. Bülow, 17.12–15; ed. Soto Bruna and Alonso Del Real, 150.2–4.

Pioneering Transformations: Gundissalinus's Philosophical Reflection | 61

movement.[148] As a consequence, God's perfect immobility is the first trait of the ontological difference between God and creature. While the creator is complete and immobile, the entirety of movement is found in his effect, i.e., in the created beings.[149]

Complete and unchangeable, God is absolutely self-sufficient. This self-sufficiency, in turn, corresponds to his necessary existence. Gundissalinus quotes dense pages from Avicenna's discussion of the Necessary Existent, quotations that comprise almost one-fifth of the entire length of *De processione mundi*.[150] Within the thematic articulation offered by al-Farabi's metaphysical procedure, Gundissalinus's discussion of modal ontology corresponds to the examination of God's being and attributes – an examination developed on a purely philosophical level, without any references to sacred texts. Through Avicenna, Gundissalinus expounds the key concepts of self-sufficiency, insufficiency, ontological necessity, possibility, and impossibility in their conceptual bond to existence and causality.

The four arguments of *De processione mundi* as presented above share a common thread in the acknowledgment that no caused being can be the cause of itself. An external cause is always required and, as an infinite regress is inadmissible, that cause is precisely the first cause of the universe. This being so, the first cause must be uncaused and self-sufficient, perfect and immobile. As the uncaused cause of everything, the first cause has a necessary existence. In comparison, any caused being has a completely different ontological status, as it has been caused by an external cause. Once its existence has been caused, that being can be said to be subsistent and concretely existing. It is necessary only as long as it exists and this only in a mediated way, as it has been caused by something external to it. The mediated and derived necessity of any caused being is rooted in its ontological possibility. The external cause of its being resolves a fundamental alternative to which each and every caused being is subject. Requiring an external cause, any caused being, in itself, could equally be or not be. Its being is utterly insufficient *per se* to resolve the alternative between its own existence or inexistence. Its possible existence, marked by this possibility of being and not being, can exist only through a cause that resolves this alternative in favour of one of its eventualities. In other words, before coming to be, every caused being has a possible existence and receives a necessary existence only after the causative

---

148 See ibid., ed. Bülow, 17.16–18.13; ed. Soto Bruna and Alonso Del Real, 150.7–24.

149 Ibid., ed. Bülow, 18.27–19.3; ed. Soto Bruna and Alonso Del Real, 152.13–16.

150 See ibid., ed. Bülow, 5.15–17.10; ed. Soto Bruna and Alonso Del Real, 126.17–148.7. In relation to Gundissalinus's attitude toward Avicenna's *Liber de philosophiae prima*, see Polloni, "Gundissalinus on Necessary Being."

62 | CHAPTER ONE

action performed by its cause.[151] Accordingly, *De processione mundi* proposes three modal states of existence:

1. The Necessary Existent (*necesse esse per se*), which is the uncaused cause of every being, and is completely self-sufficient, perfect, and complete;

2. The possible existent (*possibile esse*) proper to any caused being. It expresses the existential alternative between the existence and inexistence of that entity before being caused. It is also an ontological trait which is present in every caused being in a sort of tension and duality with the mediated necessity it acquires through the causative process;

3. The Necessary Existent through something else (*necesse esse per aliud*), which is the ontological state of acquired necessity any caused being receives as a consequence of its causation by the external cause. This necessity corresponds, in Gundissalinus's reflection, to the actual existence of the creature, but also expresses an ontological duality (possibility vs. necessity) which is directly connected by him to the hylomorphic composition of every caused being.

These three modalities of existence expound a further crucial aspect of the ontological difference between creator and creatures. While any caused being always suffers a structural ontological deficiency (possibility, potentiality, multiplicity, change) and also a duality (possibility vs. necessity), the Necessary Existent

> is neither relative nor mutable nor many but single, since no other thing participates in its being, which is proper to it. And this is none other than God alone, who is the first cause and first principle of all things, which is necessarily understood to be one only, not two or more.[152]

God's perfect immobility and necessity are accompanied by a third fundamental aspect: God is absolute unity and oneness. A specific feature of *De unitate et uno*, this doctrine is discussed in *De processione mundi*, with some peculiarities. God is the One whose unity is absolute. This crucial aspect of God's being is referred to by Gundissalinus on particular occasions but is never properly discussed – probably because he already did so in his *De unitate*. Divine oneness

---

151 See Gundissalinus, *De processione mundi*, ed. Bülow, 5.15–17.10; ed. Soto Bruna and Alonso Del Real, 126.17–148.7.

152 See ibid., ed. Bülow, 16.23–17.1; ed. Soto Bruna and Alonso Del Real, 148.8–12: " ... neque est relativum, neque est mutabile, nec multiplex, sed solitarium, cum nihil aliud participat in suo esse, quod est ei proprium; et hoc non est nisi solus deus, qui est prima causa et primum principium omnium, quod unum tantum necesse est intelligi, non duo vel plura." English translation by Laumakis, *The Procession of the World*, 44.

Pioneering Transformations: Gundissalinus's Philosophical Reflection | 63

plays a pivotal role in specific numerological reasonings like the "numerological argument" for God's existence or the justification of the duality of the first principles of the composed being, which evidently required a specific reference to One and unity.[153]

Immobile mover, Necessary Existent, and absolute One: these are classically philosophical attributes of God's being. Curiously, Gundissalinus offers only scarce references to the biblical accounts of the divine attributes and aspects. He repeatedly refers to God's wisdom and will, but usually while he quotes Ibn Gabirol's *Fons vitae*, where divine will and wisdom are in direct relation to the genesis of hylomorphic union. Matter and form, indeed, eternally exist in God's wisdom, and they are brought out and joined together by his will.[154] God's wisdom also appears as one of the *invisibilia Dei* mentioned at the beginning of the treatise. Together with divine power and goodness, these aspects of God's being are later applied to the Trinity. The entire universe is the result of a Trinitarian action.[155]

Gundissalinus's discussion of God is mainly focused on creation and grounded upon features derived from both Aristotelian and Neoplatonic

153 See Gundissalinus, *De processione mundi*, ed. Bülow, 17.1–10; ed. Soto Bruna and Alonso Del Real, 148.12–20; and ibid., ed. Bülow, 20.15–21.11 ed. Soto Bruna and Alonso Del Real, 156.6–157.6.

154 See ibid., ed. Bülow, 27.22–28.1; ed. Soto Bruna and Alonso Del Real, 170.15–17; English translation by Laumakis, *The Procession of the World*, 55: "In fact, the being of matter is in the wisdom of the creator just as the being of the concept of matter is in my soul, which, even if it is in privation with respect to you, is not, nonetheless, in privation with respect to me." ("Esse vero materiae in sapientia creatoris est, sicut esse intellectus de materia in anima mea, qui, etsi privatus est apud te, non tamen est privatus apud me.") See also Gundissalinus, *De processione mundi*, ed. Bülow, 40.16–41.1; ed. Soto Bruna and Alonso Del Real, 194.17–20; English translation by Laumakis, *The Procession of the World*, 66: "For the creation of things by the creator is only the going forth of form from his wisdom and will and the impression of his image in matter like the going forth of water emanating from its origin and its flowing out when one part follows after another." ("Creatio namque rerum a creatore non est nisi exitus formae ab eius sapientia et voluntate et impressio eius in imaginem in materiam ad similitudinem aquae exitus emanantis a sua origine et effluxio eius, cum una sequitur post aliam.")

155 Gundissalinus, *De processione mundi*, ed. Bülow, 48.7–11; ed. Soto Bruna and Alonso Del Real, 208.2–6: "Although these are the indivisible works of the Trinity, the creation, nonetheless, of matter, from which all things are made, is attributed to power; the creation of form, by which all things are made, is attributed to wisdom, but the joining of both is fittingly attributed to union so that there is also found a small sign of the Trinity in its first works." ("Quamvis autem indivisibilia sint opera trinitatis, tamen creatio materiae, ex qua omnia, potentiae, creatio vero formae, per quam omnia, sapientiae, coniunctio vero utriusque connexioni congrue attribuitur, ut etiam in primis suis operibus signaculum trinitatis inveniatur.") English translation by Laumakis, *The Procession of the World*, 71.

64 | CHAPTER ONE

traditions (immobile mover, first cause, absolute One), as well as from the Islamic (Necessary Existent), Jewish (divine wisdom and will as origins of matter and form), and Christian (Trinity) philosophical frameworks. At the same time, the absence of any reference to Plato's Demiurge – a typical inclusion in twelfth-century speculation – is meaningful. The only trace of the Demiurge in Gundissalinus's work can be found in his rejection of the doctrine of primordial chaos.[156] After having examined God's existence and attributes, Gundissalinus is ready to take the next step of his metaphysical procedure. The descendant moment begins and is marked by a demonstration that an ontological duality must proceed from God's utter oneness, as

> by creation, therefore, the first principles of things, which were created from nothing, have a beginning. These are the material principle and the formal principle. For the creator created some principle. But every created thing must be different from the creator. Since, therefore, the creator is truly one, something created certainly ought not to have been one. But just as there was nothing in the middle between the creator and the first creature, so there is nothing in the middle between one and two. For the first thing that is different from one is two. Since, therefore, the creator is truly one, the creature that is after him certainly had to be two. For diversity is not found in oneness, but in otherness. But the first principle of otherness is twoness, which first departs from oneness. If, therefore, the first created thing were one, then there would be no diversity. But, if there were no diversity, there would be no universe of creatures that was going to be. Therefore, two simple principles, from which all things were to be constituted, had to be created first by one simple principle.[157]

156 See Gundissalinus, *De processione mundi*, ed. Bülow, 36.9–38.21; ed. Soto Bruna and Alonso Del Real, 186.9–192.3.

157 Ibid., ed. Bülow, 20.13–21.3; ed. Soto Bruna and Alonso Del Real, 156.4–18: "Per creationem ergo initium habent prima principia rerum, quae de nihilo creata sunt; quae sunt principium materiale et principium formale. Creator enim aliquod principium creavit; sed omne creatum a creante debet esse diversum. Cum igitur creator vere unus sit, profecto creatum non debuit esse unum, sed, sicut inter creatorem et primam creaturam nihil fuit medium, sic inter unum et duo nihil est medium. Primum enim, quod est diversum ab uno, hoc est duo. Cum igitur creator vere sit unus, profecto creatura, quae post ipsum est, debuit esse duo. In unitate enim non est diversitas, sed in alteritate. Sed primum principium alteritatis binarius est, qui primus ab unitate recedit. Si igitur primum creatum unum esset, tunc nulla esset diversitas; si vero nulla esset diversitas, nulla esset, quae futura esset, creaturarum universitas. Quapropter duo simplicia ab uno simplici primum creari debuerunt, ex quibus omnia constituenda erant." English translation by Laumakis, *The Procession of the World*, 47–48.

In his application of the Neoplatonic principle of difference, Gundissalinus claims that an effect must be "other" than its cause. Since the first cause is absolutely one, its effect must be twofold, or better, two in number. The first thing to be different from the "one" (i.e., number 1) is "two" (number 2), which is the principle of alterity (*principium alteritatis*). As a consequence, the principles through which the universe is established must be two opposed and yet reciprocally related ontological components. They are matter and form.[158] Composing every created being, these principles also constitute an intimate duality within every caused being. This duality is another structural aspect of the ontological difference between creator and creatures:

> because the first active unity does not have *hyle*, it was necessary that the unity that follows after it have *hyle*, for contrary things agree with respect to contraries. And because form has being only by the power of matter, there had to be matter in which it would subsist. Moreover, because the Creator is perfect, he did not wish to create a perfect first product. It is more perfect, however, to create what subsists in something else and that in which something else subsists, namely, a sustainer and a thing sustained, than to create only one of them. And because the Creator is sufficient in himself, needing nothing, the created thing, because it is distinct from him, had to be insufficient and needy. And for this reason, because they were two, it was certainly necessary that they should be such that they would mutually need each other and that neither would be perfected except by the other. Therefore, one had to be matter and the other form.[159]

---

158 See Gundissalinus, *De processione mundi*, ed. Bülow, 21.3–15; ed. Soto Bruna and Alonso Del Real, 156.18–158.6.

159 Ibid., ed. Bülow, 21.16–22.9; ed. Soto Bruna and Alonso Del Real, 158.7–18: "Item, quia prima unitas agens non habet yle, oportuit, ut unitas, quae post eam sequitur, sit habens yle; contraria enim contrariis conveniunt. Et quia forma non habet esse, nisi vi materiae, tunc debuit esse materia, in qua subsisteret. Item, quia creator perfectus est, primum opus perfectum creare noluit. Perfectius autem est creare, in quo aliud et quod in alio subsistat, scilicet sustinens et sustentatum, quam alterum tantum. Et quia creator in se sufficiens est, nihilo indigens, profecto creatum, quod ab eo diversum est, debuit esse insufficiens et indigens. Et ideo necessario, quia duo erant, profecto talia esse debuerunt, ut alterum altero indigeret vicissim et neutrum perficeretur, nisi ex altero. Quapropter unum debuit esse materia et alterum forma." For the sake of the argument, I read "sufficiens" rather than "insufficiens" (Bülow) and "sustinens" (Soto Bruna and Alonso Del Real), and "insufficiens" rather than "sufficiens" (Bülow) and "insustinens" (Soto Bruna and Alonso Del Real). English translation by Laumakis, *The Procession of the World*, 49.

66 | CHAPTER ONE

Dialectically, Gundissalinus claims that creatures must have matter, as God has no matter at all. This ontological difference was something God decided to enact with creation – he chose to create something utterly different from himself and that always requires something else to exist. The bearer requires the borne, and the borne requires the bearer, from the very beginning of the universe. To bear is matter, to be borne is form, and together, they constitute the substance of any existing creature, as actual existence can be gained only through hylomorphic union. Therefore,

> since matter is the neediness for form, in every constitution of things matter is first necessary as a sustainer of the constitution of things; later, the result of the work exists by means of form. Hence, matter could not be without form nor form without matter. For it is impossible that one exist without the other, because being is perfected only from the union of both of them. Hence, one is seen to give being to the other, and each is seen to be the cause of the other in order that it may be. If, however, each gives being to the other, why doesn't each have being in itself? For what does not have being cannot give being to anything.[160]

In *De processione mundi*, universal hylomorphism is directly bound to the doctrine of act and potency. Both matter and form, before their union, have a potential being, which is actualised in their compound.[161] The efficient causality, which provides existence to every created being, actualises the potentiality proper to the possible existent. Indeed, only what is a "possible existent is made. But when it is made, everything that is a possible existent goes forth from potency to act. Therefore, everything that is made goes forth from potency to act."[162]

Gundissalinus identifies universal hylomorphism with the intrinsic duality proper to the possible existent. On the one hand, God is the Necessary Existent.

---

160 Gundissalinus, *De processione mundi*, ed. Bülow, 22.18–24; ed. Soto Bruna and Alonso Del Real, 160.7–12: "nec materia potuit esse sine forma, nec forma sine materia. Impossibile est enim, ut altera sit sine altera, quia non perficitur esse, nisi ex coniunctione utriusque. Unde altera alteri videtur dare esse, et utraque utriusque videtur causa esse, ut sit. Si autem utraque utrique dat esse, cur non utraque in se habet esse? Quod enim non habet esse, nulli dare potest esse." English translation by Laumakis, *The Procession of the World*, 50.

161 See Gundissalinus, *De processione mundi*, ed. Bülow, 22.25–23.3; ed. Soto Bruna and Alonso Del Real, 160.13–16.

162 Ibid., ed. Bülow, 35.17–19; ed. Soto Bruna and Alonso Del Real, 184.15–16: "nihil fit, nisi quod possibile est esse; sed omne, quod possibile est esse, dum fit, de potentia exit ad effectum. Ergo omne, quod fit, de potentia exit ad effectum." English translation by Laumakis, *The Procession of the World*, 62, modified.

On the other hand, every creature is a caused being, whose possibility is expressed by its composition of matter and form in potency. The actual and necessary being it acquires is the actuality of the hylomorphic compound (the *necesse esse per aliud*). With this doctrine – especially with the supposition that form is not an act, but a potency, and actualisation only is possible to the compound of matter and form – Gundissalinus opposes almost the entire Latin tradition. Possibly aware of this fact, Gundissalinus proposes what can appear as a sort of mediation. He distinguishes between matter and form, on the one hand, and material being (*esse materiale*) and formal being (*esse formale*), on the other, claiming that

> material being, which is being in potency, is distinct from formal being, which is being in act. But each of them by itself without the other has material being, just as each of them has formal being if it is united with the other. But because men have not been accustomed to say that something exists except what exists in act, while being in act is present only when form is united to matter, being does not belong to matter by itself nor to form by itself, but to both of them when joined together.[163]

Gundissalinus identifies act with "formal being," the kind of being usually identified with the role of the form. And he identifies potency with "material being," the modality of being ascribed to matter. As a consequence, a sort of bizarre concordance is established between traditional hylomorphism and the novelties presented by *De processione mundi*. Gundissalinus's distinction between hylomorphic principles and their "statuses" softens the radicality of his ontological stances.[164]

There is another problem that appears to be linked to Gundissalinus's peculiar clarification – the problem of the actualisation of matter and, particularly, form. As nothing can be the efficient cause of itself, the potentiality of matter must be actualised by something external and already in act. While a vast majority of ontological systems claims that this function is pursued – totally or par-

---

163 Gundissalinus, *De processione mundi*, ed. Bülow, 28.11–29.1; ed. Soto Bruna and Alonso Del Real, 172.2–8: "Esse enim materiale, quod est esse in potentia, diversum est ab esse formali, quod est esse in actu. Sed esse materiale utraque habet per se sine altera, sicut esse formale habet utraque, si coniuncta est cum altera. Sed quia homines non consueverunt dicere aliquid esse, nisi quod in actu est; esse vero in actu non habetur, nisi cum forma materiei coniungitur: ideo esse non convenit materiae per se, nec formae per se, sed coniunctis simul." English translation by Laumakis, *The Procession of the World*, 56.

164 Thanks to this clarification, a reader's reticence in accepting Gundissalinus's positions on matter's actuality and form's potentiality could be softened by understanding that formal and material being were standing for the traditional references to form and matter.

68 | CHAPTER ONE

tially – by the form, for Gundissalinus the form shares matter's utterly potential being. Nevertheless, Gundissalinus often repeats in *De processione* that the actuality of the compound is provided by form, which also actualises matter.[165] The claim that actuality is realised by form seems to entail an intermediate level of causality between the external cause and hylomorphic compound. Accordingly, the external efficient cause must be mediated by the form – a doctrine strikingly similar to Avicenna's discussion of form as middle cause of corporeal being.[166]

These remarks, however, raise a thorny problem. How can something in potency (a form) actualise a potency (matter)? It should be considered that Gundissalinus never identifies form and being. Being is an outcome of form joining matter. It always is together with form but does not correspond to any form ("being is something that inseparably accompanies form").[167] Created being only happens when form is joined to matter, and this emergence of being corresponds to the actualisation of the compound and the intrinsic unity of its components. Concomitant to being, form is nevertheless simultaneous to another metaphysical aspect grounding the existence of every created being. Recalling his *De unitate et uno*, Gundissalinus repeats "whatever exists, exists because it is one" and being one, it is necessary that it exists.[168] The form of unity is shared by every creature – as the foundation upon which the other forms can be stratified to realise any specific creature – and plays a primary role in the causation of being. It is from the first encounter of first matter with the forms of unity and substantiality that created being comes to exist. The actualisation of that first created being corresponds to the function performed by the form of unity, which "makes one" its intrinsic hylomorphic duality. Created unity is not absolute, but a "unity of unities," a compositional unity of two components which are matter and form.

These components are opposed and contrary to each other. As Gundissalinus stated in his second argument for God's existence, the union of matter and

165 See Gundissalinus, *De processione mundi*, ed. Bülow, 25.9–18; ed. Soto Bruna and Alonso Del Real, 166.3–11. It is worth noting that this appears to be the reason why Gundissalinus proposes to identify actual being with "formal being," as it proceeds from a function which is performed by form, not by matter.

166 See Avicenna, *Liber de philosophia prima* 2.4, ed. Van Riet, 101.98–4. See also Amos Bertolacci, "The Doctrine of Material and Formal Causality in the *Ilāhiyyāt* of Avicenna's *Kitāb al-Šifā*ʾ," *Quaestio* 2 (2002): 125–54.

167 See Gundissalinus, *De processione mundi*, ed. Bülow, 27.8–9; ed. Soto Bruna and Alonso Del Real, 170.2–3: "esse enim est quiddam, quod inseparabiliter comitatur formam." English translation by Laumakis, *The Procession of the World*, 54.

168 See ibid., ed. Bülow, 29.17–30.3; ed. Soto Bruna and Alonso Del Real, 174.2–5.

Pioneering Transformations: Gundissalinus's Philosophical Reflection | 69

form necessarily implies an external composing cause, which is God. It is God, then, as the external cause of their union, who acts as efficient cause of the hylomorphic compound. *De anima* states that God is neither potency nor act, being the origin of both ontological statuses. Accordingly, the *origin of potency* coincides – logically and cosmologically – with the creation of matter and form. Likewise, the *origin of act* corresponds – again, logically and cosmologically – to the first union of matter and form into the compound made of them. This is a compositional unity (i.e., two entities which are made "one") which corresponds to the necessary existence *per aliud* and to actuality. This original solution appears to be the only way to supersede the tensions between different explanatory devices in Gundissalinus's text, although even this is not free of problems.

Peculiarities and modalities of matter and form are thoroughly examined by the central pages of *De processione mundi*. As they cannot be accidents, both hylomorphic components are substances, although their being *per se* is in potency.[169] As matter is the bearer of form and form is what is borne by matter, matter is logically prior to form.[170] Matter is also privation (*privatio*), but not absolute privation, because matter has desire and moves toward the form in order to realise its own being. Therefore, it must have some subsistence as potential existence that can only be actualised by joining form.[171] Matter is also "potentiality of existence" (*potestas essendi*), in which every form is actualised – a rather minimal existence, yet so enveloping.[172] The potentiality of matter is a specific feature of possible existence, as "potentiality (*potestas*) is only something possible (*res possibilis*), and something possible (*possibile*) is possible only by means of potentiality (*nisi potestate possibile*)."[173] As a consequence, any supposition of a creation of matter in its sense of *potestas essendi* is inadmissible. Matter is the very possibility of existence that cannot be preceded by any other possibility.[174] Therefore matter, as well as form, eternally exists in God's wisdom, without beginning or end.[175] In their "material being," matter and form are eternal, while

169 See ibid., Bülow, 31.18–32.21; ed. Soto Bruna and Alonso Del Real, 176.15–178.16.

170 See ibid., ed. Bülow, 23.16–19; ed. Soto Bruna and Alonso Del Real, 162.8–10.

171 See ibid., ed. Bülow, 27.11–28.11; ed. Soto Bruna and Alonso Del Real, 170.5–172.2.

172 Ibid., ed. Bülow, 33.1–5; ed. Soto Bruna and Alonso Del Real, 178.17–20.

173 See ibid., ed. Bülow, 33.6–7; ed. Soto Bruna and Alonso Del Real, 180.2–3.

174 See ibid., ed. Bülow, 33.14–34.9; ed. Soto Bruna and Alonso Del Real, 180.10–182.12.

175 See ibid., ed. Bülow, 34.10–13; ed. Soto Bruna and Alonso Del Real, 182.8–11; English translation by Laumakis, *The Procession of the World*, 61: "But nothing begins to be in the wisdom of the creator, for then something new would happen to him, which is impossible. Matter, therefore, did not begin to be in potency. It was, therefore, in potency without a

70 | CHAPTER ONE

they have a beginning (as their first actualisation) only in their "formal being" that happens with their union.[176]

The cosmology of *De processione mundi* is marked by further changes in perspective. Gundissalinus detaches himself from the hypostatic cosmology, derived from Ibn Gabirol and accepted in the *De unitate*, presenting a new cosmogonic description, now based on Hermann of Carinthia's *De essentiis*. Gundissalinus calls "first composition" (*primaria compositio*) the first joining of matter and form operated by God. First composition is the second existential causation performed by God, following his creation from nothing (*creatio*) of matter and form.[177] The effect of God's first composition is a "first offspring" (*primaria genitura*), corresponding to the aforementioned angels, celestial spheres, and the four elements.[178] These three species of perpetual entities act as secondary causes in the establishment of the universe. This represents an instrumental causality dispensing divine will and through which the causality of the immobile mover is transmitted to the entire universe.[179] Any further difference among causes and agents is developed from this metaphysical distinction, since

> one of the motions of the first cause, by which the first cause moves, is called creation, whereas the other is called composition. But creation is first; composition is second. However, the motion of some secondary causes is composition only, whereas the motion of others is generation. For one type of composition is primary, whereas the other is secondary. Primary composition arises from simple things. Secondary composition arises from composed things, and one type of secondary composition is natural, whereas the other

---

beginning, because it was in the wisdom of the creator without a beginning." ("Sed nihil incipit esse in sapientia creatoris; tunc enim aliquid novi sibi accideret, quod est impossibile. Igitur materia non coepit esse in potentia; sine initio igitur fuit in potentia, quia sine initio fuit in creatoris sapientia. Materia igitur secundum esse materiale, quod est esse in potentia, non coepit esse; similiter et forma. Unde est illud esse, quod factum est, in ipso vita erat. Videtur autem materia coepisse secundum formale esse.")

176 See Gundissalinus, *De processione mundi*, ed. Bülow, 34.21–22; ed. Soto Bruna and Alonso Del Real, 182.18–19; English translation by Laumakis, *The Procession of the World*, 61: "For they were created simultaneously, because they began to be simultaneously when they were united to each other" ("simul enim creatae sunt, quia simul esse coeperunt, cum sibi coniunctae fuerunt"). Consequently, it is only under consideration of their actual/formal being that matter and form can be said to be created *ex nihilo*. See Gundissalinus, *De processione mundi*, ed. Bülow, 36.3–6; ed. Soto Bruna and Alonso Del Real, 186.3–8.

177 See ibid., ed. Bülow, 51.13–16; ed. Soto Bruna and Alonso Del Real, 214.1–4.

178 See ibid., ed. Bülow, 51.17–23; ed. Soto Bruna and Alonso Del Real, 214.5–11.

179 See ibid., ed. Bülow, 19.4–12; ed. Soto Bruna and Alonso Del Real, 152.17–154.2.

Pioneering Transformations: Gundissalinus's Philosophical Reflection | 71

is artificial. And creation, of course, arises from the very first of the first principles out of nothing. Composition, however, is the arising from those principles of the first things that, once they have been made, never perish, inasmuch as they were put together as a result of the first formation. Generation, however, arises from the same principles, and it is the renewal, not of the things that were composed, but of the things that continuously begin and perish, as if from remaining small things a drawing out of things has, once again, been produced.[180]

The universe is caused and preserved through creation (*creatio*), first composition (*primaria compositio*), secondary composition (*secundaria compositio*), and generation (*generatio*). These kinds of causality are performed by three agents: the first cause (God, responsible for creation and first composition), the secondary cause (the first offspring, responsible for secondary composition and generation), and further natural causes, as concomitant causes of generation and accidental causes.[181] It is evident that the causal concatenation makes the causality impressed by the *primaria genitura* central for the institution and governance of the universe. The *secundaria genitura* – angels, celestial spheres, and elements – are hierarchically disposed, each one acting on what is below.[182] The angels create new souls every day and move the spheres.[183] Moved by the angels, the celestial spheres blend the elements lying in the middle of the universe and every day realise new elemental aggregations.[184] The elements – or, more precisely, nature as their internal virtue – further blend and transform the elemental mixtures following the movement impressed by the heavens and realising the species

180 Ibid., ed. Bülow, 19.14–20.2; ed. Soto Bruna and Alonso Del Real, 154.5–16: "Motus igitur primae causae, quo scilicet prima causa movet, alius dicitur creatio, alius compositio; sed primus est creatio, secundus est compositio. Motus vero secundariae causae cuiusdam tantum est compositio, cuiusdam et generatio. Nam compositio alia est primaria, alia secundaria. Primaria est ex simplicibus, secundaria est ex compositis; et secundaria alia naturalis, alia artificialis. Et creatio, quidem est a primordio primorum principiorum ex nihilo. Compositio vero est primarum rerum ex ipsis principiis, quae semel factae nunquam occidunt, utpote ex prima conformatione compactae. Generatio vero est ex eisdem principiis eorum, quae nascuntur et occidunt usque, non per ea, quae composita sunt, reparatio, tamquam de residuis minutiis denuo confecta rerum protractio." English translation by Laumakis, *The Procession of the World*, 46–47.

181 Ibid., ed. Bülow, 19.10–12; ed. Soto Bruna and Alonso Del Real, 154.1–2.

182 See ibid., ed. Bülow, 51.17–23; ed. Soto Bruna and Alonso Del Real, 214.5–11.

183 See ibid., ed. Bülow, 51.24–25; ed. Soto Bruna and Alonso Del Real, 214.12–13. See also Polloni, "Gundissalinus on the Angelic Creation of the Human Soul."

184 See Gundissalinus, *De processione mundi*, ed. Bülow, 51.26–52.17; ed. Soto Bruna and Alonso Del Real, 214.16–216.8.

of natural movements – generation, corruption, increase, diminution, alteration, and local movement.[185]

Although Gundissalinus does not dedicate any space to a specific discussion of how secondary cause performs secondary composition and generation, it is possible to suggest some hypotheses.[186] He clearly distinguishes between *elementa* (the actual elements, as instantiations of the elemental qualities) and *elementata* (the elemental aggregates we usually refer to when talking about elements: fire, air, water, and earth, each of which is actually made of all the four elements).[187] Accordingly, it seems plausible that the secondary composition is reducible from the aggregation of the elements into the *elementata* and followed by their endless transmutation. Generation, therefore, seems to be specifically referred to those bodies composed of *elementata*, which are not subject to transmutation but to generation and corruption. As a consequence, Gundissalinus's description of the cosmic institution is consistently developed as a progressive ontological descent into multiplicity, from the creation of matter and form, down to the complex ontological structure of natural bodies.

An additional set of problematic questions arises from a consideration of how first composition happens. God creates matter and form and joins them into the first offspring. What form(s), though, are joined to first matter in order to cause three rather different genera of beings? First in order, the form of unity provides the compound with unity and actuality. Nevertheless, Gundissalinus distinguishes three kinds of forms: the corporeal, spiritual, and middle forms. The corporeal form has two functions: the *intrinseca habitudo* (performing the proportion of the elemental mixture) and the *extrinseca absolutio* (enacting the disposition of the corporeal figure). The corporeal form is the form which is found only in corporeal beings, and can be substantial or accidental.[188] In con-

---

185 See ibid., ed. Bülow, 52.18–24; ed. Soto Bruna and Alonso Del Real, 216.9–14.

186 A possible reason for Gundissalinus's silence could be furnished by considering that these problems are aspects engaged by natural philosophy rather than metaphysics.

187 The emergence and diffusion of the technical term "elementatum/elementata" within the Latin philosophical traditions is connected to the medical translations in Southern Italy. Nevertheless, Gundissalinus probably inherits this term through William of Conches, who uses it diffusely in his works. On his use of "elementatum," see Irene Caiazzo, "The Four Elements in the Work of William of Conches," *Guillaume de Conches: Philosophie et science au XII siècle*, ed. Barbara Obrist and Irene Caiazzo (Florence, 2011), 3–66.

188 See Gundissalinus, *De processione mundi*, ed. Bülow, 42.9–25; ed. Soto Bruna and Alonso Del Real, 198.5–21. It should be noted that this passage seems to imply a formal causation of matter: nonetheless, these apparent contradictions should be interpreted as a reference to the primary function performed by the considered form. In this way, colour is primarily referred to matter (in its equivocal meaning as substance in general), while knowledge is referred to form, since knowledge is always "through form." Otherwise it should be supposed that Gundissalinus thought that matter has a colour, and the form has another form, which shows evident doctrinal strain.

trast, the spiritual form, proper to the spiritual beings, has no parts but can still be substantial or accidental.[189] Finally, middle forms (*forma media*) are those forms, like unity and substantiality, which are not primarily bound to the spiritual or the corporeal substance, but are previous and common to them.[190] Indeed,

> the first form to which first matter was joined was substantiality, which made matter be a substance. But because everything that exists, exists precisely because it is one, substantiality alone, therefore, could not come to matter without unity as its companion, because it was impossible for matter to become a substance and not one. Hence, substantiality and unity come to matter simultaneously, and at their coming matter passes from possibility to act, from darkness to light, from deformity to comeliness, since by their union matter is made one substance.[191]

The first two forms to join first matter are exactly the form of unity and the form of substantiality, the former providing unity/actuality and the latter making the compound a non-qualified substance, i.e., a substance as such. This substance is then joined to the form of corporeity or the form of spirituality, originating the spiritual or corporeal substances. Through the reception of these different forms, the realms of bodies and spiritual entities is then established, since

> it happened that, when forms came to matter by the command of the creator, as the excellence of each form required and as the aptitude of the parts of matter desired, the various species of things were formed so that the beginnings of form, namely, corporeity and spirituality, came to matter that was already constituted, that is, made into one substance, and distinguished the whole of it completely into two kinds, namely, corporeal and incorporeal substance. Afterwards, the forms accompanying and attendant upon those two kinds subsequently divided them into the many species and orders of things by the ministry of nature. At first, therefore,

189 See ibid., ed. Bülow, 43.1–5; ed. Soto Bruna and Alonso Del Real, 198.21–200.3.

190 See ibid., ed. Bülow, 43.5–7; ed. Soto Bruna and Alonso Del Real, 200.3–5.

191 Ibid., ed. Bülow, 41.10–17; ed. Soto Bruna and Alonso Del Real, 196.8–15: "Prima autem forma, cui prima copulata est materia, substantialitas fuit, quae materiam fecit esse substantiam. Sed quia omne, quod est, ideo est, quia unum est: ideo substantialitas sola sine unitate comite non potuit venire, quia materiam substantiam fieri, et non unam, impossibile fuit. Unde substantialitas et unitas simul adveniunt, in quarum adventu materia transit de potestate ad actum, de tenebris ad lumen, de informitate ad decorem, quoniam earum coniunctione materia facta est substantia una." English translation by Laumakis, *The Procession of the World*, 66.

74 | CHAPTER ONE

what is composed of matter and form was divided into corporeal and incorporeal substance.[192]

Matter receives a progression of non-incidental forms. Later medieval philosophers like Aquinas would claim that the entirety of the ontological complexity of each substance is expressed by one substantial form only (together with its accidents). On the contrary, Gundissalinus acknowledges that only a plurality of substantial (= non-incidental) forms can explain the complex set of specific differentiations that is found in individuals. Indeed, it is this formal richness within the ontology of the individual thing that causes different species of beings.[193] Gundissalinus's approach can be said to be utterly "monohylic": there is only one matter for every caused being, which receives a plurality of forms. The first enmattered forms are the form of unity and that of substantiality. Their outcome, substance as such, is then divided into spiritual and corporeal substance, a division corresponding to the first branch of Porphyry's tree. Spiritual and corporeal substance undergo further divisions. Accordingly, spiritual substance is primarily divided into irrational and rational substances. The former is divided into nature, vegetative souls, and sensible souls.[194] The latter is divided into four species – angels, demons, human souls, and planetary spirits.[195] Similarly, corporeal substance is divided into three species: the elements, the aggregates of elements (*elementata*), and what is neither an element nor an aggre-

---

192 See Gundissalinus, *De processione mundi*, ed. Bülow, 43.11–21; ed. Soto Bruna and Alonso Del Real, 200.8–18: "Quapropter hoc factum est, ut in materia nutu creatoris formis advenientibus, prout cuiusque formae dignitas exigebat et aptitudo partium materiae appetebat, varia rerum species formaretur, ita quidem ut principia formae, corporeitas et spiritualitas, in materiam iam constitutam, hoc est factam substantiam unam, advenientes eam totam penitus in duo prima rerum genera, scilicet corpoream et incorpoream substantiam, distinguerent, quae duo genera post modum formae illarum comites et pedissequae in multimodas rerum species et ordines naturae ministerio consequenter distribuerent. Imprimis igitur ex materia et forma compositum distributum est in corpoream substantiam et incorpoream." English translation by Laumakis, *The Procession of the World*, 43.

193 On the doctrine of substantial forms, see Marienza Benedetto, "Alle origini della controversia medievale sulla pluralità delle forme sostanziali: Il *Fons vitae* di Avicebron," in *Appropriation, Interpretation and Criticism*, ed. Fidora and Polloni, 137–84; Daniel A. Callus, "Gundissalinus' *De Anima* and the Problem of Substantial Form," *The New Scholasticism* 13 (1939): 338–55; and Benedetto's introductory study to Avicebron, *Fonte della vita*, ed. Benedetto (Milan, 2007), 153–86.

194 See Gundissalinus, *De processione mundi*, ed. Bülow, 45.5–6; ed. Soto Bruna and Alonso Del Real, 204.2–3.

195 See ibid., ed. Bülow, 44.9–45.4; ed. Soto Bruna and Alonso Del Real, 202.8–204.2.

gate of elements, i.e., that which composes the substance of the heavens.[196] Gundissalinus's cosmological description can be summarised in the following diagram:

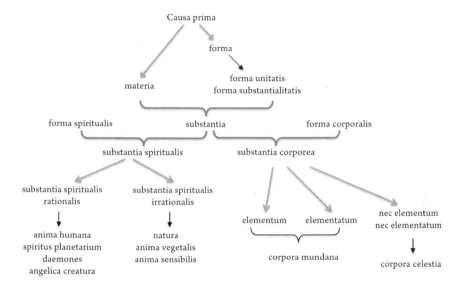

Gundissalinus closes his *De processione mundi* with a numerological digression. He presents and discusses two numerological series aimed at demonstrating that the universe is complete and perfectly ordered, since

> in this way, therefore, the constitution of the whole world proceeded from being nothing to being in possibility, from being in possibility to being in act, and from being in act to corporeal and incorporeal being; and all this happened simultaneously, not in time. For reason required that the institution of the whole world should proceed in this way: namely, that matter and form were, first of all, created from nothing; then, from matter and form the elements and the other things discussed before were composed; and finally,

---

196 See ibid., ed. Bülow, 43.22–44.7; ed. Soto Bruna and Alonso Del Real, 200.19–202.7. It should be emphasised that not every species into which spiritual and corporeal substance are divided correspond to the first offspring, which is perpetual (see ibid., ed. Bülow, 26.6–47.1; ed. Soto Bruna and Alonso Del Real, 204.13–206.11). For instance, specification of spiritual substance is necessarily progressive, since, if this were not the case, this would imply the perpetuity of vegetative and sensible souls: an outcome surely unacceptable for Gundissalinus.

76 | CHAPTER ONE

from the mixing and changing of the elements all the things composed of the elements were generated. Reason, that is, required that, first of all, the first simple things should be made from nothing by creation, and that from the simple things composed things should be made by the first union of the simple things, and then that from the composed things the things composed of the elements should be made by generation. And in this way, a progression was made from nothing to simple things, from simple things to composed things, and from composed things to generated things.[197]

This is the final stage of Gundissalinus's metaphysical procedure.[198] Combining Arabic and Latin sources, Gundissalinus's metaphysical treatise marks a shift in the twelfth century. The questions he addresses are shared by and inherited from the Latin tradition. His answers, however, belong to a different tradition. The relevance of Gundissalinus's reflection can be positively appreciated through an examination of how these two plans met in Gundissalinus's processes of assimilation, alteration, and development of different and sometimes divergent sources.

---

197 Gundissalinus, *De processione mundi*, ed. Bülow, 54.5–18; ed. Soto Bruna and Alonso Del Real, 2002.1–18: "Sic igitur processit totius mundi constitutio de nihil esse ad possibiliter esse, de possibiliter esse ad actu esse et de actu esse ad corporeum et incorporeum esse; et hoc totum simul, non in tempore. Ratio enim exigebat, ut institutio mundi universalis hoc modo progrederetur, videlicet ut primum materia et forma de nihilo crearentur, deinde de materia et forma elementa et cetera praedicta componerentur, de elementis vero commixtis et conversis elementata omnia generarentur; videlicet ut primum prima simplicia fierent de nihilo per creationem et de simplicibus composita fierent per primam simplicium coniunctionem, deinde de compositis fierent elementata per generationem. Et sic de nihilo ad simplicia, de simplicibus ad composita, de compositis ad generata facta est progressio." English translation by Laumakis, *The Procession of the World*, 74–75.

198 See Nicola Polloni, "'Natura vero assimilatur quaternario': numerologia e neoplatonismo nel *De processione mundi* di Dominicus Gundissalinus," in *De Natura: La naturaleza en la Edad Media*, ed. José Luis Fuertes Herreros and Ángel Poncela González (Ribeirão, 2015), 2: 679–88.

CHAPTER TWO

Reshaping Frameworks:
Gundissalinus and the Latin Tradition

Dominicus Gundissalinus's indebtedness to the Latin philosophical tradition is massive, and is evidently the result of his historical context. A learned Latinist, Gundissalinus had access to a vast amount of Latin scientific and philosophical sources (although a distinction between philosophy and science is often inapplicable in the Middle Ages). A good sample of the vastness of Gundissalinus's library is provided by his *De divisione philosophiae*, which is constructed upon an impressive number of quotations from Latin authors. A thorough examination of the influence of late ancient and medieval Latin sources on Gundissalinus's reflections could have a "breakthrough effect" on our understanding of his aims and speculative framework – especially in relation to the ontological implications of the logical debate on universals, which animated the twelfth century.

In this chapter I will limit my examination only to a sampling of this profound influence of Latin sources on Gundissalinus. Although potentially open to criticism, my choice here is to offer the coordinates that, if not governed, at least affected Gundissalinus's reception of Islamicate ontology which, eventually and under some restrictions, was closer to the Latin tradition than what Gundissalinus might have been expecting. Accordingly, I will discuss some major doctrinal issues that appear to have influenced Gundissalinus while he constructed his ontological descriptions, not aiming to be exhaustive but at least breaking ground regarding some problematic questions which can be properly addressed in the future. This set of doctrines are (1) Boethius's theory of unity, (2) Calcidius's theory of the three principles (and his speculative method), (3) Thierry of Chartres's and William of Conches's theories of the Holy Trinity, (4) the controversy over primordial chaos, and (5) Hermann of Carinthia's cosmological account. All of these will be contrasted with their interpretation, appropriation, and rejection by Gundissalinus as a preliminary step to an analysis of his reception of Ibn Gabirol and Avicenna.

78 | CHAPTER TWO

Aetas Boethiana

The philosophical reflection of Boethius determined many central aspects of the Latin tradition. As a translator, Boethius made available to the Latinate readership a fundamental set of Aristotelian works – the so-called *logica vetus*. As a philosopher, he commented on some of these logical works by Aristotle – including, crucially, Porphyry's *Isagoge* – and wrote a magisterial philosophical and literary masterpiece, *De consolatione Philosophiae*, in which he described his detention in Pavia and his encounter with Philosophy. Finally, as a theologian, Boethius appears to have authored five short treatises that played a primary role concerning the main problems related to the Trinity and the notion of "person," and also to the field of ontology.[1] We should not then underestimate the influence of Boethius on the Latin Middle Ages – and also on Gundissalinus. Fidora has recently pointed out the relevance Gundissalinus bestowed upon Boethius in his effort to estabish a correct classification of the sciences in *De divisione philosophiae*.[2] Traces of Boethius can be detected also in some epistemological passages of *De processione mundi*, where Gundissalinus engages with the distinction among the disciplines composing theoretical philosophy, i.e., physics, mathematics, and theology.[3] As emphasised by Fidora, in this case Gundissalinus's examination of the interrelations among these disciplines is totally dependant on Boethius's *De Trinitate*.[4]

Not far from that epistemological discussion, *De processione mundi* presents another meaningful reference to a very famous passage of Boethius's *De consolatione Philosophiae*. Arguing about the first cause, Gundissalinus claims that

---

1 On Boethius's originality and the crucial role he played in the Middle Ages, see John Marenbon, *Boethius* (New York, 2002); Henry Chadwick, *Boethius: The Consolations of Music, Logic, Theology, and Philosophy* (Oxford, 1981); and Pierre Courcelle, *La* Consolation de Philosophie *dans la tradition littéraire* (Paris, 1967). On the reference to the twelfth century as "Aetas Boethiana" see Marie-Dominique Chenu, *La théologie au douzième siècle* (Paris, 1966), 142–58.

2 See Alexander Fidora, "La metodología de las ciencias según Boecio," *Revista Española de Filosofía Medieval* 7 (2000): 127–36; and Fidora, *Domingo Gundisalvo y la teoría* (Pamplona, 2009), 53–103.

3 See Gundissalinus, *De processione mundi*, ed. Georg Bülow, *Des Dominicus Gundissalinus Schrift Von dem Hervorgange der Welt* (Münster, 1925), 2.9–19; ed. María Jesús Soto Bruna and Concepción Alonso del Real, *De processione mundi: Estudio y edición crítica del tratado de D. Gundisalvo* (Pamplona, 1999), 120.22–122.7.

4 See Boethius, *De sancta Trinitate*, ed. Claudio Moreschini in *De consolatione philosophiae / opuscula theologica* (Munich, 2005), 165–81, at 168.68–169.83. See also Fidora, *Domingo Gundisalvo y la teoría*, 53–75.

the primary cause is an efficient cause, since it moves by its own power in order that something may be developed. And this is the first and simple cause, which, although it is unmoved, is the cause of moving for all other things. Hence, it is called stable because, while remaining, it makes all things be moved. For every motion begins from rest, and for this reason it is necessary that what is unmoved should precede, by its antiquity, everything that is moved.[5]

The periphrasis defining the first cause as "stable because, while remaining, it makes all things be moved" ("stabilis, quia manens dat cuncta moveri") is a direct quotation from the third book of *De consolatione Philosophiae*, where Boethius praises God in the following terms:

O Thou, that dost the world in lasting order guide,
Father of heaven and earth, Who makest time swiftly slide,
And, standing till Thyself, yet fram'st all moving laws
("Ire iubes stabilis, quia manens dat cuncta moveri").[6]

God is the unmoved cause moving everything, the creator and cosmic orderer who shaped matter following the eidetic model of his own mind. God is also the highest good who causes every created good, which are so only for participation in true goodness. Gundissalinus inserts a reference to this well-known passage from *De consolatione* probably with the aim of establishing a connection with Boethius's authoritative position. Nevertheless, relying on Arabic sources like Avicenna and Ibn Gabirol, Gundissalinus's reflections are, at the same time, similar to and different from Boethius's.

De consolatione philosophiae describes God as utterly good and perfect. He is the origin of every goodness and perfection which can be found in the universe.[7] Completely self-sufficient and almighty, God is absolutely one, and his

---

5 Gundissalinus, *De processione mundi*, ed. Bülow, 17.11–17; ed. Soto Bruna and Alonso Del Real, 150.1–7: "Primaria causa est causa efficiens, quoniam vi propria movet, ut aliquid explicetur; et haec est prima et simplex causa, quae, cum sit immota, cunctis aliis movendi est causa. Unde dicitur stabilis, quia manens dat cuncta moveri. Omnis enim motus a quiete incipit, et idcirco necesse est, ut id, quod immotum est, omne, quod movetur, antiquitate praecedat." English translation by John Laumakis, *The Procession of the World* (Milwaukee, 2002), 44.

6 Boethius, *De consolatione Philosophiae*, ed. Moreschini, 1–163, at 79.101–103: "O qui perpetua mundum ratione gubernas, / terrarum caelique sator, qui tempus ab aevo / ire iubes stabisque manens das cuncta moveri." English translation by Hugh F. Stewart, *The Consolation of Philosophy* (Cambridge, MA, 1964), 263.

7 See Boethius, *De consolatione Philosophiae*, ed. Moreschini, 81.21–25.

80 | CHAPTER TWO

own substance is good in itself. As God's oneness is nothing but pure goodness, every created being receives its own goodness and perfection from God together with its own derived unity, which constitutes its being.[8] Every created entity, therefore, desires unity, as only through unity can something exist. Therefore, as God is the true One, everything desires God. He is pure Good and the end of everything, who has disposed the universe in the best possible way.[9]

Similar stances are expounded by Boethius in his *Opuscula sacra*.[10] There Boethius develops some of his most fundamental contributions to theology, such as his discussion of the Trinity in *De Trinitate* and his notion of the "persona" in *Contra Eutychen et Nestorium*.[11] But in his *Opuscula*, Boethius also elaborates a refined ontology grounded on a merging of Plato and Aristotle. In his *De Trinitate*, Boethius emphasises that God is purely form devoid of any matter – "the divine Substance is form without matter, and is therefore One, and is its own essence. But other things are not simply their own essences."[12] Created entities, indeed, have a derived being which is ontologically dependant on the parts of which they are composed – like the human being, who is made of soul and body. To the contrary, God's existence is utterly simple. His is the true, complete, and self-sufficient existence, always stable and perfect.[13]

God's simplicity evidently entails a complete absence of multiplicity. God is a purely formal being who does not require a substrate (i.e., matter) and

8 See ibid., 82.30–83.71 and 87.18–19.

9 See ibid., 87.26–88.40: "Do you know then, she said, that everything that exists so long remains and subsists as it is one, and perishes and is dissolved so soon as it ceases to be one? ... And in like manner it will be manifest to him that will descend to other particulars, that everything continues so long as it is one, and perishes when it loses unity." ("Nostine igitur, inquit, omne quod est tam diu manere atque subsistere, quamdiu sit unum, sed interire atque dissolvi pariter atque unum esse destiterit? ... Eoque modo percurrenti cetera procul dubio patebit subsistere unumquodque dum unum est, cum vero unum esse desinit, interire.") English translation by Stewart, *The Consolation of Philosophy*, 279, revised. See also Boethius, *De consolatione Philosophiae*, ed. Moreschini, 90.103–91.121 and 93.37–40.

10 See Christophe Erismann, "The Medieval Fortunes of the *Opuscula sacra*," in *The Cambridge Companion to Boethius*, ed. John Marenbon (Cambridge, 2009), 155–77.

11 Boethius, *Contra Eutychen et Nestorium*, ed. Moreschini, 206–41, at 214.171–72. See also Maurice Nédoncelle, "*Prosopon* et *persona* dans l'antiquité Classique: Bilan linguistique," *Revue des sciences religieuses* 22 (1948): 277–99; and Claudio Micaelli, "Teologia e filosofia nel *Contra Eutychen et Nestorium* di Boezio," in *Atti del congresso internazionale di studi boeziani (Pavia, 5–8 ottobre 1980)*, ed. Luca Obertello (Rome, 1981), 177–99.

12 Boethius, *De sancta Trinitate*, ed. Moreschini, 170.92–94: "divina substantia sine materia forma est atque ideo unum et est id quod est. Reliqua enim non sunt id quod sunt." English translation of *On the Holy Trinity* by Hugh F. Stewart and Edward K. Rand in *Theological Tractates* (Cambridge, MA, 1964), 11.

13 See Boethius, *De sancta Trinitate*, ed. Moreschini, 170.100–106.

who is not a subject for anything – differently from creatures, whose forms are substrates of accidents and are borne by matter.[14] Matter is joined to corporeal forms. These forms are nothing but images of the true forms which correspond to the eidetic contents of God's mind. Corporeal forms derive from the divine ideas, but are also ontologically "other" than the ideas. Indeed, corporeal forms always need matter to bear them while incorporeal forms cannot be joined to matter in any way and cannot be the substrate of accidental forms.[15] Accordingly, Boethius claims that there cannot be any difference or multiplicity in God's being. As God is pure form and true One, and his attributes correspond to his own being, therefore his Trinitarian existence does not contradict his perfect unity.[16] Boethius's *De Trinitate* instances a fundamental tension between God's existence and created being. This tension is primarily developed through the notions of the simplicity and complexity of being. While God's existence is simple and self-sufficient, created existence is always marked by a plurality of parts and, at heart, a duality of form and matter, the latter being joined to an immanent form which is an image of the perfect eidetic world of God's mind. Immanent forms, therefore, are ontologically different from transcendent forms, as they are characterised by different properties and functions in relation to matter and accidents – the main features of corporeal existence.[17]

A different approach is followed by Boethius in his *De hebdomadibus*.[18] This fascinating treatise aims at demonstrating how created beings are good without being the true Good – i.e., without being substantial goods. *De hebdomadibus*'s opening is a presentation of nine axioms in which Boethius's examination is

14 See ibid., 170.106–110.

15 See ibid., 170.110–171.117: "Form which is without matter cannot be a substrate, and cannot have its essence in matter, else it would not be form but a reflexion. For from those forms which are outside matter come the forms which are in matter and produce bodies. We misname the entities that reside in bodies when we call them forms; they are mere images; they only resemble those forms which are not incorporate in matter." ("Forma vero quae est sine materia non poterit esse subiectum nec vero inesse materiae: neque enim esset forma, sed imago. Ex his enim formis quae praeter materiam sunt, istae formae venerunt quae sunt in materia et corpus efficiunt. Nam ceteras quae in corporibus sunt abutimur formas vocantes, dum imagines sint: adsimulantur enim formis his quae non sunt in materia constitutae.") English translation by Stewart and Rand, *On the Holy Trinity*, 13.

16 See Boethius, *De sancta Trinitate*, ed. Moreschini, 174.197–98.

17 Immateriality of transcendental forms is also underlined by Boethius in *Contra Eutychen*. See *Contra Eutychen et Nestorium*, ed. Moreschini, 230.532–41.

18 See Jean Luc Solère, "Cercles, sphères et hebdomades: l'art platonicien d'écrire chez Boèce et Proclus," in *Boèce ou la chaîne des savoirs: Actes du colloque international de la Fondation Singer-Polignac Paris, 8–12 juin 1999*, ed. Alain Galonnier (Leuven, 2003), 55–110.

82 | CHAPTER TWO

rooted.[19] There are common conceptions (*communes animi conceptiones*) that are self-evident to the human mind without requiring a demonstration. From this starting point, Boethius distinguishes between "being" (*esse*) and "what it is" (*id quod est*). The latter exists because it has received the "form of being" (*forma essendi*), while the former "is not yet" (*nondum est*), as it is just an indeterminate being. Only what subsists, however, can participate in something and possess something other than itself – i.e., it can be the substantial subject of an accident. Every substance, indeed, participates in the *forma essendi* and in a variable number of accidents. Accordingly, through his axioms, Boethius constructs a theory of double participation. A being which is not yet, comes into existence through participation in the true being of God, which corresponds to its reception of the *forma essendi*. This created being, now existing, participates in further forms and accidents, thereby qualifying its being. This twofold dynamic is evidently inapplicable to God's being, which is the cause of the existence of any other being. Divine substance is completely simple. His "being what it is" corresponds to true being, which is the source of every participated existence, marked by an intimate compositional duality.[20]

As what is similar tends toward what is similar to it, the consideration that everything tends to what is good appears to entail that everything is good. Nevertheless, if things were good either substantially or through participation there would be inescapable contradictions. Boethius's solution resides on the consideration of the ontological duality of any created being. Created entities, indeed, are not simple in themselves, as they receive their existence from God.[21] Their being is different from their determination as good, while in God being and goodness are perfectly coincident, as God is pure being and true goodness in himself. Therefore, things are good only because they participate in God's being, from which they receive existence and, through that, goodness. Accordingly, created things are only relatively good, as they are good only through their imperfect participation in God to the degree desired by God.[22]

In general, Boethius's ontology is therefore marked by crucial reflections on the ontological difference between God and the created universe. Although they

19 See Boethius, *Quomodo substantiae in eo quod sint bonae sint cum non sint substantialia bona* [*De hebdomadibus*], ed. Moreschini, 186–94 at 187.17–188.46. Concerning this peculiar treatise, see Scott MacDonald, "Boethius's Claim that All Substances are Good," *Archiv für Geschichte der Philosophie* 70 (1988): 245–79; and Gangolf Schrimpf, *Die Axiomenschrift des Boethius (De Hebdomadibus) als philosophisches Lehrbuch des Mittelalters* (Leiden, 1966).

20 See Boethius, *Contra Eutychen et Nestorium*, ed. Moreschini, 218.250–219.264.

21 See Boethius, *De hebdomadibus*, ed. Moreschini, 186–94, at 191.114–15.

22 See ibid., 191.119–193.152.

share the same being – God's being, in which the creatures participate – only God is entitled to that being. In their numerical and ontological plurality, creatures only exist as long as they participate in God's being, from which they receive existence, goodness, and unity. Grounded upon a Platonic theory of participation, Boethius's discussion of divine and created being is developed through constant references to (corporeal) hylomorphism. Boethius radically distinguishes between immanent and transcendent form. The latter is immaterial and eidetic, corresponding to the content of God's mind while, following a tradition started by Plato himself, Boethius claims that immanent forms are nothing but images, i.e., reflections of the eidetic forms that join to matter, resulting in the body. At the same time, Boethius also distinguishes between the ontological statuses of spirits and bodies. Only the latter have matter (which is joined to immanent forms), while spiritual creatures (like human souls and angels) have a purely formal nature, although not coincident with God's mental contents.

Gundissalinus's line of reasoning is marked by a sensibility similar to Boethius's but characterised by a different set of answers. Both Boethius and Gundissalinus stress a compositional duality within created being, making what is created radically different from its creator. There is no need to underline the closeness of Boethius's doctrine of double participation to Gundissalinus's admission of a plurality of non-accidental forms within a created being and a duality of functions performed by the form of unity. As well as this, the proximity in their rhetoric about divine unity is obvious. Nevertheless, there are also many discrepancies that substantively oppose Boethius's and Gundissalinus's ontologies. The points of major disagreement are Gundissalinus's universal hylomorphism and his denial of any identification between ontological forms and the eidetic world. Although Gundissalinus refers to God's wisdom as the origin of forms, he does not appear to mean that the forms are images of a mental eidetic model as Boethius and Calcidius did. Divine will is the enactor of the cosmic creation, which is realised by the union of form and matter proceeding from God's wisdom. Nevertheless, these forms and their matter are said to be created *ex nihilo*. Matter and forms are created together. At the same time, Gundissalinus also denies any identification of God with a pure form or even an act. God cannot be a form, as a form is the effect of God's causality and, therefore, a form can exist only along with matter. Even more radically, in *De anima* Gundissalinus also rejects the hypothesis of God being the creator of human souls, by denying that God has actual being.[23] He has neither actual nor potential being, as he is beyond the characteristics which are valid only for created being, of which he is the origin.

---

23 See Gundissalinus, *De anima*, ed. María Jesús Soto Bruna and Concepción Alonso Del Real (Pamplona, 2009), 130.20–132.4.

84 | CHAPTER TWO

In comparison with Boethius's theory of hylomorphism, Gundissalinus seems to move within a slightly more Aristotelian – or maybe a much more Arabic Neoplatonist – framework. Far from Aristotle, though, and also from Boethius, Gundissalinus's extension of hylomorphic composition to spiritual creatures has almost no precedents in the Latin tradition. Consistently, for Boethius matter is a typical feature of corporeal beings only. Spiritual entities have a purely formal being which is deprived of any materiality, and consequently they do not suffer any process of generation and corruption proper to sublunary bodies. It is upon matter, therefore, that the ontological difference between spirits and bodies is established, as matter provides the character of dimensionality, multiplicity, and concreteness implied by the notion of body. Gundissalinus's position is completely different. For him, matter plays the function of ontological substrate for each and every form. In other words, there cannot be a form without being joined to matter. Therefore, every created being – both spiritual and corporeal – is composed of both form and matter. The main feature differentiating spirits and bodies must lie elsewhere in Gundissalinus's chain of being. It is the form of corporeity (*forma corporeitatis*) that performs this crucial passage from non-extension to dimensionality, as matter *per se* is completely unextended and undetermined and, precisely for this reason, can be the substrate of both three-dimensional bodies and non-extended spirits.

Beside these points of departure there are also some important points of convergence, starting with Gundissalinus's examination of God's being and its difference from created being. In the difficult discussion Boethius develops in his *De hebdomadibus*, he states the identity of *ipsum esse* and *id quod est* in God. This claim is based evidently on the acknowledgment that God's essential characteristic corresponds to his own existence. While some incidental correspondence with Avicenna's discussion of divine essence and existence is clear, it does not seem that Gundissalinus bestowed too much interest upon either of them. What appears to have interested him most is a corollary of the identity of essence and existence in God: His pure ontological simplicity is opposed to an intimate duality proper to created being as such. In Boethius's consideration, this duality is expressed by the necessity of the preliminary reception of the *forma essendi* in order to establish a being which *nondum est* as an existing – even if not yet qualified – being. Accordingly, created being cannot be simple, but it is always a conjunction of a not-yet-caused being (a "possibility of existence") and the form of being through which it participates in the only entity that truly and *per se* exists, i.e., God. Gundissalinus's created being is dual as well. Its duality, though, is dual in itself: It is a dual-duality constructed at once of necessity and possibility, and form and matter. This ontological multiplicity is proper to every created being and characterises it as completely different from the first cause, which is necessary *per se* and beyond any compositional plurality implied by matter and form. Relying on Arabic sources, Gundissalinus's ontology develops and follows different aims than Boethius's, although they agree in claiming that ontological duality is the feature specifically characterising created being as such, notwithstanding its corporeal or spiritual status.

The other term of this ontological dynamic, God's utter simplicity and unity, is the point that appears to be closest between Boethius's and Gundissalinus's metaphysical reflections. For both authors, God is primarily one and causes the existence of a manifold universe whose being tends to be dispersed into multiplicity. What is more, Boethius seems to be a leading source of inspiration for Gundissalinus's theory of metaphysical oneness. Gundissalinus's *De unitate et uno* is doctrinally grounded on the axiom that "whatever exists, therefore, exists because it is one."[24] Every created being receives the oneness it requires to subsist from the simple One that is God. It is indeed thanks to unity that an entity can be said to be one and is preserved in existence, holding together matter and form. Accordingly, every single thing exists only as long as it is one and, for this reason, everything desires to be one. And,

> as a consequence, a thing which receives its being from him is one, and therefore, the movement of every substance is toward and through the One, and none of the existing things desire to be many. To the contrary, all of them, desiring to be, desire to be one, since everything desires by nature to be, and it can be only by being one. So, everything tends to [be] one.[25]

In *De processione mundi*, this desire for oneness is further expressed by matter's desire for the form of unity which gives matter its actual existence. Although they cannot be identified, unity and being are always together, and the form of unity is the first form to join matter.[26]

---

24 See Gundissalinus, *De unitate et uno*, ed. María Jesús Soto Bruna and Concepción Alonso Del Real (Pamplona, 2015), 104.3.

25 Gundissalinus, *De unitate et uno*, ed. Soto Bruna and Alonso Del Real, 110.2–112.1: "Ac per hoc, quia ex quo res habeat esse una est, ideo motus omnium substantiarum est ad unum et propter unum; et nihil eorum, quae sunt, appetit esse multa, sed omnia, sicut appetunt esse, sic et unum esse. Quia enim omnia esse naturaliter appetunt, habere autem esse non possunt nisi sint unum, ideo omnia ad unum tendunt."

26 Gundissalinus, *De processione mundi*, ed. Bülow, 26.3–6; ed. Soto Bruna and Alonso Del Real, 166.22–168.3: "Hinc est, quod materia dicitur desiderare formam et moveri ad recipiendum illam motu scilicet naturalis appetitus, quo omnia appetunt esse unum; unum enim non possunt esse, nisi per formam." As Gundissalinus makes clear elsewhere in his treatise, this first form is the form of unity.

86 | CHAPTER TWO

Gundissalinus's theory of metaphysical unity is, nonetheless, very close to Boethius's. Both authors refer to a desire for unity, proper to created being, and establish a pivotal bond between being and oneness. While in this case Gundissalinus also appears to ground his line of reasoning on further sources, it is remarkable that the axiom "whatever exists, therefore, exists because it is one" ("quicquid est, ideo est, quia unum est") is a quotation from the famous discussion of universals in Boethius's second commentary on Porphyry's *Isagoge*.[27] While engaging with the fundamental problem of whether genera and species subsist *in re* or *in intellectu* – possibly the most debated question in the twelfth century – Boethius first expands on the refutation of their existence *in re*. A universal cannot be subsistent in reality, because what is common and shared at the same time by multiple entities must, but could not then be, one in itself. Each one of the species common to a single genus, indeed, must have at the same time the entirety of the shared genus. Nothing, though, can be at the same time in multiple entities in its entirety, while remaining one in number in itself. Indeed,

> But if this is so, then a genus cannot be one. Hence it is nothing at all. For everything that exists, exists for the reason that it is one. The same can be said about species.[28]

As a consequence, following a convertibility of unity and being, it is evident that universals cannot exist *in re*, i.e., as subsistent entities beyond their mental existence.

While Boethius's discussion goes on to consider and refute the other alternative, that universals only have a mental subsistence, Gundissalinus just quotes the short line concerning being and oneness. And although Gundissalinus does not accept the convertibility of oneness and being, as Boethius famously does, the relevance of this passage should not be underestimated. The quotation from Boethius's commentary, indeed, plays a primary role in both *De unitate* and *De processione*. It is the pillar itself of Gundissalinus's theory of metaphysical unity. The duality of interpretative levels which marks Gundissalinus's speculation appears to be rooted, in many distinctive ways, in Porphyry's *Isagoge* and, through

---

27 Concerning Boethius's discussion of universals in his second commentary on *Isagoge*, see Paul V. Spade, "Boethius Against Universals: The Arguments in the Second Commentary on Porphyry," unpublished, available at: http://www.pvspade.com/Logic /index.html.

28 Boethius, *In Isagogen Porphyrii commenta*, ed. Samuel Brandt (Vienna, 1906), 162.1– 3: "Quod si ita est, unum quiddam genus esse non poterit, quo fit ut omnino nihil sit; omne enim quod est, idcirco est, quia unum est. Et de specie idem convenit dici." English translation by Paul V. Spade, *Five Texts on the Mediaeval Problem of Universals: Porphyry, Boethius, Abelard, Duns Scotus, Ockham* (Indianapolis, 1994), 22.

it, on Aristotle's *Categories*. Nonetheless, the aforementioned quotation from Boethius's commentary on the *Isagoge*, together with a further quotation from Boethius's *Introductio ad Syllogismos Categoricos*, seems to open a new and extremely promising scenario in relation to Gundissalinus's training in logic and the interrelation between logic and ontology implied by his reflections.[29]

Boethius's influence on Gundissalinus, therefore, appears to be rather peculiar. On the one hand, considering the twelfth-century *curriculum studiorum* and philosophical debate, it is beyond doubt that Gundissalinus knew Boethius's works. His philosophical training was surely based on many of Boethius's works and, as a consequence, various aspects of his thought constitute a sort of ground in which Gundissalinus rooted his own speculation. Yet on the other hand Gundissalinus's originality and his willingness to open new perspectives for Latin speculation through a constant recourse to Arabic sources mark an undeniable distance from Boethius. Even more, Gundissalinus develops his thought in a different direction, one which leads him to accept positions which would likely be rather abhorrent for Boethius. It is questionable, though, whether Gundissalinus felt this distance from Boethius or not.

From this point of view, an examination of Gundissalinus's uncredited quotations of Boethius's works is an exemplar case of his overall attitude. He quotes few, but very well-known, passages from Boethius's writings, dispersing them throughout his own treatises without referring to their origin or truly developing them into his own reflection. As Fidora has pointed out, in the framework of *De divisione philosophiae* both Isidore of Seville and Boethius serve as main *auctoritates* to facilitate the insertion of new doctrines and theoretical points into the Latin tradition. References to their texts play a sort of corroborating role, displaying the coherence of Gundissalinus's "novelties" within the Latin tradition and its main *auctoritates*.[30] As these remarks appear to be valid also in metaphysics, although less pervasively and with some

---

29 See Boethius, *Introductio ad Syllogismos Categoricos*, ed. Christina T. Thörnqvist (Gothenburg, 2008), 50.9–11, which appears to be the source of the passage Manuel Alonso Alonso attributed to Abraham ibn Daud. See also Alonso Alonso, "Las fuentes literarias de Domingo Gundisalvo," *Al-Andalus* 11 (1946): 159–73. I will discuss in a forthcoming study the crucial tension between logical analysis and ontological description in Gundissalinus's works in relation to Boethius's logical commentaries and the twelfth-century debate.

30 See Fidora, *Domingo Gundisalvo y la teoría*, 53–103. Fidora refers to the role played by Boethius in Gundissalinus's epistemology as a "hermeneutical condition" through which the Toledan philosopher read and interpreted the Arabic sources. While I agree with Fidora about Boethius's role in Gundissalinus's epistemology, the case of his metaphysics appears to be rather different – at least inasmuch as a thorough analysis of the interrelations of logic and ontology in the twelfth century is still a *desideratum*.

88 | CHAPTER TWO

restrictions, Gundissalinus's complicated attitude toward Boethius is a magisterial example of his overall attitude toward Latin speculation, marked by a tension between his adherence to the tradition and his willingness to supersede it.

Decoding Timaeus

Plato's *Timaeus* and its commentary authored by Calcidius are a second pillar grounding vast aspects of twelfth-century cosmological reflection.[31] For centuries, Plato's *Timaeus* was the only Platonic dialogue available in Latin, thanks to the partial translation (*Timaeus*, 17a–53c) made by Calcidius.[32] The dialogue, which famously engages with a complex description of the cosmic founding, was accompanied by a dense commentary authored by its translator, Calcidius.[33] A Middle Platonist,[34] Calcidius's interest is mostly focused on the cosmogonic and metaphysical features of Plato's dialogue, peculiarly interpreted and commented upon. Together with Martianus Capella's *De nuptiis Philologiae et Mercurii*, Macrobius's *Commentarius in Somnium Scipionis*, and Boethius's writings, Calcidius's commentary played a crucial role within Latin culture up to the twelfth century.

31 On the relevance bestowed upon Plato's *Timaeus* by twelfth-century philosophers, see Eugenio Garin, "Contributi alla storia del Platonismo medievale," *Annali della Scuola Normale Superiore di Pisa: Lettere, Storia e Filosofia* (Serie II) 20 (1951): 58–97; and Tullio Gregory, "The Platonic Inheritance," in *A History of Twelfth-Century Western Philosophy*, ed. Peter Dronke (Cambridge, 1988), 54–80. See also Irene Caiazzo, "La materia nei commenti al *Timeo* del secolo XII," *Quaestio* 7 (2007): 245–64; Thomas Ricklin, "Calcidius bei Bernhard von Chartres und Wilhelm von Conches," *Archives d'histoire doctrinale et littéraire du Moyen Âge* 67 (2000): 119–41; and Anna Somfai, "The Eleventh-Century Shift in the Reception of Plato's *Timaeus* and Calcidius's Commentary," *Journal of the Warburg and Courtauld Intitutes* 65 (2002): 1–21.

32 In fact, Cicero's translation of Plato's *Timaeus* disappeared during the Middle Ages. The twelfth-century translation of Plato's *Phaedo* and *Meno* underwent a similar fate. Without disappearing, their role was superseded by Aristotle's newly translated works.

33 Indeed, Calcidius focuses his commentary mostly on *Timaeus* 40a–53c. See Béatrice Bakhouche's introduction to Calcidius, *Commentaire au* Timée *de Platon*, ed. Bakhouche (Paris, 2011), 7–88. On Plato's *Timaeus* and the peculiarities of its original contents, see Luc Brisson, *Le Même et l'Autre dans la Structure Ontologique du* Timée *de Platon* (Sankt Augustin, 1994); Mary L. Gill, "Matter and Flux in Plato's Timaeus," *Phronesis* 32 (1987): 34–53; and Thomas K. Johansen, *Plato's Natural Philosophy: A Study of the Timaeus-Critias* (Cambridge, 2004).

34 For an overall perspective, see Stephen Gersh, *Middle Platonism and Neoplatonism: The Latin Tradition* (Notre Dame, 1986).

The *Timaeus*'s description of the cosmogonic process is based on a discussion of the ordering role of the Demiurge, who produces a mixture of rationality (i.e., the separated ideas, eidetic model of the universe) and necessity (the *chora*, identified by Calcidius with matter and translated as *silva*). The progressive production of this mingling corresponds to the ordering of a primordial chaos from which the ordered universe we are living in is generated.[35] This ordering action of the *opifex deus* is correspondent to giving unity and form to the four elements, which were in a state of "squalor and deformity," just "traces" of the elements they would become. In ordering this primordial chaos, the Demiurge used an unchangeable and perfect model, which is the eidetic world – his own mind. Images of these transcendent ideas are reflected on matter, becoming the immanent forms which joined it, thus causing the existence of bodies.

Ordering cause, exemplar model, and substrate are the terms of the so-called doctrine of the three principles.[36] Among them, *chora* (matter, in Calcidius's interpretation) plays a special role. Just as gold can be shaped into different figures, matter is constantly shaped and made something else by the immanent forms joining it.[37] Accordingly, matter is a sort of nurse for every generated being, as is demonstrated by processes of elemental transmutation, in which a substrate must always persist.[38] Like a mother, matter is seeded by the form (analogous to a "father"), producing an offspring of beings.[39] Matter is the receptacle of the ideas – an invisible and shapeless entity which is able to receive whatever form is reflected on it as an eidetic image.[40] Accordingly, matter is like a place (*locus*) for these images, which constantly are born and die as the only way to continue their existence.[41] The first reflection of the images on matter, though, was a chaos that needed to be ordered through numbers and shapes, modelling the universe, as,

> at that point there was a disordered confusion of things, a confusion devoid of any such element of reason, but after taking the decision to bring every-

---

35 See Plato, *Timaeus* (Calcidius's translation), in Calcidius, *In Platonis Timaeum Commentarius*, ed. Bakhouche, 158.11–15, along with Calcidius's comments in the same place.

36 See Stephen Gersh, "Calcidius' Theory of First Principles," *Studia Patristica* 18 (1989): 85–92.

37 See Calcidius, *In Platonis Timaeum Commentarius*, ed. Bakhouche, 194.23–29 and 194.34–196.2.

38 See ibid., 192.26–27 and 194.10–23.

39 See ibid., 196.5–7.

40 See ibid., 196.23–29.

41 See ibid., 198.28–200.4.

90 | CHAPTER TWO

thing back within measure, the craftsman God first gave binding unity to fire, earth, air, and water, not in their present states but such that they exhibited the traces of the elements despite the squalor and deformity manifested by things that lack divine foresight; and once light and form had been bestowed upon each one of them, number too proceeded to follow the generation of all the things thus illuminated, with the result that they were all established in a state of beauty such as they had not previously enjoyed.[42]

The notion of matter was so important for Calcidius that he dedicates the final and largest part his commentary to this central concept.[43] In order to examine what matter is, Calcidius needs to introduce a twofold method. It is a speculative device called *compositio et resolutio*.[44] Through the two moments by which this procedure is developed, the existence of the three simple and eternal principles of the universe – matter, ideas, and cause – is demonstrated.[45] In itself, matter is characterised by a complete passivity. It is the unchangeable subject of change, like wax shaped and reshaped, but remaining the same wax in itself throughout these changes.[46] Matter, thus, is formless, shapeless, and unqualified. It has form, shape, and quality only in potency, as it is a possibility of being actualised through the forms.[47] As a result of this characterisation, matter is the possibility of every form, and it possesses every form in potency, as it can receive any form through God's moulding activity.[48]

---

42 Plato, *Timaeus* (Calcidius's translation), ed. Bakhouche, 200.23–29: "Ac tunc quidem erat huius modi rationi expers rerum inordinata confusio, sed ubi cuncta redigi ad modum placuit, ignem primo terramque et aera atque aquam continuavit opifex deus, non talia ut nunc sunt, sed quae praeferrent elementorum vestigia in eo squalore ac deformitate quae apparet in his quibus divina deest prospiscientia; nunc vero singulis luce ac specie tributa, numerus quoque illustratorum omnium genituram sequebatur, pulchris omnibus ex non talibus quondam institutis." English translation by John Magee, in Calcidius, *On Plato's Timaeus* (Cambridge, MA, 2016), 119–21.

43 See Calcidius, *In Platonis Timaeum Commentarius*, ed. Bakhouche, 496.29–584.6.

44 Bakhouche highlights that Calcidius's sources of his method of composition and resolution is Alcinous. See ibid., 858–59, n1099. See also Christina Hoenig, "Calcidius' Platonic Method: On *syllogismus*, *compositio* and *resolutio*." Paper discussed at Notre Dame University on 27 March 2015.

45 Calcidius, *In Platonis Timaeum Commentarius*, ed. Bakhouche, 532.30–31.

46 See ibid., 536.23–29.

47 See ibid., 538.1–8.

48 See ibid., 538.11–12 and 544.23–26.

Reshaping Frameworks: Gundissalinus and the Latin Tradition | 91

Provided with such a precarious existence posited "between some sort of being and non-being" ("inter aliquam et nullam substantiam"),[49] matter cannot be a body. A body is what is limited and made finite by a form. At the same time, though, matter cannot be incorporeal either. What is incorporeal, indeed, cannot become corporeal, whereas matter is precisely the origin of all bodies, once it has received a form. In addition, if matter were incorporeal, it would be intelligible, whereas matter is virtually unknowable.[50] Matter must be a possibility of both corporeal and spiritual beings. As Calcidius states,

> again, if it is body then it is a sensible; but it is not a sensible: thus it will not be body either; but if matter is to be something incorporeal then its nature is intelligible; but it is not intelligible: thus it is not incorporeal either. We are right, then, to speak, without qualification and in consideration of its proper nature, in terms of its being neither corporeal nor incorporeal but both body in potency (*possibilitate corpus*) and nonbody in potency (*possibilitate non corpus*).[51]

Eternally moved by the constant flow of immanent forms – mortal images of immortal beings, i.e., the eidetic world – matter receives beauty and order from God.[52] The ideas are reflected in matter as in a mirror. Through this reflection, the eidetic images are engrained into matter, and for this reason matter is called the immortal and ubiquitous *locus* of the universe.[53] Through the first reflection of the eidetic contents, a phase corresponding to primordial chaos, matter suffers a movement impressed by those images. That chaotic movement is ordered by the Demiurgical action, which shapes the sensible world following the most perfect model, i.e., the mind of the Demiurge himself.[54] As a result, the universe is originated, not in time but only by cause, in the timeless dimension

---

49 Plato, *Timaeus* (Calcidius's translation), ed. Bakhouche, 200.4–5. English translation by Magee, *On Plato's* Timaeus, 117.

50 See Calcidius, *In Platonis Timaeum Commentarius*, ed. Bakhouche, 544.10–17.

51 Ibid., 544.14–19: "Deinde, si corpus est, sensile est; at enim sensile non est: ne corpus quidem igitur est. Si autem incorporeum quiddam erit silva, intelligibilis eius natura est; at intelligibilis non est: ne incorporea quidem. Recte igitur eam simpliciter et ex natura sua neque corpoream neque incorpoream cognominamus, sed possibilitate corpus et item possibilitate non corpus." English translation by Magee, *On Plato's* Timaeus, 623.

52 Calcidius, *In Platonis Timaeum Commentarius*, ed. Bakhouche, 544.31–545.2 and 556.31–558.4.

53 See ibid., 570.13–22.

54 See ibid., 582.12–16.

of God. Although generated, the universe is made eternal by the unceasing temporal recreation of its parts (*partium recreatio*).[55]

There is little doubt about Gundissalinus's knowledge of the complex cosmological discussion expounded in Plato's *Timaeus* and Calcidius's *Commentarius*. These works were part of his philosophical training, wherever he might have received it. Some features of *Timaeus*'s narrative – specifically, the doctrine of primordial chaos – are explicitly engaged and refuted by Gundissalinus. Traces of the dialogue and its commentary can be detected throughout Gundissalinus's *De processione mundi*, although in many cases it seems that mediation has taken place, at least concerning their interpretation by Gundissalinus.

Yet Gundissalinus's and Calcidius's philosophical perspectives are noticeably divergent. In Gundissalinus's speculation, there is no reference to a Platonic eidetic world acting as exemplar cause on the sensible universe. In general, the doctrine of the three principles (matter, model, God) is posited by Gundissalinus in a completely different sense. Indeed, God has no Demiurgical role – there was no primordial chaos. The model is not an eidetic world reflected in matter and connected to those images by structures of participation. Whereas the forms were in God's mind – with matter – before the creation, there is no Platonic claim in Gundissalinus's position. Only concerning matter is there some proximity between Calcidius and Gundissalinus – under some considerations, at least.

Concerning the ontological characterisations of matter and form in relation to their meta-temporal dimension, Calcidius claims that

> he [i.e., Plato] compares that which receives the forms within itself to a mother, namely, to matter, for it receives the forms brought forth by nature; and that from which the element of likeness comes to a father, i.e., to the idea, for it is from it that the forms under consideration borrow their element of likeness; and that which is from the two to their offspring, namely, to the generated form, for it is situated between the nature which is truly existent, constant, and forever the same, namely, the ideas or eternal intellect of the eternal God, and the nature which indeed is but is not forever the same, i.e., matter, for by its nature matter is none of the things that are, since it is eternal. Thus that which is situated between these two natures is not truly existent. For being the image of a truly existent reality, it has to some degree the appearance of being, but in its not enduring and its undergoing change

55 See ibid., 232.11–19.

Reshaping Frameworks: Gundissalinus and the Latin Tradition | 93

within itself, it is not truly existent as exemplars are; for the exemplars thrive on a fixed and immutable constancy.[56]

For Calcidius, the transcendent forms are characterised by a true, eternal, and stable being, as they are the contents of God's mind. In turn, matter has a true and eternal being, though it is not stable, as it constantly receives the images of the ideas – i.e., the immanent forms – which, in turn, have an untrue, transient, and unstable being. For this reason, ideas and matter are like a father and a mother of transient beings. This analogy is present also in Gundissalinus's *De processione mundi*. Its direct source, though, is not Calcidius, but Hermann of Carinthia – an author profoundly indebted to Plato and Calcidius.[57] Gundissalinus claims that:

> there are three principles of everything begotten: first, an efficient cause; second, that-from-which, and third, that-in-which. That-in-which is named the matter of things, since in the role of a passive mother it is open to all the motions of the male power coming over it. Form, however, is that-from-which, since it fashions that formless neediness by the motions of the active male power into various results. For, in accord with such neediness, form is the ornament of matter. But, since matter is the neediness for form, in every constitution of things matter is first necessary as a sustainer of the constitution of things; later, the result of the work exists by means of form.[58]

56 Calcidius, *In Platonis Timaeum Commentarius*, ed. Bakhouche, 556.4–15: "Comparat enim quod percipit in se species matri, videlicet silvae – haec enim recipit a natura proditas species – illud vero ex quo similitudo commeat patri, hoc est ideae – huius enim similitudinem memoratae species mutuantur – quod vero ex his duobus est proli, generatae scilicet speciei – est enim haec posita inter naturam vere existentem, constantem eandemque semper, nimirum idean, quae intellectus dei aeterni est aeternus, et inter eam naturam quae est quidem, sed non eadem semper, id est silvam; quippe haec natura sua nihil est eorum quae sunt, cum sit aeterna. Ergo quod inter has duas naturas positum est vere existens non est. Cum enim sit imago vere existentis rei, videtur esse aliquatenus, quia vero non perseverat patiturque immutatione sui, non est existens vere, ut sunt exempla; illa quippe exempla rata et immutabili constantia vigent." English translation by Magee, *On Plato's* Timaeus, 641–43.

57 See Hermann of Carinthia, *De essentiis*, ed. and trans. Charles Burnett (Leiden, 1982), 76.21–78.4.

58 Gundissalinus, *De processione mundi*, ed. Bülow, 22.9–16; ed. Soto Bruna and Alonso Del Real, 158.18–160.7: "Tria enim sunt principia omnis geniturae: primum scilicet causa efficiens, secundum id, ex quo, tertium id, in quo. Id, in quo, quoniam, tamquam matris patientis vice, supervenientis virtutis ad omnes motus patet, rerum materia nominatur. Forma vero id est, ex quo, quoniam informem illam necessitatem agentis virtutis motibus in varios

94 | CHAPTER TWO

Gundissalinus is evidently referring here to the doctrine of the three principles. Nevertheless, the theoretical context in which this reference is introduced drastically changes its scope. In *De processione*, matter and form have a radically different being, but a rather similar existence, as they are both per se in potency and are created directly by God simultaneously. An absence of any differentiation between transcendent and immanent forms does not entail any reference to the universe as an instantiation of God's mind. Matter and form, therefore, are a mother and a father only because they are the immanent components of every caused being. While apparently close to Calcidius, then, Gundissalinus's line of reasoning is rooted in different sources and perspectives.

The correlations between the concepts of matter and body offer another point of much interest. For both Calcidius and Gundissalinus, matter is an eternal ontological possibility of existence which is perfected and actualised through the reception of forms. Both authors also agree that the union of matter and form can produce a body. Whether spiritual beings are also composed of matter and form, however, is a substantively different problem. For Gundissalinus, they surely are. As for Calcidius, the situation is much more complex. In a passage quoted above, Calcidius explicitly refers to matter as the potency of both corporeal and incorporeal things.[59] A literal interpretation of this passage would imply that, for Calcidius, matter plays a primordial role in an extended ontological version of Porphyry's tree – it would indeed precede the distinction of substance into corporeal and incorporeal, being the origin of both species. Substance as such, therefore, would be made of matter and form and, if that were the case, Calcidius's hylomorphism would be universal.

As Jacob Van Winden has pointed out in his fundamental study of Calcidius's doctrine of matter, there are more textual passages which appear to corroborate Calcidius's unspoken universal hylomorphism.[60] Without entering the intricate debate on this delicate point, it is worth noting that, whenever there might be *margins* to suppose that Calcidius sustained *a sort of* universal hylomorphism, it seems rather unlikely that he might have been an actual source of inspiration for Gundissalinus. His explicit universal hylomorphism is grounded on Ibn Gabirol's *Fons vitae* without traces of any additional rooting in Latin *auctoritates* which might have formulated similar ontological doctrines, like

---

effingit eventus. Forma enim secundum huiusmodi necessitatem ornatus est materiae. Materia vero formae necessitatis in omni siquidem rerum constitutione sustinens imprimis est necessarium; posterius est operis eventus per formam." English translation by Laumakis, *The Procession of the World*, 49–50.

59 Calcidius, *In Platonis Timaeum Commentarius*, ed. Bakhouche, 544.17–19.

60 See Jacob Van Winden, *Calcidius on Matter: His Doctrine and Sources* (Leiden, 1965), 165–72.

Calcidius or Augustine – although a thorough examination of this genetic hypothesis would be much desired. If Calcidius did play some role in Gundissalinus's reflection on matter, he is likely to have done so mainly concerning the position – and *not* the solution – of problems like the ontological composition of spiritual substances and primordial chaos.[61] In addition to this, it should be considered that Calcidius's presence (with Plato's *Timaeus*) often appears to be mediated in Gundissalinus's works. The twofold method of composition and resolution provides the best example of this fact. In his commentary, Calcidius distinguishes between two kinds of reasoning, the first of which is called *resolutio* (resolution, or analysis). Calcidius claims that:

> there is a twofold method of proof for questions that have been raised for consideration: one method provides confirmation of posterior things on the basis of prior ones, and this is proper to the syllogism, for in order the premises, which are called elements, precede the conclusion; and the other is that which on the basis of posterior things reaches the investigation of prior ones by steps, and this kind of proof is called analysis (*resolutio*). Since, then, the discussion concerns the first principles which are prior to all else, we will avail ourselves of the method of demonstration deriving from analysis ... To the extent, then, that anyone undertakes a disputation in such a way as to ascend from things which are primary in relation to us to those which are at a second remove from us, he is said to analyze the question, for beginning with things which are not truly existent but are rather images of truly existent ones he reaches those which are the first principles and causes of truly existent things.[62]

61 While many problems Gundissalinus was addressing in his works (and through his translations) were probably inherited from the twelfth-century debate, his encounter with Ibn Gabirol's doctrines must have been a sort of game-changer. He consistently, constantly, but tacitly refers to *Fons vitae* in practically all his major works, as we shall see in the next chapter.

62 Calcidius, *In Platonis Timaeum Commentarius*, ed. Bakhouche, 530.4–25: "Est igitur propositarum quaestionum duplex probatio, altera quae ex antiquioribus posteriora confirmat, quod est proprium syllogismi – praecedunt quippe ordine acceptiones, quae elementa vocantur, conclusionem – altera item quae <ex> posterioribus ad praecedentium indaginem gradatim pervenit, quod genus probationis resolutio dicitur. Nos ergo, quia de initiis sermo est quibus antiquius nihil est, utemur probationis remediis ex resolutione manantibus, ... Quotus quisque igitur in disputatione sic exordietur ut ab his, quae prima sunt ad nos versum, ascendat ad ea quae sunt a nobis secunda, resolvere dicitur quaestionem, siquidem ab his orsus quae vere non sunt sed imagines potius sunt vere existentium rerum, perveniat ad ea quae vere existentium initia causaeque sunt." English translation by Magee, *On Plato's* Timaeus, 599–601.

96 | CHAPTER TWO

While *compositio* (composition, or synthesis) demonstrates the effect from its cause, *resolutio* departs from the effect to examine its cause. Calcidius points out that any study of the first principles must start with the *resolutive method*. Principles indeed are first in order, and accordingly there is no cause through which they can be known. Therefore, any approximation to them has to start from what is closer to us. Application of *resolutio* to matter coincides with the abstraction of quantity, quality, forms, and shapes from the things. In this way, human reason deduces the existence of a common substrate of everything, which is matter.[63]

The second moment of the twofold method exposited by Calcidius is *compositio*, which is used in relation to the ideas and the *opifex*. Calcidius presents the procedure as follows.

> Let us now consider the other kind, which is called synthesis (*compositio*); for synthesis follows analysis, and concretion separation. Let us then reintegrate the things, i.e., the genera, qualities, and shapes, which in our minds we just now imagined ourselves separating from matter, and put them back into their place, as it were, not in a disorderly or haphazard way but with an eye to their pattern and order. Now, order is incapable of existing without harmony, and harmony is ultimately a concomitant of proportion, and proportion is similarly coupled with reason, and reason is ultimately found to be the inseparable concomitant of providence; but providence is not without intellect, nor intellect without mind. Thus the mind of God tempered, ordered, and adorned the whole of the corporeal structure; thus the divine origin arising from the craftsman puts into effect and adorns everything according to his rational power and the majesty of his works; but his works are his thoughts, which by the Greeks are called *ideai*; and the ideas are the exemplars of natural realities. And in this way the third, exemplary origin of things is found.[64]

---

63 Calcidius, *In Platonis Timaeum Commentarius*, ed. Bakhouche, 532.7–12.

64 Ibid., 532.13–25: "Nunc illud aliud consideremus quod compositio cognominatur; sequitur quippe resolutionem compositio et discretionem concretio. Quae igitur modo separare animo videbamur a silva, rursus ei praesentemus ac velut in suum locum reponamus, hoc est genera qualitates figuras, nec inordinate haec ipsa et utcumque sed cum cultu et ordine. Ordo autem sine harmonia esse non potest, harmonia demum analogiae comes est; analogia item cum ratione et demum ratio comes individua providentiae reperitur, nec vero providentia sine intellectu est intellectusque sine mente non est. Mens ergo dei modulavit, ordinavit, excoluit omnem continentiam corporis; inventa ergo est demum opificis divina origo. Operatur porro opifex et exornat omnia iuxta vim rationabilem maiestatemque operum suorum; opera vero eius intellectus eius sunt, qui a Graecis ideae vocantur; porro ideae sunt exempla naturalium rerum. Quo pacto invenitur tertia exemplaris origo rerum." English translation by Magee, *On Plato's* Timaeus, 603.

Reshaping Frameworks: Gundissalinus and the Latin Tradition | 97

As the characteristic method of the syllogism, as Calcidius remarks, *compositio* departs from a principle (in this case, matter) to demonstrate another principle (God and the ideas) through a sort of induction. The formal characteristics that were removed from matter during *resolutio* are now re-added to that principle, allowing the human mind to understand that there is an ordering to the way forms are joined to matter. This harmonic order shows that some intelligent principle (God and his mind) must be its origin. Therefore, it is only through an interrelation of *compositio* and *resolutio* that the principles of existence can be known. And, "thus by following the rational law of analysis (*dissolutio*) we have found Matter; and by following the precepts of synthesis (*compositio*) we have found the craftsman God himself; and from the works of the craftsman God we have found the Exemplar."[65]

In Gundissalinus's *De processione mundi* there are fifty-one occurrences of the term "compositio," compared to only five occurences of "resolutio." This discrepancy is due to Gundissalinus's use of "compositio" in relation to the ontological composition of created beings which he distinguishes into "compositio primaria" and "compositio secundaria." In at least three cases Gundissalinus uses "compositio" and "resolutio" in an eminently epistemological way. The first case reads as follows:

> But they are the first principles in composition (*in compositione*) and the ultimate limit in resolution (*in resolutione*), since, just as they are the first from which every composition (*compositio*) begins, so they are the last in which every resolution (*resolutio*) ends. Nothing precedes them except the creator alone, not in time but in causality and eternity.[66]

Gundissalinus states that matter and form are the first principles in *compositio* and the ultimate limit in *resolutio*. This statement can be interpreted in two different ways. On the one hand, it could be referred, ontologically, to the fact that matter and form are the principles composing everything and, therefore, their separation corresponds to a resolution or corruption of the composite. On the other hand, the passage might be considered as pointing at the processes of *compositio* and *resolutio* described by Calcidius. The latter seems to be the orig-

65 Calcidius, *In Platonis Timaeum Commentarius*, ed. Bakhouche, 532.25–27: "igitur silvam quidem iuxta legem rationemque dissolutionis invenimus, iuxta compositionis vero praecepta ipsum opificem deum, ex operibus porro dei opificis exemplum." English translation by Magee, *On Plato's* Timaeus, 603.

66 Gundissalinus, *De processione mundi*, ed. Bülow, 24.20–25.2; ed. Soto Bruna and Alonso Del Real, 164.12–15: "Sed prima principia sunt in compositione, finis ultimus in resolutione, quoniam, sicut sunt prima, a quibus omnis compositio incipit, ita sunt ultima, in quibus omnis resolutio finit, quae nihil, nisi solus creator, non tempore, sed causa et aeternitate praecedit." English translation by Laumakis, *The Procession of the World*, 52.

98 | CHAPTER TWO

inal sense Gundissalinus intended. Indeed, it should be recalled that, in Gundissalinus's universal hylomorphism, even perpetual creatures like the angels are composed of matter and form. They do not suffer any corruption; therefore, there is no ontological *resolutio* for them. The epistemological interpretation of this passage is corroborated by another excerpt in which Gundissalinus claims that

> in all these cases, when we say "prior," we do not wish to describe a priority in time, but in causality and in diversity of things among themselves, which composition (*compositio*) and resolution (*resolutio*) evidently reveal.[67]

Gundissalinus is discussing here the division of substance into corporeal and incorporeal. Creation of matter and form is simultaneous to their composition and, accordingly, the distinction of the substance into corporeal and incorporeal is causally, and not temporarily, prior. Gundissalinus claims that this point is made evident by *compositio* and *resolutio*. In this case, there are no alternatives. Gundissalinus is indeed referring to epistemology and the twofold method expounded by Calcidius. It is only through that method that it is possible to distinguish between a (logical) moment in which there is substance as such and another (logical) moment in which that substance has been informed by the forms of, respectively, corporeity and spirituality. This is in explicit coherence with what Gundissalinus states in the first pages of his treatise, while referring to the very aim of *De processione mundi*, i.e., the knowledge of the most intimate aspects of God. Gundissalinus claims indeed that

> Reason investigates by composing and resolving (*componendo and resolvendo*). By resolving (*in resolvendo*), it ascends; by composing (*in componendo*), it descends. For in resolution (*in resolvendo*), it begins from the last things; in composition (*in componendo*), it begins from the first things. Hence, the creature of the world sees the invisible things of God that have been understood by means of the things that were made, since reason deals with composition (*ad componendo*) in this way.[68]

---

67 Gundissalinus, *De processione mundi*, ed. Bülow, 50.10–13; ed. Soto Bruna and Alonso Del Real, 212.1–3: "in his enim omnibus, cum 'prius' dicimus, non prius tempore, sed causa et diversitate rerum inter se exprimi volumus, quod evidenter indicat compositio et resolutio." English translation by Laumakis, *The Procession of the World*, 72.

68 Gundissalinus, *De processione mundi*, ed. Bülow, 3.6–10; ed. Soto Bruna and Alonso Del Real, 122.13–15: "Ratio inquirit componendo et resolvendo; resolvendo ascendit, componendo descendit. In resolvendo enim ab ultimis incipit, in componendo a primis incipit. Unde per ea, quae facta sunt, invisibilia dei intellecta creatura mundi conspicit, cum ratio ad compositionem accedit hoc modo." English translation by Laumakis, *The Procession of the World*, 34.

Ascending through *resolutio* (from the effect to its cause) and descending through *compositio* (from the cause to its effects), the *invisibilia Dei* can be discovered. It is clear that Gundissalinus is not referring to the *ontological* processes of *compositio* and *resolutio*, but to the *epistemological* method described by Calcidius. The centrality of this reference makes clear the relevance Gundissalinus bestowed upon the twofold method of composition and resolution.

While the *Commentarius* is undoubtedly the origin of this doctrine, one could ask whether Calcidius is also the *direct* source of the epistemological procedure referred to by Gundissalinus. It is worth noting, indeed, that Thierry of Chartres, in his *Commentum* on Boethius's *De Trinitate*, also refers to and uses Calcidius's speculative method.[69] Thierry affirms that through *resolutio* it is possible to grasp what matter is. If one abstracts the shape from a statue, what is left is the material of which it is made. Likewise, if one abstracts from something its forms, therefore, what is left is just matter and its mere possibility of existence.[70] However, through *compositio* it is possible to grasp the existence of a first cause. Considering the disposition of the limbs within a human body, or even the order of the universe, it is clear that there is a rational ordering principle. In fact, as matter is the potency of everything, the actual existence of the order of nature indicates that there are forms actualising matter's potency and causing the existence of everything.[71] Accordingly, for Thierry it is through the method of *compositio* and *resolutio* that one can grasp the three principles of the universe – matter, form, and the first cause.[72]

It is evident that the source of Thierry's discussion of this speculative method is Calcidius. Nevertheless, application of this speculative device is different in Thierry's treatise than in its source. Indeed, while the aims are similar – the demonstration of the three cosmological principles – the cases considered by Thierry do not coincide with the discussion presented in Calcidius's commentary. Gundissalinus had access to both works, and it is very likely that he was influenced by them both. Calcidius's description of the twofold method is the original source. But it is probably Thierry's use of *compositio* and *resolutio* – the abstraction of this method from Calcidius's commentary and its application – that could have convinced Gundissalinus of the usefulness of this speculative procedure. Moreover, Gundissalinus's ontology seems much closer to Thierry's version of the three principles, which he demonstrates through this application of composition and resolution, than to Calcidius's.

---

69 See Thierry of Chartres, *Commentum super Boethii librum De Trinitate*, ed. Nikolaus Häring, *Commentaries on Boethius by Thierry of Chartres and His School* (Toronto, 1971), 75.29–31.

70 See ibid., 75.32–76.43.

71 See ibid., 76.44–56.

72 See ibid., 76.57–61.

100 | CHAPTER TWO

It is probably worth appreciating also that some traces of Calcidius's *Commentarius* are noticeable in Gundissalinus's *De processione mundi* – but virtually nowhere else and almost always in a mediated way. This fact can probably be connected to the relevance bestowed upon Calcidius in the twelfth century. Together with Boethius, Calcidius formed part of a cosmological paradigm which was shared by the vast majority of thinkers of that period, but which was also progressively eroded by recently translated works. Notwithstanding some points of contact, therefore, one of the outcomes of Gundissalinus's work – whether he was aware or not – is an overcoming of the world of Calcidius and, above all, the *Timaeus*.

God and Numbers

Traces of a mediation between Boethius and Calcidius, on the one hand, and Gundissalinus, on the other, are easy to detect. Boethius and Calcidius, indeed, profoundly marked the philosophical reflection of the twelfth century, particularly in Chartres.[73] In turn, Chartrean masters like William of Conches and Thierry of Chartres had a meaningful influence upon Gundissalinus. William and Thierry are among the main sources of the rhetorical and grammatical parts of the *De divisione philosophiae*. And some important influences of William of Conches on Gundissalinus's *De processione mundi* have been detected and analysed by Fidora.[74] Thierry of Chartres, too, seems to have played an important role in Gundissalinus's metaphysical reflection, as Gundissalinus's discussion of universal hylomorphism appears to be engaged with a peculiar problem arising from Thierry's doctrine of spiritual composition.[75] A brief consideration of two further theories will be worthwhile in order to assess the continuities and ruptures which marked Gundissalinus's ontol-

73 See Richard Southern, *Scholastic Humanism and the Unification of Europe* (Oxford, 1995), 1: 61–85; Peter Dronke, "New Approaches to the School of Chartres," *Anuario de estudios medievales* 6 (1969): 117–40; and Andreas Speer, "The Discovery of Nature: The Contribution of the Chartrians to Twelfth-Century Attempts to Found a *Scientia Naturalis*," *Traditio* 52 (1997): 135–51. Concerning Boethius's influence on Chartres, see also the recent study by Andrew Hicks, *Composing the World: Harmony in the Medieval Platonic Cosmos* (Oxford, 2017).

74 See Alexander Fidora, "Le débat sur la création: Guillaume de Conches, maître de Dominique Gundisalvi?" in *Guillaume de Conches: Philosophie et science au XII siècle*, ed. Barbara Obrist and Irene Caiazzo (Florence, 2011), 271–88.

75 See Nicola Polloni, "Thierry of Chartres and Gundissalinus on Spiritual Substance: The Problem of Hylomorphic Composition," *Bulletin de Philosophie Médiévale* 57 (2015): 35–57.

ogy. These theories concern God and the Trinity, and the theory of primordial chaos.

Through his influence all the way up to Nicholas of Cusa, Thierry of Chartres is one of the most well-known thinkers of the twelfth century.[76] And among Thierry's doctrines, his reflection on God and numbers plays a central role. Thierry's point of departure is the position of God as the most complete and total being (*onitas*). Creatures are provided with being through their participation in the form of being (*forma essendi*), which is the origin of every form and also coincides with God himself. Accordingly, God is the "Form of forms" (*forma formarum*), the only act not to be the result of an actualisation of a previous potency, an act *per se*.[77] It is from this first eminent being that every created being derives and, therefore, everything must have been in God before coming to be, although in a way proper to God. It is Thierry's famous doctrine of the *rerum universitas*, by which the existence of the entire universe is "complicated" in the absolute necessity of God before being unfolded into created existence.

Obviously, the presence of the entire universe in God's being in the way proper to God does not imply any plurality in his being. God's most intimate characteristic is his pure and absolute unity. As numerical unity is the origin of the infinite numerical series, so too unity is the origin of the "true numbers" whose creation corresponds to the creation of the universe. The creation of numbers, indeed, is analogous to the creation of beings. For this reason, the absolute and eternal unity must be identified with the creator of the universe.[78] Furthermore, as God is completeness of being, his unity must correspond to his own being. The provision of being to the creatures through the *forma essendi* corresponds to the provision to every creature of its own unity. In other words, created unity is a constitutive character of created being, because unity and being are one in God.[79]

According to Thierry's theory, unity is therefore the origin of every creature and every number.[80] In arithmetic, though, numbers are generated following two

76 On Thierry of Chartres's philosophical reflection, see Peter Dronke, "Thierry of Chartres," in *A History of Twelfth-Century Western Philosophy*, ed. Dronke, 358–85; Enzo Maccagnolo, "Il Platonismo nel XII secolo: Teodorico di Chartres," *Rivista di Filosofia Neo-Scolastica* 73 (1981): 283–99; and Maccagnolo, "*Rerum universitas*": *Saggio sulla filosofia di Teodorico di Chartres* (Florence, 1976). Concerning Thierry's influence on Cusa, see David Albertson, *Mathematical Theologies: Nicholas of Cusa and the Legacy of Thierry of Chartres* (Oxford, 2014).

77 See Thierry of Chartres, *Lectiones in Boethii librum De Trinitate*, ed. Häring, *Commentaries on Boethius*, 168.62–67.

78 See Thierry of Chartres, *Tractatus de sex dierum operibus*, ed. Häring, *Commentaries on Boethius*, 570.44–51.

79 See ibid., 568.93–569.1.

80 See Thierry of Chartres, *Commentum super Arithmeticam Boethii*, ed. Irene Caiazzo, *The Commentary on the "De arithmetica" of Boethius* (Toronto, 2015), 126.646–47.

102 | CHAPTER TWO

processes, i.e., from their own substance or through multiplication with other numbers.[81] While the first kind of generation gives origin to equal figures (for instance, 2 multiplied by itself – or 2^2 – gives a square), the second kind gives unequal figures (2 multiplied by 3 would give a rectangle, a *figura a parte longiori*). In other words, the creation of numbers can originate both equality (*aequalitas*) and inequality (*inaequalitas*). Equality, therefore, is *broken* at the very beginning of the numerical series, number two being the principle of inequality which, ontologically, corresponds to matter.[82]

While the tension between equality and inequality marks the numerical series starting with number two, pure equality is a characteristic of unity. Unity or oneness is radically different from any other number. It is the source of every number, as every number n multiplied by one gives the same number n. But it is also the eternal origin of equality. One multiplied by one gives something identical to itself, as the substances of both are one and the same substance.[83] This is the equality (*aequalitas*), the origin of every number, corresponding to the Son of the Holy Trinity – while unity is evidently the Father.[84] As unity corresponds to God's complete being, so too equality corresponds to the *forma essendi* providing the universe with existence. Equality is nothing but the divine wisdom, the Logos that gives everything the form and measure it deserves and, therefore, causes and establishes the order of the entire universe.[85]

Thierry's third step in his reflection on the Trinity is the identification of the Holy Spirit with the connection (*conexio*) of unity and equality. This connection is the love binding Father and Son, a love in which the entire universe is immersed.[86] The Holy Trinity creates and governs the universe through the causative dynamic expressed by the interactions among unity, equality, and con-

81 See Jean-Michel Counet, "Les mathématiques au service d'une théologie de la matière chez Thierry de Chartres et Clarembaud d'Arras," in *Vie spéculative, vie méditative et travail manuel à Chartres: Actes du colloque international des 4 et 5 juillet 1998* (Chartres, 1998), 103–14; and Agnieszka Kijewska, "Mathematics as a Preparation for Theology: Boethius, Eriugena, Thierry of Chartres," in *Boèce ou la chaîne des savoirs*, ed. Galonnier, 625–47.

82 See Thierry of Chartres, *Tractatus de sex dierum operibus*, ed. Häring, 568.86–91 and *Commentum super Arithmeticam Boethii*, ed. Caiazzo, 119.465. See also Polloni, "Thierry of Chartres and Gundissalinus on Spiritual Substance."

83 See Thierry of Chartres, *Commentum super Arithmeticam Boethii*, ed. Caiazzo, 146.1220–26.

84 See Thierry of Chartres, *Lectiones super Boethii librum De Trinitate*, ed. Häring, 225.51–53.

85 See Thierry of Chartres, *Commentum super Arithmeticam Boethii*, ed. Caiazzo, 146.1226–1232 and *Tractatus de sex dierum operibus*, ed. Häring, 573.16–39 and 574.68–80.

86 See Thierry of Chartres, *Lectiones in Boethii librum De Trinitate*, ed. Häring, 225.64–72 and 297.60–64.

Reshaping Frameworks: Gundissalinus and the Latin Tradition | 103

nection. In a world established through and rooted in numbers, traces and signs of its Trinitarian cause are everywhere.[87] And while the created universe is marked in itself by inequality, dispersion, and composition, every created being receives its own unity and being from God. It is for this reason that everything desires to return to and wholly participate in true unity.[88]

A similar sensibility (yet with different attitudes and outcomes) is shared by William of Conches's theory of the Holy Trinity. A great appreciator of new scientific texts recently translated into Latin, like Constantine's *Pantegni* and Nemesius's *De natura hominis*, William is well known for his studies on nature and his "integumental" efforts at displaying the coherence between sacred texts and (Platonic) philosophy.[89] For William, God has a simple being with a perfect existence; he is the highest Good who has created a most perfect universe whose final cause is goodness itself.[90] In his *Glosae super Boetium*, *Glosae super Platonem*, and *Philosophia mundi*, William tends to characterise God as "Maker" (*opifex*) and "world orderer" (*ordinator mundi*), in accordance with Plato's *Timaeus*.[91] Also as a consequence of this tendency, William's doctrine of the Trinity appears to be marked by a series of identifications between divine persons and attributes in specific consideration of the creation of the universe. In his *Philosophia mundi*, William explicitly claims that the Father corresponds to divine power (*potentia*), the Son to divine wisdom (*sapientia*), and the Holy Spirit to divine will (*voluntas*) as well as to God's goodness (*bonitas*).[92]

---

87 See Thierry of Chartres, *Commentum super Boethii librum De Trinitate*, ed. Häring, 80.82–81.90.

88 Ibid., 80.61–81.12.

89 For a summary of William of Conches's reflection, see Tullio Gregory, *"Anima mundi": La filosofia di Guglielmo di Conches e la scuola di Chartres* (Florence, 1955).

90 See William of Conches, *Glosae super Boetium*, ed. Lodi Nauta (Turnhout, 1999), 187.14–18 and 343.97–102; and William of Conches, *Glosae super Platonem*, ed. Édouard Jeauneau (Turnhout, 2006), 85.12–23.

91 In his *Glosae super Boetium*, William expounds two arguments for the existence of God. The first argues *per creationem mundi* that the contrariety among elements always requires a composer who assembles them, resolving their opposition – an argument very close to Gundissalinus's first argument in *De processione mundi*. William's second argument focuses on universal order to establish *per mundi gubernationem* that a cosmic Orderer is necessary. The same arguments are presented, with slight differences, also in William's *Philosophia mundi*. See William of Conches, *Glosae super Boetium*, ed. Nauta, 193.17–195.46; and William of Conches, *Philosophia mundi*, ed. Gregor Maurach (Pretoria, 1980), 19.6–20.7.

92 See ibid., 20.9–21.10. Concerning William's concept of divine mind as eidetic model and *simulacrum*, see Enzo Maccagnolo's remarks in Maccagnolo, *Il divino e il megacosmo: Testi filosofici e scientifici della scuola di Chartres* (Milan, 1980), 51–53.

104 | CHAPTER TWO

In his *Glosae super Boetium* and *Glosae super Platonem*, William further develops his theory of the creative Trinity, linking it to the Aristotelian theory of the four causes. The divine power (the Father) corresponds to the efficient causality of the universe, the divine wisdom (the Son) to the formal cause and eidetic model, while the divine will and goodness (the Holy Spirit) are the final cause. Efficient, formal, and final cosmogonic causality, therefore, are considered by William as specific expressions of each particular divine person. The fourth Aristotelian cause, i.e., matter, is not coeternal with God, but it is created in the same instant in which time and the universe were created. Ultimately, for William that matter is nothing but the four elements of bodies.[93] In his *Philosophia* William states that

> the power is called the Father, because it creates everything and everything orders with paternal love. Then, the wisdom is called the Son begotten from the Father before time and yet coeternal with him, because as the Son temporally derives from the Father, so too the wisdom derives from the power eternally and consubstantially ... Further on, divine will is called the Holy Spirit. A spirit is properly a breath, but since the human will often depends on both spirit and breath (as one who is happy breathes one way, and one who is enraged in another), we call divine will a "spirit" in a figurative way, but [we call it] Holy through antonomasia.[94]

Rooted in his examination of the creative dynamic instituting the universe, William's theory of the Trinity tends to inopportunely reduce Trinitarian persons to divine attributes and creative functions. In a somewhat smoother way than Abelard, whose doctrine of the Trinity had been condemned by the Council of Soissons in 1122, William also received some harsh criticism and probably a tacit reprimand.[95] His theory was attacked by William of Saint Thierry, who criticised

93 See William of Conches, *Glosae super Platonem*, ed. Jeauneau, 61.5–11. See also Irene Caiazzo, "The Four Elements in the Work of William of Conches," in *Guillaume de Conches*, ed. Obrist and Caiazzo, 3–66; and Gregory, *Anima mundi*, 50–51.

94 William of Conches, *Philosophia mundi*, ed. Maurach, 20.9–21.10: "Potentia dicitur Pater, quia omnia creat et paternu affectu disponit. Sapientia vero dicitur filius a patre ante saecula genitus et tamen illi coaeternus, quia ut filius temporaliter est a patre, ita sapientia aeternaliter et consubstantialiter a potentia ... Voluntas vero divina dicitur spiritus sanctus. Est autem proprie spiritus halitus, sed quia in spiritu et anhelitu saepe hominis voluntas perpenditur (aliter enim spirat laetus, aliter iratus), divinam voluntatem translative vocaverunt spiritum, sed antonomasice sanctum."

95 For a summary, see Jeff Brower, "Trinity," in *The Cambridge Companion to Abelard*, ed. Jeff Brower and Kelvin Guilfoy (Cambridge, 2004), 223–57.

William's stances as defining the Trinitarian persons in a superficial, extrinsic, and relative way.[96] As Paul Dutton has reconstructed, the controversy between William of Conches and William of Saint Thierry seems to have eventually involved even Bernard of Clairvaux and the archbishop of Chartres during the Council of Reims in 1148.[97] As an outcome, William would eventually move from Chartres to Normandy and correct his stance on the Holy Trinity. Through his earlier works, though, William's theory of the creative Trinity would spread throughout Latin Europe.

As mentioned in the historical introduction, Gundissalinus's reflection appears to be closer to Chartres's than to any other Latin speculative centre or tradition. Many points hint at a direct philosophical training that Gundissalinus could have received in Chartres earlier in his life. Nevertheless, Gundissalinus's aim of superseding some approaches and doctrines elaborated by Chartrean masters like Thierry and William makes any attempt at substantiating this fascinating hypothesis rather baffling. Yet traces of influence from both Thierry and William appear to be in place in relation to Gundissalinus's reflection on God's being and the Holy Trinity. Thierry's problem of spiritual composition, his position that matter is a principle of alterity and, under some points of view, his theory of *rerum universitas* seem to have meaningfully influenced Gundissalinus's reflection.[98] At the same time, the corollary of these theories, i.e., Thierry's doctrine of *aequalitas*, is completely absent from Gundissalinus. For Gundissalinus, God cannot be considered either as the *onitas* "which is like the being of everything"[99] or as the *forma formarum* at the origin of every form.[100] As he repeatedly states in his writings, God cannot be identified with a form, nor an act, as he is the origin of matter and forms. His being is completely different from created being, which is rooted in duality.

Notwithstanding their different attitudes on this point, Thierry's marked interest in numbers is a peculiar trait of Gundissalinus's philosophical approach as well. Besides the reference to the principle of alterity mentioned above, Gundissalinus often uses numbers to argue in favour of God's existence and the duality of the first created entities (i.e., matter and form), and he even closes his *De processione mundi* with a numerological examination of the universe.[101]

---

96 William of Saint Thierry, *De erroribus Guillelmi de Conchis*, PL 180, 333–40, at 335.

97 See Paul Dutton, *The Mystery of the Missing Heresy Trial of William of Conches* (Toronto, 2006).

98 See Polloni, "Thierry of Chartres and Gundissalinus on Spiritual Substance."

99 Thierry of Chartres, *Lectiones in Boethii librum De Trinitate*, ed. Häring, 170.39.

100 See Thierry of Chartres, *Glosae super Boethii librum* De *Trinitate*, ed. Häring, 275.92.

101 See Gundissalinus, *De processione mundi*, ed. Bülow, 20.15–22 and 55.6–56.12; ed. Soto Bruna and Alonso Del Real, 156.6–12 and 222.6–224.16.

106 | CHAPTER TWO

Although Gundissalinus's and Thierry's methods are close, and sometimes even seem to move on a common ground, in this case Gundissalinus chose to use Arabic rather than Latin sources – namely, Ibn Gabirol.

Besides their shared arithmetical sensibility and the method of *compositio* and *resolutio*, a third crucial aspect linking Thierry and Gundissalinus is the central thesis of ontological unity. So pervasive in Gundissalinus's *De unitate* and *De processione*, Boethius's ontological claim that "everything that exists, exists for the reason that it is one" ("omne enim quod est, idcirco est, quia unum est")[102] also plays a pivotal role in Thierry of Chartres's discussion of ontological unity. In his *Tractatus de sex dierum operibus*, Thierry states, referring to God's unity, that

> unity itself, indeed, is divinity. And the divinity is the form of being (*forma essendi*) of every single thing. As something is said to be luminous because of light or hot because of heat, so too every single thing receives its own being because of the divinity. Therefore, God is correctly called "being" in a most complete, essential, and all-embracing way. Unity, indeed, is the form of being of every single thing and, accordingly, it is said that whatever exists, therefore, exists because it is one.[103]

Unity is the form of being through which each and every created being has its own existence and unity/oneness. Indeed, "everything that exists, exists for the reason that it is one." The same claim is made in his commentary on Boethius's *De Trinitate*, when Thierry states that

> Indeed, whatever exists, therefore, exists because it is one in number. For this reason, whatever exists desires to be one and, necessarily, shuns division. Accordingly, it must be inferred that unity shuns division, equality loves unity, and unity [loves] equality. Love, indeed, is some connection of equality to unity and of unity to equality of being.[104]

---

102 Boethius, *In Isagogen Porphyrii commenta*, ed. Brandt, 162.1–3; and Gundissalinus, *De unitate et uno*, ed. Soto Bruna and Alonso Del Real, 104.3.

103 Thierry of Chartres, *Tractatus de sex dierum operibus*, ed. Häring, 568.93–569.1: "Unitas igitur ipsa divinitas. At divinitas singulis rebus forma essendi est. Nam sicut aliquid ex luce lucidum est vel ex calore calidum ita singule res esse suum ex divinitate sortiuntur. Unde deus totus et essentialiter ubique esse vere perhibetur. Unitas igitur singulis rebus forma essendi est. Unde vere dicitur: Omne quod est ideo est quia unum est."

104 Thierry of Chartres, *Commentum super Boethii librum De Trinitate*, ed. Häring, 80.61–66: "Omne enim quod est ideo est quia unum numero est. Omne ergo quod est unum esse desiderat. Necesse ergo est ut divisionem fugiat. Concludatur itaque ut quoniam unitas divisionem refugit, et unitatem equalitas diligit et equalitatem unitas. Amor igitur quidam est et conexio equalitatis ad unitatem et unitatis ad essendi equalitatem."

The immanent unity of created being – corresponding, in Aristotelian terms, to their individuation – is what moves every creature toward the true unity and equality which is God. This is a desire for unity which is governed by the love expressed by the Connection, i.e., the Holy Spirit. Evidently, the reference to Boethius's claim plays a grounding authoritative role in Thierry's line of reasoning. In a way similar to what has been pointed out regarding Calcidius's method of *compositio* and *resolutio*, a Chartrean mediation can be supposed concerning Boethius's claim that "everything that exists, exists for the reason that it is one" – although Boethius's influence on Gundissalinus appears much more profound and direct than Calcidius's.[105]

Concerning Gundissalinus's explicit discussion of the Holy Trinity, the problem is more complicated. First, Thierry does not appear to have had any specific influence, apart from a minor reference to the *signaculum Trinitatis*. Second, when referring to God's attributes, Gundissalinus usually mentions divine wisdom and will. Third, and most important, one might even ask if there is a theory of the Holy Trinity in Gundissalinus's works. Quite surprisingly, in his cosmogonical work *De processione mundi* there is only one explicit reference to the Holy Trinity. Gundissalinus claims that

> although these are the indivisible works of the Trinity, the creation, nonetheless, of matter, from which all things are made, is attributed to power; the creation of form, by which all things are made, is attributed to wisdom, but the joining of both is fittingly attributed to union so that there is also found a small sign of the Trinity in its first works.[106]

The doctrinal context of this passage is the perpetuity of the first composed being. These first caused beings do not suffer corruption because they are the result of God's direct creation – as *opus Trinitatis*, i.e., direct effects of the Trinity. For this reason, they are indivisible. Evidently Gundissalinus is referring to the

---

105 Some of the theoretical corollaries of Thierry's discussion of immanent unity can be found in Gundissalinus as well. Among them, the reference to the form of unity as the form providing any created entity with its own existence seems particularly meaningful. At least at a first glance. Indeed, Gundissalinus not only does not mention the *forma essendi* but, pivotally, grounds even this ontological aspect upon a radical theory of matter and form proceeding from Ibn Gabirol. As a result, any attempt at establishing a (doctrinal, not textual) mediation by Thierry inescapably encounters many difficulties.

106 Gundissalinus, *De processione mundi*, ed. Bülow, 48.7–11; ed. Soto Bruna and Alonso Del Real, 208.2–6: "Quamvis autem indivisibilia sint opera trinitatis, tamen creatio materiae, ex qua omnia, potentiae, creatio vero formae, per quam omnia, sapientiae, coniunctio vero utriusque connexioni congrue attribuitur, ut etiam in primis suis operibus signaculum trinitatis inveniatur." English translation by Laumakis, *The Procession of the World*, 71.

108 | CHAPTER TWO

creative dynamic instituting the universe, regarding which he mentions the Holy Trinity through an unspoken functional scheme, as follows:

Trinitarian Person	Attribute	Performed function
[Father]	power	creation of matter
[Son]	wisdom	creation of form
[Holy Spirit]	?	union of matter and form

While the quoted passage does not mention any further aspect of Gundissalinus's theory of the Holy Trinity, an examination of the indirect references to the Trinity in *De processione mundi* casts some light on this obscure point. The opening of Gundissalinus's treatise itself is meaningful in this regard. Referring to the invisible and most intimate aspects of God (the *invisibilia Dei*), Gundissalinus claims that "since greatness, beauty, and usefulness are set forth to be admired so much, the power, wisdom, and goodness of the creator, which are the invisible things of God, are certainly revealed."[107] Power, wisdom, and goodness, therefore, appear to be the main attributes of God. As power and wisdom are explicitly mentioned in relation to, respectively, Father and Son, should it be considered that Gundissalinus is implicitly attributing goodness to the Holy Spirit? This might very well be the case, as the text explicitly refers to the most intimate aspects of God (his *invisibilia*), corresponding to his *potentia, sapientia, bonitas*. These are three aspects which implicitly point to his Trinitarian nature. Even so, why should Gundissalinus have preferred to avoid an explicit mention of goodness as a central attribute of the Holy Spirit?

When referring to the Holy Trinity, *De processione mundi* explicitly attributes one main function to each of the three divine persons. Namely, Gundissalinus claims that God's power (= Father) creates matter, God's wisdom (= Son) creates form, and the third person supposedly joins matter and form. A few pages before, though, Gundissalinus adamantly states that

> In fact, the sealing of form in matter, when it comes from the divine wisdom, is like the sealing of a shape in a mirror when the shape is reflected in it from one who is looking at it. And, in this way, matter receives form from the

107 Gundissalinus, *De processione mundi*, ed. Bülow, 1.10–12; ed. Soto Bruna and Alonso Del Real, 120.9–11: "cum enim magnitudo, pulchritudo et utilitas tantum miranda proponitur: profecto potentia creatoris, sapientia et bonitas, quae invisibilia dei sunt, revelantur." English translation by Laumakis, *The Procession of the World*, 33.

divine will, just as a mirror receives a shape from one who is looking into it, and nonetheless, matter does not receive the essence of that from which it receives form, just as the sense does not receive the matter of a sensed thing whose form it receives.[108]

Following a redundant point of Ibn Gabirol's *Fons vitae*, Gundissalinus claims that forms are created by God's wisdom and are reflected upon matter as if they were rays of light reflected in a mirror. The union of matter and form is realised by God's will, which impresses forms upon matter, giving origin to creatures. Accordingly, it seems that Gundissalinus has divine will in mind when refering to the Trinitarian dynamic of creation. It is because matter derives from God's power, forms from God's wisdom, and they are joined together by God's will that the first composed beings have a seal (*signaculum*) of the Trinity in their being – a doctrinal point probably inspired by Thierry of Chartres. In other words, Gundissalinus's unspoken theory of the Trinity would be marked by the following set of correspondences:

Trinitarian Person	Attribute	Performed function
[Father]	power	creation of matter
[Son]	wisdom	creation of form
[Holy Spirit]	will and goodness	union of matter and form

Two consequences arise from these remarks on Gundissalinus's references (or lack of references) to the Trinity. First, there is some evident tension within *De processione mundi*, in virtue of which Gundissalinus does not seem to be keen on engaging with a discussion of the Trinity, notwithstanding the relevance of this feature for his analysis of the creation of the world and the ontological difference between God and creatures. Second, the scheme of correspondences he had in mind appears to be extremely close (although not identical) to William's doctrine of the creative Trinity. In both series, indeed, divine power, wisdom, and will are referred, respectively, to the Father, the Son, and the Holy Spirit.

---

108 Gundissalinus, *De processione mundi*, ed. Bülow, 41.2–8; ed. Soto Bruna and Alonso Del Real, 196.1–6: "Sigillatio vero formae in materia, cum sit a divina sapientia, est quasi sigillatio formae in speculo, cum resultat in eo ab aspectore, et materia sic recipit formam a divina voluntate, sicut speculum recipit formam ab inspectore, et tamen materia non recipit essentiam eius, a quo recipit formam, sicut nec sensus recipit materiam sensati, cuius recipit formam." English translation by Laumakis, *The Procession of the World*, 66.

110 | CHAPTER TWO

Gundissalinus undoubtedly knew William's works, and it is possible that the former was aware of the problematice responses that William's doctrine of the Trinity had inspired just a few years earlier . This might explain why Gundissalinus did not want to engage with a doctrine which, implicitly, could be seen as consistent with William's and why he preferred to follow a Jewish philosopher, i.e., Ibn Gabirol (again), when addressing the problem concerning God's creation. Although the results of William's and Gundissalinus's reflections seem close regarding the Trinity as cause of the universe, Gundissalinus might have deliberately chosen to conceal this proximity.

Subtly present in his writings, the Chartrean authors exert a somewhat bizarre influence on Gundissalinus's metaphysical attitude and style. He seems to have shared some main directions that marked the Chartrean approach to the study of God and nature, in particular their interest in the secondary causation of the universe and the key role played by nature. However, on most occasions Gundissalinus detached himself from the fundamental and traditional positions for which they stood, and turned the tables to embrace the *new* authors. This was most spectacularly the case in his theory of primordial chaos.

Disordered Universes

Plato's *Timaeus* provided medieval philosophers and theologians with a particular cosmogonic account connected to a plurality of physical and metaphysical assumptions. These medieval narratives often utilised the theory of primordial chaos – a rather complex point in Plato's account. Twelfth-century thinkers tried different approaches and solutions to fill some of the gaps in the account. These solutions were often based, on the one hand, on the biblical text and the ideal concordance between *Timaeus* and scripture and, on the other, on abridged and second-hand knowledge of Aristotle's physics and metaphysics. In general, the theory of primordial chaos was the object of divisive reception and development within the Latin tradition. An example of these tensions is the controversy which was animated by two very important philosophers of the first half of the twelfth century: Hugh of St Victor and William of Conches.

Centred on the creation of the universe, the first part of Hugh of St Victor's famous theological work, *De sacramentis christianae fidei*, engages with a discussion of primordial chaos. Hugh opines that the creation of the universe was pursued *per tempora intervalla*, that is, through creative phases. God firstly created matter and then he joined it to forms (= "information" of matter). The first creation of matter should then be identified with a primordial disordered state

(*Timaeus*'s chaos), and the information of matter with the cosmic institution (the Demiurgical impression of order). Consequently, the first problem to be addressed is the possibility itself of a formless matter. As Hugh claims,

> it remains [to discuss], then, if the matter of everything was created formless. I shall explain whether something could have existed with no form, what sort of essence – as we showed – it should be believed to have had before receiving [its] form, and – in a few words – what I think should be understood about that. I do not think at all that the first matter of everything was formless in such a way that it had no form in any respect, as if I believed that it had some kind of being, but not some kind of form, since nothing of this sort can exist. Indeed, it is possible to call that [matter] formless – which was in confusion and mixture – only as far as it is not meaningless. Already subsisting, that [matter] had not yet received that disposition and [that] form in which it can now be perceived as beautiful and suited. Therefore, matter was created before form, but [it was created] in form: in the form of confusion (*forma confusionis*), before [having received] the form of arrangement (*forma dispositionis*). Before all corporeal things were materially created together and at once, [matter was] in the first form of confusion; after [all corporeal things] were ordered through the time of six days, [matter was] in the second form of arrangement.[109]

Hugh's solution to the problematic supposition of a formless matter is intriguing. He claims that matter was formless only insofar as it lacked the divine disposition which would bring out of it the corporeal entities composing the world. This point is grounded on the distinction between two "forms" shaping matter. They are the form of confusion (*forma confusionis*), which is proper to matter at the beginning of its coming to be, and the form of arrangement (*forma*

---

109 Hugh of St Victor, *De sacramentis christianae fidei* 1.1.6, ed. Rainer Berndt (Frankfurt am Main, 2008), 39.1–13: "Restat enim ut si prius materiam rerum informem creatam fuisse asseruimus. Utrum ne aliquid sine forma existere potuerit, qualem ue essentiam ante formam inditam habuisse credendum sit ostendamus, et ut breviter quod super hoc sentiendum michi videtur aperiam. Certe non puto primam illam omnium rerum materiam taliter informem fuisse, ut nullam omnino formam habuerit, quia nec aliquid tale existere posse omnino quod aliquod esse habeat, et non aliquam formam crederim. Ita tamen non absurde informem eam appellari posse quod in confusione et permixtione, quedam subsistens, nondum hanc in qua nunc cernitur pulchram aptamque dispositionem et formam receperit. Ergo ante formam facta est materia, tamen in forma. In forma confusionis, ante formam dispositionis. In prima forma confusionis, prius materialiter omnia corporalia simul et semel creata sunt. In secunda forma dispositionis, postmodum per sex dierum intervalla ordinata."

dispositionis), which is the form – or better, the shape – of matter after having been ordered by God during the six days of creation. Accordingly, all corporeal things which would constitute the universe are created *simul et semel* into matter, but in a disordered state and *materialiter*. This dynamic corresponds to the first day of creation, in which God created the heavens (which are the angelic creatures, incorporeal and immaterial) and the earth (the bulk of matter). Everything the universe would be, therefore, was already present in the outcomes of the first day of creation – following *Ecclesiasticus* 18:1, which states the simultaneous creation of everything.[110]

After having clarified that (1) matter can be said to be both formless and disordered, and (2) progressive creation does not contradict the letter of the sacred text, Hugh expounds primordial chaos in vivid terms. In this chaotic mass which was matter before being ordered by God, the four elements were scattered in a dynamic mingling. The earth was in the middle, surrounded by the three other elements, which were confused in a single mixture. Like fog, they were enveloping the earth, filling the entire space which is now the universe. In the mass of earth, most of the hydrographic elements of the world were already there – river-beds, channels, and the great abyss, with no water to fill them, though, since water was mingled with air and fire in that foggy mixture enveloping everything. Accordingly, even if in a disordered state, everything was created at the beginning – heaven and earth, i.e., the matter of every celestial and earthly thing which would constitute the universe.[111]

Hugh's colourful description of primordial chaos would have a striking success in the twelfth century. At the same time, though, at least two main problems appear to affect his account. First, following the Latin Platonic tradition (without having direct access to Aristotle's physical and metaphysical works), Hugh's notion of *forma* and *materia* are grounded on Plato's and Augustine's accounts. As a consequence, once the Aristotelian corpus became available during the twelfth century, Hugh's position would be substantially affected. Moreover, Hugh does not seem to conclusively address and resolve the problem of whether primordial chaos is made of matter or of elements, and the relation between these two candidates is not duly problematised, nor is it clarified. This unresolved tension would indeed open his account to criticism during the course of that century.

The success of Hugh's theory can also be explained by considering that one of the most influential authors in accepting and quoting Hugh's account was Peter Lombard. In the second book of his *Sentences*, Peter Lombard engages with

---

110 *Ecclesiasticus* 18:1: "Qui vivet in aeternum creavit omnia simul" ("He that liveth for ever hath created all things in general," KJV).

111 See Hugh of St Victor, *De sacramentis christianae fidei* 1.1.6, ed. Berndt, 40.4–27.

Reshaping Frameworks: Gundissalinus and the Latin Tradition | 113

the creation of the universe, and his main source is Hugh's *De sacramentis*. The twelfth distinction of the *Sentences'* second book presents the main terms of the doctrine of primordial chaos. Lombard states, indeed, that

> when God in his wisdom established the angelic spirits, he also created other things, as the above-mentioned Scripture of Genesis shows. It says that in the beginning God created heaven, that is, the angels, and earth, namely the matter of the four elements, which was still confused and formless, which is called chaos by the Greeks; and this happened before any day. Afterwards, he distinguished the elements and gave their proper and distinct forms to individual things according to their kind. And he did not form them simultaneously, as it pleased some of the Fathers [to hold], but at intervals of time and in the course of six days, as it has seemed to others.[112]

Following the text of Genesis, Lombard presents the creation *ex nihilo* as the coming to be of heaven and earth, identifying the former with the angels and the latter with the formless and confused matter of the four elements, which is called *chaos* by the Greeks. This material bulk is then distinguished into the four species of elements, to originate all genera of existing things during the six days of the biblical account. Lombard's description of the bi-phasic institution of the universe (creation *ex nihilo* and ordering of chaos) is grounded upon the recognition of a *concordia* between biblical narrative and Plato's *Timaeus*, and specifically on the interpretation of the former through the latter by means of Hugh of St Victor. Indeed, the subsequent chapters of the *distinctio* develop some of the main doctrinal points Hugh expounded in the first chapters of *De sacramentis*, starting with the *intervalla temporis* of God's creation and the role played by light. Immediately following this point, Lombard addresses the pivotal question of how *formless* matter can be a *chaos*. His discussion is a synthesis of what Hugh stated on this point in the passage quoted above. Lombard claims that:

---

112 Peter Lombard, *Sentences* 2.12.1, ed. Ignatius Brady (Grottaferrata, 1971), 384.8–16: "Cum Deus in sapientia sua angelicos condidit spiritus, alia etiam creavit, sicut ostendit supra memorata Scriptura Genesis, quae dicit, in principio creasse Deum caelum, id est Angelos, et terram, scilicet materiam quatuor elementorum, adhuc confusam et informem, quae a Graecis dicta est chaos; et hoc fuit ante omnem diem. Deinde elementa distinxit et species proprias atque distinctas singulis rebus secundum genus suum dedit, quae non simul, ut quibusdam sanctorum Patrum placuit, sed per intervalla temporum ac sex volumina dierum, ut aliis visum est, formavit." English translation by Giulio Silano, *The Sentences*, 4 vols (Toronto, 2007–10), 2: 49.

114 | CHAPTER TWO

briefly responding to what was posed first, we say that that primal matter is not said to have been formless because it had no form at all, since no corporeal thing can exist which has no form. But we say that it is not absurd to call it formless because, subsisting in some confusion and mixture, it had not yet received any beautiful, clear, and distinct form such as we now see. Therefore, that matter was made in a form of confusion (*forma confusionis*) before the form of arrangement (*forma dispositionis*). All corporeal things first were created materially, simultaneously, and at once in a form of confusion; afterwards, they were set in order in six days in a form of arrangement. – See, what was first proposed for discussion has been resolved, namely why that matter is called formless.[113]

Lombard's text is evidently derived from Hugh's and presents all the main terms of the discussion exposited in *De sacramentis*, whose text is extensively quoted and probably re-adapted. For Lombard, too, matter can be said to be formless only in relation to the disordered state in which matter was, being made "in the form of confusion" before receiving the "form of arrangement." It is the *materia quattuor elementorum*, not as the matter of what *would be* the elements after the ordering, but as the actual matter of those very same elements. Back then, they were chaotically scattered far from where they would be after the Demiurgical action impressing order onto them. That corporeal entity, before being ordered and disposed through the six days of creation, was a chaos covering the entire universe:

without making any rash assertions, we say to this that that first mass of all things, when it was created, appears to have come into being in the same place where it is now after being formed. And this earthly element was in the lowest place, sinking down to the same middle position [where it now is], while the rest [of the elements] were mixed in one confusion. These spread all around it in the manner of a cloud and covered it so much that what it was

---

113 Peter Lombard, *Sentences* 2.12.5, ed. Brady, 387.15–26: "Ad illud igitur quod primo positum est, breviter respondentes dicimus, illam primam materiam non ideo dictam fore informem, quod nullam omnino formam habuerit, quia non aliquid corporeum tale existere potest, quod nullam habeat formam; sed ideo non absurde informem appellari posse dicimus, quia in confusione et permixtione quadam subsistens, nondum pulcram apertamque et distinctam receperat formam, qualem modo cernimus. Facta est ergo illa materia in forma confusionis ante formam dispositionis: in forma confusionis prius omnia corporalia materialiter simul et semel sunt creata, postmodum in forma dispositionis sex diebus sunt ordinata. Ecce absolutum est quod primo in discussione propositum fuit, scilicet quare illa materia dicatur informis." English translation by Silano, *The Sentences* 2: 52.

could not be seen. In fact those three elements, confused in one mixture and suspended all around, reached as far up as the highest point of corporeal creation does now. – And it seems to some that that mass extended beyond the firmament because it was thicker and grosser in its lower part, but thinner, lighter, and finer in the higher; some hold that the waters which are said to be above the firmament were made of this thinner substance. – Such was the face of the world in the beginning, before it received form or spatial arrangement.[114]

This passage of Lombard's *Sentences*, too, is a quotation from Hugh's description of primordial chaos expounded in *De sacramentis*.[115] Eagerly accepted and quoted by Lombard, Hugh's theory of primordial chaos spread ever further as the *Sentences* became an established text across European universities from the thirteenth century onwards. By that time, however, the theory of primordial chaos was already an outdated issue. Some problematic points intrinsic to Hugh's account had been criticised early on. Dominique Poirel has recently described the terms of the possible controversy opposing Hugh and William of Conches.[116] This controversy was based on and developed through William's refutation of the doctrine of primordial chaos, a theory that was accepted by other Chartrean authors like Thierry of Chartres.[117]

A great number of William's works deal with the problem of primordial chaos: *Glosae super Boetium*, *Philosophia*, *Glosae super Platonem*, and finally *Dragmaticon philosophiae*, where William will substantively change his stance on the problem. In the glosses on Boethius's *De consolatione Philosophiae*, on Plato's

---

114 Peter Lombard, *Sentences* 2.12.5, ed. Brady, 388.1–13. Latin text: "Ad quod nihil temere asserentes dicimus, quod illa prima rerum omnium moles, quando creata est, ibidem ad esse videtur prodiisse, ubi nunc formata subsistit; eratque terreum hoc elementum in uno loco eodemque medio subsidens, ceteris in una confusione permixtis, eisdemque circumquaque in modo cuiusdam nebulae oppansis, ita obvolutum erat, ut apparere non posset quod fuit. Illa vero tria, in una confusione permixta circumquaque suspensa, eousque in altum porrigebantur, quousque nunc summitas corporeae naturae pertingit." Et sicut quibusdam videtur, ultra locum firmamenti extendebatur illa moles, quae in inferiori parte spissior atque grossior erat, in superiori vero rarior et levior atque subtilior existebat; de qua rariori substantia putant quidam fuisse aquas, quae super firmamentum esse dicuntur." English translation by Silano, *The Sentences*, 2: 52.

115 See Hugh of St Victor, *De sacramentis christianae fidei* 1.1.6, ed. Berndt, 40.4–27.

116 See Dominique Poirel, "Physique et théologie: une querelle entre Guillaume de Conches et Hugues de Saint-Victor à propos du chaos originel," in *Guillaume de Conches*, ed. Obrist and Caiazzo, 289–327.

117 See, for instance, Thierry of Chartres, *Tractatus de sex dierum operibus*, ed. Häring, 565.10–16. See also ibid., 565.17–566.24.

116 | CHAPTER TWO

Timaeus, and in his *Philosophia*, William explains in similar terms his criticism of primordial chaos in the account given by Hugh of St Victor, as is made quite clear by intrinsic references to passages and points of Hugh's text. As Poirel has pointed out, William's criticism is grounded upon three doctrinal points, of which the first is philosophical, the second is bound to theological implications, while the third is based on hermeneutical remarks.[118] William attacks Hugh's theory by arguing that:

1. Its physical description of the chaotic state of matter/elements is implicitly contradictory.

2. Its position of a chaos created and then ordered by God is groundless and implies a deficiency in God's action and will.

3. Its application of the theory exposited in *Timaeus* to the biblical narrative is based on a wrong interpretation of the former.[119]

While the third of William's arguments follows on the preceding two, the theological implications of chaos (argument 2) appears to be a direct attack on the theme of God's displaying his power and goodness in creating *per temporum intervalla* – a doctrine developed by Hugh's *De sacramentis*, where it is presented in an implicit relation to primordial chaos. William, indeed, points out that, at the moment of God's supposed ordering of original chaos, there was no public who could possibly see it. Indeed, the angels know and knew everything by their own nature and through divine grace, while human beings were not yet created. Accordingly, there is no basis for claiming that God wanted to show anything to anyone.[120] The main argument against primordial chaos, though, is argument (1.), which engages directly with the physical implications of the theory to show its theoretical inadmissibility. William presents his arguments with slight differences in the two glosses and in his *Philosophia*. The latter explains the refutation by stating that:

We say indeed that the opinion they put forward is false, that the argument they bring in is inappropriate, and they do not understand well the authority they allege. ... Were, thus, the elements bodies or not? If they were not bodies, they would have been either spirits or properties of a spirit or a body. But matter cannot be a spirit or a property, and consequently it cannot be the

118 See Poirel, "Physique et théologie."

119 Ibid.

120 See, among other passages, William of Conches, *Glosae super Boetium*, ed. Nauta, 154.204–155.216.

elements. Were they bodies, then, and were they occupying a place, as every corporeal being is in some place? If they were not in a place, they were either where they are now, or somewhere else. Aside from the elements, though, there is no place. Therefore, the elements were where they are now. Moreover, conceding that they were not disposed as they are now, [all the same] they would have been in those four places. As a consequence, one [of them] would have occupied the lower place, another the upper [place], and two others the middle places. Therefore, if they descended together downwards – as you state – they would descend with the others; but there was no place from which they could descend. Similarly, if they ascended upwards, they would ascend with the others; but there was no place from which they could ascend. Therefore, they cannot have ascended together, and they cannot have descended together either. Therefore, the opinion of those people is false.[121]

William's refutation is based on a crucial interpretation. Following a theory of primordial chaos, it should be assumed that chaos was made of corporeal entities which, in turn, must be identified with the elements, be they in their present state or not. Since these entities are corporeal, they must be subject to the natural law of movement. William's argument, though, is not grounded upon the Aristotelian theory of the natural movement of the elements, as one might expect from a discussion of elemental movement. To the contrary, William problematises primordial chaos in relation to the doctrine of place. Since the world was filled with these elements, how could upper elements take the place of the lower ones, and the latter the place of the former, when there was no space to realise those movements? For William, this is a physical and logical contradiction, making clear that the assertion is false. Since there is no possibility of such a movement, the theory of primordial chaos is inadmissible.

121 William of Conches, *Philosophia mundi*, ed. Maurach, 26.449–27.465: "Nos vero dicimus falsam esse sententiam quam proponunt, non convenientem esse rationem quam inducunt nec bene esse intellectam auctoritatem quam praetendunt. ... Elementa tunc erant corpora vel non? Si corpora non erant, spiritus vel proprietates spiritus aut corporis erant. Sed neque spiritus neque aliqua proprietas materia esse potest, nec ergo elementa. Corpora igitur erant et loca obtinebant (omne enim corpus in aliquo loco est)? Si in loco erant, vel ubi nunc sunt vel alibi. Sed extra elementa nullus locus est. Erant ergo elementa ubi nunc sunt; etiam si sic non essent disposita ut nunc sunt, in his IIII locis erant. Aliquod ergo obtinebat inferiorem locum, aliquod superiorem, duo media loca. Si ergo, ut affirmas, simul descenderent inferius, cum aliis descenderent; sed non erat, quo descenderent. Similiter, si ascenderent superius, cum aliis ascenderent, sed non erat, quo ascenderent. Nec ergo simul ascendebant nec simul descendebant. Falsa est ergo illorum sententia."

118 | CHAPTER TWO

William's strategy is grounded upon an identification of chaos and elements. Hugh being the target of his criticism, it should be noted that William interpreted his theory as shifting the tension between material and elemental chaos toward the latter. William's criticism of primordial chaos is a *topos* of his first philosophical production, variously attested in many of his works. Probably as a consequence of the events leading him to leave Chartres, William changed his position on a conspicuous number of topics, among which was original chaos. In *Dragmaticon philosophiae*, indeed, the theory of chaos is exposited and accepted with a noticeably uneager approach. Discussing the particles (*particulas*) which are the "real" elements and the principles of bodies,[122] William presents to the Duke the main terms of the theory claiming that

> the Creator created these particles in a single great body – not distinguished locally, but commingled in that same whole – so that that body was nothing but these particles. Indeed, it occupied the entire space (*locus*) that all bodies occupy nowadays. Because of the particles' mixture, the philosophers called that [body] "chaos," which is rendered [into Latin] by "mingling" (*confusio*). The hot [particles], in fact, were opposed to the cold, since they were bound together in this [body] with neither proportion nor middle [term]. Similarly, the moist [particles were opposed to] the dry. For this reason, Ovid said [this body was]: "a crude and undeveloped mass," and then he added [that in that body] "the cold [parts] strove with the hot, and the wet with the dry." Yet, out of that great body [God] created, all at once, four bodies in [four] different places. These [bodies] are now called elements after those undefined [bodies,], in the way we are about to say.[123]

God created the elements in a confused state, which is called chaos by the "philosophers" and was filling the entire space which now is the universe. These particles were located in different places – they were bodies and all body must be in some place – and cold were opposed to hot particles, in coherence with what

122 See Caiazzo, "The Four Elements in the Work of William of Conches."

123 William of Conches, *Dragmaticon philosophiae* 1.7, ed. Italo Ronca (Turnhout, 1997), 29.4–15: "Creator istas particulas in uno magno corpore creavit, non localiter distinctas, sed per ipsum totum commixtas, ita quod ex his particulis nichil extra hoc corpus erat. Omnem vero locum obtinuit, quem omnia corpora modo obtinet. Hoc a philosophis propter particularum commixtionem chaos, quod interpretatur confusio, est nominatum. Calidae enim frigidis in eo sine proportione et medio coniunctae repugnabant, similiter humidae siccis; unde ait Ovidius: 'Rudis indigestaque moles;' deinde subiunxit: 'Frigida pugnabant calidis, humentia siccis.' Sed ex hoc magno corpore statim quattuor corpora, quae hodie a quibusdam dicuntur elementa, pro modo quem dicturi sumus, in diversis loci creavit."

Reshaping Frameworks: Gundissalinus and the Latin Tradition | 119

Ovid said regarding chaos. The main terms of William's criticism against primordial chaos not only vanish but are reversed as parts of a concise account of the theory of original chaos, now accepted by William. Traces of William's criticism can be perceived in the Duke asking William, right after the passage quoted above, why God – who had created everything and knew everything before creating it – would have created something knowing that it would not last.[124] This is one of the points of William's refutation, attacking the uselessness of God's creation and ordering of primordial chaos, and the consequent "irrationality" of divine choice in creating something which was not supposed to last. William's response in the *Dragmaticon* is rather elusive and is grounded upon his theory of the three works.[125]

In its variety of shades and also positions, William's discussion of primordial chaos left its mark on the subsequent discussions of this delicate theme. Apparently, William's account also influenced Dominicus Gundissalinus. In his *De processione mundi*, Gundissalinus includes a long digression on primordial chaos. The *casus* of this digression is to be found in the last sentences right before this thematic shift. Gundissalinus claims, "Therefore, these two, namely, first matter and first form, are prior to all the things that have a beginning, because these alone have being by creation."[126] To the contrary, any other thing following the creation of matter and form has "a beginning either by their union or by generation or by the commingling of generated things."[127] Since God's creative

---

124 See ibid., 29.16–18.'

125 See ibid., 29.19–30.25: "What you try to understand is unsuitable for anyone. We see, indeed, the works of the Creator, yet we are ignorant of [their] causes. Who could have been, indeed, his adviser? Nevertheless, we do say something we believe to be true [about the causes] following [their effects], and after that, [we will ask] what other people say about that. A work can be [made] by the Creator, or by nature, or by a craftsman. The Creator's work is the creation of elements and souls from nothing, the resurrection of the dead, the virginal conception, and the like." ("Quod quaeris, neminem decet: opera enim creatoris videmus, causa tamen ignoramus. Quis enim consiliarius eius fuit? Quod tamen inde nobis videtur, dicemus; deinde, quid alii de eodem dicant. Omne opus vel est creatoris, vel naturae, vel artificis. Opus creatoris est elementorum et animarum ex nichilo creatio, mortuorum resuscitatio, partus virginis, et similia.")

126 Gundissalinus, *De processione mundi*, ed. Bülow, 36.4–6; ed. Soto Bruna and Alonso Del Real,186.4–6: "Haec igitur duo, scilicet materia prima et forma prima, priora sunt omnibus habentibus initium eo, quod haec sola esse habent per creationem." English translation by Laumakis, *The Procession of the World*, 62.

127 Gundissalinus, *De processione mundi*, ed. Bülow, 36.6–8; ed. Soto Bruna and Alonso Del Real, 186.7–8: "Cetera vero initium habent vel per coniunctionem istarum vel per generationem vel commixtionem generatorum." English translation by Laumakis, *The Procession of the World*, 62.

120 | CHAPTER TWO

act is pursued through the creation of matter and form alone, which is followed by their first composition (*primaria compositio*), any hypothesis of a primordial chaos or a Demiurgical ordering action are left aside completely. In order to demonstrate the impossibility of such a cosmogonic moment, Gundissalinus surprisingly presents the position of the "theologians" and some poets, and claims that

theologians, nonetheless, and certain of the poets say that first matter was a kind of blending and mixture of things. In this blending of things, this earthy element resides in one and the same middle place and endowed with a better form than the other elements mixed together in the one blending, but is wrapped all around by those other elements like an opaque cloud so that what it was could not be seen. The other three elements, however, which were mixed and blended with one another and suspended all around it, were stretched out upwards to where the summit of corporeal creation now ends. This whole space that stretches from the surface of the earth, which is positioned in the middle, all the way to the edge of the highest sphere, was filled with that darkness and cloud. And the riverbeds or paths of the waters that now exist were then surely prepared in the body of the earth as future receptacles for these waters. In those times, that great abyss from which the streams of all waters flowed was also still an open and empty chasm, and a horrendous void stretched straight downward, over which the clouds of that gloomy darkness by which the whole surface of the earth was then covered were stretched out from above. It is these clouds, so they say, that Divine Scripture testifies to as having been upon the face of the deep when heaven and earth were created. The surface of the world is said to have been created as such in the beginning, before it received form and distinction into different kinds of things. In this way, it was created, as it were, formless in the same place where now it subsists as formed. When Moses says, "In the beginning, God created heaven and earth," by "heaven" and "earth" in this statement he wanted us to understand the matter of all heavenly and earthly things from which, afterwards, those things were subsequently distinguished by means of form which were earlier created at the same time in themselves through their essence. When, however, he then adds, "The earth was empty and void," "earth" signifies the element of earth. And "heaven" was that moving and light blend of the remaining three elements, which, being suspended, were carried on a course around the earth that was positioned in the middle. Then his words, "and darkness was upon the face of the deep" and the others that follow add further descriptions to the previously mentioned description. A poet also agrees with this, saying:

> "there was one countenance to all of nature in the world,
> which was called chaos, an undeveloped and disorderly mass."[128]

According to Gundissalinus's account, the "theologians" claim that first matter was a blending of things (*rerum confusio*), in which the elements were confused and mixed. But this did not include the earth, which was in the middle of this *confusio*, but the other three, which surrounded the earthy element like a cloud, covering the whole universe. This was the state of the universe at the beginning, corresponding to the creation of heaven and earth in the biblical narrative, whose words must be interpreted in relation to the chaotic state of the four elements, at least by the "theologians." The existence of an original chaos is further attested by "some poet" – Ovid's *Metamorphoses* – saying that the world was "an undeveloped and disorderly mass" which "was called chaos."

As Alonso Alonso has pointed out, Gundissalinus's presentation of the theory of primordial chaos, as applied to the biblical narrative, corresponds to a long quotation from Hugh of St Victor's *De sacramentis christianae fidei*.[129] In addition,

---

128 Gundissalinus, *De processione mundi*, ed. Bülow, 36.9–37.17; ed. Soto Bruna and Alonso Del Real, 186.9–190.2: "Dicunt tamen theologi et quidam ex poetis materiam primam fuisse quandam rerum confusionem atque permixtionem, in qua rerum confusione hoc terrenum elementum medio uno eodemque loco subsidens ceteris in una confusione permixtis forma meliore praeditum, sed eisdem circumquaque in modum cuiusdam nebulae oppansis ita involutum, ut non posset apparere, quod erat. Tria vero alia sibi permixta atque confusa circumquaque suspensa eo usque in altum porrigebantur, quo nunc summitas creaturae corporeae terminator. Totumque hoc spatium, quod a superficie terrae in medio iacentis usque ad extremum supremi ambitus extenditur, illa caligine et nebula replebatur. Et qui nunc sunt alvei sive tractiones aquarum, iam tunc in terrae corpore aquis futura receptacula parata erant. In quibus etiam illa magna abyssus, de qua omnium fluenta aquarum fluxerunt, erat patulo adhuc hiatu vacuoque et horrendum in praeceps inane proferebatur, cui quidem desuper illius tenebrosae caliginis, qua tunc tota terrae superficies obvoluta erat, nebulae tendebantur, quas, ut aiunt, divina scriptura, cum caelum et terra crearentur, super faciem abyssi fuisse testatur. Talis dicitur fuisse creata mundi facies in principio, priusquam formam susciperet et distinctionem, quae sic quasi informis creata ibidem fuit, ubi nunc formata substitit. Ubi cum Moyses dicit: 'In principio creavit deus caelum et terram,' per caelum et terram omnium caelestium terrestriumque materiam hoc loco voluit intelligi, de qua consequenter postea per formam distincta sunt, quae in ipsa prius per essentiam simul creata sunt. Deinde autem, cum addit: 'Terra autem erat inani set vacua,' illud terrae elementum designat. Et caelum erat illa mobilis et levis confusio reliquorum trium, quae in circuitu mediae iacentis terrae suspensa ferebantur. Deinde quod dicit: 'et tenebrae erant super faciem abyssi' et cetera, quae sequuntur, adaptant descriptiones praedictae descriptioni. Huic etiam consonat poeta dicens: 'Unus erat toto naturae vultus in orbe, / quem dixere chaos, rudis indigestaque moles.'" English translation by Laumakis, *The Procession of the World*, 62–63.

129 See Manuel Alonso Alonso, "Hugo de San Victor, refutado por Domingo Gundisalvo hacia el 1170," *Estudios eclesiásticos* 21 (1947): 209–16; and Hugh of St Victor, *De sacramentis christianae fidei* 1.1.6, ed. Berndt, 40.4–27. A textual comparison between Hugh's and Gundissalinus's excerpts can be found in Fidora, "Le débat sur la création," 276–78.

Fidora has recently pointed out that, among other points of contact, Gundissalinus relies on William for his criticism of Hugh's positions.[130] The controversy on primordial chaos between William and Hugh was harsh, and Gundissalinus's direct quotation of an excerpt from *De sacramentis* makes it plausible that he wanted to follow William in refuting this inadmissible theory, considering that William of Conches appears to be an important yet not principal source for Gundissalinus. Fidora has also underlined that the opposition between theologians and philosophers can be traced back to William himself, even if not in the terms used by Gundissalinus.[131]

Nevertheless, it seems likely that the mention of the *theologi* (in plural) made by Gundissalinus at the beginning of his quotation from *De sacramentis* was referring to both Hugh and Lombard, indeed two of the most important theologians of the twelfth century.[132] Peter Lombard also reported the same doctrine and quoted the first part of the text Gundissalinus quotes in *De processione*.[133] Once Gundissalinus has presented the position of "the theologians," he expounds the criticism expressed by the "philosophers claiming universal hylomorphism," stating that

> according to the philosophers, who hold that an angelic creature consists of matter and form, this chaos does not seem to have been the first matter of all creatures. For this matter could not, of course, have been something spiritual, because it was a body, and because they say that it was a mixture of both the elements and things composed of the elements, from which the heavenly bodies were distinguished through the distinction of their form, they seem to contradict the philosophers who testify that the heavenly bodies came, not from the elements, but from first matter. In the following way, however, it is seen to be proved that that blending of things was not first

130 See Fidora, "Le débat sur la création," especially 278–85.

131 See ibid., 280.

132 While a study of the influence of Lombard's *Sentences* on Gundissalinus is still a desideratum, it should be noted that Peter's *Sentences* were surely available to Gundissalinus, considering both the ecclesiastic relevance of Toledo and the presence in that town of a considerable number of French clergymen. Moreover, extending the scope of the inquiry into Gundissalinus's Latin sources might be helpful to reassess the hypotheses on Gundissalinus's "Chartres connection." At present, all clues point at establishing a direct connection between Gundissalinus and Chartres, implying his personal attendance at Chartres sometime before 1148. While no valuable alternative explanation to Gundissalinus's profound intimacy with Chartrean texts has been presented, the final proof of his "Chartrean period" is yet to be produced.

133 See Peter Lombard, *Sentences* 2.12.5, ed. Brady, 388.1–13.

Reshaping Frameworks: Gundissalinus and the Latin Tradition | 123

matter. The elements are composed of matter and form, for the elements are bodies because they are limited and have qualities. However, whatever things are composed of some other things are posterior to the things of which they are composed. Matter and form, therefore, are prior to the elements. But that chaos was a mixture of the elements and things composed of the elements. For this reason, that chaos was not created from nothing, since it was a mixture from many bodies. For a thing that is seen to be composed of so many things is not said to have been created from nothing. For this reason, that chaos could not have been first matter, because the creation of those simple things preceded it, although not by time, but by causality. Moreover, whatever is broken down into other things comes after the things into which it is broken down. But that chaos is broken down into the things composed of the elements and the things composed of the elements into the elements, while the elements are broken down into matter and form. Since, therefore, that chaos is posterior to many bodies, it certainly could not have been the matter of all bodies.[134]

Gundissalinus's criticism of primordial chaos is grounded on the notion of matter. "Philosophers claiming that the angels are made of matter and form" state that primordial chaos cannot be first matter, since the "matter" the theologians say was a chaos was necessarily a body and a mixture of elements and *elementata*. These elements were supposedly separated into the bodies of the super-

---

134 Gundissalinus, *De processione mundi*, ed. Bülow, 37.18–38.21; ed. Soto Bruna and Alonso Del Real, 190.4–192.3: "Sed secundum philosophos, qui tenent angelicam creaturam constare ex materia et forma, non videtur haec fuisse prima materia omnium creaturarum. Nam quia corpus fuit, spiritum utique materia esse non potuit; et quia permixtionem eam fuisse dicuntam elementorum, quam elementatorum, de qua celestia corpora per distinctionem formae distincta sunt, contra philosophos loqui videntur, qui corpora celestia non ex elementis, sed ex materia prima fuisse testantur. Quod autem illa confusio rerum non fuit prima materia, sic probari videtur. Elementa constat ex materia et forma; elementa enim corpora sunt, quia circumscripta sunt et qualitates habent. Quaecunque autem constant ex aliquibus, posteriora sunt eis, ex quibus constant. Materia igitur et forma priora sunt elementatis. Sed chaos illa erat permixtio ex elementis et elementatis. Quare chaos illa de nihilo creata non est, quae siquidem ex multis corporibus commixta est. Nulla enim res de nihilo creata esse dicitur, quae ex tam multis composita esse videtur. Quare chaos illa prima materia esse non potuit, quia creatio eorum simplicium eam antecessit, etsi non tempore, tamen causa. Item, quicquid resolvitur in aliqua, posterius est eis, in quae resolvitur; sed chaos resolvitur in elementata et elementata in elementa, elementa vero in materiam et formam. Cum igitur chaos multis corporibus posterior sit, profecto materia omnium corporum esse non potuit." English translation by Laumakis, *The Procession of the World*, 63–64. I have emended the Latin text to "elementata" instead of "elementa," for the sake of coherence within the text.

124 | CHAPTER TWO

and sublunary worlds, which contradicts those philosophers inferring that the celestial bodies are not composed of elements. Consequently, the hypothetical original chaos could not have been matter, because the elements are composed of matter, but they are not matter themselves. As the component precedes what it composes, matter must precede the elements, and if the chaos was made of elements (as it cannot be matter), then it was not created from nothing, but from matter, which is created *ex nihilo* together with form. At the same time, since the chaos is resolved into elements and *elementata* made of elements, and the elements are resolved into matter and form, chaos cannot have been the matter of all bodies, being posterior to their principles.

Gundissalinus's strategy in refuting the theory of primordial chaos is developed as a criticism of one of the most problematic points of the overall hermeneutics of *Timaeus* – is chaos made of matter or elements? Gundissalinus's refutation assumes that "the theologians" identify matter and elements. This point is not attested in the quotation from *De sacramentis*, but is presented by both Hugh and Lombard, in different terms, right before the excerpt quoted by Gundissalinus. While the reasons remain unclear for why Gundissalinus quoted an excerpt to refute a doctrine presented in a passage immediately preceding that quotation, his refutation of this point is based on two arguments stating that

1. There are bodies (the celestial bodies) which have matter but are not composed of elements. Therefore, elements are not matter, because they are not ontologically co-extended.

2. Elements are logically resolved in and ontologically composed of matter and form. Therefore, elements are not matter, because matter is ontologically prior to the elements.

As a consequence, chaos cannot be *primordial*. Since the entire line of reasoning of "the theologians" was grounded on the application of this theory to the biblical narrative of Genesis, when Gudissalinus argues that the supposed chaos cannot correspond to the first moment of creation, he also argues that this theory is groundless.

The two arguments Gundissalinus proposes align with the positions of "the philosophers," and he refers explicitly here to two groups of *philosophi*. The phrase "philosophers, who hold that an angelic creature consists of matter and form" ("philosophos, qui tenent angelicam creaturam constare ex materia et forma") seems to be a direct reference to the most important of Gundissalinus's sources, Ibn Gabirol. Nevertheless, and quite surprisingly, Gundissalinus's reference to Ibn Gabirol is not followed by any quotation from the *Fons vitae*, but by a discussion seemingly elaborated by Gundissalinus himself. Gundissalinus's first argument is grounded on a second reference to *philosophi*, explicitly to "the philosophers claiming that the celestial bodies are made from first matter but not of elements" ("philosophos ... qui corpora celestia non ex elementis, sed ex materia prima fuisse testantur").

Who are these philosophers? The first and most eminent candidate appears to be Aristotle, even though it is quite probable that Gundissalinus is using a third source reporting this Aristotelian theory, such as Avicenna, among other possibilities. The position held by these philosophers allows Gundissalinus to demonstrate that matter cannot be the elements. The celestial bodies, indeed, are composed of matter and form (they are bodies), but not of elements, making it impossible to identify the former and the latter as the same ontological entity. The second argument proposed by Gundissalinus, based on matter's logical and ontological priority to the elements, looks close to an argument expounded by William of Conches in his *Glosae super Platonem*. He does not refer, though, to William's argument concerning movement,[135] but to some final remarks presented in the *Glosae* on the wrongness of any identification of matter and elements. Regarding this point, William claims that

indeed, some people say that the elements in their chaos were that matter [i.e., first matter]. To the contrary, we say that the elements cannot be prime matter either in chaos or beyond the chaos, since some matter is proper to them. And this is proven as follows. Anything which has a form, has also a matter, since the form cannot be without matter. Some form, though, is proper to the elements, hence the fire is thin and the earth is thick. Moreover, Plato says that that matter does not have any quality of its own, while the elements have their own qualities: indeed, the fire is hot and dry, etc. Therefore, the elements are not the first matter, whether in chaos or beyond it. In fact, while in chaos, [the elements] had those same substantial qualities that they have, since nothing can be without having in some way its own substantial qualities. Therefore, we state that the matter of the elements is the first matter. There is no doubt about what matter is. Concerning its primacy, that is proven considering that [this matter] has no matter: if it had some matter, it would have a form, since everything which has a form also has matter, and therefore the matter of the elements would be made of some matter and some form, and by this it would be a body. Nevertheless, if it were a body, it would be an element or something made of elements: the

---

135 William of Conches, *Glosae super Platonem*, ed. Jeauneau, 88.1–89.28.

126 | CHAPTER TWO

matter of the elements, though, cannot be an element of something made of elements. For this reason, the matter of the elements is that matter which has no matter, and therefore it is the first matter. This matter cannot be *per se*, but it can be understood *per se* since "the intellect has the power to separate what is joined, and to join what is separated."[136]

Matter must not be identified with the elements, because matter is their substrate once it has received the elemental forms. Consequently, matter cannot be identified with chaos either. Matter *per se* does not have the properties required to be in a chaotic state, properties which are supposedly proper to elements and *elementata* – i.e., the aggregates of elements. Chaos, though, cannot be made by them, as William previously demonstrated. To the contrary, William states that, with the first creation, the elements originated and were located where they are nowadays, with their very same substantial qualities, even though they had particular accidents which made them different from what they are at present.[137] Accordingly, William's strategy develops through two arguments claiming the following:

1. As whatever has a form also has matter, and matter *per se* does not have any form or quality (while the elements do have form and quality) therefore the elements cannot be identified with matter.

136 William of Conches, *Glosae super Platonem*, ed. Jeauneau, 278.12–279.34: "Dicunt enim quidam quod elementa in chao fuerunt talis materia. Nos vero dicimus elementa nec in chao nec extra posse esse primam materiam, quia est aliqua eorum materia. Quod sic probatur. Cuiuscumque est forma, eiusdem est materia: forma enim sine materia esse non potest. Sed elementorum est aliqua forma: est enim ignis acutus, terra obtusa. Iterum, dicet Plato quod haec materia nullam propriam habet qualitatem. Sed elementa habent proprias qualitates: ignis enim est calidus et siccus, etc. Non sunt ergo elementa primordialis materia nec in chao nec extra. In chao enim habebant easdem substantiales qualitates quas modo habent: nichil enim sine suis substantialibus qualitatibus aliquo modo potest esse. Est ergo nostra sententia quod materia elementorum est prima materia. Quod materia sit, nulla dubitatio est. Quod prima est, probatur quia nichil est eius materia. Si enim esset aliquid illius materia, esset eiusdem et forma, quia quicquid habet formam, habet et materiam: esset ergo materia elementorum quiddam constans ex materia et forma, et sic esset corpus. Sed si esset corpus, esset elementum vel factum ex elementis. Sed neque elementum neque factum ex elementis est materia elementorum. Est ergo materia elementorum talis materia cuius nichil est materia: est ergo prima materia. Haec materia per se esse non potest, sed per se potest intelligi, quia 'vis est intellectus coniuncta disiungere et disiuncta coniungere.'"

137 See William of Conches, *Glosae super Platonem*, ed. Jeauneau, 90.1–6.

2. As bodies, like the elements, have to have both matter and form in order to be bodies, the matter of the elements cannot be the elements themselves or any *elementatum*, but it must be first matter, which is prior to them.

These two arguments allow William to demonstrate that primordial chaos cannot be said to be matter, for the elements are not matter, but are made of matter. Gundissalinus's second proof, based on the *resolutio* of the elements into matter and form, is slightly different in scope, but very close in both reasoning and wording. The main focus of Gundissalinus's and William's proofs is the demonstration of the priority of matter to the elements. Both authors assume that, to be so, chaos must be a conglomerate of elements and *elementata* (aggregates of elements). Accordingly, since the elements are made of matter (William), they are resolved into matter (Gundissalinus); likewise chaos is resolved into *elementata* and these into the elements. Implicitly for both, the priority of matter demonstrates the impossibility of primordial chaos, for matter logically and ontologically precedes every corporeal being which might possibly be part of that supposed original chaos. In Gundissalinus, this point is further made clear by the overall discussion of his cosmogony of universal hylomorphism, stating that matter and form are the first (and only) created entities, preceding anything else, a description profoundly rooted in Ibn Gabirol's *Fons vitae*. Gundissalinus might also have perceived a certain closeness with William's perspective regarding this point. William's arguments, indeed, assume that "whatever has a form, also has matter." This assumption is to be referred only to corporeal beings, for William tends to exclude any hylomorphism of spiritual substances.[138]

Nevertheless, Gundissalinus's syncretic attitude toward his sources means he usually simply ignores any disagreement between the sources and his own positions, to the extent of not even mentioning those passages. Accordingly, Gundissalinus's refutation of primordial chaos appears to be grounded on the opposition between *theologi* and *philosophi*, as Fidora has pointed out, but in a rather peculiar way. On the one hand, the theologians Gundissalinus refers to appear to be Hugh of St Victor, whose *De sacramentis* is quoted by Gundissalinus, and probably Peter Lombard, whose text quotes Hugh and establishes the identification of matter and elements, which is the main target of Gundissalinus's criticism. On the other hand, the question concerning the identity of the *philosophi* is more complicated. Reference to angelic hylomorphism makes it more than plausible that Gundissalinus is referring to Ibn Gabirol. The second

138 See Fidora, "Le débat sur la création."

128 | CHAPTER TWO

demonstration seems to be close to, but not necessarily based on William of Conches's *Glosae super Platonem*, and maybe also on the *Glosae super Boethium*, following Fidora's remarks, especially the reference to Ovid's *Metamorphoses*. Ovid is presented in both texts as the position of "the poet" regarding chaos – a position which, nonetheless, was surely well known to any learned person of that time.[139] On the other hand, the reference to some philosophers who claimed that the celestial bodies are not made of elements is still unclear. In his refutation, Gundissalinus abandoned a centuries-long core point of the Latin tradition, as it appeared useless and contradictory within his new cosmology rooted in the more recent theories of Avicenna and Ibn Gabirol. A much more positive attitude is reserved for one of his "colleagues" – Hermann of Carinthia.

Furnaces of Being

Hermann and Gundissalinus make wide use of the texts they translated in their works to build up new philosophical and scientific perspectives.[140] Both philosophers and translators, they shared a similar aim of updating the European cultural discussion on those questions that they thought were of principal relevance for Latin philosophy.[141] Notwithstanding these similarities, some meaninful differences are in place. While Gundissalinus centred his translating activity on philosophical writings, Hermann focused on scientific and mainly astronomical/astrological works. Moreover, Hermann and Gundissalinus are characterised by two rather distant philosophical perspectives. Far from Gundissalinus's approach, Hermann's main work, *De essentiis*, is a complex cosmogonic and cosmological description based on a tangled scheme woven from astronomical features and the fundamental influence of Plato's *Timaeus*.

De essentiis exposes an intricate cosmogonic description organised into two main moments and following a scheme where the different doctrinal cores derived from the Arabic and Latin scientific traditions are posited and

139 On the key role played by Ovid in the Middle Ages, see Amanda Gerber, *Medieval Ovid: Frame Narrative and Political Allegory* (New York, 2015); and the recent volume by James Clark et al., *Ovid in the Middle Ages* (Cambridge, 2011).

140 See José María Fernández Catón, *Colección documental del archivo de la catedral de León, V (1109–1187)* (León, 1990), 159–62, especially n1405; and Adeline Rucquoi, "Littérature scientifique aux frontieres du Moyen Âge hispanique," *Euphrosyne* 27 (2009): 193–210.

141 See Charles Burnett, "Literal Translation and Intelligent Adaptation amongst the Arabic-Latin Translators of the First Half of the Twelfth Century," in *La diffusione delle scienze islamiche nel Medio Evo Europeo*, ed. Biancamaria Scarcia Amoretti (Rome, 1987), 9–28.

incorporated into a Platonic framework, with specific interests in astronomy, astrology, and cosmology.[142] Hermann's point of departure is the position of the five "essences" – cause, movement, place, time, and *habitudo* – which are said to be the most stable and simple genera of existence.[143] Perfect in themselves, these five "essences" bring everything to existence, as they are ontologically complete and averse to any kind of alterity. This causative dynamic, though, is enacted by three main actors: matter, the ideas, and the efficient cause – i.e., the doctrine of three principles.[144]

Matter and form require each other. As a mother, matter embraces everything, but it needs to be shaped and ordered by a form. In turn, form requires matter to be provided with a shapeless mass in which it can be located, as "matter provides the formless and unordered bulk itself, without the presence of which form would have nowhere to establish itself."[145] Matter has no movement *per se* (it cannot change by itself). It is one in number and, without considering its forms, matter has no parts – it is in potency, while form is in act, the actualizing act which causes the actualization of matter in the composite.[146] When a form joins matter, it distinguishes matter into parts and actualises it, since "where there is form, matter itself exists in actuality" (*ubi forma, ipsa materia actu*).[147] As a consequence, matter is the substrate of existence for all created beings. While forms are like species providing differences, matter is like the genus that is specified by those forms.[148] Opposed to matter, form is an actualising principle of difference, change, and order. In itself, a form is made of two different parts, which are the internal condition (*intrinseca habitudo*) and the external

---

142 See Charles Burnett, "Astrology, Astronomy and Magic as the Motivation for the Scientific Renaissance of the Twelfth Century," in *The Imaginal Cosmos*, ed. Angela Voss and Jean Hinson Lall (Canterbury, 2007), 55–61; and Burnett, "Hermann of Carinthia's Attitude towards His Arabic Sources," in *L'Homme et son univers au Moyen Âge*, ed. Christian Wenin (Louvain, 1985), 306–22. Concerning Apollonius of Thiana, see Pinella Travaglia, *Una cosmologia ermetica: Il* Kitab sirr al-haliqua */* De secretis naturae (Naples, 2001), 283–310. See also Burnett, "Hermann of Carinthia and the *Kitab al-Istamatis*: Further Evidence for the Transmission of Hermetic Magic," *Journal of the Warburg and Courtauld Institutes* 44 (1981): 167–69; and Burnett, "Hermann of Carinthia's Attitude towards His Arabic Sources."

143 See Hermann of Carinthia, *De essentiis*, ed. Burnett, 76.7–11.

144 See ibid., 76.21–24.

145 Ibid., 78.2–4: "dat quidem materia massam ipsam informem et inordinatam, que nisi presto sit, nec habet ubi assit forma, que, cum supervenit, propositum ordinata quadam explanatione absolvit." English translation by Burnett, 79.

146 See ibid., 108.14–19.

147 Ibid., 108.17.

148 See ibid., 106.20–108.4 and 108.22–27.

130 | CHAPTER TWO

completeness (*extrinseca absolutio*). Both directly affect the hylomorphic composite through the formal causality.

Following Plato's *Timaeus* again, forms are originated by God's mind. From the pure and simple form of God irradiate a plurality of forms which are reflected in matter as in a mirror. These reflected images are the immanent forms, many in number, both in general and within a single being, and they are the first signs of any disposition (*dispositio*).[149] Matter and form, therefore, are characterised by a structural contrariety, which requires a composing cause to join them, resolving their intrinsic opposition. That causative moment is pivotal. The absolute contingency of matter and form is finally resolved by their union, because they cannot exist other than in the hylomorphic composite. For this reason, Hermann claims that matter always exists with form and form with matter.[150]

The first union of matter and form is brought about by the efficient cause of everything, which is the Primordial Cause – God, the true One. Hermann's description of the causation of this first substance is rather complex and expands the central aspects of *Timaeus*' account. God, the author of every existing thing, chose as his spouse an immortal and incorruptible entity (i.e., the universe), which is the very same entity binding mortal things together.[151] At the beginning of existence, God dispersed some seeds which had the potency of being mixed, a generative power, and which were provided with the same nature of "the Identical." When these seeds were placed together, they received the nature of "the Different." As if they were metals in a furnace ready to be melted into something else, God looked at the signs in his mind and assigned a sign to every seed following a specific order. These seeds and signs are the matter and form of everything.[152] Their union gives origin to "elements" which are not the corporeal

149 See ibid., 108.10–14; 108.33–110.4; and 110.5–10.

150 See ibid., 104.31–106.7 and 192.28–194.5.

151 Indeed, "what was first necessary for this kind of construction was the proposition of the Same and the Different" ("primum ergo necessaria fuit huiusmodi fabrice eiusdem diversique propositio"). See ibid., 90.8–9; English translation by Burnett, 91.

152 See ibid., 92.3–10. It should be noted that Hermann here identifies first matter with the seeds, but also with the elements. This identification, displaying *De essentiis*'s equivocal use of the term "matter," is based on the recognition that the union between *semina* and *notae* is stable and indestructible, and from it the elements arise. The elements constitute the substrate (and therefore matter) of any being, since they are not corporeal or incorporeal in themselves. Indeed, these *elementa* do not correspond to the four corporeal elements. They are "minimal particles" expressing the four elemental qualities which, when combined, give origin to the four corporeal elements, which in William of Conches's and Gundissalinus's lexicon are called *elementata*. See ibid., 104.5–10 and 92.10–13. Nevertheless, it is clear that Hermann follows a rather functionalist approach to matter and form, often calling them as such

Reshaping Frameworks: Gundissalinus and the Latin Tradition | 131

elements, as they are a sort of "incorporeal body" (*corpus incorporeum*).[153] The mixture of seeds and signs is then ordered by God in mathematical proportions and distinguished into two parts:

1. the Essence, higher and ontologically stable, proper to the heavens;
2. the Substance, the rough material of the sublunary world.[154]

This process corresponds to the first generation (*generatio primaria*), which is different from creation (*creatio*) – the causation of seeds and signs, i.e., the process through which the mixture of the elements "which are neither corporeal or incorporeal" is created from nothing. Indeed, Hermann distinguishes three stages of the cosmic institution. They are creation, first generation, and secondary generation, characterised as follows:

Causal Actor	Modality	Effect	Status of the Effect
Primordial Cause	Creation	Seeds + signs (= elements)	First principles
Primordial Cause	First generation (composition/disposition)	Essence and Substance	Secondary cause
Secondary Cause	Secondary generation (composition/disposition)	Sublunary world in becoming	Subject of Secondary cause

Hermann remarks that creation precedes the first generation by nature, but not concerning its order, time, and place. Secondary generation, in turn, follows

---

only in consideration of the function they perform – a function usually corresponding to "genus" and "species," respectively. For instance, comparison among the passages at ibid., 92.10–13; 102.30–104.2; and 104.5–10 (Mss L and C), makes clear that Hermann identifies the elements with both matter and form. As Burnett points out (at 252), matter should be identified with the seed, and these with the elements, while the forms are the *notae*. The ontological dynamic described by Hermann, thus, may be explained by the process through which first matter is informed by the divine signs, giving origin to the elemental matter from which the corporeal elements arise.

153 See ibid., 102.30–104.2: "Therefore it seems that one must assert that, since they are neither absolutely body nor entirely the incorporeal, they are that middle quality at least, which plainly could be called incorporeal body." ("Quare pronuntiandum videtur, cum nec absolute corpus sint, nec pure incorporeum, saltem medium illud quod plane corpus incorporeum dici possit"). English translation by Burnett, 103–5.

154 See ibid., 90.13–22. It should be noted that, accordingly, Hermann seems to consider Substance and Essence both as cosmological (i.e., supra- and sublunary worlds) and ontological entities (i.e., substance and essence in the individual being). See also ibid., 176.14–20.

132 | CHAPTER TWO

it in time and by nature, for the secondary causation of the sublunary world is already located in the immanent universe.[155] Hermann also differentiates between two correlated causal processes that are:

1. composition (*compositio*), i.e., how the ontological composite is made from the mixture of matter and form (elements);
2. disposition (*dispositio*), i.e., the position of every created being in the harmonic order of the chain of being.

The first generation gives origin to some entities which, in different ways, perform the secondary causation leading to the institution of the physical universe through secondary generation (*generatio secundaria*).[156] Secondary generation is indeed a mediated causation performed by a further cause which is the universal Essence – i.e., the heavens.[157] As secondary cause, the Essence acts upon the universal Substance, made of corporeal matter and forms, giving to it its species, division, and composition.[158] While the higher part of the Essence provides the forms, the lower level gives matter. The two hylomorphic principles are joined and mixed by the middle part of the Essence's disposition, following God's will and order.[159] The secondary causes originate the physical elements – earth, water, air, and fire – through different unions of matter and form, and,

> thus, I think, this secondary cause must be correctly understood as being itself the primary *genitura*. Since all secondary motions follow its authority, it is especially appropriate to consider its generation, which is the first coming-together of form with matter.[160]

The Essence, i.e., the celestial spheres, transmits God's causality to the sublunary world, where it is characterised as transmitted movement (i.e., formal

155 See ibid., 110.19–23.

156 See ibid., 112.14–114.29. What Hermann called "Substance," the lower level of the mixture, is the origin of the sublunary world. God separated the masculine from the feminine seeds so that they could be combined, and then he married each mixture, disposing them into the most desirable shape, the spherical one. These spherical elemental mixtures are of four species and correspond to the corporeal elements posited as spheres hierarchically and harmonically ordered.

157 See ibid., 192.13–19.

158 See ibid., 192.28–194.5.

159 See ibid., 196.11–22.

160 Ibid., 112.4–8: "Hanc itaque secundariam causam ipsam primariam genituram recte intelligendam opinor. Cuius auctoritatem quoniam omnes secundarii motus consequuntur, eius generationem – id est primum forme cum materia coitum – in primis speculari convenit." English translation by Burnett, 113.

change) from the perfect circular movement of the stars. As a consequence, the primordial cause, God, is the origin of every single being in a mediated or immediate way – immediately in creation and first generation, mediatedly in secondary generation.[161]

The progressive complication of the causal chain has a direct effect on the generated beings. The first offspring is composed and kept together by stable principles and, therefore, is characterised by ontological stability and perpetuity. To the contrary, the secondary offspring originates as an imitation of the first generation; it is nothing more than an ontological image of the true being of its cause and, accordingly, it is marked by generation and corruption, instability and time.[162] This is the transient ontological condition of the three species of sublunary beings – minerals, plants, and animals, distinguished by their animated/unanimated and sentient/insentient nature.[163]

The institution of the universe follows a threefold distinction of kinds of causation (creation, first generation, and secondary generation), two intrinsic processes (composition and disposition), and two main causal actors (primordial and secondary cause). The progressive causation of the universe can be summarised by the scheme on page 134.

While the distinction between primary and secondary cause is one of the most typical features of the Chartrean reflection on the universe, the causal scheme presented by Hermann is extremely close to Gundissalinus's cosmological description in his *De processione mundi*. In fact, Hermann is his main source in this regard. Gundissalinus's reception of Hermann of Carinthia's *De essentiis* is quite curious. On the one hand, the treatise is used and quoted only in the *De processione mundi*. On the other hand, *De essentiis* had a peculiar textual history in the Latin world, and Gundissalinus is basically the only philosopher relying on it as a primary source, as Burnett has pointed out.[164]

---

161 See ibid., 154.20–156.1.

162 See ibid., 110.12–19 and 156.19–24. As imitation, secondary offspring is subject to the threefold condition of being in the maternal womb (i.e., matter), in place, and in time: three conditions that constitute the receptacle of the secondary offspring, its corporeal existence, whose relation among parts is established by the secondary cause. See ibid., 172.17–20 and 190.17–21.

163 See ibid., 174.3–7. Applying Porphyry's tree, Hermann clarifies that the animals are a species of both the corporeal and incorporeal beings, since also souls, demons, and angels should be counted among them, even if the souls are created every day and angels and demons are created at the beginning of time. See ibid., 176.20–26.

164 See Charles Burnett, "Hermann of Carinthia," in *A History of Twelfth-Century Western Philosophy*, ed. Dronke, 386–406.

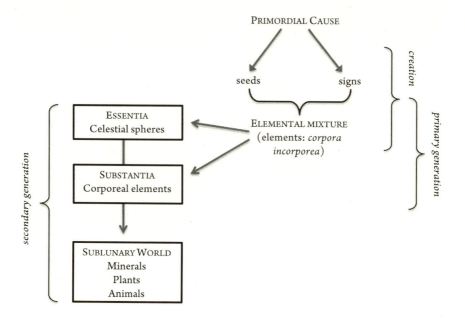

Quotations from the *De essentiis* are disseminated throughout the *De processione*, covering mostly Gundissalinus's discussion of the world instituting causality, but also important features on hylomorphism. As often with Gundissalinus, the excerpts are quoted, but on some occasions they are also reworked to fit in the overall theoretical structure of the text in which they are quoted. A good example of this attitude is provided by Gundissalinus's discussion of the duality of the first principles, grounded upon Hermann of Carinthia's text:

De essentiis	*De processione mundi*
"Plainly one principle of all things must be understood. For 'one' is prior to 'two,' since unless one comes first there is nothing to make up two. Moreover, when there are two, there must also be one, but the opposite – that if there is one, there will be two – does not hold true. How, then, can two principles even be considered, when, since each of them is struggling to be prior, the principal	"For the one is prior to two. For everything that, when eliminated, eliminates another thing and, when present, makes the other thing present is prior to that other thing. But unless one comes first there will not be two. Or, if there are two, it is necessary that there be one. But this is not reversible so that, if there is one, there are two or there must be two. Therefore, there cannot be two

place is left to neither? For unless one of the two is prior to the other, in no way could one be the principle of all things, while even one thing failed to be included in 'all things.'"[165]

principles. Each of them is said to be working to be first. But neither of them abandons the first position to the other. For unless one were prior to the other, there would by no means be a first [principle] of all things. Therefore, there is one principle, there is one efficient cause, of all things."[166]

Gundissalinus quotes this excerpt from Hermann's *De essentiis* at the end of his Avicenna-based discussion of the Necessary Existent – a fact surely displaying the relevance he bestowed upon it. The quotation signals the passage from the discussion of modal ontology to cosmogonic causation and, therefore, of matter and form as the first principle of the created being. These principles must be two in number, as the cause from which everything takes its origin is only one in number. Following the Neoplatonic assumption that the effect must be at the same time similar to and different from its cause, the first effects of God's causality must be two in number. But they must also be reciprocally interconnected, so that, from an ontological point of view, they become "one" and can exist only as "one" united thing. The latter corresponds to the ontological status of matter and form derived from Ibn Gabirol's *Fons vitae*.

Gundissalinus, though, adds to this Gabirolian scheme a crucial passage from *De essentiis*, stating that it is mathematically (or better, numerologically) necessary that a "two" is preceded by the "one," but not the other way around. These first principles are equal in existence, they exist together and come to be together. For Hermann, the dynamic of the mutual implication of matter and

165 Hermann of Carinthia, *De essentiis*, ed. Burnett, 78.17–24: "Unum autem plane omnium principium intelligi necesse est. Duobus namque prius est et unum – nisi enim precedat unum, nichil est quod duo constituat. Atque ubi duo, et unum est necessario. Non vero convertitur, ut, si unum est, et duo fore necesse sit. Duo itaque principia qui vel existimari possint, dum, utrumque prius esse laborans, neutri principalem sedem relinqueret? Nisi enim alterutrum altero prius esset, nequaquam primum omnium existeret, dum vel unum complendo omnium numero deesset." English translation by Burnett, 79.

166 Gundissalinus, *De processione mundi*, ed. Bülow, 17.1–9; ed. Soto Bruna and Alonso Del Real, 148.12–20: "Unum enim duobus prius est; omne enim illud prius est alio, quod destructum destruit et positum non ponit. Nisi autem praecedat unum, non erunt duo; aut si duo fuerint, necesse est unum esse. Sed non convertitur: si unum est, duo sunt, duo esse necesse est. Duo igitur principia esse non possunt. Dicitur utrumque prius esse laborans, neutrum neutri principalem sedem relinquit. Nisi enim alterutrum alterutro prius esset, nequaquam primum omnium existeret." English translation by Laumakis, *The Procession of the World*, 44.

136 | CHAPTER TWO

form is described through a *Timaeus*-inspired narrative of the creation of seeds and signs, a description far away from Gundissalinus's. *De processione mundi* uses this passage in implicit but clear reference to the status *in potentia* of both matter and form before their union. This is the very core of Ibn Gabirol's universal hylomorphism, alien to the discussion in the *De essentiis*. Accordingly, although textually modified and philosophically reinterpreted, *De essentiis* undoubtedly plays a central role in *De processione mundi*. Another excerpt from *De essentiis* is quoted almost word for word by Gundissalinus concerning the description of corporeal form:

De essentiis	*De processione mundi*
"Every form consists of two parts which are, as it were, 'whole,' because they perfect the complete wholeness of things. **These parts are the internal *habitudo* and the external completeness. The internal *habitudo* consists in the proportion of the mixture, but the external completeness is in the disposition of the figure** – i.e., [these two parts are] an exemplar for all things according to each kind of quantity respectively."[167]	"A form is called corporeal that is found only in bodies, as, for example, corporeity, quantity, colour, and similar things. **There are two sides to a corporeal form: intrinsic condition and extrinsic completeness. The intrinsic condition consists of the proportion of the mixture of the components of the body, and the extrinsic completeness consists of the arrangement of the shape of the body.**"[168]

In the *De essentiis*, the description of the two aspects of the form is inserted into the discussion of the reciprocal inherence between matter and form. Hermann claims that substance can be produced only through form, and that

167 Hermann of Carinthia, *De essentiis*, ed. Burnett, 110.5–10: "Constat autem omnis forma geminis quibusdam partibus tamquam integralibus, eo quod totam integraliter absolvunt. **Quarum altera intrinseca habitudo, altera extrinseca absolutio. Atque intrinseca quidem habitudo in commixtionis proportione, extrinseca vero absolutio in figure dispositione** – secundum utrumque videlicet genus quantitatis rerum omnius exemplar." English translation by Burnett, 111.

168 Gundissalinus, *De processione mundi*, ed. Bülow, 42.9–13; ed. Soto Bruna and Alonso Del Real, 198.5–10: "Corporalis forma dicitur, quae nunquam, nisi in corporibus, invenitur, ut corporeitas, quantitas, color et similia. **Cuius partes duae sunt: intrinseca habitudo et extrinseca absolutio. Intrinseca habitudo consistit in commixtionis proportione, extrinseca absolutio in figurae dispositione.**" English translation by Laumakis, *The Procession of the World*, 67.

matter is one for any existing thing and owns every form in potency.[169] It is the form which comes upon matter to distinguish it into singular and plural parts, and actualise the matter. Accordingly, form is made of two functional parts, the *intrinseca habitudo* expressing the proportion of the elemental mixture, and the *extrinseca absolutio*, which causes the external appearance of the caused substance. Gundissalinus accepts and quotes this doctrine without any relevant textual alteration but changes its overall context. Indeed, the two aspects of the *form in general* presented in *De essentiis* become, in *De processione*, aspects of the *corporeal form*. The reason for that is quite simple. In Gundissalinus's perspective it cannot be admitted that form in general causes the elemental mixture and the external appearance, as form is also the ontological principle of spiritual substances with no elements or exteriority. As a consequence, Gundissalinus has to limit Hermann's description of the form to the corporeal form, the kind of form proper to corporeal being only. In other words, he changes the scope of Hermann's doctrine of the twofold aspects of forms.

Notwithstanding these differences of perspectives and doctrinal development, Hermann certainly influenced Gundissalinus's reflection on matter and hylomorphism. From this point of view, another similarity between their approaches is their use of Porphyry's tree while engaging with the logical division of substance. Introducing a distinction between mortal and immortal animals, Hermann presents a sort of summary of his cosmogonic description, stating that

> After the primordial and efficient cause of everything, there are two principles, both for things and bodies, to which we can once again apply the names of "substance" and "essence," without incongruity. Substance is the simple fact of a thing's existence, which is founded in bodies from matter. But essence is the difference which informs this kind of simplicity in a multiple fashion. Thus, the most general category is substance, in itself one and the same for all – for both existents and accidents. When essences have approached this, a number of divisions result: in the first place, a corporeal and incorporeal division; following this, the corporeal too is immediately divided (as has been said) into a constant and a failing division.[170]

169 Hermann of Carinthia, *De essentiis*, ed. Burnett, 108.10–19.

170 Hermann of Carinthia, *De essentiis*, ed. Burnett, 176.14–23: "Post primordialem et efficientem omnium causam duo sunt tam rerum quam corporum principia, que rursus substantiam et essentiam non incongrue nuncupare possumus. Substantia quidem est ipsum simplex esse rei, quale in corporibus ex materia fondatur. Essentia vero differentie que eiusmodi simplicitatem multipliciter informant. Itaque generalissimum quidem est substantia una eademque omnibus secundum se, quecumque vel existunt vel accidunt. Quo cum essentie accesserint procedit divisionum numerus: Primo quidem loco alia corporea, alia incorporea. Consequenter et corpora statim alia (ut dictum est) constans, alia occidua." English translation by Burnett, 177.

138 | CHAPTER TWO

The primordial cause originates the existence of the two principles of everything, essence and substance – meant here not cosmologically but as the outcomes of the union of the ontological constituents (matter and form). Substance corresponds to the mere being of the things, which is granted to bodies thanks to matter. On the contrary, essence corresponds to the information differentiating the simplicity of the substance, and then it is a gradual union of the forms with matter through the five essential modalities. Accordingly, the first level of existence corresponds to the most general and unspecified substance, shared by all beings, which is specified by the essences/forms, following Porphyry's tree with its divisions into corporeal and incorporeal substance.

In *De processione mundi*, Gundissalinus too applies Porphyry's tree to his cosmological description and in a rather similar fashion, stating that

> For this reason, it happened that, when forms came to matter by the command of the creator, as the excellence of each form required and as the aptitude of the parts of matter desired, the various species of things were formed so that the beginnings of form, namely, corporeity and spirituality, came to matter that was already constituted, that is, made into one substance, and distinguished the whole of it completely into two kinds, namely, corporeal and incorporeal substance. Afterwards, the forms accompanying and attendant upon those two kinds subsequently divided them into the many species and orders of things by the ministry of nature. At first, therefore, what is composed of matter and form was divided into corporeal and incorporeal substance.[171]

Although similar, Gundissalinus's application of Porphyry's tree aims at a different purpose. Hermann uses it to present his discussion of the differ-

---

171 Gundissalinus, *De processione mundi*, ed. Bülow, 43.10–21; ed. Soto Bruna and Alonso Del Real, 200.8–18: "Quapropter hoc factum est, ut in materia nutu creatoris formis advenientibus, prout cuiusque formae dignitas exigebat et aptitudo partium materiae appetebat, varia rerum species formaretur, ita quidem ut principia formae, corporeitas et spiritualitas, in materiam iam constitutam, hoc est factam substantiam unam, advenientes eam totam penitus in duo prima rerum genera, scilicet corpoream et incorpoream substantiam, distinguerent, quae duo genera post modum formae illarum comites et pedissequae in multimodas rerum species et ordines naturae ministerio consequenter distribuerent. Imprimis igitur ex materia et forma compositum distributum est in corpoream substantiam et incorpoream." English translation by Laumakis, *The Procession of the World*, 68.

ence between corporeal and incorporeal animals – and, therefore, as a digression which does not seem completely consistent with the overall cosmology depicted by the *De essentiis*. In contrast, *De processione mundi* applies Porphyry's tree to clarify the logical progression in the causation of created being. The application of Porphyry's tree in *De essentiis* and *De processione mundi*, nonetheless, gives similar outcomes. The hylomorphic union gives origin to a preliminary and unspecified substance (substance as such, or first substrate) which is differentiated into corporeal and spiritual substances.

The point concerning which *De essentiis* exerts the strongest influence on Gundissalinus, however, is cosmogonic causality. The causative dynamic described by *De processione mundi* is based on the distinction between four kinds of causality performed by two main causal actors. Gundissalinus clearly presents the difference between these kinds of causality, stating that

> Composition, however, is the arising from those principles of the first things that, once they have been made, never perish, inasmuch as they were put together as a result of the first formation. Generation, however, arises from the same principles, and it is the renewal, not of the things that were composed, but of the things that continuously begin and perish, as if from remaining small things a drawing out of things has, once again, been produced. Creation and composition, however, are seen to be related to each other such that, although creation is seen to be prior by nature and causality, it should, nonetheless, never be understood as prior in order, time, or place. Since generation, however, comes down by means of composition, it necessarily comes later in time.[172]

Accordingly, Gundissalinus's doctrine can be summarised in the following scheme:

---

172 Gundissalinus, *De processione mundi*, ed. Bülow, 19.21–20.6; ed. Soto Bruna and Alonso Del Real, 154.11–20: "Compositio vero est primarum rerum ex ipsis principiis, quae semel factae nunquam occidunt, utpote ex prima conformatione compactae. Generatio vero est ex eisdem principiis eorum, quae nascuntur et occidunt usque, non per ea, quae composita sunt, reparatio, tamquam de residuis minutiis denuo confecta rerum protractio. Creatio autem et compositio ita se habere videntur, ut, licet creatio natura et causa prior videatur, numquam tamen et ordine, vel tempore, vel loco prior intelligenda est. Generatio autem, quoniam per compositionem descendit, necessario tempore posterior succedit." English translation by Laumakis, *The Procession of the World*, 47.

140 | CHAPTER TWO

Causal Actor	Modality	Description	Effect
First Cause	Creation	Creation *ex nihilo* of matter and form	Matter and form before their union
First Cause	First composition (*primaria compositio*)	First union of matter and form	*Primaria genitura*: angels, spheres, elements
Secondary cause	Secondary composition (*secundaria compositio*)	Composition of different hylomorphic composites	*Secundaria genitura: Elementata* and spiritual creatures
Secondary cause + Further causes	Generation	Generation and corruption of bodies	Corporeal beings composed of *elementata*

God, the first Cause, is the agent of two kinds of institutive causality. On the one hand, he performs the creation (*creatio*) of the first principles of created being, which are matter and form. On the other hand, God also joins these principles together in the first composition (*primaria compositio*), whose effect is the first offspring (*primaria genitura*), i.e., angelic creatures, celestial spheres, and elements. The first offspring is the causal agent of two further levels of causality. Secondary composition (*secundaria compositio*) corresponds to the composition of different hylomorphic composites and also to the joining of further forms with the substance, whose effect is the secondary offspring (*secundaria genitura*). Secondary cause, though, together with an imprecise number of further causes of lower degree, also governs the processes of generation (and corruption) proper to the sublunary physical world.

The origin of this causal doctrine is Hermann of Carinthia. The passage from the *De processione* is a reworked quotation from *De essentiis*, where Hermann claims that

> Creation is [the birth] of the principles of this kind; primary generation is [the birth] from such principles of the first things, which, once born, never will die, since they are put together from the first perfection; secondary generation is [the birth] from the same principles, but through the primary generation, of those things which have been coming to birth and dying up to the present day, as if for every being made anew from the left-over particles. Moreover, creation and primary generation seem to be such that, although creation appears to be prior by nature, it is not right to consider it as ever being prior in order, time or place. But secondary generation, since it

descends through primary generation, necessarily comes after it also in time.[173]

A textual comparison makes evident that Gundissalinus is relying on Hermann's discussion of cosmogonic causality. *De processione mundi* quotes an abridged version of the excerpt which covers all its details, but changes Hermann's terminology. This alteration strategy is fascinating. As Burnett has pointed out, *De essentiis* presents a logical distinction between *compositio* and *generatio* in the causal and cosmogonic ordering.[174] While the reference to composition stresses the internal ontological structure of the considered being, generation refers to the coming-to-be of that thing. Considered together, though, they are two aspects of the same causal action, performed by God in the case of primary composition/generation, and performed by the secondary cause in the case of secondary composition/generation.

Gundissalinus substantially modifies this scheme. Probably aware, through Avicenna, of the Aristotelian implication of generation, he encloses the latter into the physical world, distinguishing *generatio* and *compositio*. They are not two aspects of the same causative process anymore, but two different causations giving two different kinds of effects and entities. Composition, nonetheless, takes the very same place that generation had in Hermann's theory. Gundissalinus distinguishes between a *compositio primaria* and a *compositio secundaria*, stressing the composite nature of every created being which, at the end of any resolving process – the ontological *resolutio*, derived again from Hermann – is made of matter and form, composed together by the first cause, directly or indirectly.

The closeness between Hermann's and Gundissalinus's accounts is also expressed by the latter's discussion of the effects of these causes. Both *De essentiis* and *De processione mundi* ground their causal doctrine upon the pivotal distinction between primary and secondary cause. Gundissalinus claims that the outcomes of the first composition are three species of being, perpetual mediators

---

173 Hermann of Carinthia, *De essentiis*, ed. Burnett, 110.15–23: "Ac creatio quidem, huiusmodi principiorum; generatio primaria – primaria rerum ex huiusmodi principiis, que semel nate numquam occident, utpote ex prima perfectione compacte; secondaria vero ex isdem principiis per primariam, eorum que nascuntur et occidunt usque nunc, tamquam ex residuis minutiis denuo confecta. Ac creatio quidem et primaria generatio ita se habere videntur, ut, licet creatio natura quidem prior videatur, numquam tamen aut ordine aut tempore locove priorem intelligi fas sit; secondaria vero, cum per primariam descendat, necessario vel tempore posterior succedit." English translation by Burnett, 111.

174 See Burnett's introduction to *De essentiis*, at 10–16.

142 | CHAPTER TWO

of God's causality in the institution of the universe. They are the angelic creatures, the celestial spheres, and the elements. In the *De essentiis*, the discussion of the *constans genitura* is definitely longer and more detailed. Hermann's focus is centred on the causative power of the celestial substances which, together with the corporeal elements, are the outcomes of the first generation. Nonetheless, Hermann also states that, among these perpetual substances, angelic and demonic creatures should also be inserted, in a passage that is also quoted by Gundissalinus.[175] Gundissalinus shortens, reshapes, and inserts Hermann's passage into a different perspective. He accepts Hermann's discussion of angels and demons and quotes it. Nevertheless, while referring to it, Gundissalinus implicitly posits Hermann's discourse under a new light – that of Avicenna's and Ibn Daud's notions of separate intelligences, unassimilable within the Platonic perspective expounded in *De essentiis*.

Other aspects of the secondary causes are coincident or rather close in Hermann's and Gundissalinus's discussions. They both ascribe a pivotal role to the celestial spheres in causing processes of generation and corruption in the sublunary world through the mingling of elements. Nevertheless, Hermann's account makes no reference to the contiguity of the spheres – a central position held by Gundissalinus. In turn, the Toledan philosopher does not mention any kind of causal irradiation and makes no reference to the different kinds of influx each one of the spheres has on the sublunary world – a crucial aspect for *De essentiis*. As a consequence, although their accounts converge on both the causal agent (the spheres), the modality of their causation (secondary cause), and their effect (sublunary bodies), their development is distant in both content and perspectives.[176]

175 Compare Hermann of Carinthia, *De essentiis*, ed. Burnett, 184.13–186.8 and *De processione mundi*, ed. Bülow, 44.8–45.4; ed. Soto Bruna and Alonso Del Real, 202.8–204.2.

176 A similar scenario is offered by a comparison between Hermann's and Gundissalinus's notions of nature as principle of movement of the elements. See Gundissalinus, *De processione mundi*, ed. Bülow, 52.18–24; ed. Soto Bruna and Alonso Del Real, 216.9–14; and Hermann of Carinthia, *De essentiis*, ed. Burnett, 152.24–154.2 (version of mss L and C). It is worth noting that the authors appear to be consistent also in positing angels, spheres, and elements as the three effects of the first causation. While this point is clear in *De processione mundi*, Hermann's account states that the elements are refined into substance and essence, which can be identified with the corporeal elements and the celestial spheres, respectively. To these should be added the perpetual spiritual creatures (angels and demons), therefore arriving at three kinds of beings: angelic/demonic creatures, celestial spheres, and corporeal elements. Gundissalinus's account is extremely close. After the (logical) differentiation of the substance into corporeal and incorporeal, three kinds of beings come to be (as we already know): angels, spheres, and elements.

Looking at the bigger picture, it is beyond doubt that Hermann's *De essentiis* provides Gundissalinus with a meaningful set of theories and solutions – a cosmological framework from which he could develop his own reflection. Gundissalinus seems to be deeply inspired by Hermann, from the individuation of four kinds of causality (creation, primary and secondary composition, generation), to the position of angels, spheres, and elements/nature as secondary cause. Although solid, in Gundissalinus's eyes Hermann's framework and method were not sufficiently grounded and required the insertion of new doctrines and theories. These new doctrines are those elaborated by Ibn Gabirol, Avicenna, al-Ghazali, and Ibn Daud. As a result, Gundissalinus's use of *De essentiis* appears to be marked by a sort of contrasting attitude. It is one of the most important sources for Gundissalinus's *De processione mundi*, but also one of the most distant speculations from the perspective he matured through his study of Arabic philosophy.

This short recollection of themes, doctrines, theoretical problems, and attempted solutions has displayed both the indebtedness and remoteness of Gundissalinus's reflection in consideration of the Latin tradition closer to him. Under many considerations, Gundissalinus is bound to the twelfth-century debate and the Latin tradition. He received meaningful influences from Boethius and Calcidius, often through the mediation of the Chartrean masters. He made abundant use of Hermann's *De essentiis*, a rather peculiar source. From this point of view, Gundissalinus's speculation is rooted in the Latin philosophical tradition. Nevertheless, the sap that nourishes his reflection is from a different set of sources. They are the Arabic authors that Gundissalinus himself contributed to translating and, as a first in the Latin world, attempted to integrate within the Latin tradition. Yet his aims to renovate that tradition would imply an abandonment of many of its shared theories and, also through Gundissalinus's contributions, their substantially being superseded throughout the thirteenth century.

CHAPTER THREE

Rooting Reality:
Gundissalinus and Ibn Gabirol

The *Fons vitae* (*Font of Life*) is one of the most fascinating yet problematic philosophical works of the Middle Ages. Written by Solomon Ibn Gabirol, an Andalusian Jew, the *Fons vitae* was translated into Latin by Dominicus Gundissalinus and Johannes Hispanus, presumably in Toledo.[1] As only a few fragments of the original Arabic version of the text have survived, crucial relevance has been bestowed upon its Latin translation.[2] In contrast to a Hebrew epitome made by Shem Tob Ibn Falaquera in the thirteenth century, the Latin *Fons vitae* is indeed a complete translation of the Arabic text.[3] The three versions of the *Fons vitae* – Arabic fragments, Latin translation, Hebrew summary – display some points of textual divergence.[4] As a result, there are (sometimes radically) different interpretations of key doctrines expounded by Ibn Gabirol, as they depend on textual witnesses whose terminology is "uncertain and ambiguous."[5] Besides these problems of coherence among the three versions of the *Fons vitae*, consideration of the Latin translation posits additional difficulties. Concerning some main doctrinal points, indeed, the text appears to be not only unclear, but even internally contradictory.[6]

A valuable hypothesis on the origin of these difficulties has been recently proposed by Sarah Pessin. In her studies, Pessin considers these tensions as the

---

1 On Ibn Gabirol's biography, see I. Husik, *A History of Mediaeval Philosophy* (New York, 2002), 59–61; Julius Guttmann, *Philosophies of Judaism* (New York ,1966), 101–2; Colette Sirat, *A History of Jewish Philosophy in the Middle Ages* (Cambridge, 1985), 68; and John A. Laumakis's introduction to Ibn Gabirol, *The Font of Life* (Milwaukee, 2014), 9–14.

2 See Shlomo Pines, "Sefer 'Arugat ha-Bosem: ha-Qeta'im mi-tokh *Sefer Meqor Hayyim*," *Tarbiz* 27 (1958): 218–33; and Paul Fenton, "Gleanings from Moseh Ibn 'Ezra's *Maqalat al-Hadiqa*," *Sefarad* 36 (1976): 285–98.

3 Ibn Gabirol, *Fons vitae / Meqor hayyim*, ed. Roberto Gatti (Genoa, 2001).

4 See Ibn Gabirol, *Fons vitae / Meqor hayyim*, ed. Gatti, 107–76.

5 See Ermenegildo Bertola, *Salomon Ibn Gabirol (Avicebron)* (Padua, 1953), 71.

6 For instance, see Jacques Schlanger, *La philosophie de Salomon Ibn Gabirol: Étude d'un néoplatonisme* (Leiden, 1968), 178–79; but also Fernand Brunner, "Sur le *Fons Vitae* d'Avicembron, livre III," *Studia philosophica* 12 (1952), 171–78.

result of an insertion of external Latin and Aristotelian-based elements by the translators – an insertion allegedly due to Gundissalinus's and Johannes's hermeneutic of the original text.[7] As a consequence, both contents and context of the Latin text of the *Fons vitae* would have been positioned within a different theoretical framework by its translators.

In light of these facts, an examination of Ibn Gabirol's *Fons vitae* can consider two main problems:

the discordance among the three versions of the text;
the doctrinal tensions within the Latin version (which preserves the text in its entirety).

These two aspects, though, entail two methodologically different sets of questions and discussions of the text and its history. On the one hand, there is an examination of what is left of the *original version* in comparison with its Latin and Hebrew versions, which aims at re-constructing Ibn Gabirol's original thought and the influence the Arabic text had on its readers. This is the kind of research pursued, for instance, by Pessin. On the other hand, there is a study of the Latin reception of Ibn Gabirol's doctrines, which must be grounded on the supposedly misinterpreted translation made by Gundissalinus and Johannes Hispanus. If the discrepancies between the original and the translated texts are so meaningful, an analysis of the Latin tradition of the *Fons vitae* can and should be pursued *without* referring to the original Arabic version, which was evidently unavailable to Latin readers. The latter is the line of research on which this study is based – a methodological choice which explains, at least partially, the difference in the outcomes of this study as compared to other approaches to Ibn Gabirol.

---

7 Sarah Pessin's main supposition is that the Latin version of *Fons vitae* has been tainted by two fundamental misreadings by the translators, as well as two attempts to "Aristotelise" Ibn Gabirol's references to matter and form, and to "Augustinise" his doctrine of will. Basing her analysis on Ibn Gabirol's Arabic excerpts and their sources, Pessin shows that *Fons vitae* was originally firmly positioned in the Jewish Neoplatonic tradition, while the Aristotelian tendencies of the Latin version should be ascribed to the translators (Gundissalinus and Johannes Hispanus). From this point of view, Pessin claims that many of the doctrines traditionally ascribed to Ibn Gabirol are not actually present in the original version – universal hylomorphism, plurality of substantial forms, and divine voluntarism are all theories originated by the misunderstanding of the original text, as it is shown by the consideration of the terms *al-irada/voluntas* and *al-'unsur/materia*. It is beyond doubt that Pessin's reading of *Fons vitae* resolves many of the problems of internal coherence of the text, in which voluntarism is replaced by emanation, and hylomorphism by the reflection of God's ideas upon the first element. See Sarah Pessin, *Ibn Gabirol's Theology of Desire: Matter and Method in Jewish Medieval Neoplatonism* (Cambridge, 2013), especially 9–27 and 66–117.

146 | CHAPTER THREE

A second methodological clarification should be made concerning Gundissalinus. A central aim of the present study is an examination of how he reflected on, and consequently problematised, the *Fons vitae* along his career – that is, how Gundissalinus went on to interpret the text *after* he translated it. I have made the methodological choice to focus on Gundissalinus's philosophical interpretation and progressive problematisation of the theories he derived from *Fons vitae*, while I choose *not* to analyse, in this context, the circumstances of the translation he made of Ibn Gabirol's text.[8]

As mentioned above, *Fons vitae*'s intrinsic oscillations between different approaches and features has led to different and sometimes opposed interpretations of the text.[9] In particular, Ibn Gabirol's work is open to at least two opposite interpretative stances in relation to hylomorphism, based on *Fons vitae*'s non-univocal exposition. Indeed, Ibn Gabirol's *Fons vitae* can be read through:

1. A *compositional thesis*, claiming that, in their cosmological course, matter and form have an existence *in re* as *composing elements* of the thing of which they are components, following a strong ontological claim. As a consequence, Ibn Gabirol's ontology develops as an ontological description of the interrelation between two constitutive elements (matter and form) interacting within a *composite* compound through a series of hypostatic progressions.

2. An *analytical thesis*, focused on Ibn Gabirol's allegation that matter corresponds to the *genus generalissimum* and corporeal forms are the *speciae specialissimae*, and claiming that matter and form should be usually considered as *analogical references* to logical qualifications (genus and species), following a weak ontological claim. Accordingly, the main feature of Ibn Gabirol's discussion aims at expressing a progressive division of the first genus (first matter) into species, without necessarily entailing any reference to a composite structure of created being.

These readings evidently differ on what should be stressed most as the major point of Ibn Gabirol's reflection – a fact that, in turn, is a further sign of both the difficulty and the richness of *Fons vitae*. At the same time, none of these inter-

---

8 For some additional reflections on Gundissalinus's translation of *Fons vitae*, see Nicola Polloni, "Misinterpreting Ibn Gabirol? Questions, Doubts, and Remarks on the Latin Translation of the *Font of Life*," in *Solomon Ibn Gabirol's Philosophy and Its Impact in the Middle Ages*, ed. Nicola Polloni, Marienza Benedetto, and Federico Dal Bo, forthcoming.

9 A good example of these oscillations is offered by Ibn Gabirol's tendency to not explicitly state when he is referring to an individual rather than hypostatic intelligence and souls – a tendency which is particularly noticeable in the second book of the *Fons vitae*.

pretative approaches appear to be sufficient in providing a consistent and well-grounded account of Ibn Gabirol's perspective. They reciprocally imply each other, and in some cases both interpretations are plausible, although there are fundamental differences in the outcomes of their application. This is the case of the points in which cosmology and ontology meet in Ibn Gabirol's discussion, and particularly what I call the *reciprocal functionality* of matter and form.[10]

A Hylomorphic and Hypostatic Universe

Scholarship agrees that the discussion expounded in *Fons vitae* can be properly considered as an in-depth analysis of the metaphysical principles of reality in which the entire universe, both spiritual and corporeal, is rooted. Ibn Gabirol calls these principles matter (*materia*) and form (*forma*). Ibn Gabirol's Neoplatonic cosmos is developed through a series of hypostatic levels, each composed of matter and form and gradually constituting the corporeal tangibility of the physical world. As every being, except God, is made of matter and form, Ibn Gabirol's hylomorphism is universal, and universal hylomorphism would become the most characteristic doctrine bound to this Jewish philosopher.[11]

Ibn Gabirol adamantly claims that an understanding of the principles through which the universe has been established can be pursued only *a posteriori*. Examination of the corporeal world leads to a knowledge of their principles, which are matter and form. Through their consideration as primary effects of the constitution of the universe, it is possible to grasp a preliminary and structurally non-exhaustive knowledge of their cause, which is God.[12] Notwithstand-

10 I owe my deepest gratitude to Dominik Perler for his invaluable help regarding, among other things, the qualification of what I had elsewhere called a *circular functionality* of matter and form. I have come to the conclusion that the term *reciprocal* better qualifies this kind of functionality than *circular*, as matter and form are reciprocally needed in the definition of each of them, without necessarily implying a circularity in their definition.

11 For a general account of Ibn Gabirol's influence on scholasticism, see Hermann Adler, *Ibn Gabirol and His Influence upon Scholastic Philosophy* (London, 1964); Bertola, *Salomon Ibn Gabirol*, 187–99; as well as Marienza Benedetto's introduction to Ibn Gabirol, *Fons vitae / La fonte della vita*, ed. Benedetto (Milan, 2007), 141–97. Without being limited to it, Ibn Gabirol's impact has been profound especially on the Franciscan tradition. See Anna Rodolfi, "L'idea di materia in Dio: Essenza ed esistenza della materia nel dibattito teologico nella seconda metà del XIII secolo," *Quaestio* 7 (2007): 317–37; and Rodolfi, "Interpretazioni dell'ilemorfismo universale nella scuola francescana: Bonaventura, Bacone, Olivi," *Rivista di Filosofia Neo-Scolastica* 4 (2010): 569–90.

12 Although God in himself cannot be exhaustively known, the human intellect can rise from cause to cause up to the principles of being (matter and form), God's will, and his essence. Only God's existence can be known, as his being is utterly different from the creatural

148 | CHAPTER THREE

ing some intrinsic tensions, *Fons vitae* displays Ibn Gabirol's utterly Neoplatonic approach. His attitude can be much appreciated through a consideration of his method of analysis, which is grounded upon and developed through a constant recourse to metaphysical principles derived from the Neoplatonic Arabic tradition.[13] While all intimately interconnected, these principles can be gathered into two main groups concerning causality and structure of being. I will discuss only the most important of these principles. They are the following:

Principles of metaphysical causality (PC)

1. The *principle of the simplicity of the cause* (PC1),[14] by which a cause is always higher and simpler than its effect. In the cause, indeed, there is everything that will be transmitted to the effect, but in a way proper to the cause; thus cause and effect are similar but different under different consideration. PC1 is directly connected to the principle of the derivative nature of the manifest and the principle of conformity.

2. The *principle of the derivative nature of the manifest* (PC2),[15] by which a perspicuous or evident reality (*manifestum*) is a degraded and derived copy of a less evident but more authentic reality (*occultum*). As a result of the interaction between PC1 and PC2, the process of causation implies (a) a general ontological degradation of the cause/s into the series of its effects, and (b) a specific multiplication of simplicity into creatural multiplicity.

3. The *principle of conformity* (PC3),[16] by which two realities which are different at a lower level of reality agree at the higher level, which is their cause. This

---

being. See Ibn Gabirol, *Fons vitae* 5, ed. Clemens Baeumker (Münster, 1892–95), 301.24–25 and 322.20–323.5; ed. Benedetto, 632 and 660. Ibn Gabirol underlines that a knowledge of God is difficult, for matter and form are closed doors (*portae clausae*) beyond which human knowledge struggles to comprehend. See Ibn Gabirol, *Fons vitae* 5, ed. Baeumker, 322.7–11 and 9.24–10.22; ed. Benedetto, 658 and 220–22.

13 See David Kaufmann, *Studien über Salomon Ibn Gabirol* (Budapest, 1899), 1–63; Schlanger, *La philosophie de Salomon Ibn Gabirol*, 1–30; Bertola, *Salomon Ibn Gabirol*, 60–73; and John Dillon, "Salomon Ibn Gabirol's Doctrine of Intelligible Matter," *Irish Philosophical Journal* 6 (1989): 59–81.

14 See Ibn Gabirol, *Fons vitae* 3, ed. Baeumker, 118.21–22; ed. Benedetto, 385. Ibn Gabirol also adds, as a corollary, that if two things are similar in their concept, that concept is the same for them both. See *Fons vitae* 3, ed. Baeumker, 182.26–183.4; ed. Benedetto, 470.

15 See Ibn Gabirol, *Fons vitae* 2, ed. Baeumker, 34.10–11; ed. Benedetto, 264.

16 See Ibn Gabirol, *Fons vitae* 3, ed. Baeumker, 139.15–141.13 and 43.26–44.2; ed. Benedetto, 412–14 and 278. One of the pillars of Neoplatonic metaphysics is the claim that everything that will be transmitted to the effect is already present in its cause, but in a way proper to it. Therefore, under different considerations cause and effect are similar but not identical.

is valid for any difference (*differentia*) among opposed entities. For instance, two opposed entities at hypostatic level *c* must have a common root at the higher hypostatic level *b*. This common root is the logical substrate in which they agree (*convenientia*) and the ontological cause of their existence. Opposed differences, therefore, are but a degradation of identity. The dynamic implied is evidently similar to the agreement of two species in their common genus.

4. The *principle of subordinated causality* (PC4),[17] by which any action which is performed by a created being (i.e., anything but God) must be enacted upon a substrate, which is its matter. This principle of subordinated causality is pivotal in Ibn Gabirol's speculation, as it is the ground of universal hylomorphism through its link to the principle of formal actualisation. Also, it should be noted that the principle of subordinated causality aims at establishing a substantive and radical difference between God's causality from nothing and subordinated causality from a substrate (i.e., whose stuff is matter, not nothingness).

5. The *principle of formal actualisation* (PC5),[18] by which the complete actualisation of the compound is brought about only by a form acting upon matter, although both matter and form are said to be in potency and the act only happens through hylomorphic unity. Accordingly, matter is the substrate of any subordinated causation, i.e., any causation beside creation.

Principles of ontological structure (PS)

1. The *principle of the identification of unity and actual being* (PS1),[19] by which whatever exists in act has an intimate unity (is "one"), and what has unity also has existence in act.

2. The *principle of the ontological reciprocity of matter and form* (PS2),[20] by which matter can exist only with form and form only with matter. This implies that, although matter and form are per se in potency, they have an actual complete existence only once they are united within the hylomorphic compound, although only form is said to actualise matter (*per* PC5).

3. The *principle of the thirdness of compositional unity* (PS3),[21] by which the result of the union of matter and form cannot be reduced to any of its compos-

17 See Ibn Gabirol, *Fons vitae* 2, ed. Baeumker, 40.21–22; ed. Benedetto, 272.

18 See Ibn Gabirol, *Fons vitae* 4, ed. Baeumker, 233.17–25; ed. Benedetto, 542.

19 See Ibn Gabirol, *Fons vitae* 3, ed. Baeumker, 68.3–6; ed. Benedetto, 312.

20 For instance, see Ibn Gabirol, *Fons vitae* 1, ed. Baeumker, 13.14–14.5; ed. Benedetto, 228.

21 See Ibn Gabirol, *Fons vitae* 3, ed. Baeumker, 158.8–10; ed. Benedetto, 438. Following a traditional Aristotelian stance, Ibn Gabirol also claims that, when two opposites things are joined together, one or more *media* must be admitted, since otherwise a conjunction of the opposites would be impossible. See *Fons vitae* 3, ed. Baeumker, 79.21–22; ed. Benedetto, 328.

150 | CHAPTER THREE

ing elements, because the result of their compositional unity is a third thing (i.e., the actual substance).

4. The *principle of formal specification* (PS4),[22] by which the reception of a non-incidental form by the compound corresponds to a specification of its genus within a static ontological description of that being. Under some considerations, this principle can be considered a reflection on the ontological structure of the principle of conformity.

Through these metaphysical principles, Ibn Gabirol examines the institution and ontological composition of the universe *going up* from a consideration of corporeal beings to the next layers of reality.[23]

Although a definition of matter and form is impossible, *Fons vitae* allows some descriptions of the "roots of reality."[24] The text makes constant recourse to a set of metaphors which depict the relationship between matter and form. Among them, light is Ibn Gabirol's favourite explanatory device.[25] In a famous passage of *Fons vitae*, he states that matter can be imagined as the extreme limit of the existing things, and form as the light which gives to anything its species and properties. Possibly the closest claim to a definition of matter and form provided by *Fons vitae* states that

> Matter differs from form by the fact that the one sustains and the other is sustained ... Since matter does not sustain itself and form is not sustained by itself, but matter sustains with respect to the form that is sustained in it and form is similarly sustained only with respect to the matter that sustains it, you will know, consequently, that matter and form are distinguished by this difference only when they are considered to be united, not when the essence of either of them is considered.[26]

There are only two principles of created existence and they are a borne and a bearing element. Of them, a form must always be borne and matter always

22 See Ibn Gabirol, *Fons vitae* 3, ed. Baeumker, 168.21–169.4; ed. Benedetto, 452.

23 Ibn Gabirol also uses a twofold procedure for this analysis, rather close to Calcidius's method of *compositio* and *resolutio*. See *Fons vitae* 1, ed. Baeumker, 17.2–20.7; ed. Benedetto, 232–38.

24 See Ibn Gabirol, *Fons vitae* 5, ed. Baeumker, 298.10–21; ed. Benedetto, 628.

25 See Vincent Cantarino, "Ibn Gabirol's Metaphysic of Light," *Studia Islamica* 26 (1967): 49–71. On the metaphors of light and water flowing in the Islamic and Jewish traditions, see also Federico Dal Bo, "The Theory of 'Emanation' in Gikatilla's *Gates of Justice*," *Journal of Jewish Studies* 62 (2011): 79–104.

26 Ibn Gabirol, *Fons vitae* 5, ed. Baeumker, 259.25–260.11; ed. Benedetto, 578–80: "Materia differt a forma in eo quod altera est sustinens et altera sustentatum ... Postquam

bears. It is only through its union with matter, i.e., its being borne by matter, that a form can give its (specified) being to the hylomorphic compound following PC5. As a consequence of Ibn Gabirol's descriptions, matter can be conceived as the common substrate ("something like a genus") which is *divided* (specified) by the forms into a myriad of species. This apparently innocent claim is nonetheless accompanied by and grounded upon Ibn Gabirol's constant recourse to the principle of conformity (PC3), by which two opposed entities must have a common origin, i.e., a shared substrate. This shared substrate must also be simpler (*per* PC1) and less evident (*per* PC2) than the entities.

Consideration of the forms of the elements offers a valuable example of this dynamic of metaphysical implications. Sensible bodies are composed of elements, and elements are made of matter and form. The four elements, though, are different among themselves. As the diversity among elements derives from their forms (PS4), these forms must have something in common (PC3), a sort of residual agreement from which their difference is sorted out. This common substrate is the body, because every elemental form is corporeal and, therefore, corporeity is their hidden origin and substrate (PC2).[27] As substrate-matter of every corporeal being, the body, too, must be both subject of a form (PS2) and a specification of something logically and ontologically prior (PS4 + PC3).[28] As a consequence, the body as such

> *as matter* of the corporeal forms is called *matter bearing quantity* by Ibn Gabirol;
>
> *as form* is called "form of corporeity" and it is borne by a special and higher substrate that is called *universal spiritual matter*, which in turn is a result of the causality of the spiritual substances.[29]

---

materia non est sustinens se ipsam, et forma non est sustentata a se ipsa, sed materia est sustinens respectu formae quae sustinetur in ea, et forma similiter non est sustentata nisi respectu materiae quae eam sustinet: scies per hoc quod materia et forma non discernuntur hac differentia, nisi cum consideratur esse composita, non cum consideratur essentia cuiuslibet illarum." English translation by Laumakis, *The Font of Life*, 216.

27 See Ibn Gabirol, *Fons vitae* 1, ed. Baeumker, 17.3–19.5; ed. Benedetto, 232–36.

28 See ibid., ed. Baeumker, 20.21–21.10; ed. Benedetto, 238–40.

29 Ibn Gabirol argues in favour of the existence of the universal spiritual matter, proposing a comparison between corporeal forms and the form of corporeity – a comparison completely grounded on the metaphysical assumptions that the Jewish philosopher derives from the Neoplatonic tradition. As the sensible forms require a subject, which is the body, so the body (which is the form of corporeity at a higher level of consideration) requires a subject. That subject is the universal spiritual forms. See Ibn Gabirol, *Fons vitae* 2, ed. Baeumker,

152 | CHAPTER THREE

It should be noted that in this process there is an unspoken implication. Following PC3 and PS4, because the forms are the specific differences among every corporeal being, they must have a common substrate, i.e., a common matter. Nevertheless, Ibn Gabirol goes a bit further. As the forms are the manifest copy of what is hidden (PC2), and what is hidden coincides with a simpler and therefore higher degree of existence of the manifest (PC1), therefore the two opposed forms appear *to be* their matter at a higher level of reality. Ibn Gabirol's discussion of the cosmic progression of matter and form is rather puzzling, as the ontological reciprocity of matter and form (PS2) appears to be accompanied by a cosmological description in which Ibn Gabirol calls the same entity, respectively, *form* and *matter* in different levels of reality. The ontological reciprocity (matter and form are always together), therefore, seems to be in apparent contrast with a *compositional* reading of these passages. If matter (M) and form (F) are univocally and consistently identified with the composing elements of a thing, Ibn Gabirol's claim violates the principle of non-contradiction. Indeed, the being of matter would be identical to itself (M=M) being different from form (M≠F), yet also identical to form (M=F) and, therefore, different from itself (M≠M), at the same time and in the same hylomorphic compound, although at different levels of existence.

Consideration of the case of the *body as such* offers a useful example of the problems entailed by this line of reasoning. The body as such is said to be *matter* in regard to the sensible forms – their union with the body causes the elements. Body, though, is also said to be, at a higher level, the form of corporeity, which is the form that is joined with the universal spiritual matter. The following scheme may be helpful:

(A) higher level of reality: [(x) = F; form of corporeity] + [(y) = M; universal spiritual matter]
(B) lower level of reality: [(z) = F; elemental forms] + [(x) = M; matter sustaining quantity, or body]

where (x) is matter *and* form respectively at level (A) and (B).

Accordingly, the same entity (the body as such), depending on a consideration of it either as an ontological partner of either sensible forms or universal

---

23.13–14; ed. Benedetto, 246. It should be also noted that, as Laumakis has stressed, Ibn Gabirol uses ambiguous terminology throughout the treatise, referring to the same being with many different names. A good example of this is the "matter bearing quantity," also called matter bearing corporeity, matter bearing quantity and accidents, matter of the nine categories, and subject bearing quantity. See Laumakis, *The Font of Life*, 27.

spiritual matter, is either matter or form. Or neither of them. Consideration of matter and form through the *compositional thesis* claiming that they have a real existence *in re* as actual composing elements of the hylomorphic compound implies a fundamental tension within the onto-cosmological description of *Fons vitae*. Moreover, it should be underlined that the dynamic described by Ibn Gabirol and summarised by the scheme presented above appears to be in intrinsic contradiction with Ibn Gabirol's central application of the principle of the derivative nature of the manifest (PC2) to matter and form. Indeed, *Fons vitae* repeatedly claims that the *manifest* element is the form, while to be *hidden* is matter.[30] This would imply that it is matter (what is hidden) that becomes form (manifest) during the described process, whereas the text consistently refers to form becoming matter, as discussed above.

In contrast, an *analytical reading* would imply that matter and form are to be considered as analogical terms for genus and species. This reading substantially changes the terms of the problem. Matter is said to be the common substrate – up to first matter, which is the *genus generalissimum* bearing every form. In contrast, forms would be only the dividing factor specifying what is shared into finite sets of fewer and fewer elements. Accordingly, we would have the following scheme:

(A) higher level of reality: $[(x) = F;$ corporeity as species$] + [(y) = M;$ lower spirituality as genus$]$

(B) lower level of reality: $[(z) = F;$ species of the elements$] + [(x) = M;$ corporeity as genus$]$

The weak ontological claim entailed by the *analytical thesis* makes it possible to supersede the impasse of considering form and matter as composing elements and, accordingly, to avoid any tension with the principle of non-contradiction. Indeed, (x) can be the specifying difference at the level (A) and the generic commonality at the level (B) without any theoretical complication. To the contrary, the scheme appears to be extremely clear in itself and rooted within the logical tradition following the *Categories*. Nevertheless, the clarity of this explanatory device is limited to the present case. If we extend our consideration to the wider text of the *Fons vitae*, it seems that the *analytical thesis* drastically reduces the richness of Ibn Gabirol's perspective. It should indeed be recalled that *Fons vitae* firmly depicts a hylomorphic hypostatic universe established through progressive unions of matter and forms reciprocally interacting with each other at different hypostatic levels. Accordingly, one could even ask, naively,

---

30 See Ibn Gabirol, *Fons vitae* 2, ed. Baeumker, 34.10–11; ed. Benedetto, 264.

154 | CHAPTER THREE

what would remain of universal hylomorphism if one has to read matter and form as analogous to genus and species rather than real composing elements of the compound. Indeed, if matter is nothing but a common genus divided by a progression of species/forms, is Ibn Gabirol actually discussing a theory of universal hylomorphism?

A possible solution to the partial answers proposed by the compositional and the analytical approaches can perhaps be found as a middle position between these two extremes. That would imply a need to focus on an application of the principle of the thirdness of compositional unity (PS3) and the principle of the identification of unity and being (PS1). The ontological reciprocity of matter and form within the compound (established by PS2) entails that every created being is made of matter and form – a compositional unity which is stated repeatedly, being one of the main features of Ibn Gabirol's work. Nevertheless, PS1 implies the actual unity of being of the compound. This derived yet complete unity proper to the hylomorphic compound is coincident with its actual being. It is also a result of a duality of composing elements (matter and form).

It seems, therefore, that matter and form are not primarily to be considered as *composing elements*, but as *aspects* of their compound. They can be considered as composing elements *before* having been joined together into the compound. When they are joined, though, they become something else of which they are aspects. Indeed, PS3 claims that the result of that composition of hylomorphic duality is a third thing – not matter, not form, but not even *matter + form*. Its unity is given by a duality which is not the sum of two components, because once matter and form are joined, they become something else. Let me present an example of this ontological dynamic with an experience anyone may have had with oil paints, namely the colours blue, red, and violet.[31] The union of matter and form can be considered, accordingly, to be similar to the melding of blue and red, giving violet as a result. Violet is not blue or red, as those colours are joined into something else which is different from them. Before being joined together, blue and red can be said to be the *composing elements* of violet. Once they are joined, though, they are not parts or elements which can be delineated or extracted from violet. They are aspects of that colour instead. While they are *composing elements* of the hylomorphic compound before being joined together, after that union matter and form exist only *within* the compound. This compound is something else and matter and form are its aspects. These aspects, in turn, correspond to some functions – potentiality and actuality, materiality and formality, genus and species.

---

31 I owe my gratitude to Rosie Reed Gold for this splendid example.

Within the limits of these clarifications, a *functional thesis* can be presented. Accordingly, matter and form, within the ontological unity of the compound, are aspects performing ontological functions, existing *in re* although always together in something else which is their result. They would not be composing elements but ontological aspects expressing an intrinsic metaphysical duality which cannot be resolved into the sum of two different parts. Again, using the example of corporeity, one would have the following scheme:

(A) higher level of reality: $[(x)$ = corporeity ~ species-function$] + [(y) =$ spiritual substance ~ genus-function$]$
(B) lower level of reality: $[(z)$ = corporeal forms ~ species-function$] + [(x)$ = body ~ genus-function$]$

Accordingly, at a higher level of reality A, the entity (x) plays the function of corporeity as a species *dividing* the genus of the spiritual substance (y). That very same entity, though, is also a genus, or better, a sub-genus at a lower level of reality, where it is further divided by other forms, namely, the corporeal forms, establishing the corporeal species. At the same time, the same entity (x) can be said to perform the function of the borne element – i.e., the form – at level (A), while the same entity (x) can be consistently said to perform the function of the bearing element – i.e., matter – at level (B). The reason for that is simple. They perform different functions. Therefore, aspects of (A) can perform a form function and a matter function, and the same aspect of B can perform a different function. Matter and form indeed only exist as *functional aspects* of a radical metaphysical duality within the ontological unity of the compound. And while change and movement evidently modify the formal structure of the compound, there would never be an existence of matter and form beyond and beside the compound.[32] Therefore, an intrinsic functional reading of the reciprocal functionality of matter and form makes it possible to safeguard both a real presence *in re* of matter and form (*compositional thesis*) and an analogical value in terms of genus and species (*analytical thesis*) without, respectively, either the entry of logical *terrae incognitae* or denying the major cosmo-ontological aims of *Fons vitae*.[33]

32 Other interpretations of this tension are of course possible. See Sarah Pessin, "Chains, Trees, and the Spirit-to-Body Boundary: Substance, Spiritual Matter, and the Principle of Matter as Higher Cause in Ibn Gabirol," in *Solomon Ibn Gabirol's Philosophy and Its Impact in the Middle Ages,* ed. Polloni, Benedetto, and Dal Bo, forthcoming. It should also be noted that Ibn Gabirol's description of the hylomorphic progression has some interesting similarities to Proclus's. See Jean Trouillard, "La genèse de l'hylémorphisme selon Proclos," *Dialogue: Revue Canadienne de Philosophie* 6 (1967–8): 1–17.

33 While this analysis of the cosmological and ontological interrelations of matter and form *may* have clarified the terms of the problem and even provided a hopefully valuable

156 | CHAPTER THREE

Once this fundamental interpretative point has been clarified, a greater appreciation of Ibn Gabirol's ontology is possible. *Fons vitae* repeatedly claims that matter and form have a being in potency. The text also claims that matter and form must exist *per se*, as they are principles.[34] Matter must also have one and a single essence, because it is one and the same for every existing thing. In fact,

> If there is one universal matter of all things, these properties adhere to it: namely, that it exists through itself, has one essence, sustains diversity, and gives its own essence and name to all things ... Matter must have being, because what does not exist cannot be matter for what exists. But it is said to be subsisting through itself so that reasoning does not proceed to infinity, if matter did not exist in itself. It has one essence for the reason that we sought only one matter of all things. It sustains diversity, because diversity comes only from forms, and forms do not exist through themselves. It gives its own essence and name to all things because, since it sustains all things, it is necessary that it exists in all things, and since it exists in all things, it is necessary that it give its own essence and name to all things.[35]

---

explanation, the thorny question has only been postponed. Indeed, while I have referred to levels of reality while describing the ways in which matter and form can be interpreted, PS1 and PS3 would imply that those (A) and (B) levels are hylomorphic compounds with a *real* existence.

34 On Ibn Gabirol's theory of matter and the manifold problems arising from it, see Fernand Brunner, "Sur l'hylemorphisme d'Ibn Gabirol," *Les études philosophiques* 8 (1953): 28–38; Marienza Benedetto, "La dimensione fondante della realtà: La materia in Ibn Gabirol e Shem Tov ben Yosef ibn Falaquera," *Quaestio* 7 (2007): 229–44; Odon Lottin, "La composition hylémorphique des substances spirituelles: Les débuts de la controverse," *Revue néo-scolastique de philosophie* 34 (1932): 21–41; and María Pilar Ferrer Rodriguez, "Relación transcendental 'materia-forma' en el 'Fons vitae' de Ibn Gabirol," *Mediaevalia: Textos e Estudos* 5–6 (1994): 247–58.

35 Ibn Gabirol, *Fons vitae* 1, ed. Baeumker, 13.14–14.5; ed. Benedetto, 228: "Si una est materia universalis omnium rerum, hae proprietates adhaerent ei: scilicet quod sit per se existens, unius essentiae, sustinens diversitatem, dans omnibus essentiam suam et nomen ... Materia debet habere esse, quia quod non est ei quod est materia esse non potest. Sed dicitur subsistens per se, ideo ne ratio eat in infinitum, si materia exsisterit non in se. Unius autem essentiae, ideo quia non quaesivimus nisi unam materiam omnium rerum. Sustinens diversitatem, quia diversitas non est nisi ex formis et formae non sunt existentes per se. Dans omnibus essentiam suam et nomen, ideo quia, cum sit sustinens omnia, necesse est ut sit in omnibus, et cum fuerit existens in omnibus, necesse est ut det essentiam suam et nomen omnibus." English translation by Laumakis, *The Font of Life*, 69. See also Ibn Gabirol, *Fons vitae* 5, ed. Baeumker, 263.12–19 and 262.18–263.9; ed. Benedetto, 582–84.

Although one in number, matter must be the *bearer of diversity*, because every form requires matter and matter is shared by every created thing. Indeed, if one abstracted every form from every corporeal thing, one would find a substance which is common to every sensible entity. That substance is a compound of matter and the first form.[36]

Surprisingly, matter is also said to be the *hidden essence* of every created thing – an essence which is identical in everything (matter is indeed common to every created being) and specified by the formal diversity it receives (matter exists inasmuch as it is joined to form/s).[37] Ibn Gabirol claims that, as different golden jewels have different shapes but a common gilded substance, so too every being shares with the others its matter and essence.[38] Matter's function of providing the compound with its essence then should be tacitly linked to the role of genus that matter appears to perform within *Fons vitae*. Otherwise, one would be obliged to suppose that matter enters within the definition of every material thing – which, in Ibn Gabirol's perspective, are simply every created being. In general, it is clear that the constitution of the essence within the compound being is one of the most problematic features of Ibn Gabirol's *Fons vitae* (and possibly also for this reason, Gundissalinus appears unwilling to engage with it in his original works).

In contrast to this shared and common character of matter, form always requires something in which it can subsist. The main difference between matter and form, therefore, is ultimately posited by the complementary functions they perform in relation to each other, namely matter as the bearer of form, form as what is borne by matter. As I have mentioned, the principles of created existence, i.e., matter and form, have a potential being in themselves. This is an extremely problematic claim – a sort of major ontological puzzle, as we shall see in relation to Gundissalinus's discussion of the same doctrinal point he inherited from Ibn Gabirol. How can the union of two *potencies* give an *act*? And how it can be claimed that form actualises matter (PC5), whereas form has no actual being in itself? In other words, the potential being of both matter and form does not respect Aristotle's basic assumption about change, that only what is actual can actualise a potency. Consideration of God's being, which is beyond actuality and potency, does not help in this particular case. Divine will, though, can perhaps be considered as the mover of this dynamic. Distinguished from divine mind and divine essence, God's will is the divine aspect which *unites* matter and form in the first compound (the Intelligence). It is therefore plausible – and consistent

---

36 See Ibn Gabirol, *Fons vitae* 1, ed. Baeumker, 15.9–18; ed. Benedetto, 232.

37 See ibid., ed. Baeumker, 15.15–23; ed. Benedetto, 230.

38 See ibid., ed. Baeumker, 15.25–16.5; ed. Benedetto, 230–32.

158 | CHAPTER THREE

with the later developments of Latin voluntarism as a main feature of *Fons vitae* – to consider divine will as the actualising factor through the form. While matter lies as a subject, form is the medium used by divine will to cause the first compound, a causation that appears to correspond, accordingly, to three logically distinguished moments:

1. divine will impresses the first form into matter, which is totally permeated by it;
2. this joining creates the first compound, which exists in act;
3. matter and form are actualised and exist in act as the compound, not as matter and form.

As a result of this process, matter and form exist *per se* and *in se* inasmuch as they are separated and in potency, while they cease to exist in se and per se once they have an actual existence within the compound, as their aspects. It is a sort of reversal of the traditional consideration of matter and, especially, form. To this peculiarity, it could also be added that the actualisation of the first compound can be interpreted either as a transmission of causality from divine will (supposing that God's will is in act while his being is beyond act and potency) or, perhaps more convincingly, that the first act corresponds to the first created entity, while God is beyond the ontological characteristics of the created universe. If that were the case, further actualisations of the compound would be enacted by the following actualised (and perpetual) hypostases and the growing number of actual beings, through the impression of potential forms into the (now actualised) substrate. However, a process such as this would probably not be sufficiently grounded as to explain the course of natural change and corruptions.

In any case, Ibn Gabirol surely establishes a meaningful bond between form and actual being. They are not identical – form and being are contemporary, as actual being happens when form supervenes on matter, but they shall not be identified.[39] Accordingly, Ibn Gabirol claims that

> we understand the same thing about form that we say about unity, because unity is form, and matter deserved to have being only because of the unity that is sustained in it. It is this that gives it being, because matter without unity did not have being. But matter and unity began to be at the same time, because matter was able to exist only because of unity just

---

39 See Ibn Gabirol, *Fons vitae* 4, ed. Baeumker, 234.17–19; ed. Benedetto, 544.

as it was capable of the property of unity and form only because of unity and form.[40]

The link between form and unity, therefore, appears to be central for the causative dynamic. Ibn Gabirol identifies being and unity (PS1). This identification is complete (or overcomplete) for God, which is absolutely one and utterly being. In contrast with this, the created universe embodies a different ontology by reason of the principle of the simplicity of the cause (PC1): an ontological structure marked by dualities (act/potency, form/matter), which is a mirrored reflection of divine ontological unity. Therefore, the notion of metaphysical unity as analogous to actual being (in creatures) plays the most central role in Ibn Gabirol's created ontology. Moreover, one can distinguish in *Fons vitae* between the following:

> The *form of unity*, which is the universal form and the form constituting the Intelligence (the first hypostasis). It holds together the totality of first matter – which tends to dispersion – constituting the first being in act.
> The *function of unity*, which is performed by every form as the form unifies the essence of matter, making it *one*.[41] Under this consideration, every form is a unity and brings about unity.

While the form of unity gives the grounds for the cosmogonic course of creation, it is the function of unity to cast some light on the conundrum of the actualisation of the compound. The unity of matter and form cannot be resolved into its components, as the compound is something else – it is not a sum of numbers or a mixture of elements. This unity – the central ontological event of the created universe – corresponds to the act of the compound, and it is a function performed by the form. That is the key to the entire dynamic: unity logically precedes actuality. It is the causation of unity, once the form is joined to matter, that causes their actualisation into the compound, as it is only through unity that the compound can come to be, and then exist in act. Therefore, unity and form are some-

40 Ibn Gabirol, *Fons vitae* 5, ed. Baeumker, 272.18–25; ed. Benedetto, 596: "Quod dicimus de unitate, hoc idem intelligimus de forma, quia unitas est forma, et materia non meruit habere esse nisi propter unitatem quae sustinetur in ea; et haec est quae attribuit ei esse, quia materia absque unitate non habebat esse, sed materia et unitas coeperunt esse simul, quia materia non fuit apta esse nisi propter unitatem, sicut non fuit coaptabilis proprietati unitatis et formae nisi propter unitatem et formam." English translation by Laumakis, *The Font of Life*, 223–24. See also *Fons vitae* 5, ed. Baeumker, 271.22–26; ed. Benedetto, 594.

41 Ibn Gabirol, *Fons vitae* 4, ed. Baeumker, 234.29–235.4; ed. Benedetto, 544.

160 | CHAPTER THREE

what coincident, inasmuch as the function of unity can be performed only by the form.[42] As a consequence of this meaningful bond, Ibn Gabirol can say that, whereas form is in potency, actual being must be primarily linked to the form.[43] Form is intimately connected to being and unity. In turn, the main characteristic of matter is its potentiality, by which it can become actual only when it is joined to a form.[44] As a possibility, matter resides eternally in God's essence and wisdom, a mental existence in which matter is accompanied by, but not united to, the form.[45]

As a consequence of this crucial fact, created existence is marked by a desire for unity. Communality of the substrate implies that everything desires to be "one" because matter desires to be united to form and becomes "one" through and with the form.[46] A desire for unity – and, through unity, a desire for existence – is therefore a common feature of the entire universe since its very beginning. It all started with God. Radically different from his creatures, God is the absolute One, the infinite and unchangeable being beyond potency and act ("factor primus non est in potentia nec in effectu.")[47] His ontological completeness and teleological goodness compel every created entity to desire God and then move to receive the forms he provides the universe with.[48] God creates matter and form from nothing – although the principles are already eternally present in God's essence and mind –

42 See ibid., ed. Baeumker, 235.10–15, ed. Benedetto, 544. See also *Fons vitae* 2, ed. Baeumker, 235.18–24; ed. Benedetto, 246.

43 See Ibn Gabirol, *Fons vitae* 5, ed. Baeumker, 272.25–273.3; ed. Benedetto, 596.

44 See ibid., ed. Baeumker, 273.13–23 and 314.20–22; ed. Benedetto, 596–98 and 648.

45 See ibid., ed. Baeumker, 300.4–8; ed. Benedetto, 630: "The being of the first form, namely, to exist by itself in act, is impossible because it has being only together with matter. But this is possible in the intellect and in potency, And in this is found the difference between it and an accident, because an accident is not understood to exist by itself" ("Esse primae formae, scilicet existere per se in actu, est impossibile, quia non habet esse nisi cum materia simul; sed in intellectu et in potentia est possibile. Et in hoc differentia inter ipsam et accidens, quia accidens non intelligitur existens per se.") English translation by Laumakis, *The Font of Life*, 239. See also Ibn Gabirol, *Fons vitae* 5, ed. Baeumker, 274.19–275.3; ed. Benedetto, 598. As possibilities, matter and form are therefore eternal. The former would receive an actual being (it would be created) from God's essence while form is from divine wisdom, which is said to be "the property of the essence" – stressing again a sort of priority of matter to form. See ibid., ed. Baeumker, 333.3–6; ed. Benedetto, 672.

46 See Ibn Gabirol, *Fons vitae* 4, ed. Baeumker, 232.13–17; ed. Benedetto, 540.

47 See Ibn Gabirol, *Fons vitae* 3, ed. Baeumker, 83.17–18; ed. Benedetto, 334. On God's unchangeable perfection, see ibid., ed. Baeumker, 61.4–12; ed. Benedetto, 302.

48 See Ibn Gabirol, *Fons vitae* 5, ed. Baeumker, 319.16–18 and 319.20–320.24; ed. Benedetto, 656.

Rooting Reality: Gundissalinus and Ibn Gabirol | 161

and unites them through his will.[49] Indeed, divine will is the "provider of forms" (*largitor formarum*), the causal mover of the cosmogonic process that, as well as providing forms, also gives being, goodness, and unity to the entire universe.[50]

At the beginning, divine will joins the entirety of matter with the totality of the universal form.[51] That is the reason why matter is called the substrate of everything, as the most general of all genera (*genus generalissimum*), which is progressively specified by further forms.[52] Ontologically, the universal form is said to be the form of unity, i.e., the instance of unity which is closest to God's complete oneness. Cosmologically, though, the universal form is the form of the Intelligence, the first hypostatic being. The plurality of the forms that would come to be are "one" within it. Moreover, Ibn Gabirol makes clear that the totality of first matter is used for the creation and therefore becomes the hypostatic Intelligence. As a consequence, the form of the Intelligence is the universal form, which is *per essentiam* the form of every created being, the whole universe which is spiritually one in it.[53] After the Intelligence, every other spiritual (and hypostatic) substance – rational, sensible, and vegetative Souls, and finally nature – derives its being from the formal radiation of the preceding hypostasis.[54] Through this dynamic of secondary causation, the immediate effect of God's causality is limited to and realised by the creation of the Intelligence, the first substance from which the psychological hypostases come to be.

These substances imitate the causality of their cause. As they are caused by formal irradiation, so too they radiate their own formal contents downwards, causing a simple substance below, until the sensible world is constituted.[55] This process of causation is marked by a formal transmission which does not impoverish in any way the simple substance radiating its contents.[56] This progressively

49 See Ibn Gabirol, *Fons vitae* 4, ed. Baeumker, 226.20–227.22; ed. Benedetto, 532–34.

50 See Ibn Gabirol, *Fons vitae* 5, ed. Baeumker, 317.6–12; ed. Benedetto, 652. Using a striking metaphor, Ibn Gabirol describes the action of divine will in terms of a writer using a tablet (matter) to carve his writing (form). See Ibn Gabirol, *Fons vitae* 5, ed. Baeumker, 326.23–25; ed. Benedetto, 664.

51 Ibid., ed. Baeumker, 267.6–24; ed. Benedetto, 588–90.

52 See Ibn Gabirol, *Fons vitae* 4, ed. Baeumker, 231.21–232.30; ed. Benedetto, 540–42.

53 See Ibn Gabirol, *Fons vitae* 5, ed. Baeumker, 279.20–281.25 and 281.26–283.25; ed. Benedetto, 606–10.

54 For instance, nature is caused by the vegetative soul, its proximate higher spiritual substance. See Ibn Gabirol, *Fons vitae* 3, ed. Baeumker, 184.12–185.26; ed. Benedetto, 472–74.

55 Ibn Gabirol, *Fons vitae* 3, ed. Baeumker, 113.17–23; ed. Benedetto, 378.

56 Ibid., ed. Baeumker, 106.9–11; ed. Benedetto, 368. This transmission is understandable in terms of a gift from a lover to the beloved, in which the lover does not suffer any loss. Spiritual substances radiate their powers and rays rather than their essences, and from their rays the whole universe is instituted. See ibid., ed. Baeumker, 196.24–27; ed. Benedetto, 490.

multiplied interaction of formal radiations into the substance below which, in turn, is an actualised matter receiving a plurality of forms, corresponds to the divine *effluxio* that establishes the universe and through which God manifests himself.[57]

Since every causation is performed by forms (*per* PC5) and forms can only act upon matter, it is necessary that everything receiving the divine *effluxio* after the creation of the hylomorphic principles has matter (*per* PC4). As a consequence, Ibn Gabirol's cosmology is grounded upon universal hylomorphism, as it describes a universe in which matter is the limit of the cosmos both upwards and downwards.[58] Composed of matter and form, spiritual substances are said to be "simple" only in comparison to what follows them.[59] Having been created by God, who is purely One (hierarchically following PC1), their hylomorphic composition was necessary. The effect, indeed, cannot be identical to its cause, and can only be similar to it in some derived way, as claimed by PC3. As God is the One, the similarity which the effect receives is a unity which is united (i.e., compositional) and thus non-simple. It is the unity given by the union of matter and form, under the compositional terms described above.[60] Below the spiritual substances, the form of corporeity is borne by the universal spiritual matter – the

57 Ibid., ed. Baeumker, 113.26–114.6; ed. Benedetto, 378: "In this way, we will know the diffusion of the first power and of the first action in all the things that exist, because the powers of the simple substances and the powers of absolutely all the things that exist are infused into and penetrate through the whole. So much the more is the power of the first maker – may his name be exalted! For this reason, it was said that the first maker is in all the things that exist and nothing can exist without him." ("Et secundum hunc modum sciemus diffusionem virtutis primae et actionis primae in omnibus quae sunt, quia vires substantiarum simplicium et omnino vires omnium eorum quae sunt infusae sunt et penetrantes per totum: quanto magis virtus factoris primi, excelsum nomen eius. Et ideo dictum est quod factor primus est in omnibus quae sunt et nihil sine eo esse potest.") English translation by Laumakis, *The Font of Life*, 131.

58 See Ibn Gabirol, *Fons vitae* 3, ed. Baeumker, 106.20–28 and 106.19–20; ed. Benedetto, 368. Although matter and form are the universal constituents of created reality as such, this fact does not entail that spiritual and corporeal substances have an identical existence. The main difference between the two ontological realms is the active causality of the simple substances and the causal passivity of the corporeal beings. On the one hand, the differences among spiritual substances are due to the degradation of the hylomorphic compounds and the causal irradiation of every spiritual substance below itself. On the other hand, bodily substances are held by the *thickness* of the degraded matter, which is so corpulent and dense that it prevents bodies from performing any transmission of form (*comunicatio formalis*). See ibid., ed. Baeumker, 109,29.29–111.26 and 107.10–108.12; ed. Benedetto, 372–74 and 370.

59 See Ibn Gabirol, *Fons vitae* 4, ed. Baeumker, 218.19–24; ed. Benedetto, 522.

60 See Ibn Gabirol, *Fons vitae* 4, ed. Baeumker, 222.24–28, ed. Benedetto, 528.

last aspect of nature – which is the ontological boundary between corporeal and spiritual realms. As for corporeity, we have already seen that it corresponds to the body as such at a lower level, which is then informed by the elemental forms, giving origin to the properly natural world.

While the original Arabic text might have presented a different scenario, the hypostatic cosmology expounded in the Latin version of *Fons vitae* can be summarised by the scheme on page 164.

A fundamental aspect of the cosmogonic dynamic described by Ibn Gabirol is the gradual thickening of matter. From the initial detachment from God, a sort of degradation is implicitly caused, a deterioration which is direct for matter and indirect for the caused compound. Descending through the layers of reality, matter becomes gradually *thicker* and *more corpulent*, like the clear water that pours from its source and becomes muddy when flowing into a pond, following Ibn Gabirol's metaphor.[61] As a consequence of this thickening, the causality of form becomes less effective, as the thickness of matter makes it extremely hard for forms to penetrate it – as a light far from its source which encounters a dark and dense object. According to the metaphor of light, Ibn Gabirol observes,

> The same thing is true about light that is diffused in hyle. The reason is that the more hyle descends, it is drawn together and is made bodily, and its middle parts prevent its last parts from being penetrated completely by light ... The same thing should be said about the light that is infused in matter. The reason is that the purer, clearer, and freer from matter it is, the more perfect and stronger it will be. Similarly, it is also true that the more it is mixed with the clearer part of matter, the more it will preserve its own species, and it is stronger and firmer than the light that is mixed with the thicker part of matter ... It will consequently be established that the change that occurs in the light diffused in matter is only because of matter, not because of the light in itself.[62]

---

61 See Ibn Gabirol, *Fons vitae* 2, ed. Baeumker, 62.9–63.24; ed. Benedetto, 304–6.

62 Ibn Gabirol, *Fons vitae* 4, ed. Baeumker, 243.18–245.4; ed. Benedetto, 556–58: "Similiter et lumen quod est diffusivum in hyle; hoc est quia hyle, quo magis descenderit, constringitur et corporatur, et partes eius mediae prohibebunt ultimas partes perfecte penetrari lumine ... Similiter est dicendum de lumine quod est infusum in materia, hoc est quia, quo fuerit purius et clarius et liberius a materia, erit perfectius et fortius. Similiter etiam, quo magis fuerit commixtum clariori parti materiae, amplius servabit speciem suam, et est fortius et firmius quam illud quod est commixtum crassiori parti eius ... Et secundum hanc considerationem debet ut diminutio luminis substantiarum et diversitas non sit propter lumen in se, sed propter materiam, quia est corporalis comparatione formae, sicut iam praedictum est." English translation by Laumakis, *The Font of Life*, 207.

CHAPTER THREE

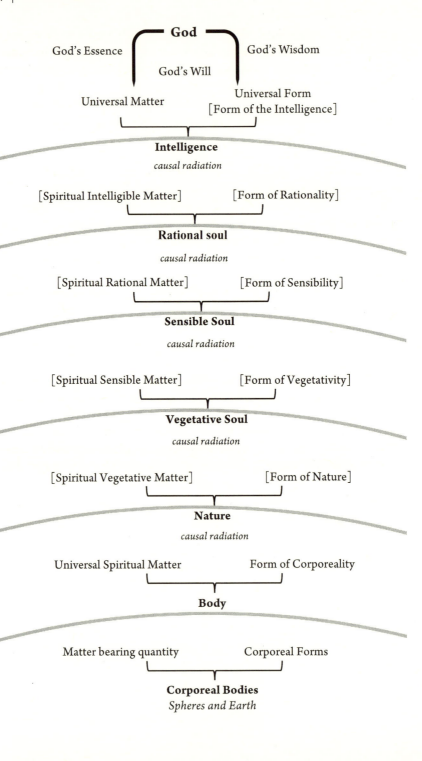

This decaying process marks the origin of the ontological differences among the levels of reality. The subtlest matter and the most perfect form bring about the strongest compound – Intelligence.[63] In contrast, the thickest matter and the feeblest form cause the weakest compound – corporeal being, the last level of existence. Efficiency of form, indeed, is intimately related to matter: throughout the different stages of formal encounters with matter, the first form is divided and multiplied into a plurality of forms.[64]

Hylomorphism Without Act and Potency

Ibn Gabirol's *Fons vitae* is the most important source of Dominicus Gundissalinus's metaphysics. This pre-eminent role can be appreciated from the first treatise written by Gundissalinus, *De unitate et uno*. The discussion on metaphysical unity expounded therein is developed in a way that follows Ibn Gabirol's doctrines closely, especially those elaborated in connection with his discussion of ontological duality and hylomorphism. Gundissalinus's primary interest in Ibn Gabirol appears to be centred on the tension between God's absolute oneness and the derived unity of creatures, which is gained through the union of matter and form.

Also for Gundissalinus's *De unitate et uno*, one of the fundamental traits of matter and form is their mutual ontological reciprocity. Notwithstanding a clear priority of form, they can exist in act only when they have joined one another in their compound, as "there is no being, in fact, except from the conjunction of matter and form, and the philosophers describe [being], thus, saying that 'being is the existence of form into matter.'"[65] For Gundissalinus, created being, therefore, is always the result of a union of matter and form. This is the position held by the "philosophers," as Gundissalinus claims in a sort of authoritative reference which, however, does not mention the name of the philosophers he is referring to. As often happens, Gundissalinus is alluding to Ibn Gabirol, or better, to those people that "described being, saying that being is the existence of form in matter," as Ibn Gabirol claims in *Fons vitae*.[66] In both *De unitate* and *Fons vitae*,

---

63 See Ibn Gabirol, *Fons vitae* 4, ed. Baeumker, 244.5–7; ed. Benedetto, 556.

64 Ibid., ed. Baeumker, 246.4–8; ed. Benedetto, 560.

65 Gundissalinus, *De unitate et uno*, ed. María Jesús Soto Bruna and Concepción Alonso Del Real (Pamplona, 2015), 104.6–106.1: "Esse igitur non est nisi ex coniunctione formae cum materia. Unde philosophi sic describunt illud dicentes: 'esse est existentia formae in materia.'"

66 Ibn Gabirol, *Fons vitae* 5, ed. Baeumker, 274.18–19; ed. Benedetto, 598: "propter hoc descripserunt esse dicentes, quod esse est existentia formae in materia." English translation by Laumakis, *The Font of Life*, 224–25.

166 | CHAPTER THREE

the claim of the "philosophers" aims at justifying the emergence of actual being from the union of form with matter. The emergence of actual existence, though, requires a unifying factor which can hold the hylomorphic compound together. Logically prior to that, unity is also required by matter, as it intrinsically tends to be dispersed and multiplied. In fact,

> considering that matter has being only through union with its form, while only unity can keep the form united to the matter, therefore matter requires unity in order to become one in itself and receive [its] being. Matter is indeed contrary to unity, for matter by itself flows away and its nature is to be multiplied, divided, and scattered, whereas unity holds together, unites, and brings it together. For this reason, it is necessary for matter to be held together by unity, so that it does not divide or scatter itself. Indeed, anything requiring something else to become one, cannot become one through itself.[67]

The emergence of actual existence in created beings, therefore, is accompanied by the accomplishment of two ontological requirements – i.e., to hold matter's tendency to division and to keep together the composed being – brought about by by a unifying factor. In *De unitate* this unifying factor is the form of unity. One of the peculiarities of this short treatise is, indeed, that it focuses almost exclusively on the first hylomorphic union (first matter + form of unity). In Ibn Gabirol the unifying factor is performed by two agents – on the one hand, by the form of unity, which unifies both matter and the hylomorphic compound as soon as it has joined matter, on the other hand, by every form as it expresses a function of unity as regards to matter (and the compound). In Gundissalinus's *De unitate* this process is sensibly simplified. Also when he mentions "unity," Gundissalinus describes how the first form joins the whole of matter enacting its unifying function throughout the further informations of matter. By this point of view, the main focus of Gundissalinus's *De unitate* appears to aim at providing an account of how a *second substrate* was created by God through a union of matter and form.

The source of Gundissalinus's account of this ontological process is Ibn Gabirol's *Fons vitae*. Nevertheless, Gundissalinus does not appear to accept the

---

67 Gundissalinus, *De unitate et uno*, ed. Soto Bruna and Alonso Del Real, 112.3–114.2: "quia materia non habet esse nisi per unitionem sui cum forma, formam autem non tenet unitam cum materia nisi unitas, ideo materia eget unitate ad uniendum se et ad suscipiendum esse. Materia enim contraria est unitati, eo quod materia per se diffluit et de natura sua habet multiplicari, dividi et spargi; unitas vero retinet, unit et colligit. Ac per hoc, ne materia dividatur et spargatur, necesse est, ut ab unitate retineatur. Quidquid autem eget alio ad uniendum se, non unitur per se."

whole of Ibn Gabirol's ontology or his main metaphysical principles. *De unitate et uno* does *not* discuss the dynamic of act and potency (the term "act" is quoted only once in the treatise, while there is not a single occurrence of "potency"). Accordingly, Ibn Gabirol's principle of formal actualisation (PC5) is used in a rather different sense. When Gundissalinus claims that "being is the existence of form into matter," it is surely possible to assume that Gundissalinus thought that form had a potential being, as in *Fons vitae* and his own later works. But there is no passage upon which such a supposition can be grounded and, accordingly, one could also assume that Gundissalinus's doctrine of the potentiality of form was a later development of his reflection. Moreover, Gundissalinus surely accepts Ibn Gabirol's principle of the identification of unity and being (PS1). This principle, though, is expressed by Gundissalinus through a sort of axiom he receives from Boethius ("whatever exists, therefore, exists because it is one") and is developed in a clear reference to actual being ("[a being] is what it is as long as unity is in it, and when it ceases to be one, it ceases to be what it is"). But the identification of unity and actual being, although referred to the hylomorphic union rather than to the form of unity, still does not provide any sufficient basis for claiming that *De unitate* acknowledged a potential status for forms. Finally, it seems that beside PC5 and PS1, the only further Gabirolian principles accepted by Gundissalinus at this stage of his career were the principle of the simplicity of the cause (PC1) and, of course, the principle of the ontological reciprocity of matter and form (PS2), upon which universal hylomorphism is based. Any other fundamental principle is left aside, at least temporarily.

Notwithstanding these limitations, *Fons vitae* plays a fundamental role in Gundissalinus's *De unitate et uno*. Gundissalinus's overall description of the cosmological and ontological course of first matter substantively depends on Ibn Gabirol's account, starting with his discussion of the unifying dynamic in which matter intrinsically tends towards dispersion and is opposed to the unifying factor performed by the form of unity. As has been abundantly discussed above, the opposition between multiplicity and unity as the characteristics, respectively, of matter and form is a central aspect of Ibn Gabirol's metaphysics. The ontological dynamic developed between *materia retenta* and *forma retinens* is also the precise object of a question by the student to his teacher, asking,

S: Why is matter preserved, and why does form preserve?
T: Because form is the unity acted upon by the first unity, which preserves everything and in which everything exists. Because unity unites a thing and joins it together so that it is neither multiplied nor dispersed, it is necessary for this reason that it is what preserves matter. But because it is the nature of

168 | CHAPTER THREE

matter to be multiplied and divided, it must be united and preserved and gathered by unity.[68]

It should be noted, however, that while Gundissalinus's discussion of the ontology of created beings relies completely on Ibn Gabirol, his main interest does not reside on matter and form in themselves, but crucially on the unifying process governing the coming to existence of a second substrate and its gradual course into multiplicity. As I have shown, unity is the key to the very *emergence of actuality* within the created universe in Ibn Gabirol's ontology. The character of *unity into duality* proper to created beings is the main term expressing the ontological difference between God's being (beyond act and potency, utterly one, other than matter and form) and created being (marked by a duality of act/potency and matter/form). This central point is only partially developed in *De unitate et uno*. A constant recourse to Ibn Gabirol's text is mainly focused on the first *union* of matter and the form of unity, leaving aside their *actualisation*. Accordingly, only the hylomorphic duality of created being is addressed by Gundissalinus in his first treatise. Unity is the key to existence – unity is existence. As God is the absolute One, everything comes to be from him and existentially moves toward him. In fact,

> since the Creator is the true One, then the things he established – each one of them – received from him, as a gift, to be one. As a consequence, a thing which receives its being from him is one, and therefore, the movement of every substance is toward and through the One, and none of the existing things desire to be many. To the contrary, all of them, desiring to be, desire to be one.[69]

Created union is caused by the complete unity of God. For this reason, every creature desires God and moves toward him. Although this position of God as

---

68 Ibn Gabirol, *Fons vitae* 5, ed. Baeumker, 305.23–306.3; ed. Benedetto, 638: "D. Cur materia est retenta, et forma retinens? M. Quia forma est unitas patiens ab unitate prima quae totum retinet et in qua totum existit, et quia unitas adunit rem et coniungit, ne multiplicetur nec dispergatur: ideo oportet ut sit retentrix materiae. Sed quia natura materiae est multiplicari et dividi, debet uniri ab unitate et retenta esse et collecta." English translation by Laumakis, *The Font of Life*, 242.

69 Gundissalinus, *De unitate et uno*, ed. Soto Bruna and Alonso Del Real, 110.1–5: "Quia enim creator vere unus est, ideo rebus, quas condidit in hoc numero, dedit, ut unaquaeque habeat esse una. Ac per hoc, quia ex quo res habet esse, una est: ideo motus omnium substantiarum est ad unum et propter unum; et nihil eorum, quae sunt, appetit esse multa, sed omnia, sicut appetunt esse, sic et unum esse."

absolute oneness is a distinctive trait of the Neoplatonic tradition – and therefore, it is shared by many authors of the four linguistic groups of the Mediterranean basin in which that tradition was developed – the source of Gundissalinus's discussion is again *Fons vitae*. Ibn Gabirol refers, throughout the five books of his work, to God's complete unity and the causative process through which he establishes the universe. The intimate and yet unidirectional bond between creatures and creator can be understood by an examination of created reality, and

> a sign of this is that the motion of everything moving is only to receive form, and form is only an impression from the One. The One, however, is goodness. The motion of everything, therefore, comes about only because of goodness, which is the One. A sign of this, however, is that none of the things that exist desires to be many but all things desire to be one. All things, therefore, desire unity.[70]

For both Ibn Gabirol and Gundissalinus, this desire for unity and existence is fulfilled by the endowment of forms, forms which are impressed into matter. Progressive unions of matter and forms establish different species of beings, hierarchically ordered. The entire universe is caused by this dynamic of information of matter. The hierarchical order among creatures, by which some are spiritual and perpetual while others are corporeal and transient, also implies that some differentiating factor is in place. Otherwise, if spiritual and corporeal beings were both composed of the same components (matter and form), there would be no justification for why some beings have a stable being while others are subject to corruption. In other words, what is the factor governing and causing the ontological shift from spirituality to corporeity, from perpetuity to corruption?

Also in this case, Gundissalinus addresses this crucial question in a rather Gabirolian fashion. God is the source of unity and existence, the cause of both the material substrate and the form of unity. The causation of the universe, though, has a vertical progression. It is an emanation which is directed downwards through a gradual detachment from the origin of matter and form. Distancing themselves more and more from God, matter and form interact in different ways.

---

70 Ibn Gabirol, *Fons vitae* 5, ed. Baeumker, 317.6–12; ed. Benedetto, 652: "Signus huius est quod motus omnis mobilis non est nisi ad recipiendum formam; et forma non est nisi impressio ab uno. Unus autem est bonitas. Ergo motus omnis rei non est nisi propter bonitatem, quae unus est. Signum autem huius est quod nihil eorum quae sunt appetit esse multa, sed omnia appetunt esse unum; ergo omnia appetunt unitatem." English translation by Laumakis, *The Font of Life*, 248.

170 | CHAPTER THREE

While the power of forms remains unaltered, its action upon matter is less effective, as matter becomes thicker, more corpulent, and contracted in its detachment from its cause. As a consequence,

> being furthest from the first unity, [this matter] is thick, corpulent, and compact, and due to its thickness and largeness, [this matter] is opposed to the superior substance, which is subtle and simple: indeed, the latter is the subject of the beginning and the start of unity, while the former is the subject of the end and the extremity of unity.[71]

Spissa et, corpulenta et constricta, matter is not able to completely receive the unifying power of the form in the lower levels of reality. For this reason, corporeal hylomorphic unions are less persistent and also subject to corruption.[72] Gundissalinus further explains this point through an intriguing analogy between form and sunlight:

> Form, indeed, is like light: for just as a thing is seen on account of light, so too cognition and knowledge of the things are provided by the form, and not by matter. This light, though, is brighter in some things and darker in others, depending on whether the matter in which it is infused comes to be brighter or darker. The more sublime matter is, the subtler it will be, and completely penetrated by light: consequently, that substance will be wiser and more perfect, such as the Intelligence and the Rational Soul. And on the contrary, the lower matter is, the thicker and darker it will be, not completely penetrated by light. As has been said already, the more matter descends, [the more] it is made compact, thick, and corpulent, and its middle parts block the last ones from being perfectly penetrated by light. It is impossible, indeed, for light to penetrate the second part as much as [it does] the first; nor does as much light reach the third part as reaches the middle part, and so on, little by little, down to the lowest part, in which the light is weakened, for it is furthest away from the source of light. Nonetheless, as has been said, this does not happen on account of the light in itself, but on account of the great density and obscurity of matter in itself. Similarly, when the sunlight is mixed with the dark air,

71 Gundissalinus, *De unitate et uno*, ed. Soto Bruna and Alonso Del Real, 122.4–8: "Quae quia a prima unitate remotissima est, ideo spissa et, corpulenta et constricta est, et propter spissitudinem et grossitudinem suam opposita est substantiae superiori, quae est subtilis et simplex, quoniam illa est subiectum principii et initii unitatis, haec vero est subiectum finis et extremitatis unitatis."

72 See ibid., 118.1–8.

it lacks the power [that it has] when it is mixed with bright air; and similarly, the whiteness of a very thin white cloth is occluded by the abundance of blackness when it is worn by a black body. Or again, similarly if three or more glass windows are set up in order one after another [and] perpendicularly to the sunlight, it is ascertained with certitude that the second [window] receives less light that the first, and the third less than the second [window], and up to the last one there is a diminution of light which is not due to the light itself, but to the distance of the glass windows from the light. In the same way, the light of the form of unity which is infused into matter becomes weak and dark while descending [through its degrees], as the light which passes through the first of these [windows] is rather different from [the light passing through] the middle one, and [that passing through] the middle [one is different] from [that passing through] the last one.[73]

As sunlight illuminates different things in different ways according to the subject of its filtration, so too the form establishes different kinds of beings according to the subject of its ontological inherence.

---

73 Ibid., 128.5–134.10: "Forma enim est quasi lumen, eo quod sicut per lumen res videtur, sic per formam cognitio et scientia rei habetur, non per materiam; sed hoc lumen in quibusdam est clarius, in quibusdam vero obscurius, prout materia cui infunditur fuerit clarior vel obscurior. Quo enim materia fuerit sublimior, fit subtilior et penetratur tota a lumine; et ideo substantia ipsa fit sapientior et perfectior sicut intelligentia et rationalis anima. Et e contrario, quo materia fuerit inferior, fit spissior et obscurior et non ita tota penetratur a lumine. Quo magis enim materia descendit, sicut iam dictum est, constringitur et spissatur et corpulentatur et partes eius mediae prohibent ultimas perfecte penetrari a lumine. Non enim est possibile ut tantum luminis penetret partem secundam, quantum primam, nec ad tertiam tantum luminis pervenit, quantum ad mediam. Et sic paulatim donec perveniatur, usque ad partem infimam. Quae, quia remotissima est a fonte luminis, lumen debilitatur in illa. Nec tamen hoc fit sicut praedictum est propter lumen in se, sed propter multam densitatem et obscuritatem materiae in se. Quemadmodum lumen solis cum admiscitur tenebroso aeri, non est illius virtutis, cuius est admixtum claro aeri, vel quemadmodum pannus albus tenuissimus, cum induitur a corpore nigro occultatur candor eius propter abundantiam nigredinis; vel quemadmodum si tres vel plures fenestrae vitreae una post aliam recte contra radium solis disponantur in ordine, constat siquidem quod secunda minus recipit luminis quam prima, et tertia minus quam secunda, et sic usque ad ultimam fit defectus luminis non propter lumen in se, sed propter elongationem fenestrae vitreae a lumine; ita et lumen formae unitatis, quod infusum est materiae, descendendo fit debile et obscurum, ita ut primum eius multum discrepet a medio et medium ab ultimo." Gundissalinus also uses Ibn Gabirol's metaphor of matter's degradation as analogous to the flowing of a river from its spring. See, for instance, Ibn Gabirol, *Fons vitae* 5, ed. Baeumker 310.14–23; ed. Benedetto, 644. See also Gundissalinus, *De unitate et uno*, ed. Soto Bruna and Alonso Del Real, 122.10–124.4, which is derived from Ibn Gabirol, *Fons vitae* 2, ed. Baeumker, 63.7–12; ed. Benedetto, 306.

172 | CHAPTER THREE

After what can be considered as a short reference to Augustine's doctrine of illumination, Gundissalinus's discussion immediately leaves gnoseological aspects aside to focus on the cosmological process alluded to by the sunlight/form analogy. As sunlight is said to be clearer or cloudier depending on the substrate receiving it, so too form acts in different ways according to the different states of its subject. Where matter is thinner, form can penetrate the substrate completely, realising a perfect hylomorphic union which is proper to perpetual spiritual beings. On the other hand, in those regions of existence where matter is thicker, form cannot entirely penetrate the substrate, and the hylomorphic union is weak and subject to separation – i.e., corruption. As a consequence, the entities that are furthest away from the source of existence receive a form/light which has a weakened effect in them ("lumen debilitatur in illa").

This weakening is caused by the thickening of matter and not by form/light itself. Gundissalinus argues this point through conspicuous examples of differences in sunlight depending on its reflection on clear/dark air and white/black cloths. The most intriguing example proposed by him is that of three windows perpendicularly disposed through which a ray of light passes. The power of this ray is progressively weakened when it goes through the second window, and even more when passing through the third window. In a similar fashion, the *efficiency* of the form of unity (not its power) upon matter changes as the latter becomes thicker and darker in its progressive detachment from God, unable to be completely joined to form. Throughout the process of material information, therefore, the form of unity remains unaltered while matter changes.

Once again, Gundissalinus's discussion of the analogy between form and light is derived from Ibn Gabirol's *Fons vitae*. Specifically, Gundissalinus applies to the form of unity some aspects of Ibn Gabirol's description of the causality of spiritual substances and their coming to be. After having introduced the problem concerning the origin of spiritual substances, Ibn Gabirol claims that

> the same thing is true about light that is diffused in *hyle*. The reason is that the more *hyle* descends, it is drawn together and is made bodily, and its middle parts prevent its last parts from being penetrated completely by light. The same thing should be said about all of the parts of matter. The reason is that it is not possible that as much light penetrates the second part as the first part or that as much light reaches the third part as the second part. The same thing should be said about the other parts, until the lower part of them is reached. For the middle parts prevent the light from penetrating into the others, and the light is then weakened because of matter, not because of itself. The certitude of this, however, is as follows: When a thing is purer, it will preserve its own species more strongly and more clearly until, when it is

Rooting Reality: Gundissalinus and Ibn Gabirol | 173

mixed with something else, that other thing acts on it and changes it from the purity and clarity in which it existed. The same thing should be said about the light that is infused in matter. The reason is that the purer, dearer, and freer from matter it is, the more perfect and stronger it will be. Similarly, it is also true that the more it is mixed with the clearer part of matter, the more it will preserve its own species, and it is stronger and firmer than the light that is mixed with the thicker part of matter. It will consequently be established that the change that occurs in the light diffused in matter is only because of matter, not because of the light in itself. This is similar to the light of the sun, when it is mixed with darkness, or to a thin white cloth, when it is put on by a black body, because its brightness will be hidden because of the abundance of blackness. Or it is similar to light penetrating three panes of glass, that is, because the second pane of glass has less light than the first, and the third has less than the second. It is known that this is not because of the weakness of the light, but because of the panes of glass hindering the penetration of the light, because they are thick bodies. According to this consideration, it is necessary that the lessening and diversity of the light of substances is not because of the light in itself, but because of matter. For it is corporeal in comparison to form, as was already said.[74]

---

74 Ibn Gabirol, *Fons vitae* 4, ed. Baeumker, 243.18–244.25; ed. Benedetto, 556–58: "Similiter et lumen quod est diffusum in hyle; hoc est quia hyle, quo magis descenderit, constringitur et corporatur, et partes eius mediae prohibebunt ultimas partes perfecte penetrari lumine. Similiter dicendum est de omnibus partibus materiae, hoc est quia non est possibile ut tantum luminis penetret partem secundam quantum primam, nec ad tertiam tantum luminis pervenit quantum ad mediam; similiter dicendum est de ceteris partibus, donec perveniatur ad partem inferiorem ex illis, quia partes mediae prohibent lumen penetrare alias et lumen debilitatur tunc propter materiam, non propter se. – Certitudo autem huius haec est, quia cum res fuerit pura magis, servabit speciem suam fortius et manifestius, donec cum alio commixta illud agat in ea et permutet a puritate et claritate in qua erat. Similiter dicendum est de lumine quod est infusum in materia, hoc est quia, quo fuerit purius et clarius et liberius a materia, erit perfectius et fortius. Similiter etiam, quo magis fuerit commixtum clariori parti materiae, amplius servabit speciem suam, et est fortius et firmius quam illud quod est commixtum crassiori parti eius. – Ac per hoc constabit quod mutatio quae cadit in lumen diffusum in materia non est nisi propter materiam, non propter lumen in se; ad similitudinem luminis solis, quando periscetur tenebris, aut panni subtilis albi, quando induitur a corpore nigro, quia occultabitur candor propter abundantiam nigredinis; vel ad similitudinem luminis penetrantis tres vitreas, scilicet quia vitrum secundum minus habet luminis quam primum, et tertium minus quam secundum; et constat quod non est hoc ex debilitate luminis, sed propter vitra prohibentia penetrationem luminis, quia sunt corpora spissa. Et secundum hanc considerationem debet ut diminuitio luminis substantiarum et diversitas non sit propter lumen in se, sed propter materiam, quia est corporalis comparatione formae, sicut iam praedictum est." English translation by Laumakis, *The Font of Life*, 207.

174 | CHAPTER THREE

A comparison between the two textual excerpts from *De unitate* and *Fons vitae* shows an overall dependence of Gundissalinus's discussion on Ibn Gabirol. Both texts present a consistent description of the progressive weakening of the form/light efficiency and the three examples of differences in sunlight. It is worth noting that, while quoting it, Gundissalinus slightly modifies the text of *Fons vitae*. On the one hand, Gundissalinus condenses the central section of Ibn Gabirol's passage in a quotation that is not very accurate. On the other hand, the three examples are discussed by Gundissalinus in a much clearer fashion. In particular, the third example displays a noticeable degree of textual insertion:

Fons vitae	*De unitate et uno*
"Or it is similar to **light penetrating three panes of glass** (*vitrae*), that is, **because the second pane of glass has less light than the first, and the third has less than the second.** It is known that this is not because of the weakness of the light, but because of the panes of glass hindering the penetration of the light, because they are thick bodies."[75]	"Or again, **similarly if three or more glass** windows (*fenestrae vitrae*) are set up in order one after another [and] perpendicular to the sunlight, it is ascertained that **the second [window] receives less light that the first, and the third less than the second** [window], and up to the last one there is a diminution of light which is not due to the light itself, but to the distance of the glass windows from the light."[76]

Gundissalinus clarifies that the three windows must be "one after another and perpendicular to the sunlight" ("una post aliam recte contra radium solis"). He also explains in detail that the differences in the light are caused by the distance of the three windows from the source of light and not by the tripling of the

75 Ibn Gabirol, *Fons vitae* 4, ed. Baeumker, 244.18–22; ed. Benedetto, 558: " ... **vel ad similitudinem luminis penetrantis tres vitreas**, scilicet quia **vitrum secundum minus habet luminis quam primum, et tertium minus quam secundum**; et constat quod non est hoc ex debilitate luminis, sed propter vitra prohibentia penetrationem luminis, quia sunt corpora spissa."

76 Gundissalinus, *De unitate et uno*, ed. Soto Bruna and Alonso Del Real, 134.3–8: " ... **vel quemadmodum si tres vel plures** fenestrae **vitreae** una post aliam recte contra radium solis disponantur in ordine, constat siquidem quod **secunda minus recipit luminis quam prima, et tertia minus quam secunda**, et sic usque ad ultimam fit defectus luminis non propter lumen in se, sed propter elongationem fenestrae vitreae a lumine." English translation revised.

reflecting surface making it thicker, which is the point made by Ibn Gabirol. Should we suppose that Gundissalinus conducted an experiment based on the description in *Fons vitae*? This does not seem to be the case. On the contrary, this is one of the many cases in which Gundissalinus interpolates material into the text he is quoting, aiming at pointing out and clarifying the aspects he thought would be more relevant to his exposition.

Ibn Gabirol also has a fundamental influence on the cosmology presented by *De unitate*. While there is no specific section dealing with cosmology, some scattered passages of *De unitate* undoubtedly refer to the hypostatic derivation of the universe, whose source is Ibn Gabirol. The first union of matter and form causes the first being, which is Intelligence. Since "every created thing must be completely different from what has created it"[77] (i.e., PC1), this first creature is completely different from its creator, and yet its unity is almost absolute in comparison to the entities following it. These are three hypostatic Souls (the rational, sensible, and vegetative Soul), and Nature, through a progressive diversification (= multiplication) of being. In fact,

> in the highest things, indeed, matter is informed by the form of Intelligence; and further on, by the form of the rational Soul; while afterwards by the form of the sensible Soul. Then, below it, [it is informed] by the form of the vegetative Soul, and after that, by the form of Nature; while finally in the lowest things [matter is informed] by the form of the body. Consequently, [we must assume that] all this does not happen for the diversity of the power of the agent, but for the aptitude of the matter receiving [it].[78]

Presenting all the hypostases of Ibn Gabirol's chain of being, this excerpt makes clear that, in his first encounter with the doctrines of the Jewish philosopher, Gundissalinus also accepts his cosmology. This is made even more clear by another passage of *De unitate* which alludes to the characteristic *matter bearing quantity* (i.e., the lowest level of hylomorphic reality), stating that

> since the unity subsisting in the matter of Intelligence is the unity of simplicity, however, the unity subsisting in the matter of the Soul – which is

77 See Gundissalinus, *De unitate et uno*, ed. Soto Bruna and Alonso Del Real, 116.14: "omne creatum omnino diversum est a quo creatum est."

78 Ibid., 128.1–5: "Quia igitur materia in supremis formata est forma intelligentiae, deinde forma rationalis animae, postea vero forma animae sensibilis, deinde inferius forma animae vegetabilis, deinde forma naturae, ad ultimum autem in infimis forma corporis, hoc non accidit ex diversitate virtutis agentis, sed ex aptitudine materiae suscipientis."

176 | CHAPTER THREE

below it [Intelligence] – necessarily grows and multiplies [itself], and so change and diversity happen to it. Unity, then, is increased and multiplied little by little while descending from what is superior through every degree of the inferior matter, until it reaches the substance which bears quantity – that is, the substance of this world.[79]

This excerpt is a direct quotation from *Fons vitae*, where Ibn Gabirol claims that

because the unity subsisting in the matter of the intelligence is the unity of simplicity, according to what was said, it was necessary for the unity subsisting in the matter of the Soul to be augmented and multiplied, because the order of this unity is below the order of the unity subsisting in the matter of the intelligence. It was, therefore, necessary for this unity to be augmented and multiplied, and change and diversity come to it among the other orders of matter sustaining it according to the descent of the level of matter to what is lower and of its separation from what is higher, until it arrives at the matter that sustains quantity, that is, the substance of this world.[80]

Gundissalinus's reference to the *matter bearing quantity* seems to certify his most complete adherence to Ibn Gabirol's cosmology – also an acceptance of controversial substances, like the *matter bearing quantity*, posited in a middle position between the traditional hypostases and the corporeal world. This is a sign of the high esteem Gundissalinus already had for Ibn Gabirol at the beginning of his reflection. The main and almost exclusive source of *De unitate et uno* is indeed Ibn Gabirol. In *Fons vitae*, Gundissalinus found a way to root reality in a *hylomorphic duality acting as a unity*. The ontological difference

---

79 Ibid., 120.9–122.3: "Sed quia unitas subsistens in materia intelligentiae est unitas simplicitatis, ideo necessario unitas subsistens in materia animae, quia infra eam est, crescit et multiplicatur et accidit ei mutatio et diversitas; et sic paulatim descendendo a superiore per unumquemque gradum materiae inferior unitas augetur et multiplicatur, quousque pervenitur ad materiam, quae sustinet quantitatem, scilicet substantiam huius mundi."

80 Ibn Gabirol, *Fons vitae* 2, ed. Baeumker, 62.10–20; ed. Benedetto, 304: "Et quia unitas subsistens in materia intelligentiae est unitas et simplicitatis, secundum quod dictum est, necesse fuit ut augmentaretur unitas subsistens in materia animae et multiplicaretur, quia ordo huius unitatis est infra ordinem unitatis subsistentis in materia intelligentiae. Et ideo fuit necesse ut augmentaretur haec unitas et multiplicaretur, et adveniret ei mutatio et diversitas inter ceteros ordines materiae sustinentis eam secundum descensum gradus materiae ad inferius et elongationis suae a superiori, donec pervenit ad materiam quae sustinet quantitatem, id est substantiam huius mundi." English translation by Laumakis, *The Font of Life*, 100.

between creator and creature is therefore established through the acknowledgment of their similarity (as it is expressed by unity) and irresolvable difference (God's unity is absolute, created unity is a tendency toward unity provided by the compositional unity of an ontological duality). This in turn is a development of the principle of the simplicity of the cause Gundissalinus found in *Fons vitae*.

This theoretical elaboration is grounded upon Ibn Gabirol. Major Gabirolian features are assimilated and exposited by Gundissalinus: universal hylomorphism, metaphysical unity, hypostatic cosmology, formal pluralism. Other crucial doctrines presented in *Fons vitae*, like the essential radiation of the simple substances, do not appear in the *De unitate*, a possible consequence of Gundissalinus's lack of interest in secondary causation in his early career or at least in this treatise. Some other Gabirolian theories, however, would soon after be developed by Gundissalinus through a new approach to *Fons vitae*, starting with his *De anima*.

Psychological Hylomorphism

Although Avicenna is undoubtedly the most important source of Gundissalinus's *De anima*, Ibn Gabirol plays a most meaningful role in that psychological treatise as well. This is particularly true concerning Gundissalinus's discussion of the ontological status of the soul at chapters five and seven of *De anima*. Addressing the questions of what the substance and origin of the souls are, Gundissalinus's answers are grounded upon universal hylomorphism. *De anima* is adamant in claiming that individual souls – human, sensible, and vegetative – are hylomorphic compounds made of matter and form. The admission of matter for souls and all spiritual creatures, however, entails some crucial implications for the origin of these entities. *De unitate et uno* describes a cosmological progression in which God created matter and form and joined them together into the first hypostasis, the Intelligence. Is God also the direct efficient cause of the souls, and the human soul in particular? Gundissalinus could not agree with this possibility, for many reasons. He changes his mind on some major doctrinal points he had previously accepted (and strikingly, the hypostatic progression mentioned in *De unitate*), but he does not elaborate a different position on the priority of matter and form.

This ontological and cosmological priority is now enlightened by a crucial consideration: God only creates from nothing (*ex nihilo*). These two assumptions, universal hylomorphism and *creatio ex nihilo*, are the two pillars of a drastic reshaping of Gundissalinus's cosmology, grounded upon the logical

178 | CHAPTER THREE

consequence entailed by these assumptions. Anything made of matter and form cannot be created directly by God, because it is made "from matter" rather than "from nothing." Emerging in *De anima*, this radical position finds its most advanced development in *De processione mundi*, in which Gundissalinus distinguishes between two different causations performed by God, i.e., creation and composition, the former *limited* by Gundissalinus to the causation of matter and form only.

Two consequences are implied by this sort of limitation of the outcomes of God's creation. On the one hand, hylomorphic compounds are the result of primary or secondary compositions of matter and form, and never the result of a divine creative act. On the other hand, the tension between a *cosmogonic description* of the coming to be of creatures and an *analytic account* of the progressive information of matter appears to give more ground to a different interpretative approach through an application of Porphyry's tree. Although these tensions would find their most eminent venue in *De processione mundi*, they are rooted in the positions Gundissalinus formulated in *De anima*. In chapter five of this treatise, Gundissalinus proposes a set of proofs aiming at demonstrating that God cannot be in any way the "maker" of souls – that is to say, that he cannot have caused their existence directly. A similar claim would entail some inadmissible consequences. The most important argument expounded by Gundissalinus is based on the abovementioned acknowledgment that "the first Maker only produces something from nothing. But it will be demonstrated later that the soul comes forth from matter. Consequently, it is not a product of the first Maker."[81] As God only creates *ex nihilo*, while the souls are made *ex materia*, God cannot be the creator of the souls. To the contrary, the souls must be created by a mediatory principle. Indeed, while it is usually assumed that God creates the soul,

> the philosophers, though, demonstrate that the souls are created not by God, but rather by the angels, in the following way. If the first Maker is the maker of the souls by himself, then the soul would always have existed with him. But the soul did not always exist with God, since new souls are created every day. Therefore, the soul is not made by the first Maker, and the first Maker is not the maker of the soul by himself. Consequently,

81 Gundissalinus, *De anima*, ed. María Jesús Soto Bruna and Concepción Alonso Del Real (Pamplona, 2009), 130.20–22: "Item alia probatio: factoris primi facere est facere aliquid ex nihilo; sed postea probabitur animam fieri ex materia; igitur non est factura primi factoris."

Rooting Reality: Gundissalinus and Ibn Gabirol | 179

between God and the soul, there is necessarily an intermediary, which is the maker of the soul.[82]

The "philosophers" to whom Gundissalinus is referring are, again, Ibn Gabirol. Both excerpts from *De anima* derive from Ibn Gabirol, who claims that "the making of the first Maker is to create something from nothing. But the substance that sustains the categories is composed from its own simple elements. It is, therefore, not created from nothing."[83] And Ibn Gabirol also adds that

> if there is not an intermediary between the first Maker and the substance that sustains the categories, it is necessary that the first Maker is the maker of that substance by himself. And if the first Maker is the maker of this substance by himself, then this substance always existed with God. But this substance did not always exist. It, therefore, was not made by the essence of the first Maker. Therefore, the first Maker is not the maker of this substance by himself. And since the first Maker is not its maker by himself, it will be necessary that an intermediary exists between them.[84]

Nevertheless, even though Ibn Gabirol is the source of these passages, it should be considered that *Fons vitae* does *not* expound any doctrine of an angelic creation of the souls, a theory which appears to be an original development of Gundissalinus's. A closer look at the excerpts from *De anima* and *Fons vitae* makes this point even clearer. Surprisingly, Gundissalinus changes the subject

---

82 Gundissalinus, *De anima*, ed. Soto Bruna and Alonso Del Real, 128.17–22: "Probant autem philosophi animas non a Deo sed ab angelis creari hoc modo: si factor primus est factor animae per se, tunc anima semper fuit apud eum; sed anima non semper fuit apud Deum quoniam cotidie creantur novae; igitur anima non est facta a primo factore, nec primus factor est factor eius per se. Igitur necesse est ut aliquid sit medium inter Deum et animam, quod sit factor animae."

83 Ibn Gabirol, *Fons vitae* 3, ed. Baeumker, 79.18–20; ed. Benedetto, 328: "Facere factoris primi est creare aliquid ex nihilo. Et substantia quae sustinet praedicamenta composita est ex suis simplicibus. Ergo non est creata ex nihilo." English translation by Laumakis, *The Font of Life*, 109.

84 Ibn Gabirol, *Fons vitae* 3, ed. Baeumker, 78.5–12; ed. Benedetto, 326: "si inter factorem primum et substantiam quae sustinet praedicamenta non est medium, opus est ut factor primus sit factor substantiae per se. Et si factor primus fuerit factor substantiae per se, tunc haec substantia fuit semper apud Deum. Sed haec substantia non fuit semper. Ergo non est facta ab essentia factoris primi. Ergo factor primus non est factor substantiae per se. Et cum factor primus non est factor eius per se, necesse erit ut sit medium inter illa." English translation by Laumakis, *The Font of Life*, 108–9.

180 | CHAPTER THREE

of Ibn Gabirol's argument. While *Fons vitae* addresses the relation between God and the substance bearing the categories, *De anima* introduces a different term into this relation, the souls. Beside this crucial change, the structure of Gundissalinus's argument is consistent with Ibn Gabirol's. Gundissalinus even uses the same terminology and phrasal structure of *Fons vitae*, altering it only minimally.

As I had the occasion to point out recently, this is not the only passage to have undergone this peculiar change of subject. The entire set of arguments against God's creation of souls in *De anima* 5 are grounded on this alteration strategy.[85] Gundissalinus consistently changes Ibn Gabirol's references to the "substantia quae sustinet praedicamenta" for his own reference to the soul – a substitution aimed at using these proofs in a different argument.[86] While quite common in Gundissalinus, this alteration strategy appears to be tougher in this section than anywhere else. In other words, Gundissalinus's substitution of the substance bearing the categories for the soul does not appear to be merely aimed at an application of Ibn Gabirol's proofs to a different argument. On the contrary, it seems to be a consequence of Gundissalinus's new approach to *Fons vitae*.

It should be recalled that the substance of the categories is caused by the last degree of the hypostatic Soul corresponding to nature. Ibn Gabirol's proofs are indeed aimed at demonstrating a mediation between God and corporeal bodies, which is performed by the spiritual substances (the Intelligence and the three hypostatic Souls). I have shown elsewhere that Gundissalinus's use of Ibn Gabirol's materials in *De anima* – and, in particular, his substitution of the substance of corporeity for the non-hypostatic soul – implies two crucial identifications by which:

1. Ibn Gabirol's *hypostatic* Souls are considered as *individual* souls.
2. Ibn Gabirol's hypostatic Intelligence is identified with the celestial intelligences of the Avicennian tradition, i.e., the angels.[87]

On the one hand, Gundissalinus identifies Ibn Gabirol's hypostatic Soul with the individual soul. On the other hand, he also tends to identify the hypostatic

---

85 See Nicola Polloni, "Gundissalinus on the Angelic Creation of the Human Soul: A Peculiar Example of Philosophical Appropriation," *Oriens* 47 (2019): 313–47.

86 See Gundissalinus, *De anima*, ed. Soto Bruna and Alonso Del Real, 134.1–18. This passage, too, is derived, with the same modalities described before, from the *Fons vitae*. See Ibn Gabirol, *Fons vitae* 3, ed. Baeumker, 91.7–21; ed. Benedetto, 346.

87 See Polloni, "Gundissalinus on the Angelic Creation of the Human Soul." I will not repeat here my account of Gundissalinus's use of Ibn Gabirol and Avicenna, and his "Avicennisation" of the former, which can be found in the article mentioned above.

Intelligence of *Fons vitae* with the separated intelligences derived from Avicenna's *De anima*, which in turn are clearly associated with the *angelica creatura*, i.e., the angels.[88] This identification of Intelligence and angels allows Gundissalinus to claim that the souls are created by the intelligence (as in Ibn Gabirol's hypostatic progression). This intelligence, though, is not a hypostasis, but an angel, which likewise causes individual rather than hypostatic Souls. A final step in Gundissalinus's strategy is a doctrinal tempering of his theory through an analogy inspired by a key Latin theologian, Peter Lombard.[89] Secondary causation of the souls by the angels can be properly understood through the notions of *ministerium* and *auctoritas* which are in place, for instance, during baptism. Accordingly,

> For what the philosophers demonstrate – namely, that the souls are not created by God, but by the angels – can be easily understood in this way, that they are created by the angel's service rather than God's. Nonetheless, when it is said that "God creates the soul," this sentence must be understood as referring to divine authority, not to his ministry, as when it is said of Christ that "he is the one who baptises," while [it is] the priest [who] baptises. Christ does so through his authority, not his ministry, and the priest does so through his ministry, not his authority. In a similar fashion, the angels also create souls through their ministry only, not their authority. Consequently, they are not said to be the creators of souls, since they do not create by authority, but [by] performing a ministry. Everything which uses not [its] authority but [its] ministry to act upon something necessarily obeys what is superior [to itself] while ministring. For this reason, it is not said that the soul is a creature of the angel, but of God, for it is created by his authority. Likewise the mighty works made by some of the servants are attributed not to them, but to their masters, for whose order [these works] have been made.[90]

88 Gundissalinus, *De anima*, ed. Soto Bruna and Alonso Del Real, 136.11–12.

89 See Peter Lombard, *Sententiae* 4.5.2, ed. Ignatius Brady (Grottaferrata, 1971), 265.7–266.

90 Gundissalinus, *De anima*, ed. Soto Bruna and Alonso Del Real, 134.19–136.9: "Hoc autem quod philosophi probant, animas non a Deo sed ab angelis creari, sane quidem potest intelligi, scilicet non Dei ministerio sed angelorum. Et tamen cum dicitur 'Deus creat animas,' intelligendum est auctoritate non ministerio, sicut cum dicitur de Christo: 'hic est qui baptizat,' cum sacerdos baptizet. Sed Christus auctoritate non ministerio; sacerdos vero ministerio tantum, non auctoritate; sic et angeli creant animas ministerio tantum, non auctoritate. Unde nec creatores animarum dicuntur quia in creando non auctoritate, sed ministerio funguntur. Qui enim in agendo aliquid non auctoritate sed ministerio utitur, in ministrando utique superiori obsequitur. Et ideo anima creatura angeli non dicitur, sed Dei, cuius auctoritate creatur, sicut et magnalia quae aliquorum ministri operantur non ipsis sed dominis suis quorum nutu faciunt imputantur."

182 | CHAPTER THREE

To sum up, Gundissalinus addresses the problem of the origin of the souls through the formulation of a theory of the angelic creation of the souls which is grounded upon a remarkable reinterpretation of Ibn Gabirol's theory on an Avicennian basis and justified through a recourse to the *auctoritas* of Peter Lombard. This attitude is the most peculiar trait of Gundissalinus's syncretic approach to both Arabic and Latin sources and is also an evident consequence of his effort to renovate some main terms of the Latin philosophical debate.

Ibn Gabirol's influence is pervasive in a further aspect in *De anima*. The root itself of Gundissalinus's theory of angelic creation of the souls is universal hylomorphism, a doctrine completely constructed upon Ibn Gabirol. *De anima* argues for the hylomorphic composition of the soul through twenty-three proofs derived from the fourth book of *Fons vitae*. In this case as well, the original context of these proofs differs from Gundissalinus's, as Ibn Gabirol proposed them to demonstrate the hylomorphic composition not of individual souls, but of spiritual substances – the hypostases.[91] Through a series of altered quotations, Gundissalinus expounds some main features of Ibn Gabirol's ontology. He also accepts more metaphysical principles than he did with *De unitate* – a sign of a more mature attitude toward Ibn Gabirol.

Again, Gundissalinus accepts Ibn Gabirol's principle of the simplicity of the cause (PC1), using it to substantiate the assertion, already claimed in *De unitate*, that divine oneness had a twofold effect, i.e., the duality of matter and form.[92] Gundissalinus also uses in *De anima* the principle of formal actualisation (PC5) and the ontological reciprocity of matter and form (PS2), as he already did in *De unitate*. Gundissalinus, however, does not refer in *De anima* to one of his later claims: the potentiality of matter *and form*. As in *De unitate*, there is no real discussion in *De anima* of the theory of act and potency in relation to matter and form. Without a specific reference to the doctrine of the potency of form, it can (and probably should) be assumed that Gundissalinus was accepting a shared doctrine of the actuality of form.[93] *De anima* also

---

91 See, in particular, Ibn Gabirol, *Fons vitae* 4, ed. Baeumker, 212.2–233.10; ed. Benedetto 512–42. Some arguments derive from books two and three of the *Fons vitae*. Nevertheless, the majority of them are taken from book four.

92 See Gundissalinus, *De anima*, ed. Soto Bruna and Alonso Del Real, 160.15–17.

93 It should be noted that in one passage of *De anima*, Gundissalinus observes that within every composed being there is something "which is in act and that is a form or something like a form" and something "which is in potency and is matter or something like matter." This statement is actually referring to the soul, not to form. Gundissalinus's argument by which a form is *quasi forma* cannot be applied to the present discussion on hylomorphism and act/potency, for a simple reason: for Gundissalinus the soul is a hylomorphic compound. See Gundissalinus, *De anima*, ed. Soto Bruna and Alonso Del Real, 100.4–10.

appears to implicitly refer, in a rather peculiar way, to the principle of subordinated causality (PC4), by which any created being can act only on a material substrate. Nevertheless, he seems to develop this assertion in a peculiar relation to God's creation *ex nihilo* and claims that if something is made from matter, its cause is subordinated and not prime (i.e., God). This development substantively reshapes PC4, as the claim that a created being can only act upon matter does not imply that God cannot *also* act upon matter. The doctrine of psychological hylomorphism and the non-divine origin of the soul "made of matter" are the outcomes of the interrelations of these principles. Gundissalinus uses these principles in his demonstrations of the materiality of the soul, for instance stating that

> consequently, although it is said that new human souls are created every day, nonetheless they appear to be created not from nothing but from first matter. If all being comes forth by form, therefore, the rational soul has being only by the form, but the form has being only when it is in matter. Consequently, the form by which the rational soul comes forth into being is in matter, and therefore, the soul appears to consist of matter and form.[94]

Gundissalinus's claims concerning psychological hylomorphism are marked by substantive theoretical development, but nonetheless still bear some problematic aspects. *De unitate* is explicitly marked by a *compositional thesis*, whether as a consequence of a compositional reading of Ibn Gabirol's *Fons vitae*, or as a result of Gundissalinus's own thematic focus. Unity is the main ontological event which is given to the compound and matter by the form of unity. Further forms give origin to the hypostases, until the matter bearing quantity is established. The latter is only mentioned *en passant* in *De unitate*, and there is no meaningful reference to any logical implications of the hylomorphic principles; but the situation changes radically in *De anima*. Here, form and matter are clearly identified as the principle of differentiation and limitation, and as the common substrate of multiple forms, respectively.[95] It should be asked, then, whether Gundissalinus also proposed a more *analytical reading* of matter and form, considering them as analogues to genus and species. The answer is definitely positive, although with some restrictions.

---

94 Ibid., 158.20–160.2: "Quamvis humanae animae cotidie novae creari dicantur, non tamen de nihilo, sed de materia prima creari videntur. Si enim omne esse ex forma est, profecto rationalis anima non habet esse nisi per formam; sed forma non habet esse nisi in materia; forma igitur qua anima rationalis est non est nisi in materia; ac per hoc anima videtur constare ex materia et forma."

95 Gundissalinus, *De anima*, ed. Soto Bruna and Alonso Del Real, 142.3–152.19.

184 | CHAPTER THREE

Gundissalinus's doctrine of the angelic creation of souls implied a problematisation of his formal pluralism. Through his radical reshaping of PC4 into a principle of limitation of God's creative power, Gundissalinus argues that souls are created by the angels because they are made of matter. However, the angels are also hylomorphic compounds and, accordingly, they should also not be created by God, as they are made *ex materia*. A solution to this *impasse* is offered by Gundissalinus's distinction between *creation* and *composition* in *De processione mundi*. The principle of limitation of God's creative power implies that he created only matter and form; and accordingly, any other divine causation is not a creation but a composition making a united hylomorphic compound. The composition of matter with a range of non-incidental forms, however, lets one ask which forms are joined to matter in order to establish the multitude of the universe. As *De anima* refers to angels, bodies, and souls, Gundissalinus had to address the problem of the division of genera and species in a much wider way than he did with the Gabirolian cosmology he presented in *De unitate*. In order to do so, Gundissalinus starts to use Porphyry's *Isagoge* as a crucial hermeneutical device to understand Ibn Gabirol's *Fons vitae*.[96]

First, this new Porphyrian approach led Gundissalinus to abandon Ibn Gabirol's hypostatic progression. The ontological difference between spiritual and corporeal realms cannot be justified by depicting a hypostatic progression of the spiritual into the corporeal, where the latter is caused by the former, as in *Fons vitae*. To the contrary, Gundissalinus follows Porphyry's tree where substance as such is divided into two realms: spirituality and corporeity. They have a common cause, out of which they are opposed effects – in coherence with Ibn Gabirol's principle of conformity (PC3), or better, with its very source, i.e., Aristotelian logic.[97] Gundissalinus's framework is still Gabirolian – the form of spirituality (*forma spiritualitatis*) is commonly used by Ibn Gabirol to address the problem of the difference among spiritual substances – but he backs away from the context of *Fons vitae* in order to insert a different articulation of reality. It is a different cosmology in which universal hylomorphism is posited as the very origin of substance, as the roots from which Porphyry's tree grows. Or better, the one root whose union is the beginning of the course of multiplicity:

---

96 See sections 4–5 of Boethius's Latin version of Porphyry's *Isagoge*, in Porphyry, *Isagoge*, trans. Alain de Libera and Alain-Philippe Segonds (Paris, 1998), 5–6. See also Pessin, "Chains, Trees, and the Spirit-to-Body Boundary"; and Christos Evangeliou, "Aristotle's Doctrines of Predicables and Porphyry's *Isagoge*," *Journal of the History of Philosophy* 23 (1985): 15–34.

97 See Gundissalinus, *De anima*, ed. Soto Bruna and Alonso Del Real, 142.2–12.

Rooting Reality: Gundissalinus and Ibn Gabirol | 185

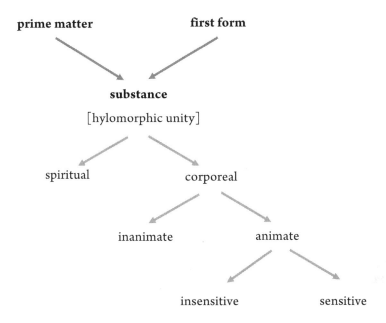

At the origin of everything, matter is joined by the first form. Then, in a second logical moment, this substance is divided into spiritual and corporeal substance, leaving aside any reference to the hypostatic progression of the universe proposed by Ibn Gabirol. These hypostases, indeed, are identified by Gundissalinus with angels and individual souls.[98] Although detaching himself from Ibn Gabirol's cosmology, Gundissalinus's new approach accepts some further metaphysical principles of *Fons vitae*. In a fascinating passage, Gundissalinus states,

> it is worth noting that, after the universal first [matter], whatever is matter for what follows, it is form for what precedes it. And what is more manifest [is] the form of what is hidden. In fact, the nearer matter is to sensation, the more similar it is to form. Therefore, it will be more manifest through the obviousness of form and the hiddenness of matter, although it is matter for a sensible form. To the contrary, the farther it is from sensation, the more similar it will be to matter on account of hiddenness, namely [the hiddenness of] matter, even though it may be a form to the simple first matter or to any other matters below it, just as quantity is the matter of color and shape while also the form of a substance. In fact, considering that a species is the form of

98 See ibid., 146.24–148.5.

186 | CHAPTER THREE

a genus, and that every genus following the first one is a species, it is clear that every genus following the first one is matter of what follows and form of what precedes it.[99]

The manifest is a copy of the hidden – this is basically the principle of the derivative nature of the manifest (PC2) in Ibn Gabirol's *Fons vitae*.[100] Applying this principle to the hylomorphic dynamic, Gundissalinus adamantly claims that the form of the higher level of reality is the matter of the lower level (*id quod est materia posteriorum, forma est priorum*). This is precisely one of the most problematic aspects of *Fons vitae* – as we have seen – and also an assertion that appears to be in implicit contradiction with Gundissalinus's detachment from Ibn Gabirol's cosmology in favour of a much more Porphyry-based reading. Indeed, if the substance is divided into two different realms (spiritual and corporeal) through a *regional ontological structure* (some regions of being are corporeal, others are spiritual), how can matter in the first place be the form of what is previous? Whatever its interpretation might be, it surely implies an *all-in-all ontological structure*, i.e., hypostases in which every substance is within every other (at least at a hypostatic level). This is the reason why Ibn Gabirol's cosmology cannot be seen as a reification of Porphyry's tree – the middle substances are *all-in-all*. Therefore, some crucial questions arise from Gundissalinus's claim. How should reciprocal functionality be interpreted in light of the Porphyrian division of the substance into spiritual and corporeal – two different regions of being, of which the latter does not derive from the former, as they do in *Fons vitae*? And why does Gundissalinus mention a plurality of matters when he usually refers to one and a single matter for every created being? A solution is offered by considering the final words of Gundissalinus's excerpt:

In fact, considering that a species is the form of a genus, and that every genus following the first one is a species, it is clear that every genus following the first one is matter of what follows and form of what precedes it.[101]

99 Gundissalinus, *De anima*, ed. Soto Bruna and Alonso Del Real, 144.10–14: "Et notandum quia post primam universalem id quod est materia posteriorum, forma est priorum et quod est manifestius, forma est occulti, quia materia quo propinquior est sensui est similior formae, et ideo fit manifestior propter evidentiam formae et occultationem materiae, quamvis sit materia formae sensibilis. Sed quo remotior fuerit a sensu, erit similior materiae propter occultationem, scilicet materiae, quamvis sit forma materiae primae simplici vel alicui aliarum materiarum quae sunt infra eam, ut quantitas, cum sit forma substantiae, materia est coloris et figurae. Nam cum species forma sit generis et omne genus post primum species sit, profecto omne genus post primum materia est posteriorum et forma priorum."
100 See Ibn Gabirol, *Fons vitae* 2, ed. Baeumker, 24.10–14; ed. Benedetto, 248.
101 See above, note 99.

Rooting Reality: Gundissalinus and Ibn Gabirol | 187

Here, Gundissalinus's *analytical reading* identifying matter and form as genus and species is clear. Gundissalinus's argument is articulated as follows:

Premise 1: a form is a species dividing a genus.
Premise 2: After the first genus (*genus generalissimum* = matter) there are only species (= forms);
Consequence: Everything after the first genus is a species (= form) which acts as genus (= matter).

De anima also offers a very good example of this line of reasoning: quantity. Gundissalinus says that quantity is form for substance and matter for colour and shape. Indeed, quantity is the special form which is joined to substance and also the sub-general substrate specified by the corporeal forms. In other words, Gundissalinus's line of reasoning would coincide with the *analytical thesis* discussed in relation to Ibn Gabirol's possible interpretations, as follows:

(A) higher level of reality: [(x) = F; quantity as species] + [(y) = M; substance as genus]
(B) lower level of reality: [(z) = F; colour and shape ~ accidents] + [(x) = M; body as genus]

Tacitly based on Porphyry, this *analytical reading* of Ibn Gabirol's doctrines is grounded upon a central quotation from the fourth book of *Fons vitae*. There Ibn Gabirol claims,

I said that what is manifest of being is the form for what is hidden only because the nearer matter is to sensation, the more similar it is to form, and it will, therefore, be more manifest because of the obviousness of form and the hiddenness of matter, although it is matter for the sensible form. The farther removed matter is from sensation, the more similar it will be to matter, and consequently, it will be more hidden according to the hiddenness of matter, although it is form for the simple first matter or any other matter that is below it.[102]

102 Ibn Gabirol, *Fons vitae* 4, ed. Baeumker, 230.7–13; ed. Benedetto, 538: "et non dixi quod manifestum de esse forma est occulti, nisi quia materia, quo propinquior est sensui, est similior fomae, et ideo erit manifestior propter evidentiam formae et occultationem materiae, quamvis sit materia formae sensibili; et quo remotior fuerit a sensu, erit similior materiae, et per hoc erit occultior secundum occultationem materiae, quamvis sit forma materiae primae simplici, aut alicui quae est infra eam ex materiis." English translation by Laumakis, *The Font of Life*, 199.

188 | CHAPTER THREE

Gundissalinus adds to this quotation a preliminary reference to matter and form that follows a few lines of this excerpt from *Fons vitae*.[103] But crucially, he re-interprets the passage as an allusion to the analogy between matter/form and genus/species, applying it to the example of substance, colour, and shape. This example is commonly used by Ibn Gabirol in books one and especially two of *Fons vitae*, to expound both the methods and contents of his examination of reality. For instance, Ibn Gabirol claims that

> an example of this is the heaven, concerning the forms of which the first to appear is colour, then shape, then corporeity, then substantiality, then the others, namely, the spiritual concepts, until you come to the concept of one created thing existing through itself and sustaining all these forms.[104]

But also, in a complex passage where the tension between different interpretative readings is remarkable, he states that

> ... quantity is diverse from the substance that sustains in itself and in the intelligence, although they are united together in being. The example of the union of quantity with substance is like the example of the union of colour and shape with quantity, although quantity is separate from substance in itself and in the intelligence, just like the separation of any colour and shape from quantity in itself and in the senses, although it is not this way in being ... That is true, and you will afterwards also see that all forms are sustained in first matter, just as colour, shape, and similar accidents are sustained in quantity and quantity in substance. It will then be clear to you that those that are manifest are an example for their hidden ones.[105]

The excerpt from *De anima*, therefore, witnesses Gundissalinus's attempt at providing a more developed interpretation of *Fons vitae*, probably to clarify some

103 Ibn Gabirol, *Fons vitae* 4, ed. Baeumker, 231.4–5; ed. Benedetto, 538: "Because I learned that whichever of the substances is matter for the lower is form for what is higher" ("Postquam innotuit mihi quod hoc quod est ex substantiis materia inferiori, est forma superiori"). English translation by Laumakis, *The Font of Life*, 199.

104 Ibn Gabirol, *Fons vitae* 1, ed. Baeumker, 14.17–21; ed. Benedetto, 230: "Huius rei exemplum caelum est, de cuius formis quae primum occurrit color est, deinde figura, post corporeitas, deinde substantialitas, deinde cetera, scilicet intellectus spirituales, donec pervenias ad intellectum rei creatae unius per se existentis, sustinentis has omnes formas." English translation by Laumakis, *The Font of Life*, 70.

105 Ibn Gabirol, *Fons vitae* 2, ed. Baeumker, 33.18–34.11; ed. Benedetto, 262: "Quia quantitas a substantia quae sustinet illam diversa est in se et apud intelligentias, etsi sint unita

non-perspicuous doctrinal points presented by the text. Matter expresses the most general genus while every species is a form. According to this point, it is undoubtedly true that every matter (= genus) of the following logical division is a form (= species), since every step of that division is just the division of a genus into its species by the special form, which divides a sub-genus which, in turn, is a species of the superior level of the only genus which is the *genus generalissimum*.

In *De anima* however, this *analytical reading* of the analogical meaning of matter and form appears to be accompanied by a firm *compositional thesis* concerning matter and form as components of the hylomorphic compound. The two plans stay separate and the analytical thesis is predominantly used as an interpretative device to join Ibn Gabirol's and Porphyry's perspectives. There are many possible reasons behind this fact. First, one should recall the nature and aims of Gundissalinus's treatise, which is a *psychological* work whose main purpose was to provide an account of the soul and its faculties which does not require a purely ontological discussion. Second, and probably connected to this remark, Gundissalinus does not appear to accept some of the crucial metaphysical principles upon which Ibn Gabirol's hylomorphic universe is built, starting with the principle of the thirdness of compositional unity. Moreover, he has not fully formulated his doctrine of the potentiality of form and matter. Without these two fundamental points, a *functional thesis* of matter and form can hardly be admitted under the circumstances of Gundissalinus's reflection.

Third, it is clear that Gundissalinus was gradually maturing his reflection in accordance with the Arabic sources he was translating. A comparison of *De unitate* with *De anima* shows in the latter a greater philosophical sensibility and the problematisation of assumptions made in the former. The same would be true regarding *De processione mundi*, a work in which Gundissalinus would finally engage with the problems of Gabirolian ontology with an enveloping and mature approach. Having detached himself from Ibn Gabirol's hypostatic cosmology, there Gundissalinus would need to construct a new perspective able to address additional doctrinal points. Gundissalinus's new cosmology would be grounded on a further re-interpretation of his own ontology through Avicenna and Hermann of Carinthia.

---

simul in esse. Exemplum autem adunationis quantitatis cum substantia tale est quale est exemplum unitionis coloris et figurae cum quantitate; quamvis sit separata a substantia in se et in intelligentia, sicut separatio uniuscuiusque coloris et figurae a quantitate in se et in sensu, etsi non sit hoc in esse .... Verum est, et videbis postea etiam quod omnes formae sustinetur in prima materia, sicut color et figura et similia accidentia sustinetur in quantitate et quantitas in substantia; et tunc patebit tibi quod manifesta eorum quae sunt exemplum sunt ad occulta eorum ... " English translation by Laumakis, *The Font of Life*, 82. See also *Fons vitae* 2, ed. Baeumker, 23.6–25.25; ed. Benedetto, 246–50.

190 | CHAPTER THREE

Structures of Functional Dualities

In many ways, *De processione mundi* can be considered as Gundissalinus's late attempt to resolve some problems and tensions arising from the doctrinal reception of Ibn Gabirol via a recourse to other sources. As a result, while a consistency of themes and sensibilities with his previous works is apparent, Gundissalinus's *De processione mundi* offers a much more developed and complex discussion than his previous works. The treatise is grounded on three main sources: Ibn Gabirol, Avicenna, and Hermann of Carinthia. The role of the former acquires some characteristic shades in *De processione mundi* – a thematic detachment marked by an improved theoretical adhesion. Parallels between Gundissalinus's and Ibn Gabirol's writings can be drawn from the very beginning of *De processione*, where Gundissalinus examines some preliminary methodological aspects, like the possibility of knowing God through his effects.[106] Nevertheless, the central point of Gundissalinus's use of *Fons vitae* is his mature development of an amended theory of universal hylomorphism.

De processione mundi first introduces matter and form in relation to their opposed properties, by stressing the ontological reciprocity of matter and form through Ibn Gabirol's principle PS2. They are ontological partners characterised by opposed properties – active and passive – which, therefore, require a composing cause to join them together into the compound. Indeed, as Gundissalinus underlines,

> form and matter, though, have opposite properties. For one sustains, and the other is sustained; one receives, and the other is received; one forms, and the other is formed. Things, however, that have opposite properties never by themselves come together in order to constitute something. Form and matter, therefore, do not come together by themselves in the constitution of a body. When, however, things that do not come together by themselves – in fact, when things opposed to each other – are found in something, they clearly reveal that they have a cause that put them together.

---

106 The opening of *De processione mundi* grounds this possibility of knowledge on Paul's *Letter to the Romans*. A similar approach is presented by Ibn Gabirol, *Fons vitae* 1, ed. Baeumker, 6.13–22; ed. Benedetto, 214–16, where it is claimed that only "ex sui operibus quae ab ea generata sunt" is it possible to know the first essence. Through this speculative procedure, "certa erit scientia occulti per manifestum" (*Fons vitae* 2, ed. Baeumker, 37.7–12; ed. Benedetto, 268). It should also be noticed that Ibn Gabirol's *modus universalis communis* and *modus particularis proprius* are close to Gundissalinus's method of *compositio* and *resolutio*, although Gundissalinus relies on Calcidius and probably Thierry, as has been observed in chapter 1.

Therefore, every body has a cause that put it together. In this way, therefore, the whole world has such a cause.[107]

This short passage from *De processione mundi* is grounded upon five different Gabirolian excerpts.[108] Gundissalinus merges them to exposit a rather concise description of the main characteristics of the hylomorphic components. Accordingly, matter and form are, respectively:

(M) what bears and (F) what is borne;
(M) what receives and (F) what is received;
(M) what is shaped and (F) what shapes.

Therefore, matter and form have opposed qualities. Accordingly, their union can be realised only by an external cause whose efficiency is able to supersede their opposition. This composing cause is the first cause, i.e., God. Matter is the "power of being" (*potestas essendi*), a "non-absolute privation" that, with Plato, is "between some substance and none" (*inter aliquam substantiam et nullam*).[109] The source of inspiration for the elaboration of these peculiar characteristics of matter is *Fons vitae*, combined with features derived from the Latin tradition.[110] Ibn Gabirol presents matter as the possibility of receiving form. His dense discussion of this point is marked by a sort of oscillation between a positive characterisation of matter as "possibility to be everything" and a negative considera-

107 Gundissalinus, *De processione mundi*, ed. Georg Bülow, *Des Dominicus Gundissalinus Schrift Von dem Hervorgange der Welt* (Münster, 1925), 3.19–4.7; ed. María Jesús Soto Bruna and Concepción Alonso del Real, *De processione mundi: Estudio y edición crítica del tratado de D. Gundisalvo* (Pamplona, 1999), 124.3–11: "Forma vero et materia oppositarum proprietatum sunt; nam altera sustinet, et altera sustinetur; altera recepit, et altera recipitur; altera format, et altera formatur. Quae autem oppositarum proprietatum sunt, nunquam ad aliquid constituendum per se conveniunt. Forma igitur et materia in constitutione corporis per se non conveniunt. Quae autem per se non conveniunt, profecto, cum in aliquo sibi opposita inveniuntur, quod compositorem habeant, evidenter ostendunt. Omne igitur corpus compositorem habet. Sic itaque totus mundus." English translation by John A. Laumakis, *The Procession of the World* (Milwaukee, 2002), 35–36.

108 See Ibn Gabirol, *Fons vitae* 5, ed. Baeumker, 299.16, 335.9–11, 307.27, 260.12–16, 316.3–6; ed. Benedetto, 630, 676, 640, 580, 650.

109 See Gundissalinus, *De processione mundi*, ed. Bülow, 27.11–20; ed. Soto Bruna and Alonso Del Real, 170.5–13. Also in this case, the direct source of Gundissalinus's remarks is Ibn Gabirol. See Ibn Gabirol, *Fons vitae* 5, ed. Baeumker, 274.8–11; ed. Benedetto, 598.

110 For instance, Chartres. See Nicola Polloni, "Thierry of Chartres and Gundissalinus on Spiritual Substance: The Problem of Hylomorphic Composition," *Bulletin de Philosophie Médiévale* 57 (2015): 35–57.

192 | CHAPTER THREE

tion of matter as "possibility to be nothing at all," stressing its aspects, respectively, of being a substrate of created existence in general and an entity with a marginal existence.[111] In this respect, while both approaches are used in *De processione mundi*, Gundissalinus's reinterpretation tends to stress more the positive aspect of matter, as the *potestas* to become any caused being.[112]

Another facet of this interpretative fluctuation is provided by the eternal existence of matter in God's wisdom. *Fons vitae* affirms that matter and form are eternally present in God's wisdom and they are "brought out" by divine will in order to create the universe. In this regard, Ibn Gabirol clarifies that matter derives from God's essence, while form is from his wisdom. This theme is only sketched in the *De processione*.[113] Gundissalinus explicitly claims only that matter eternally exists in God's *sapientia*.[114] His main interest, though, appears to lie much more in addressing how matter and form are originated *in actu* through their existential correlation, rather than expounding their divine origin.

As for form, *De processione mundi* displays Gundissalinus's change of mind concerning some main points, and particularly that form is *per se* in potency. The opposed characteristics of matter and form are indeed accompanied by a communality of their ontological status. This is a key point of Gundissalinus's approach to the problem of ontological composition. Although performing different *functions*, as we are going to see, matter and form are *both in potency*. Crucially, Gundissalinus finally and plainly accepts the doctrine of the potency of form, claiming that

111 See, for instance, Ibn Gabirol, *Fons vitae* 5, ed. Baeumker, 334.18–23; ed. Benedetto, 674: "S: ... But philosophers are in the habit of calling matter 'possibility.' T: They called matter 'possibility' only because it was possible for it to receive form, that is, to be clothed with its light. And this necessity arises only because it is below the will, and the will is above form. Hence, it is not surprising." ("D. ... Sed philosophi solent appellare materiam possibilitatem. M. Non vocaverunt materiam possibilitatem, nisi quia possibile fuit ei recipere formam, id est vestiri lumen eius; et haec necessitas non advenit nisi quia est infra voluntatem, et voluntas supra formam; unde non est mirum.") English translation by Laumakis, *The Font of Life*, 258–59.

112 Gundissalinus, indeed, distinguishes between two apparently synonymous terms, which are "possibilitas" and "potestas." On the one hand, the Toledan philosopher seems to use the term "potestas" when referring to the intrinsic capacity of matter to become everything, while "possibilitas" describes its function of bearing the forms, and "potentia" the ontological state opposed to "actus/effectus."

113 Ibn Gabirol, *Fons vitae* 5, ed. Baeumker, 275.1–3; ed. Benedetto, 598–600. Gundissalinus quotes this passage directly in *De processione mundi*. See Gundissalinus, *De processione mundi*, ed. Bülow, 27.22–28.1; ed. Soto Bruna and Alonso Del Real, 170.15–17.

114 See Gundissalinus, *De processione mundi*, ed. Bülow, 33.14–34.13; ed. Soto Bruna and Alonso Del Real, 180.10–182.11.

Hence, it should be known that being is said in two ways. For there is being in potency (*esse in potentia*), which is proper to the essence of each matter by itself and of each form by itself (*uniuscuiusque materiae per se et uniuscuiusque formae per se*), and there is being in act, which is proper simultaneously to matter and form when they are united together (*proprium materiae et formae simul coniunctarum*). For it is impossible that matter by itself or form by itself be said to be in the same way as it is said to be when one is united to the other. For, when they are understood in union, that being that is proper to them as united belongs to them, because from the union of them there is necessarily and simultaneously produced some form that was not before in each of them without the other (*fit aliqua forma, quae non prius erat in unaquaque earum sine altera*). For from the union of any different things there arises a form that was not before in either of the two things (*provenit forma, quae non prius erat in aliquo duorum*). Hence, the being of matter without form or of form without matter is understood in one way, and the being of matter and form when united is understood in another way. For the being of each of them by itself is being in potency, but the being of them when united is being in act. Hence, before being united, both have being in potency. But, when one is united to the other, both are brought forth from potency to act.[115]

This passage is of the utmost importance to understand Gundissalinus's new ontology. In *De unitate*, Gundissalinus presented a discussion of hylomorphic unity grounded mainly on *compositional* readings of the hylomorphic principles, considered as components of a dual composite. In *De anima*, the compositional thesis in ontology is accompanied by a more *analytical thesis* concerning the analogical value of matter and form in relation to genus and species, while any ref-

---

115 See Gundissalinus, *De processione mundi*, ed. Bülow, 22.25–23.15; ed. Soto Bruna and Alonso Del Real, 160.13–162.8: "Unde sciendum est, quod esse duobus modis dicitur: est enim esse in potentia, quod est proprium essentiae uniuscuiusque materiae per se et uniuscuiusque formae per se, et est esse in actu, quod est proprium materiae et formae simul coniunctarum. Impossibile est enim, quod materia vel forma per se sic dicatur esse, sicut dicitur esse, cum una coniungitur alii. Cum enim intelliguntur coniunctim, convenit eis illud esse, quod est proprium coniunctarum, quod ex coniunctione earum necessario simul fit aliqua forma, quae non prius erat in unaquaque earum sine altera. Ex coniunctione enim quorumlibet diversorum provenit forma, quae non prius erat in aliquo duorum. Unde aliter intelligitur esse materiae sine forma vel formae sine materia et aliter coniunctarum. Esse enim uniuscuiusque istarum per se est esse in potentia; esse vero illarum simul coniunctarum est esse in actu. Unde ante coniunctionem utraque habet esse in potentia. Sed cum altera alteri coniungitur, utraque de potentia producitur ad effectum." English translation by Laumakis, *The Procession of the World*, 50–51.

194 | CHAPTER THREE

erence to hypostatic cosmology is left aside. Finally, in *De processione mundi* Gundissalinus can expand on this issue.

First, Gundissalinus claims that both matter and form *per se* are in potency. This means that their own being is potential when they are not joined together within the unity of the compound. The consequences of this theory are massive, as is clearly shown by the problem of the actualisation of the compound, whereas none of its components is actual. Gundissalinus, though, now follows Ibn Gabirol not only in relation to the doctrine of the potentiality of form, but also and pivotally with the admission of the principle of the thirdness of compositional unity (PS4). Indeed, he claims, here and elsewhere, that the union of matter and form gives something which "was not before in each of them without the other." Accordingly, the compound is some third thing other than matter and form, and cannot be reduced to the sum of its components. It is the same situation exemplified by a consideration of the union of the colours red and blue into violet: their result is a third thing which is neither blue nor red, although blue and red are its *composing elements* before being joined together. These elements can be considered as shades or, in our case, aspects of the violet colour, in abstraction or even in physical manipulation when those shades are strengthened or weakened by additional components. In a similar fashion, the result of the unity of matter and form is the compound, which has actual being while matter and form *per se* do not. They are not composing elements but functional aspects of the compound.

Through the principle of the thirdness of compositional unity, therefore, Gundissalinus can substantiate a much more radical theory of hylomorphism. Accordingly, matter and form are objects of two different kinds of understanding, as Gundissalinus has pointed out in the above quoted passage, by claiming that "the being of matter without form or of form without matter is understood in one way, and the being of matter and form when united is understood in another way." These two ways of understanding the being of matter and form are *being in potency* and *being in act*. Matter and form are in potency before being joined together and they are in act within the compound. Nevertheless, a duality of understanding can also be applied to the ontological role matter and form play as *composing elements* before originating the compound and *functional aspects* once the compound has been caused.

Another point appears to be crucial. Although the wording should probably be philologically contrasted with the manuscript tradition of *De processione mundi*, due to the subtlety of the passage, it is significant to note that Gundissalinus twice refers to the result of the hylomorphic union implied by PS4 as a form. Namely, he claims that:

"... from the union of them there is necessarily and simultaneously produced some form that was not before in each of them without the other" (*fit aliqua forma, quae non prius erat in unaquaque earum sine altera*).

"For from the union of any different things there arises a form that was not before in either of the two things" (*provenit forma, quae non prius erat in aliquo duorum*).

How can the result of the union of matter and form *be a form*? This assertion seems to be an evident contradiction. Nevertheless, this problematic point appears to be connected to another thorny question within Gundissalinus's reflection: what are the *material* and the *formal functions* which are implied by a functional reading of his ontology? A possible clarification of both questions can be provided by another excerpt of *De processione mundi*, in which Gundissalinus further distinguishes among the statuses of matter and form before and after their joining. Specifically, Gundissalinus highlights the distinction between potential/actual statuses of both matter and form and the ontological entities themselves through the introduction of two rather peculiar terms for the former, i.e., *material being* (*esse materiale*) and *formal being* (*esse formale*). He points out that

> material being, which is being in potency, is indeed distinct from formal being (*esse formale*), which is being in act. But each of them by itself without the other has material being (*esse materiale*), just as each of them has formal being if it is united with the other. But because men have not been accustomed to say that something exists except what exists in act, while being in act is present only when form is united to matter, being does not belong to matter by itself nor to form by itself, but to both of them when joined together. And therefore, whatever is composed of matter and form has in a similar fashion being that is composed of being in potency, which is material being, and being in act, which is formal being. But because being and oneness are inseparable – since whatever exists, exists because it is one – just as neither has being by itself without the other, so neither is one by itself without the other.[116]

116 Gundissalinus, *De processione mundi*, ed. Bülow, 28.11–29.6; ed. Soto Bruna and Alonso Del Real, 172.2–14: "Esse enim materiale, quod est esse in potentia, diversum est ab esse formali, quod est esse in actu. Sed esse materiale utraque habet per se sine altera, sicut esse formale habet utraque, si coniuncta est cum altera. Sed quia homines non consueverunt dicere aliquid esse, nisi quod in actu est; esse vero in actu non habetur, nisi cum forma materiei coniungitur: ideo esse non convenit materiae per se, nec formae per se, sed coniunctis simul.

196 | CHAPTER THREE

Gundissalinus claims that both matter and form have a *material being (esse materiale)* which is analogous to the potential being. After their union, they acquire a *formal being (esse formale)* which is analogous to the actual being. In this case, too, the main source is Ibn Gabirol's *Fons vitae.*[117] Although further reasons for coherence with the traditions are in place – as has been signalled in the previous chapter and will be discussed again in the next – the terminologically clumsy distinction established by Gundissalinus appears to match his claim that the hylomorphic union is a *form* inasmuch as that compound is in act and, within it, matter and form are also in act. This coincidence, though, does not resolve anything by itself. A *compositional reading* of these passages, indeed, would inescapably acknowledge that the result of matter and form cannot be a form. Maybe it could if matter were considered to be an accident, which it is not. And calling the being of the compound "formal" does not make it a form.

At the same time, an *analytic reading* of these excerpts would claim that material being is but an analogical term for the genus which is actualised in and by the species. This seems to be more reasonable. Also the union of matter and form as giving origin to a form could be considered as the form dividing a genus causing a species, which has actual existence. Nevertheless, the context of the quoted passages and of many further pages of *De processione mundi* makes clear that

---

Et ideo, quicquid est non compositum ex materia et forma, habet similiter esse compositum ex esse in potentia, quod est esse materiale, et ex esse in effectu, quod est esse formale. Sed quia esse et unum inseparabilia sunt, quoniam, quicquid est, ideo est, quia unum est: idcirco, sicut neutra esse habet per se sine altera, sic neutra est unum per se sine altera." English translation by Laumakis, *The Procession of the World*, 56. Compare with Ibn Gabirol, *Fons vitae* 5, ed. Baeumker, 273.10–13 and 277.5–9; ed. Benedetto, 596 and 602.

117 See Ibn Gabirol, *Fons vitae* 5, ed. Baeumker, 276.24–277.10; ed. Benedetto, 602: "Matter does not have material being from form, but formal being, namely, the being matter has from form. For matter has the being that comes from the joining of matter and form only with form and because of form, although matter has material being in itself. If you want to say in this case that matter is in privation in comparison to formal being, I do not prohibit that, because the usual being is only what is composed of matter and form. Moreover, when you consider that the being of a thing composed of matter and form is composed of being in potency, which is the being of matter, and being in act, which is the being of form, you will see that the being of matter is a privation in comparison to the other." ("Esse materiale materia non habet ex forma, sed esse formale, scilicet quod materia habet ex forma; quia materia non habet illud esse quod est ex coniunctione materiae et formae, nisi cum forma et propter formam, quamvis materia habeat in se esse materiale. Et si volueris hic materiam dicere privatam comparatione esse formalis, non prohibeo; quia esse usitatum non est nisi quod est compositum ex materia et forma. Et etiam cum consideraveris quod esse rei compositae ex materia et forma compositum est ex esse in potentia, quod est esse materiae, et esse in actu, quod est esse formae: videbis quod esse materiae comparatione illius privatio est.") English translation by Laumakis, *The Font of Life*, 266.

Gundissalinus is not describing the specification of a genus, but the specification of a genus *together* with the ontological composition of created beings. An example of Gundissalinus's attitude is provided by the *dual* use he makes in *De processione mundi* of the terms "compositio" and "resolutio." As I have shown in chapter 2, Gundissalinus uses these terms with different meanings and in different contexts, developing them from Calcidius's and Hermann of Carinthia's discussions. Respectively, we have:

> *compositio* and *resolutio* as *epistemological devices* through which what is less common is progressively removed/added in order to progress toward what is more common (Calcidius);
> *compositio* and *resolutio* as *ontological processes* through which something is resolved into its elements or composed with additional characteristics (Hermann).

It is evident that in *De processione* both the epistemological and the ontological use of *compositio* and *resolutio* are aimed at describing one event – the hylomorphic compound – through two different points of view. These could be considered to be, respectively, an *analytical* and a *compositional* perspective. Both approaches are indeed reciprocally implied by Gundissalinus's *functional* examination of the principles of reality.

The tension between a purely compositional and a purely analytical reading of the passages mentioned above can therefore be superseded by a simple consideration. Material and formal being are considered by Gundissalinus as *functions*: namely, as material function (the material being) and formal function (the formal being). They are not matter and form – the composing elements which become the hylomorphic compound. They are the functions of potentiality and actuality that the tradition consistently yet equivocally ascribed to matter and form, but which cannot be matter and form, as the components become the compound not as its elements but its aspects. It is the emergence of metaphysics. Accordingly, material being coincides with potential being because it is the expression of the material function of the compound (but not its matter). And formal being coincides with actual being as the expression of the formal function of the compound. It seems that Gundissalinus is tacitly amending what he considered a common mistake: to identify matter and form with their functions – i.e., to identify matter with potency and form with act, as the tradition consistently has done. With the distinction between material/formal being and matter/form, Gundissalinus makes clear that there is a crucial distinction between the consideration of the hylomorphic principles as

198 | CHAPTER THREE

composing elements and *functional aspects*, as I have called them. Following his typical philosophical style, Gundissalinus not only does not explicitly attack the theories he is opposing. It seems that he also tries to find a compromise with the tradition by referring to the above-mentioned functions in terms which might have appeared as palatable for the tradition, as we have seen in the previous chapter.

Going back to the first passage from *De processione mundi* discussed above, it is clear that Gundissalinus identifies the functionality of matter and form within the compound with the traditional statuses of potential and actual being. The formal function corresponds to an act-function as well as a species-function within the compound. In turn, the material function corresponds to a potency-function and a genus-function within the compound (and before, as the potential state proper to the hylomorphic principles not yet united). In both cases, these functions are not equivalent to the composing elements, matter and form. Under this functional consideration, it can be said the hylomorphic compound is a form although it is made of matter and form. By receiving a non-incidental form, any entity is specified into a more special species. Therefore, it can be considered as expressing the function of a form inasmuch as the new compound expresses the specification of the previous and more general status of the compound from which it comes. As I said, Gundissalinus's reference to matter and form as having the being proper to the compound within the compound should be referred to matter and form not as *composing elements* but as *functional aspects* of the compound, which is a third entity unresolvable into the sum of its components.

The functional thesis also allows us to clarify a peculiar point of Gundissalinus's doctrine of the potentiality of form and matter. If both matter and form are in potency, how can the compound be actualised? As we have seen, in *Fons vitae* this problem is addressed in a rather curious way. In *De processione mundi*, Gundissalinus claims that neither matter nor form could have existed (in act) without their reciprocal ontological partner,

> for, since being comes from form, matter without form certainly could not exist for a moment. Nor did matter precede form with respect to causality, and form is rather for matter the cause of existing in order that it may be. For everything by which something exists is the cause of what exists because of it. And because being exists only by reason of form, matter never existed without form. But because form exists only by reason of the existence of formed matter, it is impossible, for this reason, that form exists without matter, since being is achieved only through the union of both of them. For

Rooting Reality: Gundissalinus and Ibn Gabirol | 199

being, as the philosophers define it, is nothing other than the existence of form in matter.[118]

This passage is the consequence of the acceptance of the principle of the ontological reciprocity of matter and form (PS2), and indeed its main and direct source is Ibn Gabirol.[119] A crucial development is Gundissalinus's fusion of ontological reciprocity with modal ontology, as the next chapter will point out. The insertion of doctrines by Avicenna in *De processione mundi*, as well as the pressure from almost the entire Latin tradition which agreed in positing form as act, seem to have concerned Gundissalinus in different ways. In turn, these concerns appear to have impacted his discussion of the *principalitas* of form, by which form is the main actor in attributing actual existence to the compound – a theme already present in Ibn Gabirol as the principle of formal actualisation (PC5). While this point was not a problem in his previous works, as *De processione* finally claims that form is *per se* in potency, Gundissalinus had to clarify the preeminent role played by the form, although in potency. Accordingly, he claims that

although, therefore, one does not precede the other in time or causality, either in being in act or being in potency, form is nonetheless said to give being to matter, and matter is not said to give being to form. The reason for this is this. At the coming of form, matter passes from potency to act. Being in potency, however, is considered like non-being in comparison to that being that is in act. Being in act, then, is first attained when matter is united to form. Therefore, on account of this primacy, matter is not seen to give being to form, but form is seen to give being to matter. Moreover, matter always remains, but form comes and goes, although not every form.[120]

---

118 Gundissalinus, *De processione mundi*, ed. Bülow, 23.18–24.3; ed. Soto Bruna and Alonso Del Real, 162.10–18: "Cum enim esse ex forma sit profecto materia sine forma nec uno momento esse potuit. Sed nec causa materia formam praecessit, cui forma est potius causa existendi, ut sit. Omne enim, per quod aliquid est, est causa eius, quod per ipsum est. Et quia esse non est, nisi per formam, tunc materia nunquam fuit sine forma. Sed quia forma non est, nisi per existentiam materiae formatae, idcirco impossibile est formam esse sine materia, quoniam non perficitur esse, nisi per coniunctionem utriusque. Esse enim, ut philosophi definiunt, nihil aliud est, quam existentia formae in materia." English translation by Laumakis, *The Procession of the World*, 51.

119 Ibn Gabirol, *Fons vitae* 5, ed. Baeumker, 334.9–13; ed. Benedetto, 674. See also *Fons vitae* 4, ed. Baeumker, 234.10–12; ed. Benedetto, 544.

120 Gundissalinus, *De processione mundi*, ed. Bülow, 25.2–12; ed. Soto Bruna and Alonso Del Real, 164.16–166.5: "Licet ergo neutra praecedat aliam tempore, vel causa, nec in esse in effectu, nec in esse in potentia: dicitur tamen forma dare esse materiae, et non dicitur

200 | CHAPTER THREE

For Gundissalinus, therefore, a central role in causing the actual existence of both matter and compound must be attributed to the form. As regards the *genus-species functions*, this claim is evident: the function of specific difference played by the form actualises the *genus-function* of matter into the species of the compound.

Consideration of the ontological causal dynamic is rather more problematic. How can a form be the cause of the actual existence of something, if that form is in potency? Indeed, while Avicenna admits, for instance, a consideration of form as a "special" cause of matter (explicitly a middle cause, *causa media*), in his ontology a form can perform that causality as it is always in act. However, in Gundissalinus's and Ibn Gabirol's perspectives, a form without matter is in potency – for this reason there are no separated forms as such, but only forms with a substrate, which is matter.[121] Nevertheless, it should be considered that Gundissalinus clarifies that, although form and being must not be identified, being (i.e., actual existence) is always a *concomitant of form* when it is joined to matter.[122] Therefore, *when* form comes to matter, actual being *happens*. A clarification of this ontological conundrum can be provided, also in Gundissalinus, by his theory of metaphysical unity. Already in *De unitate*, Gundissalinus had discussed the ontological implications linking unity and the form of unity, particularly claiming four main points:

---

materia dare esse formae. Cuius ratio haec est: namque adventu formae materia de potentia ad effectum transit, esse vero in potentia quasi non esse reputatur comparatione eius esse, quod in effectu est; esse in effectu tunc primum habetur, cum materia formae coniungitur. Ideo propter hanc principalitatem non materia formae, sed forma materiei dare esse videtur. Item materia semper permanet, sed forma advenit et recedit, licet non omnis." English translation by Laumakis, *The Procession of the World*, 52.

121 It should be recalled that, in *De anima*, Gundissalinus applies the principle by which "only an act actualises" to God in order to prove that he cannot be the cause of the actualisation of the soul, since he is not an act. See Gundissalinus, *De anima*, ed. Soto Bruna and Alonso Del Real, 132.1–4. Also, this argument derives from the *Fons vitae*, where it is referred again to the substance bearing the categories. See Ibn Gabirol, *Fons vitae* 3, ed. Baeumker, 83.15–20; ed. Benedetto, 334.

122 Gundissalinus, *De processione mundi*, ed. Bülow, 27.5–10; ed. Soto Bruna and Alonso Del Real, 168.23–170.4: "Therefore, if all being comes from form, form assuredly is not being. For whatever comes from something else is not the thing from which it comes. But all being comes from form. Therefore, no being is form, and no form is being. For being is something that inseparably accompanies form. For, when form comes to matter, it is necessary that there be being in act." ("Quapropter, si omne esse ex forma est, forma utique non est esse. Quicquid enim ex alio est, non est ipsum, ex quo aliquid est. Sed omne esse ex forma est. Nullum igitur esse forma est, et nulla forma est esse. Esse enim est quiddam, quod inseparabiliter comitatur formam. Cum enim forma in materiam advenit, necesse est, ut esse in actu sit.") English translation by Laumakis, *The Procession of the World*, 54.

Rooting Reality: Gundissalinus and Ibn Gabirol | 201

1. God is the absolute unity dispensing a derived unity into the universe.

2. Derived unity and actual existence are always together in being (Ibn Gabirol's PS1).

3. Derived unity is what holds together matter and the hylomorphic compound.

4. Derived unity is provided by the form of unity and received by matter.

De processione mundi re-elaborates these points in meaningful continuity with *De unitate*, although the former leaves aside some important details of *De unitate*. Following the principle of the simplicity of the cause (PC1) linking effect and cause ("omne creatum a creante debet esse diversum"), Gundissalinus points out that the effect of God's oneness must be a *duality*. Accordingly,

> by creation, therefore, the first principles of things, which were created from nothing, have a beginning. These are the material principle and the formal principle. For the creator created some principle. But every created thing must be different from the creator. Since, therefore, the creator is truly one, something created certainly ought not to have been one. But just as there was nothing in the middle between the creator and the first creature, so there is nothing in the middle between one and two. For the first thing that is different from one is two. Since, therefore, the creator is truly one, the creature that is after him certainly had to be two. For diversity is not found in oneness, but in otherness. But the first principle of otherness is twoness, which first departs from oneness. If, therefore, the first created thing were one, then there would be no diversity. But, if there were no diversity, there would be no universe of creatures that was going to be.[123]

Existence of an absolute unity entails that its effect is a duality made of two entities ontologically dependant on each other. The origin of this doctrine is Ibn

---

123 Gundissalinus, *De processione mundi*, ed. Bülow, 20.13–21.1; ed. Soto Bruna and Alonso Del Real, 156.4–16: "Per creationem ergo initium habent prima principia rerum, quae de nihilo creata sunt; quae sunt principium materiale et principium formale. Creator enim aliquod principium creavit; sed omne creatum a creante debet esse diversum. Cum igitur creator vere unus sit, profecto creatum non debuit esse unum, sed, sicut inter creatorem et primam creaturam nihil fuit medium, sic inter unum et duo nihil est medium. Primum enim, quod est diversum ab uno, hoc est duo. Cum igitur creator vere sit unus, profecto creatura, quae post ipsum est, debuit esse duo. In unitate enim non est diversitas, sed in alteritate. Sed primum principium alteritatis binarius est, qui primus ab unitate recedit. Si igitur primum creatum unum esset, tunc nulla esset diversitas; si vero nulla esset diversitas, nulla esset, quae futura esset, creaturarum universitas." English translation by Laumakis, *The Procession of the World*, 47–48.

202 | CHAPTER THREE

Gabirol, both in regards to the position of PC1 and the precise claim that there are only two principles and they are a matter and a form – not two matters or two forms.[124] Indeed, "since the creator of things is one, it is necessary that what is created be two."[125] Gundissalinus strictly follows this line of reasoning, applying it to demonstrate that only matter and form can be the effect of the causality of the One.[126]

The fundamental relevance of this causative process is reflected in the compounded ontology of created being. Any hylomorphic compound is made of matter and form which exist within it as a *structural duality* expressed by their functions at different levels. This ontological duality, though, requires a unity – that is why matter desires to become one through form, because the whole compound exists as long as it is one through the identification of unity and existence (PS1 in *Fons vitae*). This *unity into duality* of the compound corresponds to its actual being. Gundissalinus, indeed, claims that the formal causation of being is always accompanied (or better, logically preceded) by the causation of the compound's unity retaining matter from its own tendency toward self-multiplication. Being and unity, indeed, are always together in any existing thing,

> for whatever exists is either one or many. Therefore, because it is neither one nor many, matter in itself understood without form and form understood without matter cannot be called one. For, because oneness is form, if matter without form were one, then matter without form would certainly be matter with form, which is impossible. And because all being is called one, it is not possible that oneness exists in non-being. Hence, neither matter nor form had being in act before oneness, but they began to be simultaneously. For, when form was united to matter, oneness instantly came forth, because from the union of them something one is made. Hence, being and oneness are seen to be simultaneous by nature since, when something exists, it is one, and when it is one, it necessarily is. And consequently, just as matter without form or form without matter does not have being, so neither without the other is one by means of oneness.[127]

---

124 Ibn Gabirol, *Fons vitae* 1, ed. Baeumker, 9.1–11; ed. Benedetto, 220; *Fons vitae* 4, ed. Baeumker, 212.20–213.15 and 224.19–225.12; ed. Benedetto, 512–14 and 530. See also and in particular *Fons vitae* 4, ed. Baeumker, 222.24–28; ed. Benedetto, 528.

125 *Fons vitae* 5, ed. Baeumker, 279.3–4; ed. Benedetto, 604: "cum creator rerum sit unus, oportet ut creatum sit duo." English translation by Laumakis, *The Font of Life*, 227.

126 See also Gundissalinus, *De processione mundi*, ed. Bülow, 21.2–19; ed. Soto Bruna and Alonso Del Real, 156.16–158.10.

127 Ibid., ed. Bülow, 29.1–30.3; ed. Soto Bruna and Alonso Del Real, 172.12–174.5: "Quicquid enim est, vel est unum, vel multa. Quia igitur nec est unum, nec multa, quapropter

Through Ibn Gabirol, *De processione* posits a substantive correlation between form and unity which, in turn, is also in continuity with *De unitate et uno*.[128] Unity is the function expressed by the form of unity, the first form to join matter in the cosmological progression from which the universe arises. Going back to the problem of how a form in potency can provide matter and the compound with the act that the form itself does not have, unity provides a solution. Unity is given to the compound by the form and, through it, both matter and the compound are held together. That is the reason why unity must be the first form to logically join matter. Without unity, there would be no actual being, as actuality emerges from the first union of matter and form.

The unity of the compound, though, is not the absolute unity of God, or unity as such, but it is always a "unity-of," a derived unity that can exist only as the union of two entities, which are matter and form – a point constantly repeated by *De processione* and *De unitate*. Another thread of both treatises is the claim that actual existence originates only when matter and form are united, or better, *made one*. In other words, actual existence is equivalent to derived unity which, in turn, is a factor expressed by form – not matter, as form is what holds matter and the compound together. As a consequence, the actualisation of matter is provided by the form, not as such (not because the form is in act), but as providing the "unifying factor" which makes derived unity possible for created being.[129] Being a factor

---

materia per se intellecta sine forma et forma sine materia intellecta una dici non potest. Nam quia unitas forma est, tunc, si materia sine forma esset una, profecto materia sine forma esset materia cum forma, quod est impossibile. Et quia omne esse dicitur unum, tunc non est possibile, ut unitas existat in non-esse. Unde nec materia, nec forma habuit esse in actu ante unitatem, sed simul esse inceperunt. Cum enim forma materiei adiuncta est, statim unitas prodiit, quia ex coniunctione earum aliquid unum fit. Unde esse et unitas videntur simul esse natura, quoniam, cum aliquid est, illud est unum, et cum est unum, illud esse necesse est. Ac per hoc, sicut materia sine forma, vel forma sine materia, non habet esse, sic neutra sine altera est unitate una." English translation by Laumakis, *The Procession of the World*, 56–57.

128 Ibn Gabirol, *Fons vitae* 5, ed. Baeumker, 272.12–15; ed. Benedetto, 596: "And because form is unity and being is called 'one' and because it is not possible for unity to exist in non-being, it is evident, consequently, that something exists before unity, and it is made one by unity" ("Et quia forma est unitas, et esse dicitur unum, et non est possibile ut unitas existat in non esse: manifestum est per hoc quod aliquid est ante unitatem et fit per eam unum"). English translation by Laumakis, *The Font of Life*, 223.

129 It can be appreciated that for Gundissalinus the sum of two different entities (matter's and form's potentiality) gives something different from them (the actual being of the compound), which is only logically resolvable into the unities of which it is composed (matter and form, in their own potential state). This is the theoretical basis of what Gundissalinus would claim at the end of *De processione mundi*, where he presents two numerological series summarising the establishment of the universe. See Gundissalinus, *De processione mundi*, ed. Bülow, 55.6–56.12; ed. Soto Bruna and Alonso Del Real, 222.6–224.16.

204 | CHAPTER THREE

expressed by the first form which is joined to matter, the cause of unity/actuality is the same cause of the first union of matter and form, i.e., God. Indeed, the first cause is not the first act – as already highlighted in *De anima* – and cannot actualise a potency. He can "only" create from nothing. And accordingly, he creates the first potency (= matter and form), as well as the first act (= the first union of matter and form).

The *dynamic duality* of potency and act, therefore, is the first duality of a series of dual characteristics expressing the ontological alterity of created being from its supreme origin. The duality of genus and species is an additional *analytical duality* which corresponds to the gradual fragmentation of common being into more and more special species, until individuals are produced. Both dynamic and analytical dualities are the expression of a *compositional duality* made of the material function and the formal function that Gundissalinus calls material and formal being. And these dualities are accompanied by another *modal duality* of possibility and acquired necessity, as we will see in the next chapter. These four dualities are the expression of a rooting ontological duality: the duality of matter and form which coincides with the genesis of the substance. The rooting duality of the hylomorphic composition is made one in the compound, but persists because it takes the form of a structure of dualities expressing different functions as a result of the rooting duality from which substance originates.

In Gundissalinus's chain of being, unity and substantiality are the first forms to join matter. In an intriguing passage, *De processione* underlines that

> the first form to which first matter was joined was substantiality, which made matter be a substance. But because everything that exists, exists precisely because it is one, substantiality alone, therefore, could not come to matter without unity as its companion, because it was impossible for matter to become a substance and not one. Hence, substantiality and unity come to matter simultaneously, and at their coming matter passes from possibility to act, from darkness to light, from deformity to comeliness, since by their union matter is made one substance.[130]

---

130 Gundissalinus, *De processione mundi*, ed. Bülow, 41.10–17; ed. Soto Bruna and Alonso Del Real, 196.8–15: "Prima autem forma, cui prima copulata est materia, substantialitas fuit, quae materiam fecit esse substantiam. Sed quia omne, quod est, ideo est, quia unum est: ideo substantialitas sola sine unitate comite non potuit venire, quia materiam substantiam fieri, et non unam, impossibile fuit. Unde substantialitas et unitas simul adveniunt, in quarum adventu materia transit de potestate ad actum, de tenebris ad lumen, de informitate ad decorem, quoniam earum coniunctione materia facta est substantia una." English translation by Laumakis, *The Procession of the World*, 68. Interpretation of this point

The first union of matter and form originates substance as such, which is then divided into spiritual and corporeal substance, from which the three secondary causes (angels, spheres, and elements) arise.[131] It is a cosmologisation of Porphyry's tree, grounded in universal hylomorphism. The union of first matter and the first forms (unity, substantiality, and then, respectively, spirituality and corporeity) comes about not in time, but in a single moment – *ictu oculi*, again following Ibn Gabirol.[132]

It should be underlined that Gundissalinus is providing a cosmological description. The first part of this cosmogonic account – corresponding to God's *creatio* and *primaria compositio* – is an examination of how created being was instituted by God simultaneously and before time. It corresponds to the creation of substance and act, the coordinates of created ontology. It also corresponds to the establishment of a *regional ontological structure* of the universe. Through Porphyry, the chain of being is broken into two different series of being, respectively corporeal and spiritual. Therefore, any hypostatic tendency toward an *all-in-all ontological structure* is utterly superseded. Nevertheless, it is also a *functional* description of the ontological structures within every created being. Gundissalinus is presenting a series of *substances* (substance, hylomorphic union, corporeal substance, spiritual substance) that existed only for an instant in themselves, at the creation of the world. But they also constitute the *substrata* of every existing being, whether spiritual or corporeal. As will be pointed out in the next chapter, Gundissalinus surely considered corporeity – not matter – as the substrate of corporeal change. Still, his functional consideration of the structural duality of created being implies some peculiarities in his consideration of the natural substrate. The form of corporeity, subsisting as one within every corporeal being, informs all matter of the corporeal realm while the spiritual matter informs all the matter of the spiritual realm. And the same seems to happen, crucially, with the form of unity. Under this consideration, each and every one of these forms perform two different functions:

---

is particularly difficult, especially considering that Gundissalinus also refers to unity and substance as specific properties of form and matter. See Gundissalinus, *De processione mundi*, ed. Bülow, 30.14–31.3; ed. Soto Bruna and Alonso Del Real, 174.16–176.1. This passage, though, seems to be clearer through a comparison with the *Fons vitae*, where Ibn Gabirol makes explicit the relation between substantiality and the unity of the hylomorphic compounds. See Ibn Gabirol, *Fons vitae* 4, ed. Baeumker, 234.29–235.15; ed. Benedetto, 544–46.

131 See Gundissalinus, *De processione mundi*, ed. Bülow, 51.20–23; ed. Soto Bruna and Alonso Del Real, 214.8–11.

132 For instance, Ibn Gabirol, *Fons vitae* 3, ed. Baeumker, 113.22; ed. Benedetto, 378.

at a *cosmological level*, they establish the *substrata* of the universe;

at an *individual ontological level*, they perform the *function* of that general
form within the compound.

According to this twofold role, implied by the intersection between
Gundissalinus's doctrine of the plurality of non-incidental forms and his claim
that there is one form for every ontological universal, the form of unity appears
to be, at the same time:

the first form that is joined to matter by God at the beginning of time, establishing the universe as *one* thing in act, as *actual being* coincides with the
function of unity performed by the first form;

the form of unity that is within each and every created substance, which is
more primordial than substance itself and through which each and every
thing is in act as long as that thing is made one by the union of its matter and its forms.

And presumably, although Gundissalinus does not refer to this problem, it could
be assumed that the form of unity performs within the individual the function of
the principle of individuation – a problem that, however, will require further
examination.

With the second step in this *cosmological and particular* information of matter, the progression re-enters Porphyry's tree. Substance is divided, respectively,
into spiritual and corporeal substances, which in turn are divided by a plurality
of forms establishing species and sub-species. All these species are functions
expressed by the forms within the individual compounds. Within the compound,
therefore, there is formal richness, an *ontological structure made of enmattered
forms*. An attempt at schematising Gundissalinus's consideration of this formal
richness within matter can be seen on page 207.

Are these many forms a plurality of functions performed by one single form?
The formal richness of the compound appears to be a pivotal pillar in Gundissalinus's reflection, one which should be harmonised with the utmost necessity he
felt to ground it within the unity of the compound. Considering the structural
duality in which Gundissalinus's ontology is rooted and the functional reading it
seems to imply, I incline toward a consideration of form as the expression of a
cluster of forms, each one of which plays a functional specification (i.e., as *species-
function*). Although central, this question is not directly addressed by Gundissalinus, and I will return to it in the next chapter.

The second branch of Gundissalinus's cosmological account corresponds
to the processes of *secundaria compositio* and *generatio*. Here, his description is

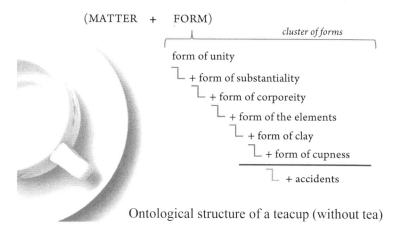

Ontological structure of a teacup (without tea)

much more cosmogonic in the traditional sense. It does not focus on the institution of the substance, but on the secondary causation of the physical universe and its spiritual actors, which are creatures rather than ontological principles. As a consequence, only this second part is a cosmology *strictu sensu* – a new cosmology, in comparison with *De unitate et uno*, as it is grounded upon a different range of sources applied to the discussion of the secondary causation Gundissalinus developed through Hermann of Carinthia, as we have seen in chapter two.[133] The influence of Ibn Gabirol's cosmology is still in place regarding the discussion of divine will as the origin of the cosmic institution. Following the vivid metaphors presented by Ibn Gabirol, Gundissalinus describes the coming to be of matter and form from God in terms of the flowing of water from a spring, and the union of form and matter as the reflection in a mirror.[134]

Nonetheless, *De processione* never extends the discussion of the role played by divine will into a real discussion of *voluntarism*. Gundissalinus refers to divine will only as the eminently efficient attribute of the first cause – an efficient cause,

[133] At first glance, it could appear that some traces of Ibn Gabirol's cosmology are still diffused throughout Gundissalinus's treatise, especially when Gundissalinus refers to intelligence and souls, quoting the *Fons vitae* in the closing numerological section of the *De processione mundi* (ed. Bülow, 56.2–12; ed. Soto Bruna and Alonso Del Real, 224.6–16 – which is a direct quotation from Ibn Gabirol, *Fons vitae*, ed. Baeumker, 239.5–12; ed. Benedetto, 550). Nonetheless, I have recently demonstrated that this passage as well should be taken not as cosmological but as psychological. See Nicola Polloni, "Nature, Souls, and Numbers: Remarks on a Medieval Gloss on Gundissalinus's *De processione mundi*," in *Causality and Resemblance: Medieval Approaches to the Explanation of Nature*, ed. María Jesús Soto Bruna (Hildesheim, 2018), 75–87; and Polloni, "Gundissalinus on the Angelic Creation of the Human Soul."

[134] Gundissalinus, *De processione mundi*, ed. Bülow, 40.16–41.9; ed. Soto Bruna and Alonso Del Real, 194.17–196.7.

208 | CHAPTER THREE

as creation "is only the going forth of form from his wisdom and will and the impression of his image in matter."[135] As a consequence, while divine will plays a crucial role in beginning the establishment of the world, Gundissalinus displays no real interest in engaging with the more theological aspects entailed by this central role or the reciprocal relations among God's will, wisdom, and essence. Generally speaking, among the many doctrines presented by *Fons vitae*, Gundissalinus had profound interest only in some main ontological and cosmological themes throughout his career, and he demonstrated almost no theological inquisitiveness beyond these.

Ibn Gabirol's ontology and cosmology are the point of departure of Gundissalinus's reflection, and they are accepted, quoted, and explained from *De unitate et uno* (his first text) onward. His initial eagerness also entailed his acceptance of Ibn Gabirol's hypostatic cosmology and was marked by a noticeable compositional reading. A gradual problematisation of the features presented in *Fons vitae* and a first attempt at binding together Avicenna's psychology with Ibn Gabirol's cosmology marks Gundissalinus's detachment from the latter in *De anima*. There, Gundissalinus also engages himself with a much more analytical reading of the two pairs of matter/form and genus/species, without addressing a possible tension between this and the compositional thesis entailed by his ontology. Finally, with *De processione mundi*, Gundissalinus appears to have found a balance with a functional reading of matter and form which allows him to properly expound the richness of his and Ibn Gabirol's ontology. This gradual maturation of Gundissalinus's approach to *Fons vitae* is therefore marked by opposed tendencies. He detaches himself from Ibn Gabirol's cosmology. But he uses much more Gabirolian doctrines and metaphysical principles here than in any of his other works. Therefore, *Fons vitae* appears to be not only the most important source of *De processione mundi*, but also a beacon leading Gundissalinus's metaphysical reflection from its very beginning. Accordingly, Gundissalinus's mature reflection corresponds to a mature and enveloping reading of *Fons vitae*.

Thanks to Ibn Gabirol, Gundissalinus could elaborate an ontology structured through functions of dualities expressed in different terms – matter and form, act and potency, genus and species. These dualities are the outcome of Gundissalinus's appropriation of Ibn Gabirol's principle of the simplicity of the cause. As the cause is more perfect and more "one" than its effect, the effect of God's complete unity of being is a created *unity into duality* (or *dualities*). As in *De anima*, Gundissalinus's first problematisation of Ibn Gabirol was pursued on

135 Ibid., ed. Bülow, 40.16–18; ed. Soto Bruna and Alonso Del Real, 194.17–19: "non est nisi exitus formae ab eius sapientia et voluntate et impressio eius in imaginem in materiam." English translation by Laumakis, *The Procession of the World*, 66.

an Avicennian basis, as too in *De processione mundi* Gundissalinus's further re-elaboration of his own ontology is marked by a discussion of a fundamental doctrine received by Avicenna. This allowed Gundissalinus to conceive God not only as absolute oneness and unity, establishing an intimately dual existence, but also as the Necessary Existent, which is other than a modal duality of possible existence and acquired necessity.

CHAPTER FOUR

Appraising Existence:
Gundissalinus, Avicenna, and Ibn Daud

Modalities of Existence

Gundissalinus's activity as translator apparently began with his encounter with Abraham ibn Daud and his involvement in the project of translating Avicenna's *Liber sufficientiae* (*Kitab aš-Šifa*) into Latin.[1] It seems that the first part of this work, which Gundissalinus and Ibn Daud translated, was *De anima*. Other translations predominantly covered parts of Avicenna's *Sufficientia* concerning epistemology and logic, natural philosophy, and metaphysics. In addition, Gundissalinus translated the sections on logic and metaphysics in al-Ghazali's *Summa theoricae philosophiae*, i.e., the Latin version of his *Maqasid al-Falasifa*, a work intimately related to Avicenna's.[2]

In these works, Gundissalinus explored a fresh new philosophical perspective that would be preeminently influential on his thought. Avicenna's impact informed the entire range of Gundissalinus's philosophical concerns, from epistemology to psychology and metaphysics.[3] Concerning the latter, a central role

---

1 It should be recalled that the manuscript tradition of these translations displays a plurality of versions (*De anima*: see Avicenna, *Liber de anima seu Sextus de naturalibus*, ed. Simone Van Riet [Louvain, 1968–72], 1: 105*–12*; *Liber de philosophia prima*: see Avicenna, *Liber de philosophia prima*, ed. Simone Van Riet [Louvain, 1977–83], 1: 128*–30*; *Physica* and *Liber de celi et mundi*: pseudo-Avicenna, *Liber celi et mundi*, ed. Oliver Gutman [Leiden, 2003], xxiii–xl). See also Charles Burnett, "Scientific Translations from Arabic: The Question of Revision," in *Science Translated: Latin and Vernacular Translations of Scientific Treatises in Medieval Europe*, ed. Michèle Goyens, Pieter de Leemans, and An Smets (Leuven, 2008), 11–31; Burnett, "The Strategy of Revision in the Arabic-Latin Translations from Toledo: The Case of Abu Ma'shar's *On the Great Conjunctions*," in *Translators at Work: Their Methods and Manuscripts*, ed. Jacqueline Hamesse (Louvain-la-Neuve, 2002), 51–113 and 529–40. Were these translations made by Gundissalinus in collaboration with his team (Abraham Ibn Daud and Johannes Hispanus)? Or maybe even alone, once he had eventually learned Arabic? See Manuel Alonso Alonso, "Coincidencias verbales típicas en las obras y traducciones de Gundisalvo," *Al-Andalus* 20 (1955): 129–52 and 345–79.

2 On al-Ghazali's use of Avicenna, see Jules Janssens, "Al-Ghazali and His Use of Avicennian Texts," in *Problems in Arabic Philosophy*, ed. Miklós Maróth (Piliscaba, 2003), 37–49.

3 While the crucial relevance of Avicenna's influence on Gundissalinus is beyond doubt, it should be recalled that Gundissalinus's "Avicenna" – i.e., the texts authored by Avicenna,

is played by Avicenna's *Philosophia prima*. Dedicated to the study of metaphysics, *De philosophia prima* is the fourth and last part of the *Sufficientia*.[4] In Avicenna's view, first philosophy inquires as to a range of entities which are characterised by separation from matter in their being and definition, and which are the first causes of natural and mathematical entities. Philosophy's first object is the study of being insofar as it is being ("ens, inquantum est ens")[5] and, pivotally, the first cause of being, which is God.[6] Another constitutive part of first philosophy is the corroboration of the principles of the sciences subordinated to it (that is, all philosophical disciplines).

Among his preliminary remarks on the contents and subjects of metaphysics, Avicenna introduces a fundamental distinction which, contextually, also grounds one of his most famous doctrines. I am referring to the distinction between essence and existence.[7] Avicenna observes that any existing thing has a being proper to itself (*esse proprium*), which is a quiddity or essence expressing the content x by which a thing is said to be x – as a squirrel is said to be a squirrel in virtue of its squirrel-essence or squirrel-quiddity. This *esse proprium* is different from the

---

plus those known and translated by him – does not correspond to the "entire" Avicenna. His works translated in Toledo, whose number would be extended by the continuation of the translation movement, provided Gundissalinus with a fundamental and yet incomplete part of Avicenna's production. Although traces of a wider knowledge of Avicenna's works by Gundissalinus can be detected in his works, it should be duly kept in mind that the "Latin Avicenna" and the "Arabic Avicenna" are neither superimposable nor interchangeable regarding either doctrines or effects.

4 For the relation between Avicenna's and Aristotle's metaphysical reflections, see Amos Bertolacci, *The Reception of Aristotle's Metaphysics in Avicenna's* Kitab al-Šifa (Leiden, 2006); and Dimitri Gutas, *Avicenna and the Aristotelian Tradition: Introduction to Reading Avicenna's Philosophical Works* (Leiden, 1988).

5 Avicenna, *Liber de philosophia prima* 1.2, ed. Van Riet, 13.36–8.

6 Avicenna, *Liber de philosophia prima* 1.1, ed. Van Riet, 5.82–8.52. For this plurality of aspects, Avicenna underlines that this science can be called by different names. It is "philosophia prima," as it studies the first cause of everything; it is "sapientia," as it is the true knowledge of God; but it is also "scientia divina," for it deals with what is utterly separated from matter. Moreover, since this discipline comes after natural philosophy and mathematics, it is also called "metaphysica," even though, considered in itself, it should be called "scientia de eo quod est ante naturam," since its object is ontologically prior to any other science. See ibid., 15.86–17.20; 20.20–23.28; 24.42–3; and 25.55–6.

7 Regarding this pivotal doctrine, see Amos Bertolacci, "The Distinction of Essence and Existence in Avicenna's *Metaphysics*: The Text and Its Context," in *Islamic Philosophy, Science, Culture, and Religion: Studies in Honor of Dimitri Gutas*, ed. Felicitas Opwis and David A. Reisman (Leiden, 2012), 257–88; Allan Bäck, "Avicenna on Existence," *Journal of the History of Philosophy* 25 (1987): 351–67; and Olga Lizzini, "*Wugud-Mawgud*/Existence-Existent in Avicenna: A Key Ontological Notion of Arabic Philosophy," *Quaestio* 3 (2003): 111–38.

esse affirmativum of that thing, corresponding to its positive or actual existence *in re* or *in intellectu*.[8] Avicenna argues for this crucial difference, pointing out that an overlay of essence and existence is impossible. Indeed, while an essential predication of a thing *x* consists of a mere tautological affirmation that "*x* is *x*," an existential predication provides supplementary information about *x*.[9] It adds something further to the essential predication, as it declares the *existence* of something – an aspect that cannot be expressed by the simple consideration of the essence of *x*.[10]

Although they are always together, essence and existence are two ontologically and logically distinguished aspects of any existing thing – with only one exception, God.[11] As they are different aspects yet together *in esse*, existence must be considered to be an added characteristic that accompanies essence without being resolvable into it. In other words, existence appears to be something assigned to an essence which makes that essence exist. If this is so, there must be a cause providing existence to essences. This cause cannot be the essence itself, as nothing can be the efficient cause of an aspect it does not already have – and the essence has no existence *per se*. Accordingly, there must be an external cause which has existence *per se* and can assign it to that essence, without being itself an essence. There must be an entity having a being completely different from the duality of essence and existence, the duality which constitutes the ontological structure of everything else. This being is the cause of that multiplicity of entities that are all marked by this ontological duality of essence and existence. In other words, it is the first cause existing by itself and for itself, the Necessary Existent.[12]

Avicenna's formulation of modal ontology (the development of an ontology entailing different modes of existence, which are necessity and possibility) is a crucial step forward for the history of philosophy. Any thing can be considered to be either necessary or possible in its existence, be it *in re* or *in intellectu*. While impossibility is not considered – evidently, a thing whose existence is

---

8 See Avicenna, *Liber de philosophia prima* 1.5, ed. Van Riet, 34.50–35.61.

9 See ibid., 35.62–36.83.

10 See Robert Wisnovsky, *Avicenna's Metaphysics in Context* (Ithaca, 2003), 145–80; and Olga Lizzini, *Avicenna* (Rome, 2012), 100–108.

11 Avicenna clarifies that existence always accompanies the essence *in re* or *in intellectu*, as it is impossible to have any knowledge of the absolutely inexistent, and therefore every knowable and affirmable quiddity always implies its existence, even if the two terms never coincide. See Avicenna, *Liber de philosophia prima* 1.5, ed. Van Riet, 36.84–37.1 and 36.78–83. See also Avicenna, *Metafisica*, trans. Olga Lizzini (Milan, 2002), 12.

12 On the sources of Avicenna's theory of necessary and possible being, see Wisnovsky, *Avicenna's Metaphysics in Context*, 197–243.

impossible both *in re* and *in intellectu* cannot be thought – Avicenna observes that ontological necessity and possibility are two radically opposed statuses of existence. On the one hand, necessity corresponds to sufficiency and, above all, self-sufficiency – something exists necessarily when it satisfies some conditions of ontological subsistence (basically corresponding to the same existence of that thing in its own subsistence either *in re* or *in intellectu*). On the other hand, the possibility of existence is intimately characterised by a fundamental alternative between the possibility of existence and non-existence. By itself, indeed, a possible entity can either be or not be. As possible things come to be, there must be an external cause providing what would otherwise be a merely possible existent with a necessary existence.[13]

This process of causation changes the possible existence of a caused entity into a necessary existence. While receiving this ontological status, the caused entity does not cease to have a possible existence in itself. Indeed, that entity was not and then came to be – its existential possibility (its being possible to exist) is an eminent characteristic of its own being. Although it could have not existed, that thing does exist. It has a necessary existence which it has acquired from an external cause having a necessary existence. Accordingly, the entity has a necessary existence *per aliud*, through its cause – an acquired necessity that, together with its own possibility, expresses the ontological duality proper to any caused being.

For the attribution of necessary existence *per aliud*, then, a cause is always required. As there cannot be a *regressus ad infinitum*, there must be a first entity in the causal series of necessitated existences. This first entity must be the cause of the entire series and, accordingly, it is not an effect, but only and completely a cause. Being uncaused, its necessity of existence is unacquired; and therefore necessity is the characteristic primarily and eminently proper to this first entity, which is necessary *per se*, by itself, rather than *per aliud*, as all other things are. Characterised by an intimate and complete ontological self-sufficiency, this first entity is the Necessary Existent. It is the Necessary Existent that causes the existence of every possible existent, providing it with an acquired existential necessity through a process that is logically correspondent to the attribution of its *esse affirmativus*. Accordingly, the Persian philosopher distinguishes among three modalities of existence:

1. The Necessary Existent *per se*, which is implicitly characterised by its own self-sufficiency and whose inexistence cannot be thought, as it is impossible to imagine a status in which it does not exist.

---

13 See Gerard Smith, "Avicenna and the Possibles," *The New Scholasticism* 17 (1943): 340–57.

214 | CHAPTER FOUR

2. The possible existent, which lacks any existential attribution and is characterised by an intimate insufficiency.

3. The necessary existent *per aliud*, which is the mode of existence proper to any caused being that acquires necessity through its cause and is marked by a twofold ontological duality of possibility and necessity and essence and existence.

From a cosmological point of view, these three modes of existence crucially correspond to, respectively:

1. God, the first and efficient cause of the universe.
2. The totality of the divine creatable, as eternal possibility of existence.
3. The eternal universe established by God.

In *Philosophia prima* 1, Avicenna develops this doctrine through five arguments.[14] The first two proofs aim at demonstrating the unrelated status of the Necessary Existent. Both proofs converge in the recognition that the Necessary Existent cannot be related to anything else in any possible way. On the one hand, a supposition of two Necessary Existents concomitant and homologous in their existence would imply that one of them is the cause of the other, or that both are causes.[15] On the other hand, a conjecture of two Necessary Existents correlative in their existence would lead to unsolvable contradictions. As a consequence, it must be said that the Necessary Existent has no relation to any other beings having a status equal to it.[16] It is self-sufficient and autonomous in its existence. Three further arguments corroborate this point. Supposition of a multiplicity of Necessary Existents invariably leads to inadmissible consequences.[17] Accordingly, the Necessary Existent is only one and is completely unrelated to anything else.[18] It is the only entity having that kind of absolute existence. Characterised by such a unique ontological status, the Necessary Existent is utterly different from any other existing thing either having a possible existence or an acquired necessity. As Avicenna remarks,

> accordingly, the property of the possible existent is already evident, i.e., that it requires a Necessary Existent to actualise it. A possible existent is whatever always has in itself (*respectu sui*) a possible existence but can acquire a necessary existence through something else (*per aliud a se*). This [necessity

14 For a detailed examination of Avicenna's proofs, see Nicola Polloni, "Gundissalinus on Necessary Being: Textual and Doctrinal Alterations in the Exposition of Avicenna's *Metaphysics*," *Arabic Sciences and Philosophy* 26 (2016): 129–60, at 132–36.

15 See Avicenna, *Liber de philosophia prima* 1.6, ed. Van Riet, 46.72–47.11.

16 See ibid., 48.12–38.

17 See Avicenna, *Liber de philosophia prima* 1.7, ed. Van Riet, 49.40–54.43.

18 See ibid., 54.38–43.

Appraising Existence: Gundissalinus, Avicenna, and Ibn Daud | 215

of existence] can happen to it always or occasionally. What happens [to be necessary only] occasionally must have a matter whose existence precedes it in time, as we have shown. But what always happens [to be necessary] does not have a simple quiddity [either]. Indeed, what it has in itself is different from what it receives from its cause – and it is what it is from both [existential aspects]. As a consequence, nothing is devoid of potency and possibility in itself, but the Necessary Existent.[19]

A pivotal difference is posited here. The Necessary Existent is one, simple, and completely self-sufficient. In contrast, the necessary existents *per aliud* have an acquired, mediated necessity which is an addition to their own possibility of existence. They are intimately *dual*, as they are made of a *duality of possibility and necessity* (their modalities of existence) and a *duality of essence and existence*. From this point of view, every additional difference among caused beings – like, for instance, their eternal or limited duration in time – is utterly secondary.

As Avicenna claimed elsewhere in *Philosophia prima*, the Necessary Existent is God.[20] He has no composition, no quiddity (for he is the cause of every quiddity), neither genus nor definition. God is not a substance, nor can be demon-

---

19 Ibid., 54.44–55.55: "Eius autem quod est possibile esse, iam manifesta est ex hoc proprietas, scilicet quia ipsum necessario eget alio quod faciat illud esse in effectu; quicquid enim est possibile esse, respectu sui, semper est possibile esse, sed fortassis accidet ei necessario esse per aliud a se. Istud autem vel accidet ei semper, vel aliquando. Id autem cui aliquando accidit, debet habere materiam cuius esse praecedat illud tempore, sicut iam ostendemus. Sed id cui semper accidit, eius quidditas non est simplex: quod enim habet respectu sui ipsius aliud est ab eo quod habet ab alio a se, et ex his duobus acquiritur ei esse id quod est. Et ideo nihil est quod omnino sit exspoliatum ab omni eo quod est in potentia et possibilitate respectu sui ipsius, nisi necesse esse."

20 Avicenna identifies the Necessary Existent with God in *Liber de philosophia prima* 8. His point of departure is an analysis of the finitude of the four series of causes and the distinction among caused, middle cause, and absolute cause. Every caused being has a proximate cause of which it is a direct effect. This cause, too, has its own cause and, as every proximate cause is always caused, the only way to avoid a *regressus ad infinitum* is to suppose a first uncaused cause. This first cause is the absolute cause of any caused effect and the first cause of the four orders of causality (material, formal, efficient, and final). As a consequence, a caused effect, its proximate cause, and the absolute cause are characterised by specific properties of which the caused and the remote/absolute cause are the extreme terms, the former being only the effect, the latter being the cause of everything different from it. Examination of the four causal chains, though, displays a fundamental difference. On the one hand, material and formal cause always refer to an agent causality and, therefore, they are proximate (*mediae*) causes of the efficient and final orders. On the other hand, efficient and final cause are two aspects of the same causality, which is characterised by a complete unity and unicity. In other words, efficiency and finality are traits of the first cause, the Necessary Existent, which is one and existent per se. See *Liber de philosophia prima* 8.1, ed. Van Riet, 376.16–377.31 and 8.3, ed. Van Riet, 395.12–396.23.

216 | CHAPTER FOUR

strated, as he is uncaused.[21] The Necessary Existent is purely one and absolutely true, characterised by the over-completeness of an over-abundant being which comes from him and constitutes the universe, with no contrariety, and is completely unrelated to anything else.[22] God is also a pure intelligence knowing himself – and, through himself, the entire universe. His knowledge does not entail any duality between intelligent and intelligible.[23] He is the *excellentior apprehensor* having the most excellent apprehension of the worthiest object of apprehension, and the *excellentior delectator* having the most excellent delight of what is most worthy of being delighted in.[24] He is powerful and generous, pure beauty, splendour, and perfection, among other attributes; God is exceedingly powerful and generous.[25] His existence corresponds to the pure goodness toward which everything tends – as caused existence is always a lack of being and, therefore, a lack of goodness.[26]

Cosmologically, the Necessary Existent is the efficient (and final) cause of the universe. His priority to the universe is not temporal, but essential.[27] As Avicenna underlines, God is the true cause, and the causality of a true cause resides in its own being, and its effect is simultaneous to it. Avicenna's example is striking. It is clear to anyone that, when opening a door, both the movement of the hand and that of the lock are simultaneous, but it is clear that the hand is the cause and the opening of the lock its effect. In a similar fashion, God and the universe are simultaneous in their eternity, but they are also respectively cause and effect.[28]

21 See Avicenna, *Liber de philosophia prima* 8.5, ed. Van Riet, 406.33–411.48. There Avicenna expounds an additional argument for the unrelatedness of the Necessary Existent. See especially 406.40–410.24.

22 Avicenna, *Liber de philosophia prima* 8.4 and 8.5–6, ed. Van Riet, 397.58–398.77 and 411.39–412.67. See also 8.6, 413.83–94 concerning God as Truth.

23 See ibid., 414.7–14 and 418.91–420.16.

24 Avicenna, *Liber de philosophia prima* 8.7, ed. Van Riet, 432.70–73.

25 See ibid., 429.21–431.49 and 431.50–432.75. See also Peter Adamson, "From the Necessary Existent to God," in *Interpreting Avicenna: Critical Essays*, ed. Adamson (Cambridge, 2013), 170–89.

26 See Avicenna, *Liber de philosophia prima* 8.6, ed. Van Riet, 412.59–61. Moreover, it should be considered that an identification of being and goodness implies evil as lack of being, in a Neoplatonic fashion. See also 412.67–413.78.

27 See Avicenna, *Liber de philosophia prima* 8.3, ed. Van Riet, 397.46–51.

28 See Avicenna, *Liber de philosophia prima* 4.1, ed. Van Riet, 184.3–187.69. The point of Avicenna's position that God's causality is essentially prior is to demonstrate that the universe is co-eternal with God but, all the same, it is caused by God. This kind of anteriority, indeed, must not be understood as a succession in a series, but as a logical and ontological precedence which leaves out any consideration of time and place. And thanks to this, Avicenna can eventually ground his doctrine of the eternal but caused universe. See Jon McGinnis, "The Eternity of the World: Proofs and Problems in Aristotle, Avicenna and Aquinas," *American Catholic Philosophical Quarterly* 88 (2014): 271–88.

The simultaneity of God and universe, however, does not imply the latter to be established instantaneously. To the contrary, consideration of the causal order of movement, which is always gradual and mediate, suggests that the cosmic institution has been gradual and mediated.[29]

The circularity of celestial movements also insinuates that the movement of the heavens is a kind of voluntary movement performed by a spiritual agent, which eternally moves the spheres tending toward something.[30] This agent cannot be an intelligence because an intelligence is, in itself, stable. Accordingly, it must be a soul which moves its sphere as it is moved by always new estimative representations.[31] Above the moving soul, though, there must be an intelligence, which is the anterior cause of the sphere's movement, as the immobile principle of movement of both the soul and the sphere. Every planetary sphere is brought into this threefold moving dynamic governed by the desire these entities have for the first cause of everything. In each sphere, everything moves toward God in different ways: the intelligence through intellection, the soul through representations, and the body through movement.[32]

God is indeed both the origin and end of their existence. The universe is established by the overabundance of the absolute One having intellection of himself. From this eternal and simple intellection starts the existential flow constituting the universe and originating a first intelligence.[33] From this first intelligence, which is possible *per se* and necessary *per aliud*, a crucial duality is established, and it radically expresses the difference between God and his effect. It marks the existence of the entire universe. The divine dynamic is indeed replicated in its own way by the first intelligence through three intellections, as,

> from the first intelligence, as it has intellection of the First [i.e., God], another intelligence proceeds below that. And as [the first intelligence] has intellection of itself, the form of the highest heaven and its perfection, i.e., [its] soul, proceeds from it. And, having intellection of itself through the nature of the possible existence that is proper to it and is retained in it, [from

29 See Avicenna, *Liber de philosophia prima* 9.1, ed. Van Riet, 436.37–438.82.

30 See Avicenna, *Liber de philosophia prima* 9.2, ed. Van Riet, 448.84–449.1.

31 See ibid., 454.86–90.

32 See Avicenna, *Liber de philosophia prima* 9.3, ed. Van Riet, 475.4–19. For an overall analysis of this doctrine and the peculiarities though which it is developed by the three major Arabic philosophers, see Herbert Davidson, *Alfarabi, Avicenna, and Averroes on Intellect: Their Cosmologies, Theories of the Active Intellect, and Theories of Human Intellect* (New York, 1992), especially 74–81.

33 See Avicenna, *Liber de philosophia prima* 9.4, ed. Van Riet, 481.51–482.64.

218 | CHAPTER FOUR

the first intelligence] the existence of corporeity of the highest heaven –
which is contained within the totality of the highest heaven – comes to be.[34]

The cosmogonic flow establishing the universe is grounded on a causal chain
which implements the *ontological duality* proper to every caused being. The first
intelligence has intellection of the three ontological modalities upon which Avicenna grounds his metaphysics. Indeed,

1. It has intellection of the unconditioned necessity of its cause (*necesse esse
per se*), from which another intelligence comes to be.
2. It has intellection of the acquired necessity of its being (*necesse esse per
aliud*), caused by the Necessary Existent, from which the celestial soul comes to
be.
3. It has intellection of the intrinsic possibility of its being (*possibile esse*),
from which the celestial sphere comes to be.

This threefold intellective activity corresponds to the causative dynamic
instituting the world. The threefold dynamic is indeed replicated by the second
intelligence, which has intellection of God and its twofold being, giving origin
to another intelligence, a second sphere and its soul. The process will end with
a tenth and last intelligence, which is the giver of forms (*dator formarum*) from
which the sensible world arises.[35] Avicenna's description of the causative derivation of the universe can be better understood through the scheme on page 219.

God's cosmogonic causality is realised through a *direct* causation of the first
intelligence only. The cosmogonic process has its beginning from this first caused
entity. Accordingly, the establishment of the universe is marked by a series of
mediated causations through which the cosmos finds its origin, while the sublunary world is governed by additional causes presided over by nature.[36]

---

34 Ibid., 483.85–91: "Igitur ex prima intelligentia, inquantum intelligit primum, sequitur
esse alterius intelligentiae inferioris ea, et inquantum intelligit seipsam, sequitur ex ea forma
caeli ultimi et eius perfectio et haec est anima, et propter naturam essendi possibile quae est
ei et quae est retenta inquantum intelligit seipsam, est esse corporeitatis caeli ultimi quae est
contenta in totalitate caeli ultimi."

35 See Dag Nikolaus Hasse, "Avicenna's 'Giver of Forms' in Latin Philosophy, Especially in the Works of Albertus Magnus," in *The Arabic, Hebrew and Latin Reception of Avicenna's Metaphysics*, ed. Dag N. Hasse and Amos Bertolacci (Berlin, 2012), 225–50.

36 See Avicenna, *De causis et principiis naturalium* 1.6, ed. Simone Van Riet, *Liber primus
naturalium: Tractatus primus de causis et principiis naturalium* (Louvain, 1992), 59.3–10.
Nature is specified by a crucial correspondence with form, i.e., the essence through which
something is what it is. In the simple beings, such as the elements, nature and form explicitly

Appraising Existence: Gundissalinus, Avicenna, and Ibn Daud | 219

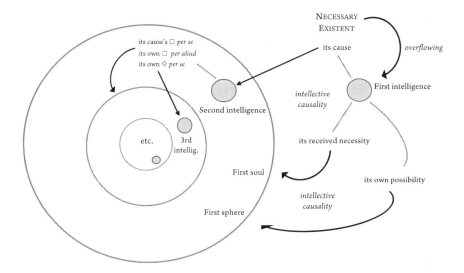

This caused yet eternal universe is furthermore organised – ontologically – through a distinction between the immaterial being of intelligences/angels and souls, on the one hand, and the material existence of bodies, on the other. Spiritual creatures are substantial quiddities.[37] They are not hylomorphic compounds, as they are not bodies – for Avicenna, matter is indeed a principle of corporeal beings only. In turn, different genera of bodies have different kinds of persistence in being. For instance, celestial spheres, which are perfectly constituted, do not suffer generation or corruption, which, to the contrary, are a typical feature of the sublunary world. Notwithstanding a causation of the matter of the celestial spheres by the intelligences, sublunary matter enters the cosmo-ontological progression only in a *logically* subsequent phase, i.e., once the celestial realm has been established.

In Avicenna's ontology, therefore, matter does not play an enveloping and grounding role as it does in Ibn Gabirol's. While *Fons vitae* bases its discussion of the ontological difference between God and the created universe upon the hylomorphic composition of the latter, the same differentiating function is pursued, in Avicenna's perspective, by the modal duality of the caused being. Accordingly, there is no need to posit matter and form at the beginning of the chain of created

---

coincide; and indeed, when one refers to what gives them their movement, one calls it "nature," otherwise form. In the composed bodies, on the contrary, there is no perfect correspondence between nature and form, since in them nature is expressed by further factors derived from the ontological complexity of the composed being. See also ibid., 60.30–37.

37 See Avicenna, *Liber de philosophia prima* 6.4, ed. Van Riet, 324.13–24.

being, as in *Fons vitae*.[38] The first entity to be caused by God is the first intelligence, whose being has no matter and, consequently, is not instantiated into a plurality of individuals.[39] Intrinsically, the simplicity of the intelligences is constituted by the modal duality of their ontological possibility *per se* and necessity *per aliud*.

Modal duality – not compositional duality – is the characteristic structure of caused being in general, both spiritual and corporeal. Only for the bodies is this duality doubled by a compositional duality of matter and form, of which they are made. The celestial spheres have matter, and their matter (as well as their form) appears to be a consequence of the intelligence's reflection on its own possible existence, establishing a meaningful bond between modal possibility and hylomorphic composition (in particular, matter). This dynamic is repeated until the celestial spheres are established in a causal descent toward the middle. Then, within the realm of nature, matter and form finally pursue a most enfolding ontological role, as the sublunary world is for the most part made of hylomorphic entities which are exposed to the four kinds of Aristotelian movements – generation and corruption included. Accordingly, sublunary corporeal beings can also be considered as instantiations of a progressive pluralisation of the ontological flow of simple being started by God, which progressively declines into plurality.[40]

---

38 It is worth noting that Avicenna uses the metaphysical principle that "ex unum non fit nisi unum" (*Liber de philosophia prima* 9.4, ed. Van Riet, 479.88–94) to deny that from the One two entities or a being composed of two entities could have derived. If that were the case, a series of contradictions would arise. On the one hand, it should be admitted that those two different aspects were in the simple One, which is a contradiction. On the other hand, the supposition that these two "aspects" were essential concomitants of the One would entail the same upshot, i.e., a plurality in what is utterly simple. See ibid., 479.97–6. Avicenna also claims that the first effect of God's causation cannot be a material form, for it would imply that matter is the middle cause of everything. Matter, though, cannot be such, as it is only receptive. If this were the case, "matter" would be matter only equivocally – not truly matter, but something else, leading us to admit that corporeal forms do not require matter. This cannot be the case, as the middle cause of matter is the form. See ibid., 480.12–481.39.

39 Indeed, species are particularised into a plurality of individuals only through matter. Being substantial quiddities, for Avicenna each and every celestial intelligence is one in its species, i.e., a singular individual which expresses the totality of that species. See ibid., 481.39–42. As is well known, this doctrine would dramatically influence the Latin tradition, although it does not seem to have had any impact on Gundissalinus.

40 As Lizzini has pointed out, Avicenna grounds his notion of matter upon two pivotal functions. In metaphysics, matter corresponds to the absolute and undetermined possibility of receiving forms and, accordingly, it also coincides with the "limit" of the cosmic flow. Nevertheless, matter also plays the role of the principle of determination and individuation of form. Matter is the ontological partner of form, and it is prepared to receive its form by the celestial spheres and the interactions among different material complexions which act upon each other. See Lizzini, *Avicenna*, 177–84.

Appraising Existence: Gundissalinus, Avicenna, and Ibn Daud | 221

Leaving the problem of celestial matter aside,[41] the world below the sphere of the Moon is made of one common matter caused by the last intelligence, the giver of forms (*dator formarum*). This common matter is the substrate of change. Avicenna follows Aristotle by claiming that matter, form, and privation are the principles of natural bodies, out of which principles matter is what persists through the processes of change. As change always involves act and potency, matter is also said to be the substrate of what is possible, as,

We now demonstrate, then, that whatever has a beginning has a material principle. And I say this with certitude, as whatever begins to be after not having been surely has matter. Indeed, whatever begins to be, before it is, is certainly possible in itself. And if it were not possible in itself, then it would not have been in any way. The possibility of its being, though, does not derive from it by the power of the agent above it, as if it were not possible in itself [already]. Do you not see that we can say that the impossible is not possible, but what has a possible existence is possible?[42]

Processes of coming to be and passing away inevitably entail a persisting substrate preceding any generation and corruption. That substrate is matter, which corresponds to both potentiality and the possibility of any natural body.[43] Such an anteriority of possibility to effective existence, though, is limited to a logical ordering only.[44] Matter, indeed, is characterised by an utter potentiality and possibility of existence which is realised only through the reception of a form. Matter is in potency, and it is *the* potency of every corporeal being, as the substrate of possibility, although under different considerations.[45] Its actuality, and the actuality of the corporeal body as well, is a consequence of its reception of a

---

41 On this point, see Andreas Lammer, *The Elements of Avicenna's Physics: Greek Sources and Arabic Innovations* (Berlin, 2018), 179–201, where the author remarkably reconstructs the problem of the communality of matter in Avicenna.

42 Avicenna, *Liber de philosophia prima* 4.2, ed. Van Riet, 208.50–58: "Certificemus igitur nunc quod omne quod incipit habet principium materiale. Et dico omnino quia omne quod incipit esse post non esse sine dubio habet materiam. Omne enim quod incipit esse, antequam sit, necesse est ut sit possibile in se. Si enim fuerit non possibile in se, illud non erit ullo modo; non est autem possibilitas sui esse eo quod agens sit potens super illud, cum ipsum non fuerit in se possibile. Nonne enim vides quia possumus dicere quod super impossibile non est posse, sed posse est super id quod possibile est esse?"

43 See ibid., 210.89–96. See also Jon McGinnis, *Avicenna* (Oxford, 2010), 187–89.

44 This kind of anteriority is only valid from a logical point of view and it is proper to corporeal beings only, as the intelligible substances are not preceded by any potency and do not have matter. See Avicenna, *Liber de philosophia prima* 4.2, ed. Van Riet, 211.12–213.69.

45 See Avicenna, *Liber de philosophia prima* 6.4, ed. Van Riet, 320.26–321.46.

form. Matter is the capacity itself of receiving a form, which is impressed on it by an external cause.[46] Reception of that form corresponds to the actualisation of the hylomorphic compound and, within it, of its matter. Form is indeed an actualizing act. Both substantial and accidental forms are always in act and have the capacity to actualise either the entirety or some aspect of the hylomorphic compound.

Substantial forms are also the principle of difference expressing the species.[47] Matter must be originally disposed to receive one form rather than any other, whatever form could join whatever part of matter. Matter, therefore, must be prepared to be joined to a particular form in one of its *regions*, and it is prepared as such by the celestial spheres.[48] Specifically, this pre-detetermination of matter is performed by the movement of the celestial spheres and by the interactions among sensible principles as well. Their effect is to make matter apt to receive the forms it shall be joined to through a perfect preparation.[49] The *principia praepatatoria*, however, are accompanied by a perfecting principle which specifically causes the union of prepared matter with its form. In other words, once matter is prepared, it needs to be joined to the form by an external cause, which is the tenth intelligence, or *dator formarum*. The giver of forms is the efficient cause of the hylomorphic compound, which impresses forms on matter once it has been prepared to receive them, and also conserves matter throughout the constant processes of change.[50]

46 See ibid., 324.2–3.

47 See ibid., 324.13–24.

48 In other words, matter cannot be conceived as being utterly undifferentiated as for its reception of forms. Otherwise, any form could join any region of matter without rhyme or reason, an eventuality which is inadmissible and is proven false by the order of nature. Therefore, matter must be preemptively prepared for the reception of one particular form, in a moment logically but not temporally prior to the joining of that form. See Avicenna, *Liber de philosophia prima* 9.5, ed. Van Riet, 488.98–494.30.

49 See ibid., 489.31–490.42. See also Avicenna, *De causis et principiis naturalium* 1.9, ed. Van Riet, 83.44–84.49. It is worth noticing that, from a certain point of view, matter preexists its union with the form. As Lizzini has pointed out, this is one of the most complex points of Avicenna's reflection, as the author seems to claim, on the one hand, that matter and form are simultaneous and, on the other hand, that matter must already be conditioned to receive its form, which cannot be emanated by the *dator formarum* until the matter is prepared to receive it. See Avicenna, *Metafisica*, trans. Lizzini, 363–64.

50 See Avicenna, *Liber de philosophia prima* 2.4, ed. Van Riet, 99.61–70. See also Avicenna, *De causis et principiis naturalium* 1.11, ed. Van Riet, 96.20–26. The pivotal relevance of the tenth intelligence, which is the main formal actor of the sublunary world, should be appreciated. Indeed, the *dator formarum* provides the immanent formal principles of the corporeal beings and the formal intellectual contents of human intellection.

Avicenna also posits a third cause of matter. In what has been defined as *extrinsécisme radical* and *formalisme,* Avicenna claims that the proximate cause of the existence of matter is its form.[51] Matter's utterly potential being can be actualised only through its union with a form. For this reason, matter can be in act only through the form and as long as it is joined to a form – accordingly, matter cannot ever be without a form *in re.*[52] Avicenna also makes clear that the peculiar relationship between matter and form cannot be understood as if they were two homologous entities or two correlatives.[53] To the contrary, consideration of such a hypothesis shows that the relation of matter and form is a causal relation in which one of the two terms is the cause of the other. Matter, though, cannot be the cause of form, as it is prepared to receive its form, and whatever is prepared to something cannot be its cause. In addition, as matter is in potency, it cannot be conceived as the cause of form, which is in act. Actuality, indeed, is prior to potency both essentially and temporally.[54] Therefore, the cause of both matter and the hylomorphic compound must be the form. The form actualises matter and is essentially prior to matter, being its cause.[55]

As a consequence, while the giver of the forms and the preparatory principles are the remote causes of both matter and the hylomorphic compound, their proximate cause is the form.[56] Its causality is a mediated causality (form is the *causa media* of matter) which realises the actuality of the body. Form, therefore, always accompanies matter, without being dependent on it in any way. Indeed, while matter always depends on both its form and its preparatory and perfecting

51 See Étienne Gilson, *Le thomisme: Introduction au système de Saint Thomas d'Aquin* (Paris, 1922), 256; and Jean Michot, *La destinée de l'homme selon Avicenne: Le retour à Dieu (ma'ad) et l'imagination* (Louvain, 1986), 68–86.

52 See Avicenna, *Liber de philosophia prima* 2.3, ed. Van Riet, 82.46–7.

53 See Avicenna, *Liber de philosophia prima* 2.4, ed. Van Riet, 92.30–95.91. Indeed, if matter and form were correlatives, it would be impossible to have intellection of one of them without the other, while we daily have cognition of forms abstracted from matter. At the very same time, if matter and form were two beings homologous in their existence, the removal of one of them would imply the removal of the other. If so, they would be correlatives or reciprocally dependent on each other: but since they both are possible in themselves, they must be caused by something external, whose removal would remove them both, a hypothesis contrary to the initial supposition, which therefore was false. For a detailed analysis of this point and its theoretical implications, see Olga Lizzini, "The Relation Between Form and Matter: Some Brief Observations on the 'Homology Argument' (*Ilahiyyat,* II.4) and the Deduction of Fluxus," in *Interpreting Avicenna, Science and Philosophy in Medieval Islam,* ed. Jon McGinnis (Paris: 2004), 175–85.

54 See Avicenna, *Liber de philosophia prima* 2.4, ed. Van Riet, 95.91–97 and 96.99–3.

55 See ibid., 97.19–22.

56 Ibid., 101.98–4.

224 | CHAPTER FOUR

principles, form only depends on the *dator formarum*, which is its cause.[57] Ultimately, both matter and form also ontologically depend on the Necessary Existent, on whom all caused beings depend, as God is the first and final cause of everything.

Once the form has joined matter, then, it realises the actuality of the compound and its matter. Nevertheless, as Avicenna's hylomorphism is a *corporeal hylomorphism*, the union of form and matter has an additional immediate consequence, i.e., corporealisation. The problem of how corporeity, or dimensionality and extension, derives from unextended and undetermined matter has marked the history of Aristotelianism since late antiquity at the very least.[58] Avicenna's solution is his famous doctrine of corporeal form (*forma corporeitatis*) – a doctrine which would have great success in the Latin Middle Ages.[59]

For Avicenna, a body is "one continuous substance not composited of indivisible parts" (*substantia una continua non composita ex partibus indivisibilibus*).[60] Since the body is continuous and always indefinitely divisible, it must be enmattered. Its actuality is caused by its form, but its potency as an object of further modifications is due to its matter.[61] Being so, a body is always characterised by three-dimensionality as such: a body is three-dimensional notwithstanding the three dimensions it has in a particular case and moment.[62] The specific characteristic of the body, therefore, is its three-dimensionality, a common feature shared by every corporeal being. Nevertheless, as matter *per se* is not extended

---

57 See Avicenna, *Liber de philosophia prima* 9.5, ed. Van Riet, 490.49–491.56.

58 On the late ancient Aristotelian development of theories of matter, see Frans A.J. de Haas, *John Philoponus' New Definition of Prime Matter: Aspects of Its Background in Neoplatonism and the Ancient Commentary Tradition* (Leiden, 1997); and Richard Sorabji, *Matter, Space and Motion: Theories in Antiquity and Their Sequel* (London, 1988).

59 On the reception of Avicenna's physical theories, see Jules Janssens, "The Reception of Avicenna's *Physics* in the Latin Middle Ages," in *O ye Gentlemen: Arabic Studies on Science and Literary Culture in Honour of Remke Kruk*, eds. Arnoud Vrolijk and Jan P. Hogendijk (Leiden, 2007), 55–64; Janssens, "The *Physics* of the Avicenna Latinus and Its Significance for the Reception of Aristotle's *Physics* in the Latin West," in *The Letter before the Spirit: The Importance of Text Editions for the Study of the Reception of Aristotle*, ed. Aafke M.I. van Oppenraay (Leiden, 2012), 311–30; Janssens, "The *Liber primus naturalium*, i.e. the *Physics* of the Avicenna Latinus," *Documenti e Studi sulla Tradizione Filosofica Medievale* 28 (2017): 219–38. See also Ayman Shihadeh, "Avicenna's Corporeal Form and Proof of Prime Matter in Twelfth-Century Critical Philosophy: Abu l-Barakat, al-Ma'sudi and al-Razi," *Oriens* 42 (2014): 364–96; Arthur Hyman, "Aristotle's 'First Matter' and Avicenna's and Averroes' 'Corporeal Form,'" in *Essays in Medieval Jewish and Islamic Philosophy*, ed. Arthur Hyman (New York, 1977), 335–406.

60 Avicenna, *Liber de philosophia prima* 2.2, ed. Van Riet, 69.87–8.

61 Ibid., 77.44–6.

62 See ibid., 69.90 and 71.32–3.

and has no dimensionality, it must be assumed that the first form to be received by matter is the form of corporeity, whose primary function is to extend the body into the three dimensions.

Bódy as such (or "absolute body") is the result of the union of matter and the form of corporeity. In other words, before being qualified, body as such is just extended and quantified matter:

> Accordingly, it is evident that the form of corporeity as such requires matter. And [it is also evident] that the nature of the form of corporeity, as it is a corporeal form, is not differentiated in itself, as it has a simple nature that cannot be specified following the differences which are added to it because it is corporeal.[63]

Qualities would join the bodies in a subsequent logical or ontological moment, specifying that "first body" into a plurality of different bodies, together with their accidents.[64]

As one of the first Latin translators of Avicenna's works, Gundissalinus had privileged access to these theories. He accepted and developed only some of them, while leaving completely unaddressed some substantive parts of Avicenna's metaphysics. He never explicitly criticised Avicenna. He never mentioned Avicenna's name in his metaphysical works, *De unitate* and *De processione*. In addition, Gundissalinus's interpretation of Avicenna appears to have been strongly influenced by one of the most intriguing interpreters of Avicenna – and Gundissalinus's most esteemed colleague in Toledo, Abraham ibn Daud.

Theoretical Crossroads

The main promoter of a Latin translation of *Kitab aš-Šifa*, Abraham Ibn Daud was also an eager follower of Avicenna's philosophy. Mostly known as author of the *Book of Tradition (Dorot 'Olam)*,[65] Ibn Daud also authored an intriguing

---

63 Ibid., 78.77–79.84: "Manifestum est igitur ex hoc quod forma corporeitatis inquantum est forma corporeitatis eget materia et quod natura formae corporeitatis inquantum est forma corporea, ipsa in se non diversificatur, quia est una natura simplex, quae non potest specificari differentiis supervenientibus sibi inquantum corporea."

64 Avicenna, *De causis et principiis naturalium* 1.2, ed. Van Riet, 20.33–46 and 28.80–87.

65 See Abraham Ibn Daud, *Sefer ha-Qabbalah: The Book of Tradition*, ed. Gerson D. Cohen (London, 1967) and *Dorot 'Olam*, ed. Katja Vehlow, *Abraham Ibn Daud's Dorot 'Olam (Generation of the Ages): A Critical Edition and Translation of Zikhron Divrey Romi, Divrey Yisra'el and the Midrash on Zechariah* (Leiden – Boston, 2013).

226 | CHAPTER FOUR

philosophical work, *The Exalted Faith* (al-'Aqidah al-Rafi'ah, or ha-Emunah ha-Ramah in Hebrew).[66] This text is marked by two characteristics which are central in the consideration of Gundissalinus's speculation. On the one hand, Ibn Daud's reflection is grounded upon Avicenna. On the other, it is also developed through a harsh criticism of Ibn Gabirol's *Fons vitae*. *The Exalted Faith* aims at demonstrating that there is an intimate although often unspoken concordance between (mainly Aristotelian and Avicennian) philosophy and (firmly Jewish) religion.[67] Ibn Daud develops many doctrinal points derived from Avicenna's reflection, often combining it with al-Ghazali's and al-Farabi's perspectives. Accordingly, many aspects of Ibn Daud's ontology and cosmology are very close to Avicenna's, starting with his modal ontology.

66 This work is only extant in Hebrew, while there are no traces pointing at a Latin translation of *The Exalted Faith*. Krizstina Szilágyi, however, has recently signalled the discovery of a Hebrew colophon of a "Physics" authored by Ibn Daud, which she connects to a reference made by Albert the Great to a writing that might be identified with this lost work by Ibn Daud. If that were the case, it could possibly be supposed that Ibn Daud and Gundissalinus might have decided, while translating Avicenna into Latin, to translate one or more writings authored by the former. Although not improbable, especially in consideration of the peculiarities of that intellectual circle, this hypothesis still lacks enough evidence to be relied upon. See Szilágyi, "Ibn Daud and Avendauth? Notes on a Lost Manuscript and a Forgotten Book," *Aleph* 16 (2016): 10–31. As for Gundissalinus, Ibn Daud's ideas and theories expounded in *The Exalted Faith* evidently did not require a Latin translation of the text. He is likely to have had access to the Arabic original, and besides that, a daily exchange of thoughts and perspectives surely marked the collaboration between him and Ibn Daud. As has been pointed out in the previous pages, Gundissalinus likely learnt Arabic later in his career, making himself able to translate Arabic without the aid of a second collaborator. All the same, the lack of both a Latin translation and the original Arabic version of Ibn Daud's work makes impossible a comparative textual analysis of Gundissalinus's and Ibn Daud's treatises. Even more, the only extant version is the only one Gundissalinus did not have access to, i.e., the Hebrew translation. For this reason, I will proceed with a comparative analysis based only on theoretical cores, referring to the text of Ibn Daud's work only if strictly necessary.

67 For Ibn Daud, religion and philosophy are but two different approaches to the knowledge of the truth. At first glance, their methods and outcomes seem to be contrasting, but this opposition is only apparent. The articulation of *The Exalted Faith* reflects Ibn Daud's aims: each chapter expounds a philosophical discussion which is followed by sets of biblical authorities, displaying the intrinsic coherence between the two branches of wisdom. *The Exalted Faith* is divided into three books, of which the first deals with Aristotelian physics and metaphysics. The second presents the basic principles of religion – the source of faith (God, as necessary and incorporeal being), the unity of God, the divine attributes, God's actions (and thus the secondary causation performed by the angels), the religious tradition, and divine providence. Unfortunately, only the first chapter of the third book has survived, so we do not know its contents.

Appraising Existence: Gundissalinus, Avicenna, and Ibn Daud | 227

For Ibn Daud, human beings can and must know God, and they can do so through an examination of creation. While God's essence can be known only once the human soul is freed from its body, the human intellect can only acknowledge that God exists.[68] God, indeed, is the first cause actualising the intimate potentiality of every caused being which, whether perpetual or transient, is characterised by the possibility of existence. In this respect, creation is opposed to God, the Necessary Existent.[69] The Necessary Existent is completely unrelated, utterly simple, and brings about an absolute causality.[70] God is also the pure One, provided with the most complete being.[71] Unity and oneness are his absolute characteristics and, accordingly, only God can be said to be One *per se*. All other beings are only incidentally "one." On the one hand, angels and spiritual creatures have a being which is composed of necessity and possibility. On the other, bodies are composed of matter and form. Therefore, while divine unity is absolute and essential, any other unity is said and known as such only *per accidens*, since it has in itself an intrinsic duality which is opposed to the true One.[72] The doctrinal proximities with Avicenna could not have been closer.

As God is purely one, the origin of the universe must be justified in terms of a series of intermediaries which mediate between God's oneness and creaturely plurality.[73] Mirroring Avicenna, Ibn Daud describes the establishment of the universe as a noetic cosmological process.[74] From God's complete oneness a first

68 See Ibn Daud, *The Exalted Faith* 121b16–122b2, trans. Norbert M. Samuelson (Rutherford, 1986), 131. See also Resianne Fontaine, *In Defense of Judaism: Abraham Ibn Daud* (Maastricht, 1990), 83–85.

69 See Ibn Daud, *The Exalted Faith* 126a3–7, trans. Samuelson, 136: "It is clear that many existents exist potentially but do not exist actually, such as plants in seeds and birds in eggs. This state of affairs is more true of what is called by the term *possible* than anything else. The reason for this is that the impression of the possible is that it is something that does not exist now and if it were posited afterward that it does or does not exist, no absurdity necessarily follows from this claim." See also ibid., 125b17–126a3, trans. Samuelson, 136.

70 See ibid., 129b4–6, trans. Samuelson, 143: "it is not possible that there is multiplicity in any respect in what is first, upon which the existence of everything depends whose existence does not depend on anything, and which has no need for anything, but everything needs it." See also ibid., 129a8–b4, trans. Samuelson, 142–43.

71 See ibid., 129b6–16, trans. Samuelson, 143.

72 See ibid., 128b8–15, trans. Samuelson, 141; and 130b3–131a7, trans. Samuelson, 144–45. Ibn Daud specifically examines ten senses in which something is said to be "one." See 128a1–b8, trans. Samuelson, 140–41.

73 See Ibn Daud, *The Exalted Faith* 152b8–12, trans. Samuelson, 173.

74 See ibid., 153a9–b2, trans. Samuelson, 174: "Next, this entity that goes forth by a primary departure from the First, may He be exalted, also is in their contention a mover that is not moved. From it goes forth a third mover that is not moved, a substance that is at the grade of soul for the Right Sphere, and the body of the Right Sphere. From the third mover

228 | CHAPTER FOUR

intelligence is originated. It is an angel who moves while resting and who, although similar to God in some respects, utterly depends upon him. This first effect of God's causality, called the "Essence of the Throne," has intellection of its own dual being. From this intellection, the first celestial sphere – the *sphera recta* – and its soul originate.[75] The first angel also has intellection of his cause, intellection which causes the existence of a second intelligence. This second intelligence would perform the same noetic causality, causing a third intelligence, and so on up to the tenth and last angel.

Angels have a mediating function within divine causality, for they administer God's will.[76] Through their noetic causality, the angels establish the spiritual universe and, through the proximate causality of the giver of forms, also the corporeal world. Angels, though, also exercise a fundamental causality regarding souls.[77] Ibn Daud points out that souls, before being joined to their bodies, have a possible existence, as,

> prior to the creation of the body the state of a soul does not escape from being one of three things. The consequence of this is that if it is the case that the soul's state of existence is necessary, then it would exist prior to the body, and we already refuted this claim. Or its existence is impossible, and if this is so then the soul of a man never exists. What remains is that the state of

---

goes forth a fourth mover, the sphere of Saturn and its mover. Similarly, the process of overflow continues to that from which is generated the sphere of the Moon, its mover, and the mover of its mover. Next, the mover for the mover of the sphere of the Moon, that is, that which is the mover for the sphere of the Moon at the grade of intellect for the human soul, exists in the order of that substance which is called 'Active Intellect.' Neither an angel nor a sphere is overflowed from this entity."

75 It should be appreciated that the terms "sphera recta" and "sphera obliqua" are astronomical technical terms referring to the view of the sky from the equator (*sphera recta*) and from every other place rather than the equator (*sphera obliqua*). A good example of this is displayed by Grosseteste's use of these terms in his *De sphera*: see Cecilia Panti, *Moti, virtù e motori celesti nella cosmologia di Roberto Grossatesta: Studio ed edizione dei trattati 'De sphera,' 'De cometis,' 'De motu supercelestium'* (Florence, 2001). Ibn Daud, though, seems to mean something completely different. Being two positional perspectives, *sphera recta* and *sphera obliqua* are not identifiable with two celestial entities, that is, with two existing spheres rotating over the Earth. On the contrary, Ibn Daud names the *sphera recta* – and the Zodiac – but he seems to bear in mind a different system, i.e., the Platonic cosmological distinction between the "sphere of the Identical" and the "sphere of the Different." This hypothesis seems to be corroborated by the claim that matter is originated by the former, while the forms come to be from the latter. A similar scenario is presented also by Hermann of Carinthia. I have to thank Cecilia Panti for her help with this curious passage.

76 Ibn Daud, *The Exalted Faith* 91b2–4, trans. Samuelson, 103.

77 See ibid., 54b7–121b4, trans. Samuelson, 88–126.

Appraising Existence: Gundissalinus, Avicenna, and Ibn Daud | 229

existence of souls is possible and their existence is potential. Now, every-thing that goes forth from potentiality to actuality is in motion, and motion only arises from a mover. This mover is what causes forms to overflow upon instances of matter, and souls to overflow upon bodies.[78]

Every possible existent always requires a cause to become necessary. Under this consideration, the soul also requires a cause, which is the mover that "causes forms to overflow upon instances of matter and souls upon bodies." The cause of the souls, therefore, appears to be the giver of forms, which impresses the souls into the bodies similarly to what happens with the forms of human cognition.[79] The constant movement of the spheres acts on sublunary matter, preparing it for the reception of the corporeal forms impressed by the *dator formarum*.[80]

Matter and form can be understood in reference to everyday experiences. As a gold bar can be melted to make a gold dinar, and this into a gold ring, it can be said that gold is the "matter," while the different figures into which it is shaped are its "forms." These kinds of forms, though, are "artificial forms" and are dif-ferent from the "divine forms" which are impressed by God into the universe, providing everything with its name and definition.[81] Elemental transmutation offers a crucial example of this process. When water becomes air, and then fire, its transmutation is complete, as divine forms give the element a whole new essence.[82] When a new elemental form takes the place of the previous one, though, there must be a subject that persists through the transmutation. This subject cannot be the previous form, since it completely disappears. It also can-not be the privation of that form, as it could be said that every form different from that one is its cause, even nothingness. Therefore, there must be a com-mon substance hidden to the senses which is potentially each one of the four ele-ments, and that entity is matter.[83]

Matter and form, though, are corporeal features only. Defined as "a sub-stance that has some mass and some rigidity, in which it is possible to posit three dimensions that intersect at right angles,"[84] body is made of matter and form. Body as such – i.e., the "absolute body" – is made of matter and the form of cohe-

---

78 Ibid., 102b18–103b6, trans. Samuelson, 113.

79 In this passage, Ibn Daud is clearly referring to the soul in general, i.e., the rational, sensitive, and vegetative souls, all of them caused by the giver of forms, whose function is, in fact, pursued through the continuous information of matter in the sublunary world.

80 See ibid., 157b1–158b10, trans. Samuelson, 176–77.

81 See ibid., 21b12–17, trans. Samuelson, 60.

82 See ibid., 21b17–22b1, trans. Samuelson, 60.

83 See ibid., 23b10–17, trans. Samuelson, 61.

84 See ibid., 28b10–13, trans. Samuelson, 63.

230 | CHAPTER FOUR

sion extending matter into dimensionality. Indeed, matter in itself has neither a complete (actual) existence nor quantitative or qualitative determination. Its first determination is cohesion, through which matter becomes three-dimensional. As a consequence, matter cannot be an ontological component of *every* existing being, but only of those beings spatially extended – hylomorphism cannot be universal, but corporeal, as in Avicenna. Admission of the contrary would be an inexcusable mistake, theoretically ungroundable and theologically inadmissible.

If matter were among the first effects of God's causation, there would be an abrupt emergence of complexity from complete oneness – an outcome which cannot be agreed upon. Moreover, as knowledge is always and only *per formam*, human beings can know both substantial and accidental forms, but cannot know matter, which can be grasped only by an abstraction which posits it as the mere and complete possibility which it is.[85] Accordingly, any attempt to ground the establishment of the universe upon matter would be in vain. This is exactly the case of Ibn Daud's nemesis – Solomon Ibn Gabirol. As we shall see, Ibn Daud repeatedly attacks *Fons vitae*, refuting the doctrine of universal hylomorphism due to its series of series of unsolvable contradictions and misunderstandings.[86]

According to these ontological limitations, matter and form are the characteristics of corporeal being and, specifically, of sublunary bodies marked by coming-to-be and passing-away.[87] Spiritual creatures are not hylomorphic compounds, and yet they have a duality which is similar to the hylomorphic duality proper to bodies. While the latter are made of matter and form, spiritual beings are made of something "like matter" and something "like form." They are, respectively, possible and necessary existence, which can be considered analogous to matter and form, but never as matter and form – as Ibn Gabirol considered them.[88] Consideration of the fact that for Ibn Daud matter is always in potency and form always in act makes clear that the author had in mind the following series of analogies:

---

85 See ibid., 26b16–17, trans. Samuelson, 62: "prime matter is a substance that the intellect considers abstracted from every form, which is not a determinate thing, but is something from which it is possible for any body to come to be."

86 See for instance, 26b17–27b14, trans. Samuelson, 62–63, which will be discussed at the end of this chapter.

87 See ibid., 27b15–20, trans. Samuelson, 63.

88 See ibid., 152b14–153a9, trans. Samuelson, 174. The next section will cast some additional light upon this relevant aspect of Ibn Daud's interpretation of Avicenna's modal ontology in relation to al-Ghazali. See also ibid., 126a3–7, trans. Samuelson, 136, in relation to matter as potency and form as act.

Modality	Act/Potency	Spiritual Substance	Corporeal Substances
possible existence *per se*	Potency	like matter	matter
necessary existence *per aliud*	act	like form	form

To the contrary, if a non-analogical equivalence between hylomorphism and modal ontology were established, two main aspects would inescapably require a further justification which, in Ibn Daud's opinion, Ibn Gabirol was not able (and could not have been able) to provide. They are:

the progressive descent of simplicity into multiplicity, which appears to require degrees of ontological intermediation between oneness and matter;

the ontological leap between spiritual and corporeal being, which in Ibn Daud is expressed by the material composition of the latter.

Ibn Daud's cosmological description is fairly engaged with these two problems. Matter is the main aspect of the corporeal bodies, on account of its extensibility into three dimensions through the form of corporeity.[89] The reception of this form gives origin to the "absolute body," the substrate of elemental forms. The elements, then, are moved towards their natural place by nature, which corresponds to their intrinsic principle of movement.[90] The preliminary reception of the form of corporeity, however, is prior only from a *logical* point of view to the reception of the elemental forms, and matter's reception of the elemental forms corresponds to its extension into three-dimensionality.[91]

Ibn Daud's ontology and cosmology are very close to those parts of Avicenna's corpus that Gundissalinus (and partially Ibn Daud himself) had translated into Latin. While they are close, Ibn Daud's theories cannot be resolved into Avicenna's, as he originally developed some of the crucial points of Avicenna's doctrines in a different direction. Moreover, Ibn Daud's acquaintance with Avicenna's works most probably extended far beyond those in Latin translation – and the same is probably true for al-Farabi, al-Ghazali, and for different reasons Ibn Gabirol. Could Ibn Daud's Avicennism have influenced Gundissalinus's reading of Avicenna? And if so, how does it relate to Gundissalinus's grad-

89 See ibid., 24b2–6, trans. Samuelson, 61.
90 See ibid., 118b9–12, trans. Samuelson, 123.
91 Ibid., 25b17–26b2, trans. Samuelson, 62.

232 | CHAPTER FOUR

ual re-thinking and problematisation of important points he had previously accepted?

Gundissalinus's Ontology of Possible Being

The most important work by Avicenna to have influenced Gundissalinus's ontology is clearly the *Philosophia prima*. While traces of an early influence of this work can also be detected in *De unitate et uno* and, more importantly, in *De divisione philosophiae*, it is only with *De processione mundi* that its core metaphysical doctrines play a central role.[92] These doctrines are developed by Gundissalinus in a rather peculiar way. Indeed, he quotes long excerpts from the first book of Avicenna's *Philosophia prima*, gathering them in only one section of *De processione mundi*. Almost no other quotations from that or any other section of Avicenna's work are presented at the same length and with the same function elsewhere in Gundissalinus's treatise.[93] These excerpts, however, are crucial passages from *Philosophia prima* 1:6–7, in which Avicenna argues in favour of the uniqueness and un-relatedness of the Necessary Existent.[94] Moreover, the dense pages of these quotations in Gundissalinus's *De processione* suffer the effects of his alteration strategy. Gundissalinus often changes the quoted text (its terms, syntax, and even the order of the reasoning), aiming at making it doctrinally consistent with the perspective exposited by *De processione mundi*.[95]

---

92 While no doctrinal influence of *Liber de philosophia prima* appears to be in place with Gundissalinus's *De unitate*, a short excerpt from Avicenna's work seems to be the source of one passage of *De unitate* (Gundissalinus, *De unitate et uno*, ed. María Jesús Soto Bruna and Concepción Alonso Del Real [Pamplona, 2015], 136.5–7). Concerning this point, see Nicola Polloni, "Gundissalinus and Avicenna: Some Remarks on an Intricate Philosophical Connection," *Documenti e Studi sulla Tradizione Filosofica Medievale* 28 (2017): 515–52, at 521–22.

93 This fact does not imply that the doctrine of necessary and possible being plays a marginal role in Gundissalinus's discussion. To the contrary, the constant references to the possibility of existence proper to matter and form is the result of a theoretical merging between Avicenna's modal ontology and Ibn Gabirol's universal hylomorphism, the base for which is provided by the very position of God as Necessary Existent.

94 See Gundissalinus, *De processione mundi*, ed. Georg Bülow, *Des Dominicus Gundissalinus Schrift Von dem Hervorgange der Welt* (Münster, 1925), 5.15–17.3; ed. María Jesús Soto Bruna and Concepción Alonso del Real, *De processione mundi: Estudio y edición crítica del tratado de D. Gundisalvo* (Pamplona, 1999), 126.17–148.12.

95 For instance, and in relation to the considered quotations, Gundissalinus changes the order of Avicenna's line of reasoning at least once. While *De processione mundi* presents a description of the Necessary Existent as the consequence of five arguments (ed. Bülow, 16.23–17.1; ed. Soto Bruna and Alonso del Real, 148.8–20), in the original text the order is inverted

Appraising Existence: Gundissalinus, Avicenna, and Ibn Daud | 233

It should be recalled that the internal organisation of Gundissalinus's *De processione mundi* follows al-Farabi's metaphysical procedure. From this point of view, the quotations from Avicenna's *Philosophia prima* describing the Necessary Existent as opposed to possible existence coincide with Gundissalinus's description of God – the apex of the first ascending moment of that procedure, from which departs the second and descending phase.[96] As a consequence of being developed through this set of quotations, the only section of *De processione mundi* in which Gundissalinus expands on a discussion of God's most intimate characteristics defines the creator in the terms of Necessary Existent. Indeed, Gundissalinus's interest is primarily ontological and cosmological, rather than theological.

Covering most of chapters six and seven of the first book of Avicenna's *Philosophia prima*, Gundissalinus's set of quotations can be considered as a single large quote covering almost one-fifth of *De processione mundi*. The discussion is developed through five arguments that the Necessary Existent is one and completely unrelated in existence. The first proof is the so-called "homology argument."[97] Gundissalinus's (and Avicenna's) initial premise is the supposition of two Necessary Existents which are *coaequalia*, i.e., homologous in their being and inseparable in their existence. Following this supposition, either of them would have a necessary existence *per se* or *per aliud*. Nevertheless, as their concomitance always implies the existence of the other one, neither of them can be a necessary existent. Rather, at least one of them is – or both are – caused by an external cause. In other words, whatever two *coaequalia* are posited, either one is the cause of the other or both are caused by an external cause, and it is this external cause which is then the Necessary Existent.

The second argument supposes the existence of two Necessary Existents *per se* which are correlative to each other and whose ontological necessity is always accompanied by the existence of the other being without any causal bond implied. That cannot be the case, though. Any ontological correlation between two entities always implies them to be either a cause and a caused being or to be both caused by an external cause (the Necessary Existent). Accordingly, the Necessary Existent *per se* cannot be related to anything else in its existence.

(see *Liber de philosophia prima* 1.6, ed. Van Riet, 43.21–23), as the description of the Necessary Existent is, for Avicenna, preliminary to the demonstration of its uniqueness and unrelatedness. An analysis of Gundissalinus's alteration strategy can be found in Polloni, "Gundissalinus on Necessary Being."

96 See Nicola Polloni, "Gundissalinus's Application of al-Fārābī's Metaphysical Programme: A Case of Epistemological Transfer," *Mediterranea: International Journal on the Transfer of Knowledge* 1 (2016): 69–106.

97 See Lizzini, "The Relation Between Form and Matter."

234 | CHAPTER FOUR

As it is completely unrelated, the Necessary Existent cannot be either a duality or a plurality. This point is made clear through three further arguments. First, Gundissalinus focuses on the essential definition of the Necessary Existent. As it is impossible to apply that definition to two or more different entities with necessary existence per se – their difference cannot be posited through their essential definition, which is coincident or relies on accidents – therefore there must be only one Necessary Existent. Second, because the definition of necessity does not act as a genus which is divided into species or as a species particularised into individuals, therefore a multiplicity of necessary existents cannot be posited. Third, as a distinction between the definition of ontological necessity and the Necessary Existent is impossible, ontological necessity and necessary existence must coincide in the Necessary Existent.

As a result, the Necessary Existent is only one in existence. It is completely other from the opposite ontological state of possible existence. The possible existent is always qualified as a caused being with a structural ontological deficiency, such that it requires an external cause for its existence. Indeed,

> we have displayed the property of that which is a possible existent. For its property is that it does not lack something else by which it might have being in act. But everything that is a possible existent, when it is considered through itself, is always a possible existent. At times, however, it happens that it is necessary through another thing. And what exists in that way either does not have the necessity of being always but only at certain times – and what exists in that way must have matter, which precedes it in time, as we will soon show – or it has the necessity of being always and through another thing – and what exists in that way is not entirely simple. For what it has, when it is considered in itself, is one thing, and what it has from another thing is something else. For it has the fact that it exists from both – namely, from itself and from something else. And on this account, nothing is so first and so simple that it does not have some possibility and potency in itself except the Necessary Existent alone.[98]

98 See Gundissalinus, *De processione mundi*, ed. Bülow, 16.9–22; ed. Soto Bruna and Alonso Del Real, 146.15–148.7: "ostendimus proprietatem eius, quod est possibile esse. Proprietas enim eius est, quod non eget alio, per quod habeat esse in actu. Omne autem, quod possibile est esse, cum consideratur per se ipsum, semper est possibile esse. Contingit autem aliquando ipsum necessarium esse per aliud, et quod sic est, aut non habet necessitatem essendi semper, sed aliquotiens, et quod sic est, opus habet materia, quae ipsum praecedit tempore, sicut mox ostendemus, aut necessitatem essendi habet semper et per aliud, et quod sic est, omnino non est simplex. Aliud est enim, quod habet consideratione sui ipsius, et aliud, quod habet ex alio. Id ipsum enim, quod est, habet ex utroque, scilicet ex se et alio; et propter hoc

Appraising Existence: Gundissalinus, Avicenna, and Ibn Daud | 235

In its own being, a possible existent always has a possible existence, which becomes necessary only sometimes (*aliquotiens*) and always through something else (*per aliud*). Therefore, the possible existent is radically different from the Necessary Existent *per se*, as it always and intimately has some reference to its own possibility and potency in its being. To the contrary, the Necessary Existent has a complete self-sufficient existence, as

> The Necessary Existent is neither relative nor mutable nor many but single, since no other thing participates in its being, which is proper to it. And this is none other than God alone, who is the first cause and first principle of all things, which is necessarily understood to be one only, not two or more.[99]

Completely unrelated and single, the Necessary Existent is one, simple, and immutable. He is God, the first cause and the first principle of everything.[100] Aside from some slight modifications, the text Gundissalinus quotes from Avicenna's *Philosophia prima* covers all the main aspects of Avicenna's discussion presented in the first book of that work. Nevertheless, there are at least two main points which characterise Gundissalinus's acceptance of Avicenna's modal ontology as being rather peculiar.

First, the examination in book one of *Philosophia prima* is a rather preliminary discussion of the attributes of the Necessary Existent and, consequently, of modal ontology. Avicenna indeed comes back to this fundamental aspect of his reflection later on in his writing. In particular, it is quite curious that Gundissa-

---

nihil est adeo primum, adeo simplex, quod non habeat aliquid possibilitatis, et potentiae in se ipso nisi necessarium esse tantum." English translation by John A. Laumakis, *The Procession of the World* (Milwaukee, 2002), 43–44, modified. This passage derives from Avicenna, *Liber de philosophia prima* 1.7, ed. Van Riet, 54.44–55.55.

99 See Gundissalinus, *De processione mundi*, ed. Bülow, 16.23–17.1; ed. Soto Bruna and Alonso Del Real, 148.8–12 (this passage derives from Avicenna, *Liber de philosophia prima* 1.6, ed. Van Riet, 43.21–23): "necesse esse neque est relativum, neque est mutabile, nec multiplex, sed solitarium, cum nihil aliud participat in suo esse, quod est ei proprium; et hoc non est nisi solus deus, qui est prima causa et primum principium omnium, quod unum tantum necesse est intelligi, non duo vel plura." English translation by Laumakis, *The Procession of the World*, 44, modified.

100 It should be noted that Gundissalinus does not seem to be interested in a theological description of the divine attributes. Besides the meagre references to God's goodness and wisdom at the beginning of the treatise – one reference to the Trinity, and another one to the role played by divine will for the union of matter and form – Gundissalinus does not engage with the rich Christian and the Islamic traditions of discussion on divine attributes. Avicenna himself discusses divine attributes in both a philosophical and a more theological fashion, but the latter does not appear to have influenced Gundissalinus.

236 | CHAPTER FOUR

linus does not consider the contents of *Philosophia prima* 8, in which Avicenna further expands on the considered topic, adding much more detail to his discussion of God as Necessary Existent.[101]

A second aspect worth noting is the silence with which Gundissalinus passes over Avicenna's crucial distinction between essence and existence. This doctrine is not only one of the most important aspects of Avicenna's ontology but also the ground in which his modal ontology is rooted. The impossibility of reducing essence to existence in caused entities implies that every essence has received its existence from an entity whose being is beyond that distinction, i.e., the Necessary Existent.[102] It is from the exigency of establishing what this entity is that Avicenna develops, in *Philosophia prima* 1, a discussion of modal ontology and the description of the Necessary Existent that Gundissalinus quotes in *De processione mundi*. Gundissalinus, though, does not refer or hint in any way to this crucial ontological distinction. Within the *De processione*, God's description is required as the outcome of four arguments pointing out that a first composing cause of the universe is necessary. This first cause must be completely simple and purely one – the One from which every caused unity derives. As metaphysical unity (the conceptual correlative of created duality) is one of the most important features Gundissalinus cared about, it is probable that he bestowed a special relevance upon Avicenna's discussion of the uniqueness and un-relatedness of the Necessary Existent. Indeed, although it does not explain why Gundissalinus chose to quote that particular passage from the first book of *Philosophia prima*, his choice must evidently have been led by specific considerations concerning the aim of *De processione mundi*. The quotation from Avicenna in *De processione mundi* could have been aimed at establishing God's oneness and utmost simplicity, and therefore necessity. This is what the four arguments that open *De processione mundi*

---

101 See Avicenna, *Liber de philosophia prima* 8.5, ed. Van Riet, 411.39–48. The reasons behind Gundissalinus's choice are open to much speculation. On the one hand, it is possible that the Latin translation of that part was not completed while Gundissalinus was writing his *De processione mundi*. Nevertheless, even if that were the case, it should be assumed that Gundissalinus had access to the original Arabic version of Avicenna's works. On the other hand, it could also be the case that Gundissalinus had simply assessed the contents presented in the first book as sufficient for his aims – i.e., as sufficiently expanding on the points he wanted to present in *De processione*. If that were the case, he might have judged Avicenna's further discussions of the same topic as redundant or unnecessary for his theoretical aims, a possibility which is far from demonstrable.

102 Regarding this crucial point, see Jean Jolivet, "Aux origines de l'ontologie d'Ibn Sina," in *Études sur Avicenne*, ed. Jean Jolivet and Roshdi Rashed (Paris, 1984), 221–37; Amélie-Marie Goichon, "Avicenne: le philosophe de l'être," *Revue de l'Institut des Belles Lettres Arabes* 15 (1952): 49–62; and Guy Jalbert, "Le nécessaire et le possible dans la philosophie d'Avicenne," *Revue de l'Université d'Ottawa* 30 (1960): 89–101.

Appraising Existence: Gundissalinus, Avicenna, and Ibn Daud | 237

required, that is, a "One" which causes a created unity, which is dual in itself. This duality, though, is not expressed by the distinction between essence and existence, as it is in Avicenna, but by a varied set of dualities – compositional (matter and form), dynamic (act and potency), and analytical (genus and species).[103]

Although explicit references to the opposition between necessary and possible existence disappear after the long quotation from *Philosophia prima*, thanks to it Gundissalinus makes a crucial theoretical gain. Indeed, through this pivotal distinction *De processione mundi* can merge modal ontology with the doctrine of act and potency and, through that, with universal hylomorphism. In other words, besides establishing the most absolute oneness and simplicity of the creator, Gundissalinus's discussion of the Necessary Existent also aims at grounding the hylomorphic composition of every caused being in its own duality of acquired necessity and structural possibility. This is the fourth duality characterising created being as such – *modal duality*.

Accordingly, while demonstrating the existence of the first cause, Gundissalinus states that

> everything that is made, before it is made, can be made. For, if it were not, at first, able to be made, then it could not be made and, thus, never would be made. Therefore, the possibility of being of everything that was made preceded its being in act. But the possibility of being (*possibilitas essendi*) comes only from matter, whereas the act of being (*effectus essendi*) comes from form.[104]

Gundissalinus establishes here a meaningful connection between two different ontological statuses, i.e., possibility and potency. It should be noted that Gundissalinus contrasts *possibilitas essendi* and *effectus essendi*. This *possibility of being* expresses the subject of the ontological causation performed by the cause. It coincides with matter before its union with the form, through which it is actualised. But it also corresponds to the very status of the form before being joined to matter: the *effectus essendi* comes from the form, but does not coincide with the

---

103 A fourth and central kind of duality is derived from Avicenna, as we shall see – the modal duality of acquired necessity and possibility.

104 Gundissalinus, *De processione mundi*, ed. Bülow, 25.20–24; ed. Soto Bruna and Alonso Del Real, 166.12–17: "Omne, quod fit, antequam fiat, possibile est fieri. Si enim non esset prius possibile fieri, tunc impossibile esset fieri, et ita nunquam fieret. Omne igitur, quod factum est, possibilitas essendi praecedit illud esse in actu; sed possibilitas essendi non est nisi ex materia, effectus vero essendi ex forma." English translation by Laumakis, *The Procession of the World*, 53.

238 | CHAPTER FOUR

ontological status of the form. Neither its nor matter's statuses, as we have seen, should be confused with privation or non-existence. They share the same mode of existence – possible being – which provides matter and form with a marginal not-yet-actual existence.

It should be appreciated that this excerpt from *De processione* is based on two main sources. The first is the final argument for the existence of spiritual substances, presented in Ibn Gabirol's *Fons vitae*.[105] The second and most influential source is Avicenna's discussion of act and potency in the fourth book of *Philosophia prima*.[106] For Avicenna, matter is the substrate of possibility. This pivotal ontological role, however, is valid only within natural bodies, i.e., corporeal beings. Avicenna's hylomorphism is indeed a corporeal hylomorphism, which required Gundissalinus to develop and universalise the scope of Avicenna's doctrine to cover a much more extended region of being. Accordingly, Gundissalinus seems to rethink the bond between potency and possibility to establish not only a connection between but a subtle identification of these two ontological statuses. As a consequence, the actualised possibility corresponds to the acquisition of necessary existence proper to any caused being, while its possible existence is the modal status which is referred to as potency in consideration of movement and change.

Already in Avicenna's *Philosophia prima* it is possible to discern a connection between modal ontology (possibility and necessity) and the doctrine of act and potency.[107] Gundissalinus, however, takes an additional step forward. For him the bond between possibility and potency implies another meaningful link between potency and matter (and form as well, considering that, for Gundissalinus, both hylomorphic partners are *per se* potential). The interaction between these two connections allows Gundissalinus to provide a broader basis – i.e., that possibility is the universal characteristic of caused being in general – for what in Avicenna is the principle only of a restricted region of being – i.e., matter and form, proper to corporeal beings only. Matter and form, therefore, are the potency expressing a *duality* proper to any and every possible existent. This duality is the ontological structure proper to created being and it is expressed through a series of meaningful *functional dualities*. Matter and form express the ontological duality under a compositional consideration. The duality is expressed by acquired necessity and potency (as modal duality) when we consider the caused being under modal ontology. And the very same duality is manifested through

---

105 See Ibn Gabirol, *Fons vitae*, ed. Clemens Baeumker (Münster, 1892–95), 100.20–21; ed. Marienza Benedetto, *La fonte della vita* (Milan, 2007), 360.

106 Avicenna, *Liber de philosophia prima* 4.2, ed. Van Riet, 208.50–58.

107 See Avicenna, *Liber de philosophia prima* 1.7, ed. Van Riet, 54.44–46 and 55.53–55.

the distinction between genus and species (analytic duality) and potency and act (dynamic duality). One could probably say that these dualities are just instantiations (or, all the more, epiphenomena) of the primal duality which is the ontological structure of created being as such. In other words, matter and form correspond to the compositional structure of any possible existence which has become actual – necessary *per aliud* – once matter and form are joined. Radically opposed in their nature to the utter simplicity and unity of the Necessary Existent, creatures are intimately characterised by this series of dualities.

This pillar of Gundissalinus's ontology also appears to be connected to an additional source, one which provides him with a specific hermeneutic of *Philosophia prima* – Abraham ibn Daud. In Avicenna's work, Gundissalinus has surely found important hints toward the first identification of modal ontology and the doctrine of act and potency. Connecting the dots in *Philosophia prima*, Gundissalinus could easily build the following scheme of identifications:

modal ontology	act and potency	cause
Necessary Existent *per se*	beyond act and potency	first cause
possible existent	existential potency	subject of causation
necessary existent *per aliud*	actual existence	effect

The basis of this set of identifications is the intrinsic existential duality of any possible existence, which can either exist or not exist. This existential cogency is elaborated by Gundissalinus through his doctrine of potency.[108] Once the potency is actualised, its outcome is an actual being which is completely other than, yet similar to, its first cause (through Ibn Gabirol's principle of the simplicity of the cause, or PC1, which is also shared by Avicenna).[109] From this point of view, Gundissalinus's ontology appears to be an original interpretation of Avicenna's discussion of *possibilitas* and *potentia essendi* leading to the identification

108 See, for instance, Gundissalinus, *De processione mundi*, ed. Bülow, 33.14–34.13; ed. Soto Bruna and Alonso Del Real, 180.10–182.11.

109 One might wonder why my analysis *per principia* of Ibn Gabirol's philosophy has not been followed by a similar speculative approach to Avicenna's reflection. The reason is quite simple. While I found that methodology extremely useful in clarifying some of the problematic tensions within Ibn Gabirol's text, its application to Avicenna's would have made the proposed analysis more difficult rather than simplifying it. Indeed, Gundissalinus appears to use only parts of Avicenna's *Liber de philosophia prima*, problematising its outcomes only in consideration of universal hylomorphism. Accordingly, an exposition *per principia* of Avicenna's metaphysics would have exceeded the present circumstances and possibly misled the reader.

240 | CHAPTER FOUR

of these ontological statuses.[110] What separates Gundissalinus's version of this principle from Avicenna's own is the relation he establishes between modal ontology and hylomorphism. Indeed, a complete chart of Gundissalinus's identifications should also include matter and form, as follows:

modal ontology	act and potency	universal hylomorphism	being
Necessary Existent *per se*	beyond act and potency	beyond matter and form	[absolute being]
possible existent	existential potency	matter and form not yet united	Material being (*esse materiale*)
necessary existent *per aliud*	actual existence	matter and form united	Formal being (*esse formale*)

Accordingly, for Gundissalinus possible existence corresponds to the potential being proper to matter and form prior to their union – the kind of being proper to anything before coming to be. In contrast, acquired necessity corresponds to the actual being of any caused entity and is the outcome of the union of matter and form actualising the hylomorphic compound. The actor of this dynamic is the composing cause that joins together matter and form – God, the Necessary Existent.

A connected aspect to this theory is Gundissalinus's distinction between material and formal being. As we have seen, this distinction expresses the functionality of matter and form in terms of actuality and potentiality. It corresponds to Gundissalinus's theoretical and textual development of a passage from Ibn Gabirol's *Fons vitae*. It also appears to be connected to Gundissalinus's concerns about consistency with the Latin tradition, univocally claiming that form is act while matter is potency. In addition to all that, following the proposed set of identifications, material being corresponds to possible existence and formal being to the acquired necessary existence proper to the caused hylomorphic compound. In this respect, the distinction between material and formal being seems to be also connected to two further sources: al-Ghazali and Abraham ibn Daud.

Gundissalinus translated the metaphysical and logical parts of al-Ghazali's *Maqasid al-Falasifa*, which circulated in Latin Europe as *Summa theoricae philosophiae*. The transmission of this work to Latin Europe is a perfect example of a heterogenesis of ends. Al-Ghazali wrote his *Maqasid* as a sort of résumé of

110 Avicenna, *Liber de philosophia prima* 4.2, ed. Van Riet, 210.89–92.

Appraising Existence: Gundissalinus, Avicenna, and Ibn Daud | 241

Avicenna's philosophy in order to play an explanatory function preliminary to the harsh criticism of Avicenna that al-Ghazali would articulate in his *Tahafut*. Once translated into Latin, though, *Summa theoricae* was read in coherence with Avicenna, as a useful device to interpret the latter's dense pages.[111]

It is beyond doubt that Gundissalinus had already translated *Maqasid* before writing *De processione mundi*, as he quotes a passage from his Latin translation in this work.[112] While many doctrines expounded by al-Ghazali are close, at least to some degree, to Avicenna's exposition in *Philosophia prima*, several aspects are presented in a rather different, simplified, and sometimes even deliberately misinterpreted fashion.[113] It is interesting that al-Ghazali explicitly refers to the duality proper to any caused being as a twofold duality of, on the one hand, necessary and possible existence and, on the other, matter and form. Indeed, while corporeal beings have a duality of matter and form, simple beings have an ontological duality of something which is "like matter" and something which is "like form" – respectively, the possibility and necessity of existence. Al-Ghazali claims that,

Considering [its] quiddity, it is a possible existent while, considering [its] cause, it is a necessary existent. Indeed, we have shown that whatever is possible in itself is made necessary through something else. Accordingly, [that being] has two aspects (*duo iudicia*), because it has necessity in one way and possibility in some other way. As regards [its] possible existence, indeed, it is in potency and, as regards [its] necessary existence, it is in act. Nevertheless, possibility belongs to it properly, while necessity from something else. As a consequence, [that being] has in itself a multiplicity [made out of] one [aspect] that is like matter and another that is like form. [Its] possibility is

111 See Manuel Alonso Alonso, "Influencia de Algazel en el mundo latino," *Al-Andalus* 23 (1958): 371–80; Marie-Thérèse D'Alverny, "Algazel dans l'occident latin," in *Un trait d'union entre l'orient et l'occident: Al-Ghazzali et Ibn Maimoun. Agadir 27–29 Nov. 1985* (Agadir, 1986), 125–46; Dominique Salman, "Algazel et les latins," *Archives d'histoire doctrinale et littéraire du Moyen Âge* 10 (1935): 103–27; and Anthony H. Minnema, "Algazel Latinus: The Audience of the Summa Theoricae Philosophiae, 1150–1600," *Traditio* 69 (2014): 153–215. See also Minnema, "A Hadith Condemned at Paris: Reactions to the Power of Impression in the Latin Translation of Al-Ghazali's Maqasid al-Falasifa," *Mediterranea* 2 (2017): 145–62.

112 See Gundissalinus, *De processione mundi*, ed. Bülow, 33.14–19; ed. Soto Bruna and Alonso Del Real, 180.10–19; which derives from al-Ghazali, *Metaphysica*, ed. Joseph T. Muckle (Toronto, 1933), 44.6–13.

113 These discrepancies are also connected to the sources used by al-Ghazali, which were not limited to Avicenna's *Kitab aš-Šifa*. See Janssens, "Al-Ghazali and His Use of Avicennian Texts."

242 | CHAPTER FOUR

like matter while the necessity that belongs to it from something else is like form.[114]

The relevance of this passage should not be underestimated. Al-Ghazali's *Summa* explicitly connects modal ontology with the doctrine of potency and act, claiming that every spiritual substance is *per se* possible and potential, while *per aliud* it is necessary and actual. Moreover, al-Ghazali refers to this dynamic claiming that the first caused beings have something "like matter" (*simile materiae*) and something "like form" (*simile formae*), corresponding respectively to possibility and necessity. These series of analogies can be summarised in the following chart:

Modality	Act/Potency	Spiritual Substance	Corporeal Substances
possible existence *per se*	potency	like matter	matter
necessary existence *per aliud*	act	like form	form

These series of analogies and identifications seem to be the missing element in explaining Gundissalinus's interpretation of Avicenna and his theoretical synthesis with Ibn Gabirol. Al-Ghazali's text states that every caused being has a dual structure, whose components are possibility (which is potency and something like matter) and necessity (which is actuality and something like form). These identifications are extremely close to Gundissalinus's, but with two fundamental changes. First, spiritual substance is not composed of something *like matter* and something *like form*, but of *matter* and *form* themselves. Second, for Gundissalinus matter and form are both in potency. Concerning the latter, we have already seen that the reference to material and formal being can be correctly understood through a functional reading. At the same time, Gundissalinus's distinction can be considered as an attempt to find a common ground with Avicenna. On the one hand Gundissalinus identifies al-Ghazali's potential status,

114 Al-Ghazali, *Metaphysica*, ed. Muckle, 120.12–23: "Igitur secundum consideracionem quiditatis erit possibile essendi, et secundum consideracionem cause, erit necesse essendi eo quod ostensum est quod quicquid possibile est in se, necesse est propter aliud a se; habet igitur duo iudicia scilicet, necessitatem uno modo, et possibilitatem alio modo. Ipsum igitur secundum quod est possibile, est in potencia, et secundum quod est necesse, est in effectu; possibilitas vero est ei ex se, et necessitas ex alio a se; est igitur in eo multitudo unius quidem quod est simile materie et alterius quod est simile forme. Quod autem est simile materie est possibilitas, et quod est simile forme est necessitas, que est ei ex alio a se."

"which is *like matter*," with material being (i.e., the potency of both matter and form). And on the other, he identifies the actual status, "which is *like form*," with formal being (the act of both matter and form within the compound). This is summarised by the following chart:

Act/Potency	Al-Ghazali	Gundissalinus
Potency	like matter	material being (both matter and form)
Act	like form	formal being (both matter and form)

While al-Ghazali appears to be one of the sources of Gundissalinus's combination of modal ontology and universal hylomorphism, there is another aspect to be considered in relation to material and formal being and the analogical relation established by al-Ghazali between hylomorphism and modal ontology. In fact, the misunderstanding of matter and form as only analogically *like matter* and *like form* corresponds to one of the major criticisms against Ibn Gabirol expounded by Ibn Daud. Indeed, Ibn Daud claims, a corporeal being is always composed of matter and form while, on the contrary, spiritual substances cannot be said to be truly "one" because they have in themselves a duality of necessity and possibility. Accordingly,

> rather, the dependence of the intellect's existence on something else indicates that it does not have in itself what is necessary of existence. Rather, it has what is possible of existence. Thus, in its substance there is what is complex for the intellect, and it is like a composite of matter and form. The reason for this is that what it has from its substance is like matter, that is, possibility, and what it has from something else is like form. The thing that it contains is what it is, that is, necessity. Of the many substances that contain this attribute [i.e., the spiritual substances], some are ordered by others of them in order. They are the entities for which Ibn Gabirol (may he be remembered for a blessing) tried to establish the existence of *hyle* and form in the fifth book of his treatise. He did not explain that what they have is something like hyle and something like form. Rather, he ordained that they have matter and form, and when he tried to establish this, he could not do it.[115]

---

115 Ibn Daud, *The Exalted Faith* 152b14–153a9, trans. Samuelson, 174. See also 28b16–29b5, trans. Samuelson, 63, and 128b8–15, trans. Samuelson, 141.

244 | CHAPTER FOUR

In comparison to al-Ghazali, Ibn Daud's excerpt displays something more. The Jewish philosopher explicitly refers to universal hylomorphism and attacks Ibn Gabirol's position, which misinterpreted the analogy by understanding that there was a *real* composition of matter and form even for spiritual substances. In other words, Ibn Daud claims that Ibn Gabirol did not understand that the simple spiritual substances have a duality of something *like matter* and *like form* (possibility and necessity) and he tried to establish that they are composed of matter and form, without achieving it. Ibn Daud's refutation of Ibn Gabirol through Avicenna and al-Ghazali is the exact opposite of Gundissalinus's attempt at realising a synthesis between Ibn Gabirol and Avicenna through al-Ghazali. Considering that Ibn Daud and Gundissalinus were colleagues, it would be rather unlikely that their perspectives, opposed yet based on the same sources, were not connected in some way. Could Gundissalinus's distinction between *esse materiale* and *esse formale* have been a result of his effort to address some of the problems signalled by Ibn Daud? An examination of the relation between Gundissalinus's and Avicenna's hylomorphism is required to properly address this question.

Contrasting Hylomorphisms

In many ways, Avicenna's and Gundissalinus's hylomorphisms are opposed. Their opposition is primarily related to the different scope of matter and form (limited to corporeal beings for Avicenna, and universal for Gundissalinus) and their mutual relationship (actualising form vs. potentiality of both). This fact does not entail that Gundissalinus does not use Avicenna's works while he is discussing matter and form. In fact, one of the central passages describing the different ways in which matter can be referred to is a direct quotation from the first book of Avicenna's *Physics*, or *De causis et principiis naturalium*. Gundissalinus underlines that there are different names referring to the substrate,

> for it is called "matter" when it is referred to form, but it is called "substance" when it is considered by itself. For matter itself is called by different names when it is viewed in different respects. For, from the fact that it is in potency as receptive of forms, it is called "hyle," and from the fact that it is already in act as sustaining form, it is called "subject." But when a substance is described, "subject" is not understood in the same sense as it is in logic. For hyle is not a subject in this way, but it is a subject of form. And from the fact that it is common to all forms, it is called either "mass" or "matter." And from the fact that other things are broken down into it, since it is the simple part

Appraising Existence: Gundissalinus, Avicenna, and Ibn Daud | 245

of every composite, it is called "element," and it is the same way in other things. And from the fact that composition begins from it, it is called "origin." But when we begin with a composite and come to it, it is called "element."[116]

This passage is a direct (and almost unaltered) quotation from Avicenna's *De causis et principiis naturalium* 2, where Avicenna discusses the different meanings of the subject of change, i.e., matter.[117] In *De processione mundi*, the passage is aimed at clarifying the meanings of matter. Nevertheless, while in Avicenna this discussion expounds the different predicable senses of matter concerning the corporeal world, in Gundissalinus those same distinctions are extended to every existing being. Accordingly, Gundissalinus uses Avicenna to ground his own doctrine of matter without paying much attention to the discrepancies which distinguish his and Avicenna's theory. In other words, the notions of matter accepted by Avicenna and Gundissalinus are primarily opposed by their stances on what is the scope of matter – i.e., what regions of being are made of matter.

While their answers to this question are radically different, their explicit descriptions of matter as principle are rather similar. Both Avicenna and Gundissalinus present matter as a potential substrate of change, which is *per se* undetermined until it receives a form. Matter is principle and subject. It is a sub-

116 Gundissalinus, *De processione mundi*, ed. Bülow, 31.3–16; ed. Soto Bruna and Alonso Del Real, 176.1–12: "Materia enim dicitur, cum ad formam refertur, substantia vero dicitur, cum per se accipitur. Ipsa enim materia diversis respectibus diversis nominibus appellatur. Ex hoc enim, quod est in potentia receptibilis formarum, vocatur yle, et ex hoc, quod iam in actu est sustinens formam, subiectum vocatur. Sed non sicut in logica subiectum accipitur, cum substantia describitur. Yle enim non est subiectum hoc modo, sed est subiecta formae, et ex hoc, quod est communis omnibus formis, vocatur vel massa vel materia; et ex hoc, quod alia resolvuntur in illam, quoniam ipsa est simplex pars omnis compositi, vocatur elementum, quemadmodum et in aliis. Et ex hoc, quod ab illa incipit compositio, vocatur origo; sed cum incipitur a composito, et pervenitur ad illam, vocatur elementum." English translation by Laumakis, *The Procession of the World*, 58.

117 Avicenna, *De causis et principiis naturalium* 1.2, ed. Van Riet, 21.60–22.72: "Et haec hyle, secundum hoc quod est in potentia receptibilis formae aut formarum, vocatur hyle et, secundum hoc quod est in actu sustinens formam, vocatur subiectum. Non autem hic accipimus subiectum sicut in logica quando definiebatur substantia, quia hyle non est subiectum ex hoc intellectu ullo modo et, secundum hoc quod est communis omnibus formatis, vocatur materia vel massa et, secundum hoc quod resolvuntur in illa et est ipsa pars simplex receptibilis formae totius compositi, vocatur elementum. Similiter etiam quicquid est sicut illud et secundum hoc quod ab illa incipit compositio, vocatur origo; similiter etiam quicquid est aliud quod est sicut illa: fortasse enim, quando incipitur ab ea, vocatur origo, quando autem incipitur a compositio et pervenitur ad illam, vocatur elementum quia elementum est simplicior pars compositi."

stance as it cannot be an accident, and it is one principle shared by a plurality of entities.[118] From this point of view, far from being a mere taxonomic digression, Gundissalinus's quotation from Avicenna's *De causis et principiis naturalium* displays an incomplete yet meaningful agreement between their notions of matter, both of which are rooted in the Aristotelian tradition, although in different ways.[119] For Gundissalinus, matter's possibility to become anything through its form(s) is characterised by three main features: matter is a potency (*potentia*), an ontological possibility (*possibilitas*), and a positive potentiality (*potestas*) – following a sensibility different than Avicenna's. Nevertheless, it is evident that the process of theoretical merging and doctrinal assimilation was surely much easier in relation to the concept of matter than with other theories of Avicenna's.

While the notion of privation is almost absent from Gundissalinus's discussion – a fact which is probably related to the *metaphysical* rather than *physical* analysis pursued by *De processione mundi* and *De unitate* – it is with the third Aristotelian principle of change (form) that the differences between Gundissalinus and Avicenna appear to be most profound.[120] In this regard, there are at least four aspects which are opposed in Avicenna's and Gundissalinus's notions of form:

1. The scope of form – at what logical/cosmological stage does form join matter?

2. Singularity vs. plurality of form(s) within a single substance – how many forms are there in a substance?

---

118 See Gundissalinus, *De processione mundi*, ed. Bülow, 33.5–13; ed. Soto Bruna and Alonso Del Real, 178.20–180.9.

119 The question of how profoundly Gundissalinus knew Aristotle is a central aspect of the problem concerning his philosophical training and background. In many ways, it seems that Gundissalinus had philosophical training through or in Chartres, where he could have received an Aristotelian training even without having access to many texts authored by Aristotle. It could also be the case that Gundissalinus read Aristotle in Toledo, maybe through the Latin translations made by Gerard of Cremona. This seems to be the case at least for Aristotle's *Physics*, even though the role played directly by Aristotle appears to be rather minor in comparison to its indirect influence through Avicenna, al-Farabi, and the Arabic texts translated by Gundissalinus.

120 In Gundissalinus's *De processione mundi* and *De anima* the term "privatio" appears only in relation to the ontological dynamic of hylomorphism. Matter is said to be a privation, but not in absolute terms (see Gundissalinus, *De processione mundi*, ed. Bülow, 27.11–18; ed. Soto Bruna and Alonso Del Real, 170.5–12). Nevertheless, it should be recalled that *De processione mundi* is a metaphysical treatise in which Gundissalinus follows a strict procedure (derived from al-Farabi) which implies not dealing with aspects belonging to other (and subordinated) sciences. Accordingly, Gundissalinus engages with matter and form as principles of caused being in general, and not as principles of change.

Appraising Existence: Gundissalinus, Avicenna, and Ibn Daud | 247

3. The actuality of form – is form always in act?

4. The causal role of form – is form a concomitant cause of matter and the compound?

The problems concerning the scope and number of forms are directly connected to Avicenna's discussion of the form of corporeity, the first form joining matter. For Avicenna matter is pre-conditioned by the preparatory function performed by the celestial spheres, which determines the unqualified matter as *that* matter capable of receiving *that* form. Once the process of the preparation of matter is complete, the *dator formarum* gives forms off into matter, originating the corporeal beings. The logical moment between the preparation of matter and the impression of form is the extension of matter into three-dimensionality through its union with the *forma corporalis*, or form of corporeity. Accordingly, between the preparation of matter and the causation of the individual there are at least four *logical* steps:

1. Preparation of matter by celestial spheres and causal interactions.

2. Union of the form of corporeity with matter, extending the latter into three-dimensionality.

3. Reception of the specific form from the giver of forms, providing essence and species.

4. Particularisation of the species into *that* individual.

As some scholars, including recently Andreas Lammer, have pointed out, the distinction between points 2 and 3 is particularly tricky.[121] On the one hand, if the form of corporeity is considered as a *real* form, then Avicenna's theory would imply that a body receives a duality of non-accidental forms, the first of which is the *forma corporeitatis*. On the other hand, if the form of corporeity is considered as a sort of function performed by whatever corporeal form, then corporealisation could be performed by the one substantial form which actualised a single body, with no need to assume a plurality of forms. As Lammer has remarked, it would probably be more correct to consider the extension of matter into three-dimensionality as a *function of corporealisation* performed by each and every substantial form which has joined matter.[122] Consideration of the form of corporeity as a function rather than a "real" form makes it possible to supersede the difficult implication of a plurality

---

121 A brilliant discussion of this problem is developed by Andreas Lammer in Lammer, *The Elements of Avicenna's Physics: Greek Sources and Arabic Innovations* (Berlin, 2018), 154–79.

122 See ibid., 165–201.

248 | CHAPTER FOUR

of substantial forms within the compound, a stratification of forms among which the form of corporeity would be the first. As a consequence, the "body as such," which is made of matter and the form of corporeity, can also be considered as a logical abstraction of any qualification from matter except that of extension.

Arguments in favour of viewing the corporeal form as a *functional aspect* of the one single substantial form's formal determination of matter are well-founded, and I find Andreas Lammer's interpretation of this point acutely persuasive.[123] In contrast, Gundissalinus appears to have firmly developed a pluralist theory of non-incidental forms, although matter and form are considered to be functional, as we have seen. In some ways, his pluralism is grounded on functionality, while functionality apparently allows Avicenna to avoid pluralism. Like the form of spirituality, the form of corporeity is for Gundissalinus the form which expresses the difference between bodies and spirits, and it is counted among a plurality of non-incidental forms within the hylomorphic compound. Under a purely hylomorphic consideration, these are forms joined to matter and they specify it in relation to the specific quality they express.

For Gundissalinus, every hylomorphic compound is the union of matter with a series of forms that progressively specify matter. As we have seen, the first forms to join matter are the forms of substantiality and unity.[124] The function of

123 This might be an outcome of the Latin rendering of Avicenna's text – translated into Latin by Gundissalinus himself. A clarification of how the Arabic and Latin receptions of Avicenna have engaged with this delicate point of his reflection might dramatically contribute to our understanding of both Avicenna's original position and the peculiarities of its influence in the Middle Ages.

124 Gundissalinus, *De processione mundi*, ed. Bülow, 42.3–7; ed. Soto Bruna and Alonso Del Real, 196.21–198.4: "substantiality and unity are certainly the first of all forms, because they come before all forms with respect to causality, and without them no forms suddenly subsist in a subject. They are the first of all forms because, by constituting it and making it appear, they come before to a substance, which is a subject of all [other] forms." ("Profecto substantialitas et unitas primae omnium formarum sunt, quia omnes formas causa praeveniunt, et sine quibus nullae in subiecto subito subsistunt. Primae omnium sunt, quia substantiam, quae est subiectum omnium formarum, constituendo et apparendo praeveniunt.") English translation by Laumakis, *The Procession of the World*, 67. And Gundissalinus, *De processione mundi*, ed. Bülow, 41.10–14; ed. Soto Bruna and Alonso Del Real, 196.8–12: "however, the first form to which first matter was joined was substantiality, which made matter be a substance. But because everything that exists, exists precisely because it is one, substantiality alone, therefore, could not come to matter without unity as its companion, because it was impossible for matter to become a substance and not one." ("Prima autem forma, cui prima copulata est materia, substantialitas fuit, quae materiam fecit esse substantiam. Sed quia omne, quod est, ideo est, quia unum est: ideo substantialitas sola sine unitate comite non potuit venire, quia materiam substantiam fieri, et non unam, impossibile fuit.") English translation by Laumakis, *The Procession of the World*, 66. On this point, see also Ibn Gabirol, *Fons vitae* 2, ed. Baeumker, 42.20–24; ed. Benedetto, 276.

the form of substantiality is to produce substance out of matter. This form accompanies the form of unity in the inaugural information of matter from which created existence emerges. This inaugural phase also coincides with the start of Porphyry's tree, whose division into species is applied by Gundissalinus in *De processione mundi*, beginning with the distinction of substance as such into spiritual and corporeal.[125] As we have seen, this application constitutes one important point of development of (and also partial detachment from) Ibn Gabirol's positions.[126] From a logical point of view, Gundissalinus justifies universal hylomorphism as the very root of Porphyry's tree. It is only through the union of matter and the forms of unity and substantiality that the *substance* from which Porphyry's tree departs can be posited.

Gundissalinus's line of reasoning, however, could not have been more peculiar. He is not only positing a plurality of forms, he is naming among them a form of substantiality whose role is to produce substance from the hylomorphic union – a role that would be played by the substantial form, for Aristotle, or by different substantial forms, for the pluralists. Why should Gundissalinus posit a form whose only function is to make the compound a substance, when the tradition consistently agrees in claiming that substantialisation is realised by any substantial form? I cannot find any other explanation than to consider Gundissalinus's references to the forms of substantiality and unity as *functions performed within the hylomorphic compound by the ontological structure of the same compound*. In other words, it is an outcome of Gundissalinus's application of the principle of the thirdness of compositional unity (PS3). Form and matter only exist in potency as themselves and in act as the compound. An *a posteriori* examination of what the compound is entails a series of forms which, in act, are only functions of that very compound. Accordingly, the same remarks I made on Gundissalinus's form of unity as a theoretical device, applied to both a cosmological and an ontological level, are also valid for the form of substantiality. Cosmologically, it corresponds to the initial stage of God's creation while, in the ontological description of the individual being, it corresponds to a function expressed by the formal structure of the compound. As I said, therefore, within the compound there is formal richness corresponding to an *ontological structure made of enmattered forms* which perform a different set of dual functions. In some ways, the formal aspect of the compound (the formal richness made of a plurality of forms) can be considered

125 See Gundissalinus, *De processione mundi*, ed. Bülow, 43.10–21; ed. Soto Bruna and Alonso Del Real, 200.8–18.

126 On Porphyry's interpretation of Aristotle's *Categories*, see Christos Evangeliou, *Aristotle's Categories and Porphyry* (Leiden, 1988); and Sten Ebbesen, "Porphyry's Legacy to Logic: A Reconstruction," in *Aristotle Transformed: The Ancient Commentators and Their Influence*, ed. Richard Sorabji (Ithaca, 1990), 141–71.

250 | CHAPTER FOUR

as a single formal cluster expressing a formal function. This is probably the reason why Gundissalinus repeatedly oscillates between references to *forma* (singular) and *formae* (plural), whereas an ontological description of the compound would have entailed a plural reference to a plurality of forms. When these formal determinations are considered in relation to matter, they can be referred to as a single cluster, a form. When they are considered in relation to the form, they are referred to as to a plurality of forms, as they express different specific contents which qualify the compound. Singularity or plurality of forms, though, is only apparent. In both cases, they are an expression of functionalities proper to the compound, as only the compound exists in act as one. Therefore, to the question of whether one or many forms exist in act *with* the compound, it would be consistent to answer, with a strong ontological claim, that none exist. Form only exists as an aspect of the compound – not as one of its parts, not as something added to it. *Within* the compound these forms (or the one form as a cluster) are something other than themselves – they are nothing but functions expressing the ontological richness of the compound.

Gundissalinus's interpretation of Avicenna's theory of the form of corporeity goes in the same direction. Many of his references to the form of corporeity explicitly hint at Avicenna's *De causis et principiis naturalium*. For instance, while examining the perpetuity of the effects of the first composition, Gundissalinus claims that

> even if water changes over into a stone, it is, nonetheless, not changed in terms of corporeity, but in terms of the form of aqueousness (*forma aqueitatis*), and for its form to be corrupted into that is nothing other than for the form of stoneness (*forma lapideitatis*) to be substituted in its place. In every change, it remains the same. I say "the same," however, according to the genus body; it is not the same according to the species water. Hence, the water that was at first and the stone that was made afterwards certainly differ in species, but they wholly agree in the genus of body. For every change of bodies according to generation and corruption comes about only through the form of corporeity. Hence, generation and corruption take place only according to the second genera and according to the third genera and so forth, namely, according to living and sensible and so forth all the way to Socrates.[127]

127 Gundissalinus, *De processione mundi*, ed. Bülow, 47.1–48.2; ed. Soto Bruna and Alonso Del Real, 206.11–22: "Nam etsi aqua transit in lapidem, non mutatur tamen secundum corporeitatem, sed quantum ad formam aqueitatis, quam formam in eam corrumpi nihil aliud est, quam vice eius formam lapideitatis substitui; in omni permutatione manet idem. Idem

Appraising Existence: Gundissalinus, Avicenna, and Ibn Daud | 251

While what is subject to generation and corruption will be eventually destroyed, what is received as an effect of divine causality will persist. Gundissalinus's example is quite bizarre: water becoming stone. Gundissalinus claims that when water becomes a stone, it does not change as regards its corporeity, but only as regards its form – the *forma aqueitatis* is substituted by the *forma lapideitatis*, while corporeity remains the same. These two forms are opposed in their species, but agree in their genus, which is corporeity. As a consequence, Gundissalinus states that generation and corruption happen only in relation to the form of corporeity and in the subsequent sub-genera up to the individual.

The source of this passage appears to be Avicenna's *De causis et principiis naturalium* 1, perhaps along with the Arabic version of Avicenna's *De generatione et corruptione*.[128] Gundissalinus, though, applies Avicenna's doctrine of the corporeal form to his own ontology. The outcome is a clear position of corporeity as the substrate of change, the same function that matter was called to perform in Aristotle's natural philosophy. Through this identification of corporeity with the substrate of physical change, Gundissalinus can keep matter at the highest level of his chain of being. Accordingly, corporeity is nothing but the substrate of any process of generation and corruption, whose substrate cannot be first matter because first matter is an ontological principle also shared by perpetual spiritual beings – a stance very close to Roger Bacon's theory of *materia naturalis*.[129] Considering corporeity as a function expressed within the compound, Gundissalinus's assertion does not necessarily imply the admission of a body as such (= corporeity) as subsisting *ut res*, as a real stratum subsisting in nature. In contrast, it can be read as an acknowledgment that only *some lower aspects* of the ontological structure of a particular being undergo processes of physical change – not any of the qualifications above corporeity.

Notwithstanding their opposite perspectives, it is clear that we should not underestimate the impact of Avicenna on Gundissalinus's hylomorphism. While

autem dico, quantum ad hoc genus 'corpus'; non idem est, quantum ad hanc speciem 'aqua.' Unde aqua, quae prius erat, et lapis, qui postea factus erat, specie quidem differunt, sed in genere corporis omnino conveniunt. Omnis enim permutatio corporum secundum generationem et corruptionem non, nisi per formam corporeitatis, fit; unde generatio et corruptio non fit, nisi secundum secunda et secundum tertia genera et deinceps, scilicet secundum animatum et sensibile et deinceps usque ad Socratem." English translation by Laumakis, *The Procession of the World*, 70.

128 See Nicola Polloni, "L'acqua che si trasforma in pietra: Gundissalinus e Avicenna sulla generazione dei metalli," in *Vedere nell'ombra: Studi su natura, spiritualità e scienze operative offerti a Michela Pereira*, ed. Cecilia Panti and Nicola Polloni (Florence, 2018), 103–19.

129 See Michela Pereira, "Remarks on *materia naturalis*," in *Roger Bacon's* Communia Naturalium*: A Thirteenth-Century Philosopher's Workshop*, ed. Paola Bernardini and Anna Rodolfi (Florence, 2014), 103–38.

252 | CHAPTER FOUR

their approaches are in many ways different, Avicenna's influence on Gundissalinus was profound and enveloping. Traces of this influence, however, are feebler in relation to two final aspects, aspects which appear to place Avicenna and Gundissalinus in opposition: the actuality and causality of form as regards matter. Avicenna's ontology reserves a special role for form, which plays two crucial roles in relation to matter, as form is an act which actualises and is the proximate cause of matter. Nevertheless, Gundissalinus's theory of being implies that both matter and form are in potency before becoming the compound. As we have seen, Gundissalinus also claims a specific role for form in the causation of actual being, the coming of the form to matter being the necessary step for the constitution of actual being.[130] Actuality indeed only happens when form and matter are joined and "made one" through the function of unity expressed by the form. Matter desires form because it wants to be "one" and therefore have actual existence.[131] The instance of unity is borne and expressed by form, and specifically by the first form, the form of unity.[132]

Although some proximity with Avicenna can be appreciated in the role the form plays (that of a proximate cause toward the existence of matter), there is not much else. Any closeness between Avicenna's and Gundissalinus's discussions ends here. For Gundissalinus, form has no actual being *per se*, and its causality is

130 See Gundissalinus, *De processione mundi*, ed. Bülow, 25.3–11; ed. Soto Bruna and Alonso Del Real, 164.16–166.4: "although, therefore, one does not precede the other in time or causality, either in being in act or being in potency, form is nonetheless said to give being to matter, and matter is not said to give being to form. The reason for this is this. At the coming of form, matter passes from potency to act. Being in potency, however, is considered like non-being in comparison to that being that is in act. Being in act, then, is first attained when matter is united to form. Therefore, on account of this primacy, matter is not seen to give being to form, but form is seen to give being to matter." ("Licet ergo neutra praecedat aliam tempore, vel causa, nec in esse in effectu, nec in esse in potentia: dicitur tamen forma dare esse materiae, et non dicitur materia dare esse formae. Cuius ratio haec est: namque adventu formae materia de potentia ad effectum transit, esse vero in potentia quasi non esse reputatur comparatione eius esse, quod in effectu est; esse in effectu tunc primum habetur, cum materia formae coniungitur. Ideo propter hanc principalitatem non materia formae, sed forma materiei dare esse videtur.") English translation by Laumakis, *The Procession of the World*, 52.

131 See Gundissalinus, *De processione mundi*, ed. Bülow, 26.1–13; ed. Soto Bruna and Alonso Del Real, 166.20–168.9.

132 Ibid., ed. Bülow, 29.13–30.3; ed. Soto Bruna and Alonso Del Real, 172.21–174.5: "Unde nec materia, nec forma habuit esse in actu ante unitatem, sed simul esse inceperunt. Cum enim forma materiei adiuncta est, statim unitas prodiit, quia ex coniunctione earum aliquid unum fit. Unde esse et unitas videntur simul esse natura, quoniam, cum aliquid est, illud est unum, et cum est unum, illud esse necesse est. Ac per hoc, sicut materia sine forma, vel forma sine materia, non habet esse, sic neutra sine altera est unitate una." English translation by Laumakis, *The Procession of the World*, 57.

pursued through its function of unity and, through this, of actuality, as we saw in chapter three. Form cannot be an actualising act because it is the required component, the only way through which something can be "one" – i.e., through the union of two different and simple principles, matter and form. Avicenna's and Gundissalinus's notions of formal causality, therefore, are only incidentally and marginally close to each other.

It is beyond doubt that Gundissalinus was aware of some major disagreements with Avicenna's ontology. Among these oppositions, the actuality or potentiality of form was probably the most evident, as it is for readers nowadays. A "reduction" of form into a potential status is a daring move which could – and indeed had – provoked harsh reactions. It is probable that Gundissalinus, following al-Ghazali, also introduced his distinction between material and formal beings as identical to the potential and actual statuses of both matter and form before and after their union, in an attempt to soften his stance. Nonetheless, there seems to be another factor to consider in relation to this and similar points of Gundissalinus's ontology.

Matter for Bodies

Abraham ibn Daud often expresses criticism against central points of Ibn Gabirol's reflection. His favoured target is the ontology expounded in *Fons vitae* and, in this regard, an excerpt from the first book of *The Exalted Faith* is especially interesting. Ibn Daud refers to Ibn Gabirol claiming that,

> when Ibn Gabirol wanted to describe prime matter, he said the following in Book I of the *Source of Life*: "If all things have a universal element, it necessarily follows that the universal element has some properties, namely that it exists, it persists by itself, it is essentially one, it is a subject of change, and it gives to each thing its essence and its name." Thus, Ibn Gabirol committed six errors at the beginning of his discourse. He erred because prime matter does not exist, since existence is said only of what actually exists. Aristotle said in his explanation of this claim that what does not exist is said only of three things: namely, of absolute privation, of the privation of the opposite of a certain form, and of matter. Furthermore, Ibn Gabirol erred because prime matter does not persist by itself. Furthermore, he erred because prime matter is neither one nor many, since what does not have existence has neither number nor unity. Furthermore, he erred because prime matter is not a subject of change, since changes are accidents and matter is not a subject

254 | CHAPTER FOUR

of accidents, because accidents extend only to the existence of what has complete existence. However, prime matter is a subject of what changes, that is, of bodies that change. Furthermore, Ibn Gabirol erred because prime matter does not give to anything its definition and its name. However, the form does do this. Furthermore, he erred because prime matter needs to have properties, since properties are accidents that necessarily are joined to an actual existent. All of his discourse in the *Source of Life* is of this kind.[133]

Ibn Daud points out six main errors that plague the theoretical edifice of *Fons vitae*, as follows:

Ibn Gabirol's Claim	Ibn Daud's Criticism
matter exists	only what is in act exists, while matter is in potency. Accordingly, matter cannot exist except within the hylomorphic compound
matter subsists in itself	matter cannot exist without a form
matter is one in essence	matter cannot be one or many, as number and unity can be said only of something in act
matter is subject to change	change occurs only in substances in act
matter gives name and definition to anything	form provides the hylomorphic compound with its essential features
matter has some properties	to have properties, matter must be in act

The six "mistakes" Ibn Daud abstracts from Ibn Gabirol's work all refer to the ontological status of prime matter. Grounding his criticism upon a direct quotation from the first book of Ibn Gabirol's *Fons vitae* and straining the meaning of some of Ibn Gabirol's positions, Ibn Daud's appraisal relies on the notion of matter as pure potency of being, completely deprived of any actuality and, therefore, of any determination. Five of these mistakes could be subsumed in one unspoken error made by Ibn Gabirol, that he supposedly has confounded matter with form. In fact, it is the form which, being in act, exists and subsists in itself (err. 1–2), is one in essence (err. 3), has some properties (err. 6) and, therefore, gives to any entity its name and definition (err. 5). In addition to this tendency, error 4 refers to another case of Ibn Gabirol's misinterpretation of matter, not with form but with the first substrate. In other words, for Ibn Daud prime matter cannot be

133 Ibn Daud, *The Exalted Faith*, trans. Samuelson, 1.62.26b17–63.27b14.

the substrate of change because change is a subsequent ontological event whose substrate is the body as such, i.e., the "absolute body" made of matter and the form of corporeity. Accordingly, prime matter is not the substrate of change, but the subject of three-dimensionality – a function matter also performs in Ibn Gabirol's perspective, but only in a later moment in the chain of being.

Ibn Daud's criticism appears to be surprisingly close to a passage from Gundissalinus's *De processione mundi*. While debating on the interrelations between matter and form, Gundissalinus introduces a string of definitions of matter, claiming that

> when, nonetheless, philosophers describe first matter and form, they say: First matter is a substance existing through itself, the sustainer of diversity and one in number. Moreover, first matter is a substance receptive to all forms. First form, however, is a substance constituting the essence of all forms. Although one is shown to differ from the other by this and yet every difference is by means of form, it should not be said that one differs from the other by something different from themselves. On the contrary, each one differs from the other by itself, not by a difference that belongs to things in agreement, but one that belongs to opposition and true contrariety, since each of them is other than the other. For if substantiality and oneness are forms, then since each of them is said of a substance that is one in number, matter in itself is certainly not entirely formless, and form is not entirely simple, since substantiality and oneness are properties of them. Hence, it must not be said that substantiality and oneness are forms of matter and form as if they were different from them, but they are matter and form, not something other than them.[134]

134 Gundissalinus, *De processione mundi*, ed. Bülow, 30.4–31.3; ed. Soto Bruna and Alonso Del Real, 174.6–176.1: "Et tamen philosophi, cum describunt primam materiam et formam, dicunt: Materia est prima substantia per se existens, sustentatrix diversitatis, una numero. Item: materia prima est substantia receptibilis omnium formarum. Forma vero prima est substantia constituens essentiam omnium formarum. Quamvis autem per hoc ostendatur una differre ab alia, omnis autem differentia forma est, non tamen dicendum est, quod una differat ab alia per aliquid aliud a se diversum. Immo per se ipsam unaquaeque differt ab alia, non per differentiam, quae est convenientium, sed quae est oppositionis et verae contrarietatis, quoniam unaquaeque illarum aliud est ab alia. Si enim substantialitas et unitas formae sint, tunc, cum utraque dicitur de substantia una numero, profecto nec materia in se omnino informis est, nec forma omnino simplex, cum substantialitas et unitas sint earum proprietates. Unde dicendum est, quod substantialitas et unitas non sunt formae materiae et formae quasi ab eis diversae, sed sunt ipsum et materia et forma, non aliquid aliud ab eis; nec est aliud materia quam substantia, quae aliquando materia et aliquando substantia dicatur." English translation by Laumakis, *The Procession of the World*, 57–58.

256 | CHAPTER FOUR

Gundissalinus's excerpt is fascinating. The first part of the text is a collection of definitions derived from Ibn Gabirol, while the second part develops them in an original way.[135] First, it should be noted that the first quotation from *Fons vitae* is both lexically and doctrinally close to the opening of Ibn Daud's excerpt on Ibn Gabirol's mistakes. Nonetheless, while Gundissalinus quotes from the fifth book of *Fons vitae*, Ibn Daud refers to a passage from the first book of that work, in which Ibn Gabirol states that

> matter must have being, because what does not exist cannot be matter for what exists. But it is said to be subsisting through itself so that reasoning does not proceed to infinity, if matter did not exist in itself. It has one essence, for the reason that we sought only one matter of all things. It sustains diversity, because diversity comes only from forms, and forms do not exist through themselves. It gives its own essence and name to all things because, since it sustains all things, it is necessary that it exists in all things,

135   See Ibn Gabirol, *Fons vitae* 5, ed. Baeumker, 298.13–21; ed. Benedetto, 628; English translation by John A. Laumakis, *The Font of Life* (Milwaukee, 2014), 238: "Therefore, the description of first matter that is taken from its properties is this, namely, that it is a substance existing through itself that sustains diversity and is one in number; and again it will be described in this way, namely, that it is the substance receptive of all forms. But the description of universal form is this, namely, that it is a substance constituting the essence of all forms … " ("Ergo descriptio materiae primae, quae sumpta est ex eius proprietate, haec est, scilicet quod est substantia existens per se, sustentatrix diversitatis, una numero; et iterum describitur sic, quod est substantia receptibilis omnium formarum. Sed descriptio formae universalis haec est, scilicet quod est substantia constituens essentiam omnium formarum"). And Ibn Gabirol, *Fons vitae* 5, ed. Baeumker, 260.12–20; ed. Benedetto, 580; English translation by Laumakis, *The Font of Life*, 216–17: "S: In what way does matter differ from form when the essence of each of them is considered? T: Each of them differs from the other through itself. And I do not mean here a difference of things that agree, but I mean a difference of opposition and true contrariety, because there is not something above them in which they agree. S: How will it be known that matter differs through itself? T: By their difference in the intelligence, and because one of them sustains and the other is sustained." ("D. In quo differt materia a forma, cum consideratur essentia cuiusque illarum? M. Unaquaeque illarum differt ab alia per se ipsam. Et non intelligo hic differentiam convenientium, sed intelligo differentiam oppositionis et verae contrarietatis, scilicet quia non est aliquid super illas in quo conveniunt. D. Quomodo scietur quod materia differt per se ipsam? M. Per differentiam earum apud intelligentiam, et quia una earum est sustinens et altera sustentatum"). Another source is Ibn Gabirol, *Fons vitae* 5, ed. Baeumker, 242.9–12; ed. Benedetto, 554. For a detailed examination of this passage, see Nicola Polloni, "Toledan Ontologies: Gundissalinus, Ibn Daud, and the Problems of Gabirolian Hylomorphism," in *Appropriation, Interpretation and Criticism: Philosophical and Theological Exchanges between the Arabic, Hebrew and Latin Intellectual Traditions*, ed. Alexander Fidora and Nicola Polloni (Barcelona, 2017), 19–49, at 42–45.

Appraising Existence: Gundissalinus, Avicenna, and Ibn Daud | 257

and since it exists in all things, it is necessary that it give its own essence and name to all things.[136]

The second part of the excerpt from *De processione mundi* appears to be an original development of the definitions of matter that he quotes from *Fons vitae* in relation to unity and substantiality – the first forms to join matter. Gundissalinus claims that oneness and substantiality are intimate properties of form and matter.

A question arises from a comparison between these excerpts. Was it Gundissalinus's aim to answer Ibn Daud's criticism of Ibn Gabirol? Is the summarised account of Ibn Gabirol's notion of matter a sort of response and counter-refutation of Ibn Daud? Indeed, Gundissalinus's text seems to touch almost all the points highlighted by Ibn Daud. Gundissalinus clarifies that matter is one and existing *per se* (Ibn Daud's errors 1–3), as it is shared by all caused beings (one in number) and exists in its own modality of being as *potestas essendi*, the positive possibility of being anything which makes matter's existence eternal. Elsewhere in his treatise, Gundissalinus also explains that "just as matter without form or form without matter does not have being, so neither without the other is one by means of oneness."[137] This remark corrects Ibn Daud's first criticism, for which matter would need an actual being in order to exist. On the contrary, the proper modality of matter's existence is that of possibility (= marginal existence), without entailing an actual existence before its union with the form. Matter is also the bearer of diversity as the potentiality of receiving every form. It is, therefore, the substrate of diversity and, remotely, the substrate of change.

This point is made even clearer by Gundissalinus's consideration of substantiality and unity in reference to matter and form (err. 6). The quoted excerpt claims that substantiality coincides with matter. Accordingly, it "must not be said that substantiality and oneness are forms of matter and form as if they were dif-

---

136 Ibn Gabirol, *Fons vitae*, ed. Baeumker, 13.23–14.5; ed. Benedetto, 220: "Materia debet habere esse, quia quod non est ei quod est materia esse non potest. Sed dicitur subsistens per se, ideo ne ratio eat in infinitum, si materia exstiterit non in se. Unius autem essentiae, ideo quia non quaesivimus nisi unam materiam omnium rerum. Sustinens diversitatem, quia diversitas non est nisi ex formis et formae non sunt existentes per se. Dans omnibus essentiam suam et nomen, ideo quia, cum sit sustinens omnia, necesse est ut sit in omnibus, et cum fuerit existens in omnibus, necesse est ut det essentiam suam et nomen omnibus." English translation by Laumakis, *The Font of Life*, 69.

137 Gundissalinus, *De processione mundi*, ed. Bülow, 30.2–3; ed. Soto Bruna and Alonso Del Real, 174.4–5: "sicut materia sine forma, vel forma sine materia, non habet esse, sic neutra sine altera est unitate una." English translation by Laumakis, *The Procession of the World*, 57.

258 | CHAPTER FOUR

ferent from them, but they are matter and form." On the one hand, this claim could be read in relation to the remarks made above on the functional nature of unity and substantiality. Being functions expressed by the compound within the compound, they could be considered as mainly referring to one or another of the two compositional aspects which make the compound – matter and form. Nevertheless, this would be in open tension with Gundissalinus's mention of a *form* of substantiality, not matter. Evidently, substantiality cannot be matter, but it does correspond to the first substrate, the substance as such, which would later be divided into corporeal and incorporeal substances. This fact is made clear by Gundissalinus's discussion immediately after the abovementioned excerpt, i.e., the plurality of names for matter which he derived from Avicenna's *De causis et principiis naturalium*.[138] Right before quoting from Avicenna's work, though, Gundissalinus inserts a short reference to *Fons vitae*.[139] And this quotation makes clear that substantiality can be said to be a property of matter, "for it is called 'matter' when it is referred to form, but it is called 'substance' when it is considered by itself."[140] In other words, matter and substance correspond to the same underlying ontological aspect under different considerations, "for matter itself is called by different names when it is viewed in different respects."[141] Accordingly, the notions of matter and substance are different considerations of the functions performed by "matter" when it is considered without form, and by "substance" when matter is considered together with form (after the inaugural first union of matter and the forms of unity and substantiality).

However, because matter cannot be in act without form even for the blink of an eye, any reference to "matter" should be considered as a reference to the functionality performed by this aspect of the compositional duality. This is a crucial fact which, supposedly, Gundissalinus thought Ibn Daud did not understand. And accordingly, if one were to consider this passage as a response to Ibn Daud's criticism, that would imply that Gundissalinus is defending Ibn Gabirol against Ibn Daud, and rejecting the "mistakes" that Ibn Daud spotted in *Fons vitae*.

138 See ibid., ed. Bülow, 31.3–17; ed. Soto Bruna and Alonso Del Real, 176.1–14.

139 Ibn Gabirol, *Fons Vitae*, ed. Baeumker, 269.15–21; ed. Benedetto, 592: "D. Nonne vides quod substantialitas est forma materiae, et materia forma rei? M. Substantialitas non est separata a sua essentia. Unde non est possibile ut sit forma eius, quia essentia substantiae ipsa est essentia materiae; et non dividuntur nomina nisi in relatione. Ergo tunc dicitur materia, cum refertur ad formam; et tunc dicitur substantia, cum per se stat."

140 Gundissalinus, *De processione mundi*, ed. Bülow, 31.3–4; ed. Soto Bruna and Alonso Del Real, 176.1–2: "materia enim dicitur, cum ad formam refertur, substantia vero dicitur, cum per se accipitur." English translation by Laumakis, *The Procession of the World*, 58.

141 Ibid., ed. Bülow, 31.5–6; ed. Soto Bruna and Alonso Del Real, 176.2–3: "ipsa enim materia diversis respectibus diversis nominibus appellatur." English translation by Laumakis, *The Procession of the World*, 58.

Moreover, if that were the case, it is possible that Gundissalinus felt that his own philosophical reflection had been attacked by Ibn Daud's criticism of Ibn Gabirol and, therefore, he needed to defend his theories. But is a controversy between Gundissalinus and Ibn Daud even plausible? Recently, Gad Freudenthal has pointed out a meaningful case in which Ibn Daud appears to criticise Gundissalinus's activity.[142] It is quite probable that some kind of dialectic engagement between Gundissalinus and Ibn Daud was in place in Toledo. Many of Gundissalinus's emendations of his previous positions in *De processione mundi* appear to be close to Ibn Daud's perspectives. On some occasions, as with the distinction between *esse materiale* and *esse formale*, it seems that Gundissalinus's emendations were aimed at addressing problems pointed out by Ibn Daud – in this case, the analogical relation between modal ontology and hylomorphism. In general, one has the impression that Gundissalinus is trying to address Ibn Daud's criticism while developing some points of Ibn Gabirol's theory and mediating them with aspects of Ibn Daud's Avicennism – a hypothesis that future scholarship should carefully assess.

Indeed, the proximities between Gundissalinus's and Ibn Daud's reflections are conspicuous, although sometimes incidental. Some doctrines they share are derived from a common source, usually Avicenna. Other doctrines might have received some influence (probably univocal, i.e., Ibn Daud on Gundissalinus). A certain degree of closeness between Ibn Daud's and Gundissalinus's cosmologies can be appreciated in the scheme on page 260.

The processes of cosmological derivation described by *The Exalted Faith* and *De processione mundi* are similar and display some commonality of approach and sensibility which, however, are developed through two different perspectives on ontology. They share a similar solution to the problem of the information of matter, which corresponds to the position of a first substrate which is corporeity for Ibn Daud and substantiality for Gundissalinus. What irremediably separates their accounts is the different scope of hylomorphism: it is universal for Gundissalinus, but limited to corporeal beings for Ibn Daud. The latter can introduce matter only as a theoretical device to explain corporeal change, by which the first substrate corresponds to corporeity. On the contrary, Gundissalinus's hylomorphism requires matter to be posited at the beginning of the chain of being, before corporeal existence. In this case, the first substrate corresponds to substantiality, whose specification follows Porphyry's *Isagoge*.

This fundamental difference produces a series of discrepancies between their cosmologies. The priority of matter in substance requires Gundissalinus to place

---

142 See Gad Freudenthal, "Abraham Ibn Daud, Avendauth, Dominicus Gundissalinus and Practical Mathematics in Mid-Twelfth Century Toledo," *Aleph* 16 (2016): 60–106.

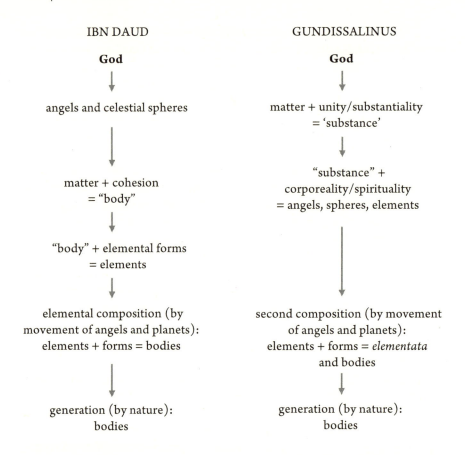

matter at the beginning of his cosmology. He mentions three secondary causes – angels, spheres, and elements – which are exactly the same secondary causes accepted by Ibn Daud. Nonetheless, *De processione mundi* does not describe the process of cosmological causation by which these entities were originated, but how substance is qualified. Crucially, though, Gundissalinus seems to hint at a much more Avicennian universe which he accepts in his *De processione*, without describing it.[143] Ibn Daud's cosmology goes exactly in that direction. It is an Avicennian progression which starts with the first angel causing a sphere, its soul, and another angel, up to the giver of forms and the sublunary world. Celestial spheres aside, for Ibn Daud, matter is a specific characteristic of sublunary bodies subject to generation and corruption and made of elements, as they are in Gundissalinus's universe.

143 See Nicola Polloni, "Gundissalinus on the Angelic Creation of the Human Soul: A Peculiar Example of Philosophical Appropriation," *Oriens* 47 (2019): 313–47.

Besides the recognition of reciprocal influences, the closeness between Ibn Daud's and Gundissalinus's perspectives indicates that Gundissalinus and Ibn Daud were aiming at providing answers to similar problems, starting with the explanation of how sensible and contingent multiplicity derives from God's absolute unity and necessity. In general, Ibn Daud seems to have had some influence in Gundissalinus's progressive problematisation of his positions on universal hylomorphism, and perhaps also regarding cosmology. The exact range of this influence, though, is still to be ascertained. Their daily activity and collaboration surely made possible many occasions of philosophical discussion between Gundissalinus and Ibn Daud. From a certain point of view, the very tension between the divergent systems upon which Gundissalinus's metaphysics is built can be considered as part of the development of a more solid position which receives some and contrasts with other aspects of Ibn Daud's Avicennian anti-Gabirolism. Accordingly, Gundissalinus's effort also appears to be aimed at establishing a new perspective that might mediate between the two opposed perspectives – i.e., Avicenna's doctrine of necessary and possible being, after having detached himself from his earlier adherence to Ibn Gabirol's cosmology.

The peculiarity of this effort is reflected in Gundissalinus's attitude towards Avicenna. On the one hand, Gundissalinus is eager to assimilate and develop his own version of Avicenna's modal ontology, reading and using it as a fundamental theoretical device. On the other hand, while Avicenna is surely the main source of both Gundissalinus's psychology and epistemology, Gundissalinus's ontology is grounded on Ibn Gabirol, yet is Avicennised in *De processione mundi* through Gundissalinus's recourse to modal ontology. As a consequence, the theoretical merging of Avicenna and Ibn Gabirol is realised to the detriment of the former. In other words, Gundissalinus's emendation of his own ontology is a sort of theoretical update of Ibn Gabirol's ontology rather than a development of Avicenna's positions. Gundissalinus's and Avicenna's hylomorphisms are opposed in many ways. While surely aware of the great distance between them, Gundissalinus avoids any explicit criticism of Avicenna's positions. He never starts a dialogue with Avicenna in any of his writings, but just cherry-picks doctrines and passages, without feeling any need to justify their insertion – nor their origin, for Avicenna is quoted by name only once, and in *De divisione philosophiae*.[144]

While it seems that Gundissalinus approached Avicenna's texts aiming at resolving some doctrinal problems he detected in his previous positions, this restriction in his aims and the limits mentioned above should not diminish the influence Avicenna has had on the elaboration of *De processione mundi*. The main

---

144 See Gundissalinus, *De divisione philosophiae*, ed. Ludwig Baur (Münster, 1903), 124.9.

factor causing Gundissalinus's detachment from *some* of the outcomes of Ibn Gabirol's *Fons vitae* is Avicenna's *Philosophia prima*, together with the likely influence of Ibn Daud. The resulting coalescence of modal ontology and universal hylomorphism corresponds to the most developed stances of *De processione mundi*.

The special relationship between Gundissalinus, Avicenna, and Ibn Daud also provides further valuable insights. In Toledo, Avicenna's works were translated and discussed not only following the requirements of the archbishopric's sponsorship of the translations, or the mere demand of new texts to be translated by the scholastic centres in Europe. It seems that a sort of speculative circle was active in that time, a circle that led Gundissalinus and Ibn Daud to work on a selected list of authors who are the main sources for them both. Did Ibn Daud play a key role in the choice of what author and work to translate into Latin, following his personal speculative perspective while leading the translating group? This might very well be the case, as the choice of texts does not appear to be random. There would be, however, only one crucial exception: Ibn Gabirol's *Fons vitae*. The translation of this work should have been realised before that of Avicenna's *Philosophia prima*. The reasons why Ibn Daud supposedly let his group translate the work of his philosophical nemesis remains a mystery at present, regarding which little or nothing can be said.[145] At the very same time, the gradual problematisation of Gundissalinus's accounts in *De unitate et uno*, *De anima*, and (later) *De processione mundi* seems to be connected with the remarkable speculative milieu in which his reflection had developed. That milieu was the Toledan circle, where discussions and debates among its members could have made clear to Gundissalinus that some of his positions needed to be revised in favour of the new *auctoritas* they were working on – Avicenna, whose stances Gundissalinus needed to harmonise with Ibn Gabirol's. This was a most fortunate choice for the course of medieval philosophy.

---

145 See Nicola Polloni, "Misinterpreting Ibn Gabirol? Questions, Doubts, and Remarks on the Latin Translation of the *Font of Life*," in *Solomon Ibn Gabirol's Philosophy and Its Impact in the Middle Ages,* ed. Nicola Polloni, Marienza Benedetto, and Federico Dal Bo, forthcoming.

CONCLUSION

Unity into Duality

The opening of Gundissalinus's *De processione mundi* founds the possibility of knowing God's most intimate aspects (the *invisibilia Dei*) on the study of the effects of divine creation. The *glimpses of the Invisible* that the present study has provided, hopefully with some success, are aspects of Gundissalinus's great appreciation of the simplest yet almost unintelligible attribute of God: his complete oneness and unity. This unity of God is invisible to human beings because God's is a different kind of unity, as Gundissalinus eminently claimed in his *De unitate et uno*. God is purely and absolutely one, under any consideration. Therefore, he is the Necessary Existent, a statement Gundissalinus makes via Avicenna's theory of modality. This claim, however, is not grounded on a consideration of God himself, but rather on a consideration of the effect of the divine causation.

What is the direct effect of God's creation? Following the letter of Gundissalinus's works, that effect is nothing but matter and form. As we have seen, that effect is actually the substance, the created being which is structured as a *unity into duality*. Matter and form are the roots of substance as such. They exist as matter and form only in potency and before being joined into the compound. Once they are united, they are *made one*, they become something else. They are the compound and exist in act only within the compound and as the compound. The *compositional duality* of matter and form is rooted in this genetic moment, temporally non-subsistent yet logically substantive, which is the emergence of substance from nothingness. As potential *composing elements* of the substance, matter and form only subsist as a possibility of existence, and for not a single instant. Their actual mode of being is functional, as it is expressed by the statuses of material being and formal being, which are nothing else but a material and a formal aspect within the unity of substance, the hylomorphic compound.

The compound is one. It is the result of matter and form made one. It is the effect of the function of unity performed by the form when it joins matter. It is a union as the union of two different elements which are made one – like blue and red paints making the colour violet. This derived unity of the substance is radically different from the absolute unity of God – a unity which is not a unity-of but a unity *in se* and *per se*. Although unified (made one), substantial unity is a metaphysically fragmented unity. The effect is always similar to and different from its cause: similar in unity, different in its structure. Substantial unity is indeed marked by a series of functional dualities that are reflections of the dual genesis of its being. While one, then, substance expresses a *compositional duality* of material and formal functions (what Gundissalinus refers to as *esse materiale* and *esse formale*). This compositional duality is accompanied by a *dynamic duality* which marks the world of becoming: that of being in act and in potency. As a substance is in potency and in act only under some respect, act and potency play the role of functions within the constant transformation of the sublunary world, a process of change instigated by the movement of the heavens which, in turn, are moved by the angels.

However, hylomorphic and dynamic duality coincide. The material being is potential and the formal being is actual. They are two different expressions of the same kind of rooting duality, derived from but not coincident with matter and form. The same thing can be said about a third kind of duality, the *analytic duality* expressing a genus- and a species-function within the compound. The genus-function is also a material function, while the species-function is a formal function. Again, they do not coincide with matter or form as composing elements, but with the compound's aspects of materiality and formality. Accordingly, the material aspect expresses the genus-function of communality. And the formal aspect expresses the species-function into a plurality of species which can be predicated of the compound. These species are the "plurality of forms" that Gundissalinus describes in his *De processione mundi*, from the forms of unity and substantiality to the individual. This formal richness within the compound corresponds to what one may call a functional cluster of the formal aspect. It coincides with the different variables which can be expressed by the formal through its species-function. And therefore, it corresponds to the different species the human mind considers while analysing the compound.

Finally, connected to these three ontological dualities is a *modal duality* as expressed by possible existence and necessary existence *per aliud*. Derived from Avicenna, this duality of modes of existence has an enveloping role in Gundissalinus's metaphysics. It expresses the most radical duality within created substance: the duality of (1) a possibility-of-being proper to any created being and (2) its acquired necessity, which partially amends its absolute cogency. Before the emergence of substance, matter and form are the bearers of this existential possibility. And that possibility persists within the compound as a mark of what is caused and created, insufficient and in need of something to provide being and existence to it – a mark of God's causation of the universe within each and every created substance. This modal duality, though, also expresses the Neoplatonic traits characterising the relationship between cause and effect. The world is radically different from its cause, as radically different as the possibility of being from the complete necessity of existence. But the universe is also similar to its cause, as God caused it and made it possess some necessity, acquired and in tension, yet similar under some respect to his utmost necessity.

Substance can be ontologically described as a unity of *structural dualities*. The meaning of universal hylomorphism for Gundissalinus is now clear. It expresses the intimate duality of created substance in contrast with the utter oneness of God. It was not his examination of the being of the soul that led Gundissalinus to claim that the spiritual substances are also made of matter and form. It was not a consideration of the number of the angels that made him claim that they are also made of matter. It was not an identification of first matter and the first genus that made him conclude that God alone is not made of matter and form. To the contrary, universal hylomorphism is the outcome of Gundissalinus's examination of the *invisible aspects of God* departing from and in contrast with the structural duality marking the being of the universe. It is God's unity and the universe's duality that implied the claim that each spirit and each body, each angel and each element is the result of enmattered forms in which God's oneness is reflected.

Gundissalinus's complex metaphysical reflection is grounded on a specific set of sources, only the most important of which have been discussed in this study. A short analysis of the use Gundissalinus has made of main authors from the Latin tradition has shown that many points of his speculation are explicitly or implicitly related to the twelfth-century discussions on natural philosophy and metaphysics. This seems to be particularly true concerning Thierry of Chartres and William of Conches. Gundissalinus appears to receive important and profound influence from their writings, although he always tends to improve and supersede the positions these masters held. This can also be said in consideration of the use Gundissalinus makes of Hermann of Carinthia's *De essentiis*. The role played by this work is crucial, as a vast part of the cosmology discussed in *De processione mundi* relies on the kinds of causation therein expounded. Nevertheless, Gundissalinus jettisons almost all the rest in a sort of doctrinal plundering which is a rather typical trait of this peculiar Toledan author.

Gundissalinus's thought, however, can be mostly appreciated through the use he made of Ibn Gabirol and Avicenna. The former accompanies Gundissalinus's reflection from the very beginning. From *Fons vitae* Gundissalinus received fundamental ideas in his elaboration of the main ontological tension between God

266 | CONCLUSION

and the universe. Ibn Gabirol's theory of God's oneness is indeed the first theme to be received by Gundissalinus and the main pillar on which his metaphysical edifice is constructed. The theory of hylomorphism described by *Fons vitae* did the rest. It provided Gundissalinus with the principles of a substantive yet intricate theory explaining the duality of the universe's constitution through recourse to matter and form as both composing elements and functional aspects. Gundissalinus's encounters with Ibn Gabirol show a process of gradual acknowledgment and discovery of interpretations and implications of his doctrines.

This process is accompanied by Gundissalinus's use of other sources, among which are Avicenna, al-Ghazali, and Abraham ibn Daud. The former in particular played a late yet crucial role in Gundissalinus's ontology through his theory of necessary and possible existence. As I have pointed out, this theory is central for Gundissalinus as it allowed him to express a most meaningful existential duality in contrast with the Necessary Existent. In this respect, although secondary in importance, al-Ghazali and Abraham ibn Daud also played an important role. Their theories helped Gundissalinus reconcile different ontological perspectives. And in the case of Ibn Daud, his criticism of Ibn Gabirol was likely a substantive contribution to Gundissalinus's elaboration of his mature ontology in *De processione mundi*.

Gundissalinus cherry-picks and quotes from hundreds of excerpts from these authors in his original writings. He almost never names the source. Contrary to contemporary understandings, this does not imply a lack of originality on his part. As for the accusation of stealing, regarding his appropriation of doctrines and theories elaborated by the texts he himself had translated into Latin, this seems to me rather far-fetched. His reticence in naming the authors he is using does not appear to me as motivated by such a purpose. To the contrary, it is a manifestation of Gundissalinus's lack of interest in authoritativeness. He was not interested in accepting or discussing a doctrine only because an important *auctoritas* had sustained it. His concern was to construct a speculative perspective that allowed him to express his philosophical position, and simultaneously to provide a synthesis of the helpful novelties which he had made available through his translations. The point is not the individual authors but the ideas. Ideas can be valid no matter the period, the religion, the geographical area, or their author. This, I would contend, lay at the root of Gundissalinus's somewhat peculiar philosophical style, which is very different from what would become mainstream just a few decades later.

A history of how Gundissalinus's metaphysics was received and discussed in the Latin world has yet to be written. The data in our possession shows a fragmented reception of his metaphysical treatises in Europe throughout the thirteenth century. Gundissalinus's *De anima* is the work whose reception has been most studied, thanks to the brilliant contribution of Dag Nikolaus Hasse.[1] It is also one of the first works relying on Avicenna to be discussed and used in the Latin West, as John Blund certainly used it in his own *De anima*.[2] Gundissalinus's psychological treatise was also used by Albert the Great in his *De homine*. There the Dominican often refers to Gundissalinus as "the Toledan" (*Toletanus*), as has been pointed out by Henryk Anzulewicz in the new critical edition of that work.[3] In all these cases, the metaphysical discussions expounded by Gundissalinus in that work do not appear to have played a relevant role, and were sometimes criticised for the hylomorphic theory therein.

The specifically metaphysical treatises authored by Gundissalinus (*De unitate et uno* and *De processione mundi*) had a rather different circulation. *De unitate et uno* for some reason circulated, probably from an early date, as a work of Boethius. This fact significantly affected its appropriation and interpretation by the Latin tradition. On the one hand, its attribution to Boethius boosted the circulation of *De unitate*, whose influence during the first half of the thirteenth century is central. On the other hand, it profoundly complicated the interpretation of both Boethius and the ontology expounded in *De unitate* itself. As we have seen, many doctrinal points oppose Gundissalinus's and Boethius's perspectives, starting with universal hylomorphism. Thirteenth-century philosophers had to find a way to reconcile the exposition of *De unitate* with that of Boethius's original works – a rather difficult task in many ways. Traces of this problematic connection can be appreciated, for instance, in William of Auvergne and the *Summa* by pseudo–Alexander of Hales.[4] It would be Thomas Aquinas who would make clear, twice, that Boethius could not have been the author of *De unitate et uno*, evident from the great doctrinal inconsistencies that claim would entail.[5] Notwithstanding Aquinas's criticism, Nicholas of Cusa would refer again to *De unitate et uno* as authored by Boethius.[6]

---

1 See Dag Nikolaus Hasse, *Avicenna's* De anima *in the Latin West: The Formation of a Peripatetic Philosophy of the Soul 1160–1300* (London, 2000).

2 See John Blund, *Treatise on the Soul*, ed. Daniel A. Callus and Richard W. Hunt (Oxford, 2013).

3 See Albert the Great, *De homine*, ed. Henryk Anzulewicz and Joachim R. Söder (Münster, 2008).

4 See for instance, William of Auvergne, *De universo* 2.1.7–8, in *Opera omnia* (Paris, 1674), 850a–852b; and pseudo–Alexander of Hales, *Summa theologiae* 2.1, ed. Patres Collegii Sancti Bonaventurae (Quaracchi, 1928), 657.

5 See Thomas Aquinas, *Quaestiones de quolibet 9*, ed. René-Antoine Gauthier (Rome, 1996), 103.144–48. See also *De spiritualibus creaturis*, ed. Joseph Cos (Rome, 2000), 1.21.

6 See Nicholas of Cusa, *De venatione sapientiae*, ed. Raymond Klibansky and Hans G. Senger (Hamburg, 1982), 21.56.5–6.

268 | CONCLUSION

As for *De processione mundi*, the Latin reception of this work is still somewhat mysterious. The manuscript tradition often refers to this work with the title *Liber de creatione celi et mundi*. The title *De processione mundi* was ascribed to this work by the first editor, Georg Bülow, following palaeographic and philological considerations of only four of the manuscript witnesses. Bülow chose the Parisian codex as the most relevant because of the clumsiness of its copyist: that codex is the only witness I am aware of naming Gundissalinus's treatise as *De processione mundi*. The history of the Latin reception of this work clearly shows the limits of Bülow's choice, as the thirteenth-century authors tend to refer to Gundissalinus's work as *De creatione mundi*. The solution to this limitation would be for scholarship to consistently change the work's title. It would be a daring choice, one that I did not make myself in this book; neither did I opt to use Gundissalinus's real name. While epistemologically irrelevant, practical considerations often have to lead scholarly discussion.

The circulation of *De processione mundi* appears to be substantively bound to the English tradition via Paris. This is a rather curious fact. The vast majority of the authors using this work, as I was able to find them, are Britons. Nevertheless, they seem to have had access to this work in Paris, rather than Oxford. This is a hypothesis that needs further research and data, in order to be extended and correctly substantiated. While no explicit reference to Gundissalinus's *De processione mundi* is found in Grosseteste's works, Gundissalinus's treatise appears twice in Roger Bacon's *Questions on Aristotle's Physics* (specifically the questions "Utrum materia sit medium inter ens et non ens" and "An aliquid addat supra materiam").[7] Surprisingly, in both cases Bacon refers to Gundissalinus in the negative part of the quaestio, together with Calcidius. Rather unsurprisingly, both questions discuss matter. At first sight, it seems that Bacon was not very keen on Gundissalinus's ontology. This fact appears to be in tension with many aspects of Bacon's ontology as it would be developed later in works like his *Communia naturalium*, where Gundissalinus's influence is remarkable. A wider textual and doctrinal influence is in place with another English thinker, Thomas of York. The second book of his *Sapientiale* presents a sort of summary of almost the entire *De processione mundi* (referred to again as *De creatione*).[8] The new critical edition *Sapientiale*, edited by Fiorella Retucci, will surely cast further light on Thomas of York's reception of Gundissalinus. He saw pivotal relevance in the

7 See Roger Bacon, *Questiones supra libros octo Physicorum Aristotelis*, ed. Ferdinand M. Delorme and Robert Steele (Oxford, 1935), 44.3–21 and 59.11–36.

8 See Thomas of York, *Sapientiale* 2, ed. Carlo A. Grassi, *The Doctrine of Creation in the Sapientiale of Thomas of York*, Ph.D. dissertation (University of Toronto, 1952), vol. 2.

"elegant exposition" of *De processione* ("eleganter prosequitur Gundissalinus"),[9] discussing and accepting central points of Gundissalinus's theories, though not without some criticism.[10]

The important role played by Gundissalinus within the English Franciscan tradition is also displayed by the *Summa* of pseudo-Grosseteste. The opening of this work offers a list of the most important philosophers, and Gundissalinus is named among the "most famous Arabic and Spanish philosophers."[11] A reference to the stances presented in *De processione mundi* is also made by Geoffrey of Aspall in his *Questions on Aristotle's Physics*, concerning the eternal existence of matter as potency.[12] In all these cases, Gundissalinus's doctrines are primarily connected to the efforts by Latin thinkers to construct well-grounded and consistent matter-theories and in relation to the manifold tensions between Aristotle's treatment of matter in his *Physics* and his *Metaphysics*.

This acknowledgment leads to a further consideration of the role Gundissalinus's treatises may or may not have played soon after Gundissalinus's death, in the final decade of the twelfth century, especially in the context of the Parisian condemnations of 1210 and 1215. In 1210 (or possibly 1209) the archbishop of Sens, Peter of Corbeil, gathered a synod to promulgate the excommunication of Amaury of Bène and David of Dinant. Contextually, the synod also banned public and private reading of Aristotle's books on natural philosophy and their commentaries.[13] While forthcoming studies by Irene Caiazzo will cast further light on

9 Thomas of York, *Sapientiale*, ed. Grassi, 2.10.126–27.

10 See, for instance, Thomas of York, *Sapientiale*, ed. Grassi, 2.27.376, where Thomas calls Gundissalinus an "imitator, immo compilator" of al-Ghazali and Avicenna.

11 See pseudo–Robert Grosseteste, *Summa philosophiae*, ed. Ludwig Baur, *Die philosophische Werke des Robert Grosseteste, Bishofs von Lincoln* (Münster, 1912), 279.28–42.

12 See Geoffrey of Aspall, *Questions on Aristotle's* Physics, ed. Silvia Donati and Cecilia Trifogli (Oxford, 2017), 1.198.23–28.

13 See *Chartularium Universitatis Parisiensis*, ed. Heinrich Denifle (Paris, 1889), 1: 70, no. 11: "Let the body of master Amaury [of Bène] be removed from the cemetery and cast into unconsecrated ground, and the same be excommunicated by all the churches of the entire province. Bernard, William of Arria the goldsmith, Stephen priest of Old Corbeil, John priest of Occines, master William of Poitiers, Dudo the priest, Dominic de Triangulo, Odo and Elinans clerks of Saint Cloud – these are to be degraded and left to secular arm. Urricus priest of Lauriac and Peter of Saint Cloud, now a monk at Saint Denis, Guarinus priest of Corbeil and Stephen the clerk are to be degraded and imprisoned for life. The writings of David of Dinant are to be brought to the bishop of Paris before the Nativity and burned. Neither the books of Aristotle on natural philosophy nor their commentaries are to be read at Paris in public or secret, and this we forbid under the penalty of excommunication. He in whose possession the writings of David of Dinant are found after the Nativity shall be considered a heretic." ("Corpus magistri Amaurici extrahatur a cimeterio et proiciatur in terram non

270 | CONCLUSION

Amaury's role, David's positions are well known.[14] His most problematic stance was his identification of God, matter, and mind as the origin of every created being. David's materialism seems to have been the main reason for his condemnation. Nevertheless, many points of this condemnation are still obscure, starting with which author's commentaries on Aristotle's natural books were banned.

As we have seen, Gundissalinus's theory of matter has many controversial points, like the position of God as beyond act and potency, the material composition of spiritual substances, and the angelic creation of the human souls. Are these doctrines connected to the Parisian condemnation, especially in consideration that the 1215 statutes also include a "Mauritius Hispanus"? The available data is insufficient to substantiate a well-grounded hypothesis in this respect. On the one hand, David of Dinant was bound to Greek-to-Latin translations and traditions rather than to Arabic sources, as Gundissalinus was. Accordingly, it seems that the 1210 ban was primarily connected to the translations from the Greek and related doctrinal contents. On the other hand, however, the most likely commentators on Aristotle's books for the ban to refer to are Avicenna (and perhaps al-Ghazali, in relation to metaphysics), whose works started to circulate in Latin translation in those years, as Amos Bertolacci has pointed out.[15] Therefore, it is impossible either to exclude or to assess an involvement of the "Toledan ontologies" in the Parisian condemnations of 1210, at least at present. While the reference to "Mauritius Hispanus" has fascinated generations of scholars, I prefer not to consider it in these closing remarks.[16]

---

benedictam, et idem excommunicetur per omnes ecclesias totius provincie. Bernardus, Guillelmus de Arria aurifaber, Stephanus presbyter de Veteri Corbolio, Stephanus presbyter de Cella, Johannes presbyter de Occines, magister Willelmus Pictaviensis, Dudo sacerdos, Dominicus de Triangulo, Odo et Elinans clerici de S. Clodoaldo, isti degradentur penitus seculari curie relinquendi. Urricus presbyter de Lauriaco et Petrus de S. Clodoaldo, modo monachus S. Dionysii, Guarinus presbyter de Corbolio, Stephanus clericus degradentur perpetuo carceri mancipandi. Quaternuli magistri David de Dinant infra natale episcopo Parisiensi afferantur et comburantur, nec libri Aristotelis de naturali philosophia nec commenta legantur Parisius publice vel secreto, et hoc sub penae excommunicationis inhibemus. Apud quem invenientur quaternuli magistri David a natali Domini in antea pro heretico habebitur ... "). English translation by L. Thorndike, *University Records and Life in the Middle Ages* (New York, 1944), 26–27.

14 See for instance Enzo Maccagnolo, "David of Dinant: Aristotelianism in Paris," in *A History of Twelfth-Century Western Philosophy*, ed. Peter Dronke (Cambridge, 1988), 429–42.

15 See Amos Bertolacci, "On the Latin Reception of Avicenna's *Metaphysics* before Albertus Magnus: An Attempt at Periodization," in *The Arabic, Hebrew and Latin Reception of Avicenna's* Metaphysics, ed. Dag N. Hasse and Amos Bertolacci (Berlin, 2012), 197–223.

16 See Marie-Thérèse D'Alverny, "Deux traductions latines du Coran au Moyen Âge," *Archives d'histoire doctrinale et littéraire du Moyen Âge* 16 (1948): 69–131, in particular 128–29.

What can certainly be said about Gundissalinus and David of Dinant is that both authors share a common and profound interest in the enveloping role that the notion of matter can play in both natural philosophy and metaphysics. Their reflections are invaluable witnesses of a changing philosophical landscape, a reshaping of the Latin speculative framework through the insertion of large amounts of new sources from the Greek and the Arabic traditions. Departing from Plato's and Calcidius's expositions, the notion of matter was one of the most central concepts to be substantively reshaped by this paradigm shift. David's and Gundissalinus's syntheses are attempts at establishing a new ground on which their radical theories of matter could flourish. Accordingly, David and Gundissalinus indicate that *prime matter* was the shared problem at the end of the twelfth and the beginning of the thirteenth century.

Matter would never cease to be a problematic notion. The thirteenth century would discuss every aspect of its peculiar existence and its shadowy presence in human understanding. Matter would be one of the most important issues leading to a gradual detachment from Aristotle's natural philosophy and metaphysics in the Renaissance, until this "fairy matter" (*materia phantastica*), as Francis Bacon would call it, would be abandoned by most philosophers in early modernity.[17] From this point of view, Gundissalinus's role should not be underestimated. It is my hope that this book has shown to the reader the originality of his thought, the curiosity guiding his approach, the existential tensions he perceived in the universe, and the open-mindedness of a unique character of the Middle Ages.

17 Francis Bacon, *De principiis atque originibus*, in *The Works of Francis Bacon*, ed. James Spedding, Robert L. Ellis, and Douglas D. Heath (Boston, 1860–64), 5: 289–346, at 297.

Bibliography

Works by Gundissalinus

This list of works, in roughly chronological order of composition, contains references to critical editions of the Latin texts as well as medieval and modern translations.

De unitate et uno
Critical editions of the Latin text:

Alonso Alonso, Manuel, ed. "El Liber 'De unitate et uno.'" *Pensamiento* 12 (1956): 179–202.

Correns, Paul, ed. *Die dem Boethius fälschlich zugeschriebene Abhandlung des Dominicus Gundisalvi De unitate*, 3–11. Beiträge zur Geschichte der Philosophie und Theologie des Mittelalters 1.1. Münster: Aschendorff, 1891.

Soto Bruna, María Jesús and Concepción Alonso Del Real, eds. *De unitate et uno de Dominicus Gundisalinus*. Pamplona: EUNSA, 2015.

Critical edition of the medieval Hebrew translation:

Schwartz, Yossef, ed. *Maamar ha-Ehad ve-ha-Ahdut (De unitate et uno)*. In *Latin-into-Hebrew: Texts and Studies*, vol. 2: *Texts in Contexts*, ed. Alexander Fidora, Harvey J. Hames, and Yossef Schwartz, 282–87. Leiden: Brill, 2013.

Modern translations:

Fidora, Alexander and Andreas Niederberger, trans. In *Vom Einen zum Vielen – Der neue Aufbruch der Metaphysik im 12. Jahrhundert*, 66–79. Frankfurt am Main: Klostermann, 2002. (German translation)

Polloni, Nicola. "On Unity and the One." In *Medieval Philosophy and the Jewish, Islamic, and Christian Traditions: Essays in Honor of Richard Taylor*, ed. Luis Xavier López Farjeat, Katja Krause, and Nicholas Oschman, forthcoming. (English translation)

De immortalitate animae
Critical edition of the Latin text:

Bülow, Georg, ed. *Des Dominicus Gundissalinus Schrift Von der Unsterblichkeit der Seele*, 1–38. Beiträge zur Geschichte der Philosophie und Theologie des Mittelalters 2.3. Münster: Aschendorff, 1897.

De scientiis
Critical edition of the Latin text:
> Alonso Alonso, Manuel, ed. *De scientiis*. Madrid: CSIC, 1954.

Modern translation:
> Schneider, Jakob, trans. *De scientiis secundum versionem Dominici Gundisalvi*. Freiburg im Breisgau: Herder, 2006. (German translation)

De divisione philosophiae
Critical edition of the Latin text:
> Baur, Ludwig, ed. *De divisione philosophiae*, 3–142. Beiträge zur Geschichte der Philosophie und Theologie des Mittelalters 4.2. Münster: Aschendorff, 1903.

Modern translation:
> Fidora, Alexander and Dorothée Werner, trans. *Über die Einteilung der Philosophie*. Freiburg: Herder, 2007. (German translation)

De anima
Critical editions of the Latin text:
> Muckle, Joseph T., ed. "The Treatise *De anima* of Dominicus Gundissalinus." *Mediaeval Studies* 2 (1940): 23–103.
> Soto Bruna, María Jesús and Concepción Alonso Del Real, eds. *El* Tractatvs de anima *atribuido a Dominicvs Gvndi[s]salinvs*. Pamplona: EUNSA, 2009.

Critical edition of the medieval Hebrew translation:
> Schwartz, Yossef, ed. *Sefer ha-Nefeš (Tractatus de anima)*. In *Latin-into-Hebrew: Texts and Studies*, vol. 2: *Texts in Contexts*, ed. Alexander Fidora, Harvey J. Hames, and Yossef Schwartz, 227–79. Leiden: Brill, 2013.

De processione mundi
Critical editions of the Latin text:
> Bülow, Georg, ed. *Des Dominicus Gundissalinus Schrift von dem Hervorgange der Welt*, 1–56. Beiträge zur Geschichte der Philosophie und Theologie des Mittelalters 24.3. Münster: Aschendorff, 1925.
> Soto Bruna, María Jesús and Concepción Alonso Del Real, eds. *De processione mundi: Estudio y edición crítica del tratado de D. Gundisalvo*. Pamplona: EUNSA, 1999.

Modern translation:
> Laumakis, John A., trans. *The Procession of the World*. Milwaukee: Marquette University Press, 2002. (English translation)

274 | Bibliography

Primary Sources

Albert the Great. *De homine*. Ed. Henryk Anzulewicz and Joachim R. Söder. Münster: Aschendorff, 2008.

Alexander of Aphrodisias. *De intellectu et intellecto*. In *Autour du décret de 1210: II Alexandre d'Aphrodise*, ed. Gabriel Théry, 68–83. Le Saulchoir: Vrin, 1926.

Pseudo-Alexander of Hales. *Summa theologiae*. Ed. Patres Collegii S. Bonaventurae. Quaracchi: Collegii S. Bonaventurae, 1928.

al-Farabi. *De intellectu et intellecto*. Ed. Étienne Gilson. *Archives d'histoire doctrinale et littéraire du Moyen Âge* 4 (1929): 115–41.

—. *Ihsa' al-'Ulum li-al-Farabi*. Ed. 'Uthman Amin. Cairo: Librairie Anglo-Egyptienne, 1949.

—. *Über die Wissenschaften / De scientiis: Nach der lateinischen Übersetzung Gerhards von Cremona*. Trans. Franz Schupp. Hamburg: Meiner, 2005.

Pseudo-al-Farabi. *De ortu scientiarum*. Ed. Clemens Baeumker. *Über den Ursprung der Wissenschaften*. Beiträge zur Geschichte der Philosophie und Theologie des Mittelalters 19.3. Münster: Aschendorff, 1916.

al-Ghazali. *Logica*. Ed. Charles H. Lohr. *Traditio* 21 (1965): 223–90.

—. *Maqasid al-falasifa o Intenciones de los filósofos*. Trans. Manuel Alonso Alonso. Barcelona: CSIC, 1963.

—. *Metaphysica*. Ed. Joseph T. Muckle. *Algazel's Metaphysics: A Medieval Translation*. Toronto: Pontifical Institute of Mediaeval Studies, 1933.

Aquinas, Thomas: *see* Thomas Aquinas

Augustine of Hippo. *Epistula* 190. PL 33.

Avicenna. *De viribus cordis*. Ed. Simone Van Riet. In *Liber de anima seu sextus de naturalibus* 2: 187–210.

—. *Liber de anima seu Sextus de naturalibus*. 2 vols. Ed. Simone Van Riet. Louvain: Peeters, 1968–72.

—. *Liber de philosophia prima sive Scientia divina*. Ed. Simone Van Riet. 3 vols. Louvain: Peeters, 1977–83.

—. *Liber primus naturalium: Tractatus primus de causis et principiis naturalium*. Ed. Simone Van Riet. Louvain: Peeters, 1992.

—. *Liber primus naturalium: Tractatus secundus de motu et de consimilibus*. Ed. Simone Van Riet. Brussels: Académie Royale du Belgique, 2006.

—. *Liber tertius naturalium: De generatione et corruptione*. Ed. Simone Van Riet. Louvain-La-Neuve: Peeters, 1987.

—. *Metafisica*. Trans. Olga Lizzini. Milan: Bompiani, 2002.

—. *Prologus discipuli et capitula*. Ed. Aleksander Birkenmajer. In "Avicennas Vorrede zum 'Liber Sufficientiae' und Roger Bacon," *Revue néoscolastique de philosophie* 36 (1934): 308–20.

Pseudo-Avicenna. *Liber celi et mundi*. Ed. Oliver Gutman. Leiden: Brill, 2003.

Bacon, Francis. *De principiis atque originibus*. In *The Works of Francis Bacon*, ed. James

Bibliography | 275

Spedding, Robert L. Ellis, and Douglas D. Heath, 5: 289–346. Boston: Houghton, 1860–64.

Bacon, Roger. *Questiones supra libros octo Physicorum Aristotelis.* Ed. Ferdinand M. Delorme and Robert Steele. *Opera Hactenus Inedita Rogeri Baconi* 13. Oxford: Clarendon, 1935.

Blund, John. *Treatise on the Soul.* Ed. Daniel A. Callus and Richard W. Hunt. Trans. Michael W. Dunne. Oxford: The British Academy, 2013.

Boethius, Anicius Manlius Severinus. *The Consolation of Philosophy.* Trans. Hugh F. Stewart. Cambridge, MA: Harvard University Press, 1964.

—. *Contra Eutychen et Nestorium.* In *De consolatione philosophiae / opuscula theologica,* ed. Claudio Moreschini, 206–41. Munich: DeGruyter, 2005.

—. *De consolatione philosophiae.* In *De consolatione philosophiae / opuscula theologica,* ed. Claudio Moreschini, 1–162. Munich: DeGruyter, 2005.

—. *De sancta Trinitate.* In *De consolatione philosophiae / opuscula theologica,* ed. Claudio Moreschini, 165–81. Munich: DeGruyter, 2005.

—. *In Isagogen Porphyrii commenta.* Ed. Samuel Brandt. Vienna: Tempsky, 1906. Translated as *Five Texts on the Mediaeval Problem of Universals: Porphyry, Boethius, Abelard, Duns Scotus, Ockham* by Paul V. Spade, 20–25. Indianapolis: Hackett, 1994.

—. *Introductio ad syllogismos categoricos: Critical Edition with Introduction, Commentary, and Indexes.* Ed. Christina T. Thörnqvist. Gothenburg: University of Gothenburg, 2008.

—. *Quomodo substantiae in eo quod sint bonae sint cum non sint substantialia bona* [*De hebdomadibus*]. In *De consolatione philosophiae / opuscula theologica,* ed. Claudio Moreschini, 186–94. Munich: DeGruyter, 2005.

—. *Theological Tractates.* Trans. Hugh F. Stewart and Edward K. Rand. Cambridge, MA: Harvard University Press, 1964.

Calcidius. *Commentaire au* Timée *de Platon.* Ed. Béatrice Bakhouche. Paris: Vrin, 2011.

—. *On Plato's* Timaeus. Trans. John Magee. Cambridge, MA: Harvard University Press, 2016.

Chartularium Universitatis Parisiensis. Ed. Heinrich Denifle. Paris, 1889.

Conrad of Prussia. *Commentary on the* De unitate et uno. In *The Commentary of Conrad of Prussia on the* De unitate et uno *of Dominicus Gundissalinus,* ed. Joseph Bobik. Lewiston: Edwin Mellen, 1989.

Daniel of Morley. *Philosophia.* Ed. Gregor Maurach. *Mittellateinisches Jahrbuch* 14 (1979): 204–55.

Geoffrey of Aspall. *Questions on Aristotle's* Physics. Ed. Silvia Donati and Cecilia Trifogli. Oxford: Oxford University Press, 2017.

Grosseteste, Robert: *see* Robert Grosseteste

Hermann of Carinthia. *De essentiis.* Ed. Charles Burnett. Leiden: Brill, 1982.

Hugh of St Victor. *De sacramentis christianae fidei.* Ed. Rainer Berndt. Münster: Aschendorff, 2008.

Ibn Daud, Abraham. *Dorot 'Olam.* In *Abraham Ibn Daud's Dorot 'Olam (Generation of the Ages): A Critical Edition and Translation of Zikhron Divrey Romi, Divrey Yisra'el and the Midrash on Zechariah,* ed. Katja Vehlow. Leiden: Brill, 2013.

276 | Bibliography

—. *Ha-Emunah ha-Ramah*. Translated as *The Exalted Faith* by Norbert M. Samuelson. Translation edited by Gershon Weiss. Rutherford: Fairleigh Dickinson University Press, 1986.

—. *Sefer ha-Qabbalah: The Book of Tradition*. Ed. Gerson D. Cohen. London: Littman Library, 1967.

Ibn Gabirol, Solomon. *Fons vitae*. In *Avencebrolis (Ibn Gabirol) Fons Vitae, ex Arabico in Latinum Translatus ab Johanne Hispano et Dominico Gundissalino*, ed. Clemens Baeumker. Beiträge zur Geschichte der Philosophie und Theologie des Mittelalters 1.2–4. Münster: Aschendorff, 1892–95.

—. *Fons vitae / Meqor hayyim*. Ed. Roberto Gatti. Genoa: Il Melangolo, 2001.

—. *Fons vitae*. Ed. Marienza Benedetto. *La fonte della vita*. Milan: Bompiani, 2007.

—. *The Font of Life*. Trans. John A. Laumakis. Milwaukee: Marquette University Press, 2014.

—. *Improvement of the Moral Qualities*. Ed. Stephen S. Wise. New York: Columbia University Press, 1902.

—. *The Kingly Crown (Keter Malkhut)*. Ed. Bernard Lewis. Notre Dame: Notre Dame University Press, 2003.

Ibn Luqa, Qusta. *De differentia animae et spiritus*. Ed. Carl S. Barach. Bibliotheca Philosophorum Mediae Aetatis 3: 120–39. Innsbruck: Verlag der Wagnerschen Universitaets Buchhandlung, 1878.

Le Liber mahameleth. Ed. Anne-Marie Vlasschaert. Stuttgart: Franz Steiner, 2010.

The Liber mahameleth. Ed. Jacques Sesiano. Berlin: Springer, 2014.

Nicholas of Cusa. *De venatione sapientiae*. Ed. Raymond Klibansky and Hans G. Senger. Hamburg: Meiner, 1982.

Peter Lombard. *The Sentences*. Trans. Giulio Silano. 4 vols. Toronto: Pontifical Institute of Mediaeval Studies, 2007–10.

—. *Sententiae in IV libris distinctae*. Ed. Ignatius Brady. Grottaferrata: Typographia Collegii S. Bonaventurae ad Claras Aquas, 1971.

Porphyry. *Isagoge*. Trans. Alain de Libera and Alain-Philippe Segonds. Paris: Vrin, 1998.

Robert Grosseteste. *De luce*. In *La luce*, ed. Cecilia Panti. Pisa: Pisa University Press, 2011.

Pseudo–Robert Grosseteste. *Summa philosophiae*. In *Die philosophische Werke des Robert Grosseteste, Bishofs von Lincoln*, ed. Ludwig Baur, 275–643. Beiträge zur Geschichte der Philosophie und Theologie des Mittelalters 9. Münster: Aschendorff, 1912.

Thierry of Chartres. *The Commentary on the "De arithmetica" of Boethius*. Ed. Irene Caiazzo. Toronto: Pontifical Institute of Mediaeval Studies, 2015.

—. *Commentum super Boethii librum de Trinitate*. In *Commentaries on Boethius by Thierry of Chartres and His School*, ed. Nikolaus Häring, 55–116. Toronto: Pontifical Institute of Mediaeval Studies, 1971.

—. *Glosa super Boethii librum*. In *Commentaries on Boethius by Thierry of Chartres and His School*, ed. Nikolaus Häring, 259–300. Toronto: Pontifical Institute of Mediaeval Studies, 1971.

—. *The Latin Rhetorical Commentaries by Thierry of Chartres*. Ed. Karin M. Fredborg. Toronto: Pontifical Institute of Mediaeval Studies, 1988.

—. *Lectiones in Boethii librum de Trinitate*. In *Commentaries on Boethius by Thierry of*

Chartres and His School, ed. Nikolaus Häring, 125–229. Toronto: Pontifical Institute of Mediaeval Studies, 1971.

—. *Tractatus de sex dierum operibus*. In *Commentaries on Boethius by Thierry of Chartres and His School*, ed. Nikolaus Häring, 553–75. Toronto: Pontifical Institute of Mediaeval Studies, 1971.

Thomas Aquinas. *De spiritualibus creaturis*. Ed. Joseph Cos. Rome: Commissio Leonina; Paris: Cerf, 2000.

—. *Quaestiones de quolibet*. Ed. René-Antoine Gauthier. Rome: Commissio Leonina; Paris, Cerf, 1996.

Thomas of York. *Sapientiale*. In *The Doctrine of Creation in the* Sapientiale *of Thomas of York*, ed. Carlo A. Grassi. Ph.D. dissertation. University of Toronto, 1952.

William of Auvergne. *The Immortality of the Soul*. Trans. Roland Teske. Milwaukee: Marquette University Press, 1991.

—. *Opera omnia*. Paris: Iohannem Dupuis, 1674.

William of Conches. *Dragmaticon philosophiae*. Ed. Italo Ronca. Turnhout: Brepols, 1997.

—. *Glosae super Boetium*. Ed. Lodi Nauta. Turnhout: Brepols, 1999.

—. *Glosae super Platonem*. Ed. Édouard Jeauneau. Turnhout: Brepols, 2006.

—. *Philosophia mundi*. Ed. Gregor Maurach. Pretoria: University of South Africa, 1980.

William of Saint-Thierry. *De erroribus Guillelmi de Conchis*. PL 180: 333–40.

Secondary Works

Abrahamov, Binyamin. "Al-Ghazālī's Theory of Causality." *Studia Islamica* 67 (1988): 75–98.

Adamo, Luigi. "Boezio e Mario Vittorino traduttori e interpreti dell'*Isagoge* di Porfirio." *Rivista critica di storia della filosofia* 22 (1967): 141–64.

Adamson, Peter. *The Arabic Plotinus: A Philosophical Study of the* Theology of Aristotle. London: Duckworth, 2002.

—. "From the Necessary Existent to God." In *Interpreting Avicenna: Critical Essays*, ed. Peter Adamson, 170–89. Cambridge: Cambridge University Press, 2013.

Adler, Hermann. *Ibn Gabirol and His Influence upon Scholastic Philosophy*. London: University College Essays, 1964.

Albertson, David. *Mathematical Theologies: Nicholas of Cusa and the Legacy of Thierry of Chartres*. Oxford: Oxford University Press, 2014.

Alessio, Franco. "La filosofia e le 'artes mechanicae' nel secolo XII." *Studi medievali* 6/1 (1965): 71–111.

Allard, Baudoin C. "Note sur le *De immortalitate animae* de Guillaume d'Auvergne." *Bulletin de philosophie médiévale* 18 (1976): 68–72.

—. "Nouvelles additions et corrections au *Répertoire* de Glorieux: À propos de Guillaume d'Auvergne." *Bulletin de philosophie médiévale* 10–12 (1968–70): 212–24.

Alonso Alonso, Manuel. "Coincidencias verbales típicas en las obras y traducciones de Gundisalvo." *Al-Andalus* 20 (1955): 129–52 and 345–79.

278 | *Bibliography*

—. "Domingo Gundisalvo y el *De causis primis et secundis.*" *Estudios eclesiásticos* 21 (1947): 367–80.

—. "El traductor y prologuista del 'Sextus Naturalium.'" *Al-Andalus* 26 (1961): 1–35.

—. "Las fuentes literarias de Domingo Gundisalvo." *Al-Andalus* 11 (1946): 159–73.

—. "Homenaje a Avicena en su milenario: Las traducciones de Juan González de Burgos y Salomón." *Al-Andalus* 14 (1949): 291–319.

—. "Hugo de San Victor, refutado por Domingo Gundisalvo hacia el 1170." *Estudios eclesiásticos* 21 (1947): 209–16.

—. "Influencia de Algazel en el mundo latino." *Al-Andalus* 23 (1958): 371–80.

—. "Influencia de Severino Boecio en las obras y traducciones de Gundisalvo." In *Temas filosóficos medievales: Ibn Dawud y Gundisalvo*, ed. Manuel Alonso Alonso, 369–96. Santander: Universidad Pontificia Comillas, 1959.

—. "Notas sobre los traductores toledanos Domingo Gundisalvo y Juan Hispano." *Al-Andalus* 8 (1943): 155–88.

Alonso Del Real, Concepción. "*De processione mundi* de D. Gundisalvo: Texto del Codex Oxoniensis Coll. Oriel no. 7." *Cuadernos de filología clásica* 21 (2001): 95–114.

Alper, Ömer Mahir. "Avicenna's Argument for the Existence of God: Was He Really Influenced by the Mutakallimun?" In *Interpreting Avicenna, Science and Philosophy in Medieval Islam*, ed. Jon McGinnis, 129–41. Paris: Brill, 2004.

Alpina, Tommaso. "Knowing the Soul from Knowing Oneself: A Reading of the Prologue to Avicenna's *Kitāb al-Nafs* (*Book of the Soul*)." *Atti e Memorie dell'Accademia Toscana di Scienze e Lettere "La Colombaria"* 82 (2018): 443–58.

—. "The Soul of, the Soul in Itself, and the Flying Man Experiment." *Arabic Sciences and Philosophy* 28 (2018): 187–224.

Anawati, George C. "Le néoplatonisme dans la pensée musulmane: État actuel des recherches." In *Plotino e il Neoplatonismo in Oriente e in Occidente*, 339–405. Rome: Accademia Nazionale dei lincei, 1974.

—. "La notion de création dans l'Islam." *Studia Missionalia* 18 (1969): 271–95.

Annala, Pauli. "The Function of the *Formae Nativae* in the Refinement Process of Matter: A Study of Bernard of Chartres's Concept of Matter." *Vivarium* 35 (1997): 1–20.

Aronadio, Francesco. "L'orientamento filosofico di Cicerone e la sua traduzione del *Timeo.*" *Méthexis* 21 (2008): 111–29.

Asztalos, Monika. "Boethius as a Transmitter of Greek Logic to the Latin West: The Categories." *Harvard Studies in Classical Philology* 95 (1993): 367–407.

Ayse Akasoy, Anna, and Alexander Fidora. "Ibn Sab'in and Raymundus Lullus: The Question of the Arabic Sources of Lullus' Logic Revisited." In *Islamic Thought in the Middle Ages: Studies in Text, Transmission and Translation in Honour of Hans Daiber*, ed. Anna Ayse Akasoy and Wim Raven, 433–58. Leiden: Brill, 2008.

Bäck, Allan. "Avicenna on Existence." *Journal of the History of Philosophy* 25 (1987): 351–67.

Baeumker, Clemens. "Dominicus Gundissalinus als philosophischer Schriftsteller." In *Studien und Charakteristiken zur Geschichte der Philosophie, insbesondere des Mittelalters*, 255–75. Beiträge zur Geschichte der Philosophie und Theologie des Mittelalters 25.1–2. Münster: Aschendorff, 1927.

—. "Les écrits philosophiques de Dominicus Gundissalinus." *Revue Thomiste* 5 (1897): 723–45.

Baffioni, Carmela. "Il *Liber introductorius in artem logicae demonstrationis*: Problemi storici e filologici." *Studi filosofici* 17 (1994): 69–90.

Beale-Rivaya, Yasmine. "The History and Evolution of the Term 'Mozarab.'" *Imago Temporis* 4 (2010): 51–72.

—. "The Written Record as Witness: Language Shift from Arabic to Romance in the Documents of the Mozarabs of Toledo in the Twelfth and Thirteenth Centuries." *La Corónica* 40/2 (2012): 27–50.

Beaujouan, Guy. "À l'affût des rapports entre sciences et techniques au Moyen Âge." *Technologia: Quarterly Review Devoted to Historical and Social Studies in Science, Technology and Industry* 11 (1988): 5–11.

Bédoret, Henri. "Les premières versions tolédanes de philosophie: Œuvres d'Avicenne." *Revue Néoscolastique* 41 (1938): 380–98.

Belo, Catarina. "Essence and Existence in Avicenna and Averroes." *Al-Qantara* 30 (2009): 403–26.

Benedetto, Marienza. "Alle origini della controversia medievale sulla pluralità delle forme sostanziali: Il *Fons vitae* di Avicebron." In *Appropriation, Interpretation and Criticism: Philosophical and Theological Exchanges Between the Arabic, Hebrew and Latin Intellectual Traditions*, ed. Alexander Fidora and Nicola Polloni, 137–84. Barcelona: FIDEM, 2017.

—. "Avicebron." In *Encyclopedia of Medieval Philosophy Between 500 and 1500*, ed. Henrik Lagerlund, 135–38. Dordrecht: Springer, 2010.

—. "La dimensione fondante della realtà: La materia in Ibn Gabirol e Shem Tov ben Yosef ibn Falaquera." *Quaestio* 7 (2007): 229–44.

—. "Sapienza e filosofia nel *Fons vitae* di Ibn Gabirol." *Quaestio* 5 (2005): 259–72.

Bertola, Ermenegildo. "È esistito un avicennismo latino nel Medioevo?" *Sophia* 35 (1967): 318–34 and 39 (1971): 278–320.

—. *Salomon Ibn Gabirol (Avicebron): Vita, opere e pensiero*. Padua: Cedam, 1953.

Bertolacci, Amos. "Albert the Great, *Metaph.* IV, 1, 5: From the *Refutatio* to the *Excusatio* of Avicenna's Theory of Unity." In *Was ist Philosophie im Mittelalter? Akten des X. Internationalen Kongresses für mittelalterliche Philosophie der Société Internationale pour l'Étude de la Philosophie Médiévale, 25. bis 30. August 1997 in Erfurt*, ed. Jan A. Aertsen and Andreas Speer, 881–87. Berlin: De Gruyter, 1998.

—. "A Community of Translators: The Latin Medieval Versions of Avicenna's *Book of the Cure*." In *Communities of Learning: Networks and the Shaping of Intellectual Identity in Europe, 1100–1500*, ed. Constant J. Mews and John N. Crossley, 37–54. Turnhout: Brepols, 2011.

—. "The Distinction of Essence and Existence in Avicenna's *Metaphysics*: The Text and Its Context." In *Islamic Philosophy, Science, Culture, and Religion: Studies in Honor of Dimitri Gutas*, ed. Felicitas Opwis and David A. Reisman, 257–88. Leiden: Brill, 2012.

—. "La divisione della filosofia nel primo capitolo del *Commento* di Alberto Magno alla *Fisica*: Le fonti avicenniane." In *La divisione della filosofia e le sue ragioni: Lettura di testi medievali (VI–XIII secolo)*, ed. Giulio D'Onofrio, 137–55. Cava de' Tirreni: Avagliano, 2001.

280 | Bibliography

—. "The Doctrine of Material and Formal Causality in the *Ilāhiyyāt* of Avicenna's *Kitāb al-Šifā*'." *Quaestio* 2 (2002): 125–54.

—. "From al-Kindi to al-Farabi: Avicenna's Progressive Knowledge of Aristotle's *Metaphysics* According to His Autobiography." *Arabic Sciences and Philosophy* 11 (2001): 257–95.

—. "From Athens to Buhara, to Cordoba, to Cologne: On the Transmission of Aristotle's *Metaphysics* in the Arab and Latin Worlds during the Middle Ages." In *Circolazione dei saperi nel Mediterraneo: Filosofia e Scienze (secoli IX–XVII)*, ed. Graziella Federici Vescovini and Ahmed Hasnaoui, 217–33. Florence: Edizioni Cadmo, 2013.

—. "*Metafisica* A, 5, 986 a 22–26 nell'*Ilahiyyat* del *Kitab al-Šifa*' di Ibn Sina." *Documenti e Studi sulla Tradizione Filosofica Medievale* 10 (1999): 205–31.

—. "'Necessary' as Primary Concept in Avicenna's *Metaphysics*." In *Conoscenza e contingenza nella tradizione aristotelica medievale*, ed. Gianfranco Fioravanti and Stefano Perfetti, 31–50. Pisa: ETS, 2008.

—. "On the Arabic Translations of Aristotle's *Metaphysics*." *Arabic Sciences and Philosophy* 15 (2005): 241–75.

—. "On the Latin Reception of Avicenna's *Metaphysics* before Albertus Magnus: An Attempt at Periodization." In *The Arabic, Hebrew and Latin Reception of Avicenna's* Metaphysics, ed. Dag N. Hasse and Amos Bertolacci, 197–224. Berlin: De Gruyter, 2012.

—. *The Reception of Aristotle's Metaphysics in Avicenna's* Kitab al-Šifa. Leiden: Brill, 2006.

—. "The Reception of Avicenna in Latin Medieval Culture." In *Interpreting Avicenna: Critical Essays*, ed. Peter Adamson, 242–69. Cambridge: Cambridge University Press, 2013.

—. "La ricezione del libro Γ della *Metafisica* nell'*Ilahiyyat* del *Kitab al-Šifa*' di Avicenna." In *Aristotele e i suoi esegeti neoplatonici: Logica e ontologia nelle interpretazioni greche e arabe*, ed. Vincenza Celluprica, Cristina D'Ancona Costa, and Riccardo Chiaradonna, 173–210. Naples: Bibliopolis, 2004.

—. "The Structure of Metaphysical Science in the *Ilahiyyat* (*Divine Science*) of Avicenna's *Kitab al-Šifa*' (*Book of the Cure*)." *Documenti e Studi sulla Tradizione Filosofica Medievale* 13 (2002): 1–69.

Betton, Efrem. "Avicebron è l'unica fonte dell'ilemorfismo universale?" In *Actas del V Congreso internacional de filosofía medieval*, 619–29. Madrid: Editora Nacional, 1979.

Bianchi, Luca. "L'acculturazione filosofica dell'Occidente." In *La filosofia nelle Università: Secoli XIII–XIV*, ed. Luca Bianchi, 1–23. Florence: La Nuova Italia, 1997.

—. "Aristotle among Thirteenth-Century Franciscans: Some Preliminary Remarks." In *Philosophy and Theology in the 'Studia' of the Religious Orders and at Papal and Royal Courts*, ed. Kent Emery Jr., William J. Courtenay, and Stephen Metzger, 237–59. Turnhout: Brepols, 2012.

—. "Cosmologia e fisica fra XIII e XIV secolo." In *Luoghi e voci del pensiero medievale*, ed. Mariateresa Fumagalli Beonio Brocchieri and Riccardo Fedriga, 222–30. Milan: Encyclomedia, 2010.

—. "Students, Masters, and 'Heterodox' Doctrines at the Parisian Faculty of Arts in the 1270s." *Recherches de théologie et philosophie médiévales* 76 (2009): 75–109.

Bignami-Odier, Jeanne. "Le manuscrit Vatican Latin 2186." *Archives d'histoire doctrinale et littéraire du Moyen Âge* 11 (1938): 133–66.

Black, Deborah L. "Knowledge (*'ilm*) and Certitude (*yaqin*) in al-Farabi's Epistemology." *Arabic Sciences and Philosophy* 16 (2006): 11–45.

Blake, Anthony G.E. "Implications of Avicebron's Notion of Will." *Systematics* 4 (1966): 1–41.

Blau, Joshua. *The Emergence and Linguistic Background of Judaeo-Arabic: A Study of the Origins of Neo-Arabic and Middle Arabic*. Jerusalem: Brill, 1981.

Bos, Egbert P. "Some Notes on the Meaning of the Term 'Substantia' in the Tradition of Aristotle's Categories." In *L'élaboration du vocabulaire philosophique au Moyen Âge*, ed. Jacqueline Hamesse and Carlos Steel, 511–27. Turnhout: Brepols, 2000.

Brentjes, Sonja, Alexander Fidora, and Matthias Tischler. "Towards a New Approach to Medieval Cross-Cultural Exchanges." *Journal of Transcultural Medieval Studies* 1 (2014): 9–50.

Brisson, Luc. *Le Même et l'Autre dans la Structure Ontologique du Timée de Platon*. Sankt Augustin: Akademia, 1994.

Brower, Jeff. "Trinity." In *The Cambridge Companion to Abelard*, ed. Jeff Brower and Kelvin Guilfoy, 223–57. Cambridge: Cambridge University Press, 2004.

Brunner, Fernand. "Creatio numerorum rerum est creatio." In *Mélanges offerts à R. Crozet*, ed. Pierre Gallais and Yves Jean Rion, 719–25. Poitiers: Société d'études médiévales, 1966.

—. "Création et émanation: Fragment de philosophie comparée." *Studia philosophica* 33 (1973): 33–63.

—. "La doctrine de la matière chez Avicébron." *Revue de théologie et de philosophie* 6 (1956): 261–79.

—. "Études sur le sens et la structure des systèmes réalistes: Ibn Gabirol, l'école de Chartres." *Cahiers de Civilisation Médiévale* 1 (1958): 259–317.

—. *Platonisme et aristotélisme: La critique d'Ibn Gabirol par St. Thomas d'Aquin*. Louvain: Publications universitaires de Louvain, 1965.

—. "Réflexion sur le réalisme de l'idée à propos d'Ibn Gabirol." In *L'art des confins: Mélanges offerts à Maurice de Gandillac*, ed. Anny Cazenave and Jean-François Lyotard, 99–120. Paris: Presses universitaires de France, 1985.

—. "Sur la philosophie d'Ibn Gabirol." *Revue des études juives* 128 (1967): 58–71.

—. "Sur le *Fons Vitae* d'Avicembron, livre III." *Studia Philosophica* 12 (1952): 171–83.

—. "Sur l'hylemorphisme d'Ibn Gabirol." *Les études philosophiques* 8 (1953): 28–38.

—. "La transformation des notions de matière et de forme d'Aristote à ibn Gabirol." In *Métaphysique d'ibn Gabirol et de la tradition platonicienne*, ed. Fernand Brunner, 1–17. Aldershot: Ashgate, 1997.

Brunschvig, Robert. "Encore sur la doctrine du Mahdi Ibn Tumart." *Folia Orientalia* 12 (1970): 33–40.

—. "Sur la doctrine du Mahdi Ibn Tumart." *Arabica* 2 (1955): 137–49.

282 | Bibliography

Burnett, Charles. *Adelard of Bath: An English Scientist and Arabist of the Early Twelfth Century*. London: The Warburg Institute, 1988.

—. *Arabic into Latin in the Middle Ages: The Translators and Their Intellectual and Social Context*. Farnham: Ashgate, 2009.

—. "Arabic into Latin in Twelfth-Century Spain: The Works of Hermann of Carinthia." *Mittellateinisches Jahrbuch* 13 (1978): 100–134.

—. "Arabic into Latin: The Reception of Arabic Philosophy into Western Europe." In *The Cambridge Companion to Arabic Philosophy*, ed. Peter Adamson and Richard C. Taylor, 370–404. Cambridge: Cambridge University Press, 2005.

—. "Astrology, Astronomy and Magic as the Motivation for the Scientific Renaissance of the Twelfth Century." In *The Imaginal Cosmos: Astrology, Divination and the Sacred*, ed. Angela Voss and Jean Hinson Lall, 55–61. Canterbury: University of Kent, 2007.

—. "The Blend of Latin and Arabic Sources in the Metaphysics of Adelard of Bath, Hermann of Carintia, and Gundisalvus." In *Metaphysics in the Twelfth Century: On the Relationship among Philosophy, Science and Theology*, ed. Matthias Lutz-Bachmann, Alexander Fidora, and Andreas Niederberger, 41–66. Turnhout: Brepols, 2004.

—. "The Coherence of the Arabic-Latin Translation Programme in Toledo in the Twelfth Century." *Science in Context* 14 (2001): 249–88.

—. "Communities of Learning in the Twelfth-Century Toledo." In *Communities of Learning: Networks and the Shaping of Intellectual Identity in Europe, 1110–1500*, ed. Constant J. Mews and John N. Crossley, 9–18. Turnhout: Brepols, 2011.

—. "The Contents and Affiliation of the Scientific Manuscripts Written at, or Brought to, Chartres in the Time of John of Salisbury." In *The World of John of Salisbury*, ed. Michael Wilks, 127–60. Oxford: Blackwell, 1984.

—. "Dialectic and Mathematics According to Ahmad ibn Yusuf: A Model for Gerard of Cremona's Programme of Translation and Teaching?" In *Langage, sciences, philosophie au XIIe siècle: Actes de la table ronde internationale organisée les 25 et 26 mars 1998 par le Centre d'histoire des sciences et des philosophies arabes et médiévales (UPRESA 7062, CNRS/Paris VII/EPHE)*, ed. Joël Biard, 83–92. Paris: Vrin, 2000.

—. "The Establishment of Medieval Hermeticism." In *The Medieval World*, ed. Peter Linehan and Janet Nelson, 111–30. London: Psychology, 2001.

—. "Euclid and al-Farabi in ms. Vatican, Reg. Lat. 1268." In *Words, Texts and Concepts Cruising the Mediterranean Sea: Studies on the Sources, Contents and Influences of Islamic Civilization and Arabic Philosophy and Science Dedicated to Gerhard Endress on His Sixty-Fifth Birthday*, ed. Rüdiger Arnzen and Jörn Thielmann, 411–36. Leuven: Peeters, 2004.

—. "European Knowledge of Arabic Texts Referring to Music: Some New Material." *Early Music History* 12 (1993): 1–17.

—. *Glosses and Commentaries on Aristotelian Logical Texts: The Syriac, Arabic and Medieval Latin Traditions*. London: The Warburg Institute, 1993.

—. "A Group of Arabic-Latin Translators Working in Northern Spain in the Mid-Twelfth Century." *Journal of the Royal Asiatic Society* (1977): 62–108.

Bibliography | 283

—. "Hermann of Carinthia." In *A History of Twelfth-Century Western Philosophy*, ed. Peter Dronke, 386–406. Cambridge: Cambridge University Press, 1988.

—. "Hermann of Carinthia and the *Kitab al-Istamatis*: Further Evidence for the Transmission of Hermetic Magic." *Journal of the Warburg and Courtauld Institutes* 44 (1981): 167–69.

—. "Hermann of Carinthia's Attitude towards His Arabic Sources, in Particular in Respect to Theories of the Human Soul." In *L'Homme et son univers au Moyen Âge*, ed. Christian Wenin, 306–22. Louvain: Peeters, 1985.

—. "Humanism and Orientalism in the Translations from Arabic into Latin in the Middle Ages." In *Wissen über Grenzen: Arabisches Wissen und Lateinisches Mittelalter*, ed. Andreas Speer and Lydia Wegener, 22–31. Berlin: De Gruyter, 2006.

—. "The Impact of Arabic Science on Western Civilisation in the Middle Ages." *Bulletin of the British Association of Orientalists* 11 (1979–80): 40–51.

—. "Innovations in the Classification of the Sciences in the Twelfth Century." In *Knowledge and the Sciences in Medieval Philosophy: Proceedings of the Eighth International Congress of Medieval Philosophy (SIEPM)*, ed. Simo Knuuttila, Reijo Työrinoja, and Sten Ebbesen, 25–42. Helsinki: Yliopistopaino, 1990.

—. "The Institutional Context of Arabic-Latin Translations of the Middle Ages: A Reassessment of the 'School of Toledo.'" In *Vocabulary of Teaching and Research Between Middle Ages and Renaissance: Proceedings of the Colloquium London, Warburg Institute, 11–12 March 1994*, ed. Olga Weijers, 214–35. Turnhout: Brepols, 1995.

—. *The Introduction of Arabic Learning into England*. London: The British Library, 1997.

—. "John of Seville and John of Spain: A Mise au Point." *Bulletin de philosophie médiévale* 44 (2002): 59–78.

—. "The Latin and Arabic Influences on the Vocabulary Concerning Demonstrative Argument in the Versions of Euclid's *Elements* Associated with Adelard of Bath." In *Aux origines du lexique philosophique européen: L'influence de la latinitas, actes du colloque international (Rome, 23–25 mai 1996)*, ed. Jacqueline Hamesse, 175–201. Louvain-la-Neuve: FIDEM, 1997.

—. "Literal Translation and Intelligent Adaptation amongst the Arabic-Latin Translators of the First Half of the Twelfth Century." In *La diffusione delle scienze islamiche nel Medio Evo Europeo*, ed. Biancamaria Scarcia Amoretti, 9–28. Rome: Accademia dei Lincei, 1987.

—. "Magister Iohannes Hispalensis et Limiensis and Qusta ibn Luqa's *De differentia spiritus et animae*: A Portuguese Contribution to the Arts Curriculum?" *Quodlibetaria Mediaevalia: Textos e Estudos* 7–8 (1995): 221–67.

—. "Magister Iohannes Hispanus: Towards the Identity of a Toledan Translator." In *Comprendre et maîtriser la nature au Moyen Âge, Mélanges d'histoire des sciences offerts à Guy Beaujouan*, ed. Georges Comet, 425–36. Geneva: Droz, 1994.

—. "Michael Scot and the Transmission of Scientific Culture from Toledo to Bologna via the Court of Frederick II Hohenstaufen." *Micrologus* 2 (1994): 101–26.

284 | *Bibliography*

—. "A New Source for Dominicus Gundissalinus's Account of the Science of the Stars?" *Annals of Science* 47 (1990): 361–74.

—. *Numerals and Arithmetic in the Middle Ages.* Farnham: Ashgate, 2010.

—. "Physics before the *Physics*: Early Translations from Arabic of Texts concerning Nature in MSS British Library, Additional 22719 and Cotton Galba E IV." *Medioevo* 27 (2002): 53–109.

—. "Plato amongst the Arabic-Latin Translators of the Twelfth Century." In *Il Timeo: Esegesi greche, arabe, latine,* ed. Francesco Celia and Angela Ulacco, 269–306. Pisa: Pisa University Press, 2012.

—. "Robert of Ketton." In *Oxford Dictionary of National Biography.* Oxford: Oxford University Press, 2004. Online edition.

—. "Scientific Translations from Arabic: The Question of Revision." In *Science Translated: Latin and Vernacular Translations of Scientific Treatises in Medieval Europe,* ed. Michèle Goyens, Pieter De Leemans, and An Smets, 11–31. Leuven: Leuven University Press, 2008.

—. "The Second Revelation of Arabic Philosophy and Science." In *Islam and the Italian Renaissance,* ed. Charles Burnett and Anna Contadini, 185–98. London: The Warburg Institute, 1999.

—. "*Sefer ha-Middot*: A Mid-Twelfth-Century Text on Arithmetic and Geometry Attributed to Abraham Ibn Ezra." *Aleph* 6 (2006): 57–238.

—. "Some Comments on the Translating of Works from Arabic into Latin in the Mid-Twelfth Century." In *Orientalische Kultur und Europäisches Mittelalter,* ed. Albert Zimmerman, 161–71. Berlin: De Gruyter, 1985.

—. "Stephen of Messina and the Translation of Astrological Texts from Greek in the Time of Manfred." In *Translating at the Court: Bartholomew of Messina and Cultural Life at the Court of Manfred, King of Sicily,* ed. Pieter De Leemans, 123–32. Leuven: Leuven University Press, 2014.

—. "The Strategy of Revision in the Arabic-Latin Translations from Toledo: The Case of Abu Maʿshar's *On the Great Conjunctions.*" In *Les traducteurs au travail: Leurs manuscrits et leurs méthodes,* ed. Jacqueline Hamesse, 51–113 and 529–40. Louvain-la-Neuve: Brepols, 2002.

—. "Talismans: Magic as Science? Necromancy among the Seven Liberal Arts." In *Magic and Divination in the Middle Ages: Texts and Techniques in the Islamic and Christian World,* ed. Charles Burnett, 1–15. Aldershot: Routledge, 1996.

—. "The Toledan *Regule* (*Liber Alchorismi,* pt. II): A Twelfth-Century Arithmetical Miscellany." *Sciamus* 8 (2007): 141–231.

—. "The Translating Activity in Medieval Spain." In *The Legacy of Muslim Spain,* ed. Salma Khadra Jayyusi, 1036–58. Leiden: Brill, 1992.

—. "Translating from Arabic into Latin in the Middle Ages: Theory, Practice, and Criticism." In *Éditer, traduire, interpreter: Essais de méthodologie philosophique,* ed. Steve G. Lofts and Philipp W. Rosemann, 55–78. Louvain-la-Neuve: Éditions de l'Institut supérieur de philosophie, Louvain: Peeters, 1997.

—. "The Translation of Arabic Science into Latin: A Case of Alienation of Intellectual Property?" *Bulletin of the Royal Institute for Inter-Faith Studies* 4 (2002): 145–57.

—. "Translations and Transmission of Greek and Islamic Science to Latin Christendom." In *Cambridge History of Science*, vol. 2: *Medieval Science*, ed. David C. Lindberg and Michael H. Shank, 341–64. Cambridge: Cambridge University Press, 2013.

—. "The Transmission of Science and Philosophy." In *The Cambridge World History*, vol. 5: *Expanding Webs of Exchange and Conflict, 500 CE–1500 CE*, ed. Benjamin Z. Kedar and Merry E. Wiesner-Hanks, 339–58. Cambridge: Cambridge University Press, 2015.

—. "The Twelfth-Century Renaissance." In *Cambridge History of Science*, vol. 2: *Medieval Science*, ed. David C. Lindberg and Michael H. Shank, 365–84. Cambridge: Cambridge University Press, 2013.

—. "Two Approaches to Natural Science in Toledo of the Twelfth Century." In *Christlicher Norden – Muslimischer Süden: Ansprüche und Wirklichkeiten von Christen, Juden und Muslimen auf der Iberischen Halbinsel im Hoch- und Spätmittelalter*, ed. Matthias Tischler and Alexander Fidora, 69–80. Münster: Aschendorff, 2011.

Burnett, Charles, and Danielle Jacquart, eds. *Constantine the African and 'Alī Ibn al-'Abbās al-Maǧūsī: The Pantegni and Related Texts*. Leiden: Brill, 1994.

Burnett, Charles, and Pedro Mantas España, eds. *'Ex Oriente Lux': Translating Words, Scripts and Styles in the Medieval Mediterranean World*. Córdoba: UCO Press, 2016.

—. *Mapping Knowledge: Cross-Pollination in Late Antiquity and the Middle Ages*. Córdoba: UCO Press, 2014.

Burrell, David B. "Creation and Emanation: Two Paradigms of Reason." In *God and Creation: An Ecumenical Symposium*, ed. David B. Burrell and Bernard McGinn, 27–37. Notre Dame: Notre Dame University Press, 1990.

Caiazzo, Irene. "L'âme du monde: Un thème privilégié des auteurs chartrains au XIIe siècle." In *Les temps de Fulbert: Actes de l'Université d'été du 8 au 10 juillet 1996*, 79–89. Chartres: SAEL, 1996.

—. "La forme et les qualités des éléments: Lectures médiévales du *Timée*." In *Il Timeo: Esegesi greche, arabe, latine*, ed. Francesco Celia and Andrea Ulacco, 307–45. Pisa: Pisa University Press, 2012.

—. "The Four Elements in the Work of William of Conches." In *Guillaume de Conches: Philosophie et science au XII siècle*, ed. Barbara Obrist and Irene Caiazzo, 3–66. Florence: SISMEL, 2011.

—. "Un inedito commento sulla *Isagoge Iohannitii* conservato a Parigi." In *La scuola medica salernitata: Gli autori e i testi*, ed. Danielle Jacquart and Agostino Paravicini Bagliani, 93–123. Florence: SISMEL, 2007.

—. *Lectures médiévales de Macrobe: Les* Glosae Colonienses super Macrobium. Paris: Vrin, 2002.

—. "La materia nei commenti al *Timeo* del secolo XII." *Quaestio* 7 (2007): 245–64.

—. "Il rinvenimento del commento di Teodorico di Chartres al *De arithmetica* di Boezio." In *Adorare caelestia, gubernare terrena: Atti del Colloquio Internazionale in onore di Paolo Lucentini (Napoli, 6–7 Novembre 2007)*, ed. Pasquale Arfé, Irene Caiazzo, and Antonella Sannino, 183–204. Turnhout: Brepols, 2011.

286 | Bibliography

Callus, Daniel A. "Gundissalinus' *De Anima* and the Problem of Substantial Form." *The New Scholasticism* 13 (1939): 338–55.

Campi, Luigi. "*In ipso sunt idem esse, vivere et intelligere*: Notes on a Case of Textual Bricolage." *Viator* 45/3 (2014): 89–100.

Cantarino, Vincent. "Ibn Gabirol's Metaphysic of Light." *Studia Islamica* 26 (1967): 49–71.

Carlotta, Vincenzo. "La morte e la resurrezione dei corpi nel *Dialogo dei filosofi e di Cleopatra* e nel *Liber de compositione alchemiae* di Morieno." In *Appropriation, Interpretation and Criticism: Philosophical and Theological Exchanges Between the Arabic, Hebrew and Latin Intellectual Traditions*, ed. Alexander Fidora and Nicola Polloni, 92–120. Barcelona: FIDEM, 2017.

Cavaleiro de Macedo, Cecilia C. "Neoplatonismo e aristotelismo no hilemorfismo universal de Ibn Gabirol (Avicebron)." *Veritas* 52/3 (2007): 132–48.

—. "A unidade da matéria em Ibn Gabirol." *Seara Filosófica* 13 (2016): 52–68.

Chadwick, Henry. *Boethius: The Consolations of Music, Logic, Theology, and Philosophy.* Oxford: Oxford University Press, 1981.

Châtillon, Jean. "Les écoles de Chartres et de Saint-Victor." *Settimane di studio del centro italiano di studi sull'alto medioevo* 19 (1972): 795–839.

Chenu, Marie-Dominique. "Nature ou histoire? Une controverse exégétique sur la création au XIIème siècle." *Archives d'histoire doctrinale et littéraire du Moyen Âge* 28 (1953): 25–30.

—. "Notes de Lexicographie Philosophique Médiévale: Disciplina." In *Studi di lessicografia filosofica medievale*, ed. Marie-Dominique Chenu, 93–99. Florence: Leo S. Olschki, 2001.

—. *La théologie au douzième siècle.* Paris: Vrin, 1966.

Chisholm, Roderick M. *A Realistic Theory of Categories: An Essay on Ontology.* Cambridge: Cambridge University Press, 1996.

Chroust, Anton-Hermann. "The Definitions of Philosophy in the *De Divisione Philosophiae* of Dominicus Gundissalinus." *The New Scholasticism* 25 (1951): 253–81.

Clark, James G., Frank T. Coulson, and Kathryn L. McKinley, eds. *Ovid in the Middle Ages.* Cambridge: Cambridge University Press, 2011.

Colley, Caleb. *John Pecham on Life and Mind.* Würzburg: Königshausen, 2015.

Counet, Jean-Michel. "Les mathématiques au service d'une théologie de la matière chez Thierry de Chartres et Clarembaud d'Arras." In *Vie spéculative, vie méditative et travail manuel à Chartres: Actes du colloque international des 4 et 5 juillet 1998*, 103–14. Chartres: Association des Amis du Centre Médiéval Européen de Chartres (AACMEC), 1998.

Courcelle, Pierre. *La Consolation de Philosophie dans la tradition littéraire.* Paris: Études Augustiniennes, 1967.

Courtine, Jean François. "Essenza, sostanza, sussistenza, esistenza." *Quaestio* 3 (2003): 27–59.

Crisciani, Chiara. "Alchemy and Medicine in the Middle Ages: Recent Studies and Projects for Research." *Bulletin de philosophie médiévale* 38 (1996): 9–21.

—. "L'alchimia dal Medioevo al Rinascimento: 'Scientia' o 'ars'?" In *Il Rinascimento italiano e l'Europa*, vol. 5, *Le scienze*, ed. Antonio Clericuzio and Germana Ernst, 111–28. Treviso: Angelo Colla Editore, 2008.

Crowley, Theodore. "Alfarabi and Avicenna on the Active Intellect." *Viator* 3 (1972): 109–78.

Cruz Hernández, Miguel. *La metafísica de Avicena*. Granada: Universidad de Granada, 1949.

Dal Bo, Federico. "The Theory of 'Emanation' in Gikatilla's *Gates of Justice.*" *Journal of Jewish Studies* 62 (2011): 79–104.

D'Alverny, Marie-Thérèse. "Algazel dans l'occident latin." In *Un trait d'union entre l'orient et l'occident: Al-Ghazzali et Ibn Maimoun*, 125–46. Agadir: Academie Royale du Maroc, 1986.

—. "Anniyya-anitas." In *Mélanges offerts a Étienne Gilson*, 59–91. Toronto: Pontifical Institute of Mediaeval Studies, 1959.

—. "Avendauth?" In *Homenaje a Millás Vallicrosa*, 1: 19–43. Barcelona: CSIC, 1954.

—. "Le cosmos symbolique du XIIe siècle." *Archives d'histoire doctrinale et littéraire du Moyen Âge* 20 (1953): 31–81.

—. "Deux traductions latines du Coran au Moyen Âge." *Archives d'histoire doctrinale et littéraire du Moyen Âge* 16 (1948): 69–131.

—. "L'introduction d'Avicenne en Occident." *La Revue du Caire* 27 (1951): 130–39.

—. "Notes et observations au sujet des éditions des textes médiévaux." In *Probleme der Edition mittel- und neulateinischer Texte Kolloquium d. Dt. Forschungsgemeinschaft, Bonn, 26.–28. Februar 1973*, ed. Ludwig Hödl and Dieter Wuttke, 41–54. Boppard am Rhein: Boldt, 1978.

—. "Les pérégrinations de l'âme dans l'autre monde d'après un anonyme de la fin du XIIe siècle." *Archives d'histoire doctrinale et littéraire du Moyen Âge* 13 (1940–1942): 280–99.

—. "Les traductions à deux interprètes, d'arabe en langue vernaculaire et de langue vernaculaire en latin." In *Traduction et traducteurs au Moyen Âge: Actes du colloque international du CNRS organisée à Paris, Institut de recherche et d'histoire des textes, les 26–28 mai 1986*, ed. Geneviève Contamine, 193–206. Paris: Éditions du CNRS, 1989.

—. "Translations and Translators." In *Renaissance and Renewal in the Twelfth Century*, ed. Robert Benson and Giles Constable, 421–62. Cambridge, MA: Harvard University Press, 1982.

D'Ancona Costa, Cristina. "Alexander of Aphrodisias, 'De unitate': A Pseudepigraphical Testimony of the 'De unitate et uno' by Dominicus Gundissalinus." In *Islamic Thought in the Middle Ages: Studies in Text, Transmission and Translation in Honour of Hans Daiber*, ed. Anna Ayse Akasoy and Wim Raven, 459–88. Leiden: Brill, 2008.

—. "Avicenna and the *Liber de Causis.*" *Revista Española de Filosofía Medieval* 7 (2000): 95–114.

—. "Dalla metafisica greca al Medioevo latino: La mediazione araba." In *Storia della*

288 | Bibliography

teologia nel medioevo, ed. Giulio D'Onofrio, 1: 669–702. 3 vols. Casale Monferrato: Piemme, 1996.

—. "*Ex uno non fit nisi unum*: Storia e preistoria della dottrina avicenniana della prima intelligenza." In *Per una storia del concetto di mente*, ed. Eugenio Canone, 29–55. Florence: Leo S. Olschki, 2007.

—. "Primo principio e mondo intelligibile nella metafisica di Proclo: Problemi e soluzioni." *Elenchos* 12 (1991): 271–302.

—. *Recherches sur le* Liber de Causis. Paris: Vrin, 1995.

Daniel, Norman. *The Arabs and Mediaeval Europe*. London: Longman, 1975.

Davidson, Herbert A. *Alfarabi, Avicenna, and Averroes on Intellect: Their Cosmologies, Theories of the Active Intellect, and Theories of Human Intellect*. New York: Oxford University Press, 1992.

—. "Arguments from the Concept of Particularization in Arabic Philosophy." *Philosophy East and West* 18 (1968): 299–314.

Decorte, Jos. "Proofs of the Immortality and Mortality of the Soul in the Renaissance of the 12th and Late 15th Centuries." In *Mediaeval Antiquity*, ed. Andries Welkenhuysen, Herman Braet, and Werner Verbeke, 95–126. Leuven: Leuven University Press, 1995.

De Haas, Frans A.J. *John Philoponus' New Definition of Prime Matter: Aspects of Its Background in Neoplatonism and the Ancient Commentary Tradition*. Leiden: Brill, 1997.

De Rijk, Lambertus M. "Boèce logicien et philosophe: Ses positions sémantiques et sa métaphysique de l'être." In *Atti del congresso internazionale di studi boeziani (Pavia, 5–8 ottobre 1980)*, ed. Luca Obertello, 141–55. Rome: Herder, 1981.

De Vaux, Roland. *Notes et textes sur l'avicennisme latin aux confins des XII–XIII siècles*. Paris: Vrin, 1934.

De Wulf, Maurice. *Histoire de la philosophie médiévale*. Louvain: Institut supérieur de philosophie, 1900.

Dhanani, Alnoor. "The Impact of Ibn Sīnā's Critique of Atomism on Subsequent Kalam Discussions of Atomism." *Arabic Sciences and Philosophy* 25 (2015): 79–104.

Di Donato, Silvia. "Les trois traductions latines de la *Météorologie* d'Avicenne: Notes pour l'histoire du texte." *Documenti e Studi sulla Tradizione Filosofica Medievale* 28 (2017): 331–48.

Dillon, John M. *The Middle Platonists: A Study of Platonism 80 B.C. to A.D. 220*. Ithaca: Cornell University Press, 1977.

—. "Salomon Ibn Gabirol's Doctrine of Intelligible Matter." *Irish Philosophical Journal* 6 (1989): 59–81.

Di Stasi, Giuseppina. *La struttura del reale nel* De essentiis *di Ermanno di Carinzia*. Ph.D. Dissertation. Università degli Studi di Salerno, 2012.

Di Vincenzo, Silvia. "Avicenna's *Isagoge*, Chap. I, 12, *De Universalibus*: Some Observations on the Latin Translation." *Oriens* 40 (2012): 437–76.

—. "Avicenna's Reworking of Porphyry's 'Common Accident' in the Light of Aristotle's *Categories*." *Documenti e studi sulla tradizione filosofica medievale* 27 (2016): 163–94.

Donati, Silvia. "La dottrina delle dimensioni indeterminate in Egidio Romano." *Medioevo* 14 (1988): 149–233.

—. "Materia e dimensioni tra XIII e XIV secolo: La dottrina delle *dimensiones indeterminatae.*" *Quaestio* 7 (2007): 361–93.

D'Onofrio, Giulio. "La scala ricamata: La *Philosophiae divisio* di Severino Boezio tra essere e conoscere." In *La divisione della filosofia e le sue ragioni: Lettura di testi medievali (VI–XIII secolo)*, ed. Giulio D'Onofrio, 11–63. Cava de' Tirreni: Avagliano, 2011.

Dronke, Peter, ed. *A History of Twelfth-Century Western Philosophy.* Cambridge: Cambridge University Press, 1988.

—. "New Approaches to the School of Chartres." *Anuario de estudios medievales* 6 (1969): 117–40.

—. "Thierry of Chartres." In *A History of Twelfth-Century Western Philosophy*, ed. Peter Dronke, 358–85. Cambridge: Cambridge University Press, 1988.

—. "William of Conches and the New Aristotle." *Studi medievali* 43 (2002): 157–63.

Dutton, Paul E. "The Little Matter of a Title: *Philosophia Magistri Willelmi de Conchis.*" In *Guillaume de Conches: Philosophie et science au XIIe siècle*, ed. Barbara Obrist and Irene Caiazzo, 467–86. Florence: SISMEL, 2011.

—. *The Mystery of the Missing Heresy Trial of William of Conches.* Toronto: Pontifical Institute of Mediaeval Studies, 2006.

Ebbesen, Sten. "Boethius as an Aristotelian Commentator." In *Aristotle Transformed: The Ancient Commentators and Their Influence*, ed. Richard Sorabji, 373–91. Ithaca: Cornell University Press, 1990.

—. "Porphyry's Legacy to Logic: A Reconstruction." In *Aristotle Transformed: The Ancient Commentators and Their Influence*, ed. Richard Sorabji, 141–71. Ithaca: Cornell University Press, 1990.

Elford, Dorothy. "William of Conches." In *A History of Twelfth-Century Western Philosophy*, ed. Peter Dronke, 308–27. Cambridge: Cambridge University Press, 1988.

El-Madkouri Maataoui, Mohamed. "Las escuelas de traductores en la Edad Media." In *La enseñanza en la Edad Media: X semana de estudios medievales (Nájera 1999)*, ed. José Ignacio De La Iglesia Duarte, 97–127. Logroño: Instituto de Estudios Riojanos, 2000.

Endres, Joseph A. "Die Nachwirkung von Gundissalinus' *De immortalitate animae.*" *Philosophisches Jahrbuch* 12 (1899): 382–92.

Endress, Gerhard. "Du grec au latin à travers l'arabe: La langue, créatrice d'idées dans la terminologie philosophique." In *Aux origines du lexique philosophique européen: L'influence de la latinitas, actes du colloque international (Rome, 23–25 mai 1996)*, ed. Jacqueline Hamesse, 137–63. Louvain-la-Neuve: FIDEM, 1997.

Erismann, Christophe. "The Medieval Fortunes of the *Opuscula sacra.*" In *The Cambridge Companion to Boethius*, ed. John Marenbon, 155–77. Cambridge: Cambridge University Press, 2009.

Evangeliou, Christos. *Aristotle's Categories and Porphyry.* Leiden: Brill, 1988.

—. "Aristotle's Doctrines of Predicables and Porphyry's *Isagoge.*" *Journal of the History of Philosophy* 23 (1985): 15–34.

290 | Bibliography

Evans, Gillian. "Introductions to Boethius's *Arithmetica* of the Tenth to the Fourteenth Century." *History of Science* 16 (1978): 22–41.

—. "John of Salisbury and Boethius on Arithmetic." In *The World of John of Salisbury*, ed. Michael Wilks, 161–67. Oxford: Oxford University Press, 1984.

—. "The Uncompleted *Heptateuchon* of Thierry of Chartres." *History of Universities* 3 (1983): 1–13.

Faes De Mottoni, Barbara. *Il platonismo medievale*. Turin: Loescher, 1979.

Farmer, Henry G. "The Influence of Al-Farabi's "Ihsa' al-'Ulum" ("De scientiis") on the Writers on Music in Western Europe." *The Journal of the Royal Asiatic Society of Great Britain and Ireland* 3 (1932): 561–92.

—. "Who Was the Author of the *Liber introductorius in artem logicae demonstrationis*?" *Journal of the Royal Asiatic Society* 3 (1934): 553–56.

Federici Vescovini, Graziella. *Le teorie della luce e della visione ottica dal IX al XV secolo*. Perugia: Morlacchi Editore, 2003.

Fenton, Paul B. "Gleanings from Moseh Ibn 'Ezra's *Maqalat al-Hadiqa*." *Sefarad* 36 (1976): 285–98.

Fernández Catón, José María. *Colección documental del archivo de la catedral de León, V (1109–1187)*. León: Centro de Estudios e Investigación San Isidoro, 1990.

Fernández Conde, Francisco Javier. *La religiosidad medieval en España: Plena Edad Media (siglos XI–XIII)*. Oviedo: Trea, 2005.

Ferrari, Franco. "La *chora* nel *Timeo* di Platone: Riflessioni su 'materia' e 'spazio' nell'ontologia del mondo fenomenico." *Quaestio* 7 (2007): 3–23.

—. "Commentari specialistici alle sezioni matematiche del *Timeo*." In *La filosofia in età imperiale*, ed. Aldo Brancacci, 169–224. Naples: Bibliopolis, 2000.

Ferreiro Alemparte, Jaime. "La escuela de nigromancia de Toledo." *Anuario de Estudios Medievales* 13 (1983): 205–68.

Ferrer Rodriguez, María Pilar. "Relación transcendental 'materia-forma' en el 'Fons vitae' de Ibn Gabirol." *Mediaevalia: Textos e Estudos* 5–6 (1994): 247–58.

Fidora, Alexander. "Abraham Ibn Daud und Dominicus Gundissalinus: Philosophie und religiöse Toleranz im Toledo des 12. Jh." In *Juden, Christen und Muslime: Religionsdialoge im Mittelalter*, ed. Matthias Lutz-Bachmann and Alexander Fidora, 10–26. Darmstadt: WBG, 2004.

—. "The Arabic Influence on the Classification of Philosophy in the Latin West: The Case of the Introductions to Philosophy." *Micrologus* 28 (2020), forthcoming.

—. "Arabic into Latin into Hebrew: Aristotelian Psychology and Its Contribution to the Rationalisation of Theological Traditions." In *Philosophical Psychology in Medieval Arabic and Latin Aristotelianism*, ed. Luis Xavier López-Farjeat and Jörg Alejandro Tellkamp, 17–39. Paris: Vrin, 2013.

—. "Le débat sur la création: Guillaume de Conches, maître de Dominique Gundisalvi?" In *Guillaume de Conches: Philosophie et science au XII siècle*, ed. Barbara Obrist and Irène Caiazzo, 271–88. Florence: SISMEL, 2011.

—. "Les différentes approches des traducteurs: De la perception des textes à la réception des traductions." In *Une conquête des savoirs: Les traductions dans l'Europe latine (fin XIe siècle – milieu XIIIe siècle)*, ed. Max Lejbowicz, 45–66. Turnhout: Brepols, 2009.

—. "Domingo Gundisalvo y la Sagrada Escritura." *Estudios eclesiásticos* 76 (2001): 243–58.

—. "Dominicus Gundissalinus and the Introduction of Metaphysics into the Latin West." *The Review of Metaphysics* 66 (2013): 691–712.

—. "La metodología de las ciencias según Boecio: Su recepción en las obras y traducciones de Domingo Gundisalvo." *Revista Española de Filosofía Medieval* 7 (2000): 127–36.

—. "La recepción de San Isidoro de Sevilla por Domingo Gundisalvo (ca. 1110–1181): Astronomía, Astrología y Medicina en la Edad Media." *Estudios eclesiásticos* 75 (2000): 663–77.

—. "A tripartiçao da filosofia práctica na obra *De divisione philosophiae* de Domingos Gundisalvo." In *Idade Média: Tempo do mundo, tempo dos homens, tempo de Deus*, ed. José Antônio de Camargo Rodrigues Souza, 417–28. Porto Alegre: Est Ediçõe, 2006.

—. "Der wissenschaftliche Ort der Mantik in der Schule von Toledo (12. Jahrhundert)." In *Mantik, Schicksal und Freiheit im Mittelalter*, ed. Loris Sturlese, 33–49. Cologne: Böhlau, 2011.

—. *Die Wissenschaftstheorie des Dominicus Gundissalinus: Voraussetzungen und Konsequenzen des zweiten Anfangs der aristotelischen Philosophie im 12. Jahrhundert*. Berlin: Akademie, 2003. Spanish Translation: *Domingo Gundisalvo y la teoría de la ciencia arábigo-aristotélica*. Pamplona: EUNSA, 2009.

Fidora, Alexander, and Nicola Polloni. *Appropriation, Interpretation and Criticism: Philosophical and Theological Exchanges Between the Arabic, Hebrew and Latin Intellectual Traditions*. Barcelona: FIDEM, 2017.

Fidora, Alexander, and María Jesús Soto Bruna. "Gundisalvus ou Dominicus Gundisalvi? Algunas observaciones sobre un reciente artículo de Adeline Rucquoi." *Estudios eclesiásticos* 76 (2001): 467–73.

Fierro, Maribel. "Le mahdi Ibn Tûmart et al-Andalus: L'élaboration de la légitimité almohade." *Revue des mondes Musulmans et de la Méditerranée* 91–94 (2000): 107–24.

Filippani-Ronconi, Pio. "I concetti di 'quiddità' ed 'esistenza' in al-Farabi ed Avicenna." In *Studi in onore di Francesco Gabrieli nel suo ottantesimo compleanno*, ed. Francesco Gabrieli and Renato Traini, 315–21. Rome: Università di Roma "La Sapienza," Dipartimento di studi orientali, 1984.

Fisher, Humphrey J. "What's in a Name? The Almoravids of the Eleventh Century in Western Sahara." *Journal of Religion in Africa* 22 (1992): 290–317.

Fletcher, Madeleine. "Ibn Tumart's Teachers: The Relationship with al-Ghazali." *Al-Qantara* 18 (1997): 305–30.

Fliche, Augustin. *La réforme grégorienne et la reconquête chrétienne*. Paris: Bloud et Gay, 1940.

Fontaine, T.A.M. (Resianne). "Abraham Ibn Daud: Sources and Structures of *ha-Emunah ha-Ramah*." *Zutot* 2 (2002): 156–63.

292 | *Bibliography*

—. "For the Dossier of Abraham Ibn Daud: Some Observations on an Anonymous Commentary on His *ha-Emunah ha-Ramah*." *Zutot* 7 (2010): 35–40.

—. *In Defense of Judaism: Abraham Ibn Daud: Sources and Structure of* ha-Emunah ha-Ramah. Assen: Uitgeverij Van Gorcum, 1990.

Fontaine, T.A.M. (Resianne), and Steven Harvey. "Jewish Philosophy on the Eve of the Age of Averroism: Ibn Daud's Necessary Existent and His Use of Avicennian Science." In *In the Age of Averroes: Arabic Philosophy in the Sixth/Twelfth Century*, ed. Peter Adamson, 215–27. London: Warburg Institute, 2011.

Franceschini, Ezio. "Ricerche e studi su Aristotele nel Medioevo Latino." In *Aristotele nella critica e negli studi contemporanei*, 144–66. Milan: Vita e Pensiero, 1956.

Frank, Richard M. *Creation and the Cosmic System: Al-Ghazali and Avicenna*. Heidelberg: Carl Winter Universitätsverlag, 1992.

Fredborg, Karin Margareta. "The Dependence of Petrus Helias' *Summa super Priscianum* on William of Conches' *Glosae super Priscianum*." *Cahiers de l'Institut du Moyen Âge grec et latin* 11 (1973): 1–57.

—. "Petrus Helias on Rhetoric." *Cahiers de l'Institut du Moyen Âge grec et latin* 13 (1974): 31–41.

Freudenthal, Gad. "Abraham Ibn Daud, Avendauth, Dominicus Gundissalinus and Practical Mathematics in Mid-Twelfth Century Toledo." *Aleph* 16 (2016): 60–106.

—. "Abraham Ibn Ezra and Judah Ibn Tibbon as Cultural Intermediaries: Early Stages in the Introduction of Non-Rabbinic Learning into Provence in the Mid-Twelfth Century." In *Exchange and Transmission across Cultural Boundaries: Philosophy, Mysticism and Science in the Mediterranean World*, ed. Haggai Ben-Shammai, Shaul Shaked, and Sarah Stroumsa, 58–81. Jerusalem: Israel Academy of Sciences and Humanities, 2013.

Freudenthal, Gad, and Rémi Brague, eds. "Ni Empédocle, ni Plotin: Pour le dossier du Pseudo-Empédocle arabe." In *Agonistes: Essays in Honour of Denis O'Brien*, ed. John Dillon and Monique Dixsaut, 267–83. Aldershot: Routledge, 2005.

Fromherz, Allen J. *The Almohads: The Rise of an Islamic Empire*. London: Tauris, 2010.

Galonnier, Alain. *Le "De scientiis Alfarabii" de Gérard de Crémone: Contribution aux problèmes de l'acculturation au XIIe siècle*. Turnhout: Brepols, 2016.

—. "Dominicus Gundissalinus et Gérard de Crémone, deux possibles stratégies de traduction: Le cas de l'encyclopédie farabienne du *De scientiis*." In *Une lumière venue d'ailleurs: Héritages et ouvertures dans les encyclopédies d'Orient et d'Occident au Moyen Âge*, ed. Godefroid de Callataÿ and Baudouin Van den Abeele, 103–17. Turnhout: Brepols, 2008.

García Fayos, Juan. "El colegio de traductores de Toledo y Domingo Gundisalvo." *Revista de la Biblioteca, Archivo y Museo* 34 (1932): 109–23.

García Gallo, Alfonso. *El Concilio de Coyanza: Contribución al estudio del derecho canónico español en la Alta Edad Media*. Madrid: BOE, 1951.

Gargatagli, Marietta. "La historia de la escuela de traductores de Toledo." *Quaderns* 4 (1999): 9–13.

Garin, Eugenio. "Contributi alla storia del Platonismo medievale." *Annali della Scuola Normale Superiore di Pisa: Lettere, Storia e Filosofia* (Serie II) 20 (1951): 58–97.

Gerber, Amanda J. *Medieval Ovid: Frame Narrative and Political Allegory*. New York: Palgrave Macmillan, 2015.

Gersh, Stephen. "Calcidius' Theory of First Principles." *Studia Patristica* 18 (1989): 85–92.

—. *Concord in Discourse: Harmonics and Semiotics in Late Classical and Early Medieval Platonism*. Berlin: De Gruyter, 1996.

—. *From Iamblichus to Eriugena: An Investigation of the Prehistory and Evolution of the Pseudo-Dionysian Tradition*. Leiden: Brill, 1978.

—. *Middle Platonism and Neoplatonism: The Latin Tradition*. Notre Dame: Notre Dame University Press, 1986.

—. *Reading Plato, Tracing Plato: From Ancient Commentary to Medieval Reception*. Aldershot: Ashgate, 2005.

Gersh, Stephen, and Martin Hoenen. *The Platonic Tradition in the Middle Ages: A Doxographic Approach*. Berlin: De Gruyter, 2002.

Gibson, Margaret, ed. *Boethius: His Life, Thought and Influence*. Oxford: Blackwell, 1981.

—. "The Study of the *Timaeus* in the Eleventh and Twelfth Centuries." *Pensamiento* 25 (1969): 183–94.

Gigante, Marcello. "Enrico Aristippo, un interprete platonico del secolo XII." *Studi italiani di filologia classica* 9 (1991): 244–59.

Gill, Mary Louise. "Matter and Flux in Plato's *Timaeus*." *Phronesis* 32 (1987): 34–53.

Gilson, Étienne. "Avicenne en Occident au Moyen Âge." *Archives d'histoire doctrinale et littéraire du Moyen Âge* 44 (1969): 89–121.

—. *La philosophie au Moyen Âge*. Paris: Vrin, 1944.

—. "Pourquoi saint-Thomas a critiqué saint-Augustin." *Archives d'histoire doctrinale et littéraire du Moyen Âge* 1 (1926–7): 5–129.

—. "Les sources gréco-arabes de l'augustinisme avicennisant." *Archives d'histoire doctrinale et littéraire du Moyen Âge* 5 (1930): 1–107.

—. *Le thomisme: Introduction au système de Saint Thomas d'Aquin*. Paris: Vrin, 1922.

Glasner, Ruth. *Averroes' Physics: A Turning Point in Medieval Natural Philosophy*. Oxford: Oxford University Press, 2009.

Goheen, John. *The Problem of Matter and Form in the 'De ente et essentia' of Thomas Aquinas*. Cambridge: Cambridge University Press, 1940.

Goichon, Amélie-Marie. "Avicenne: Le philosophe de l'être." *Revue de l'Institut des Belles Lettres Arabes* 15 (1952): 49–62.

—. *La philosophie d'Avicenne et son influence en Europe médiévale*. Paris: Librairie d'Amérique et d'Orient Adrien-Maisonneuve, 1951.

—. "La théorie des formes chez Avicenne." In *Aristotelismo padovano e filosofia aristotelica: Atti del XII Congresso Internazionale di Filosofia (Venezia, 12–18 Settembre 1958)*, 131–38. Florence: Sansoni, 1960.

González Palencia, Ángel. *Los mozárabes de Toledo en los siglos XII y XIII*. Madrid: Maestre, 1926.

294 | Bibliography

Goodman, Lenn Evan. *Avicenna*. London: Routledge, 1992.

—. *Neoplatonism and Jewish Thought*. Albany: SUNY Press, 1992.

Graetz, Heinrich. *History of the Jews*. 6 vols. Philadelphia: Jewish Publication Society of America, 1891–98.

Grant, Edward. "Celestial Incorruptibility in Medieval Cosmology, 1200–1687." In *Physics, Cosmology and Astronomy, 1300–1700: Tension and Accommodation*, ed. Sabetai Unguru, 101–28. Dordrecht: Springer, 1991.

Gregory, Tullio. *"Anima Mundi": La filosofia di Guglielmo di Conches e la scuola di Chartres*. Florence: Sansoni, 1955.

—. *"Mundana Sapientia": Forme di conoscenza nella cultura medievale*. Rome: Edizioni di storia e letteratura, 1992.

—. "Note sul platonismo della scuola di Chartres: La dottrina delle specie native." *Giornale critico della filosofia italiana* 32 (1953): 358–62.

—. "The Platonic Inheritance." In *A History of Twelfth-Century Western Philosophy*, ed. Peter Dronke, 54–80. Cambridge: Cambridge University Press, 1988.

—. *Platonismo medievale: Studi e ricerche*. Rome: Istituto Storico Italiano per il Medio Evo, 1958.

Grignaschi, Mario. "Le *De divisione philosophiae* de Dominicus Gundissalinus et les *Questiones II–V in Sextum Metaphysicorum* de Jean de Jandun." In *Knowledge and the Sciences in Medieval Philosophy: Proceedings of the Eighth International Congress of Medieval Philosophy (SIEPM)*, ed. Simo Knuuttila, Reijo Työrinoja, and Sten Ebbesen, 53–56. Helsinki: Yliopistopaino, 1990.

Guijarro González, Susana. "Las escuelas y la formación del clero de las catedrales en las diócesis castellano-leonesas (siglos XI al XV)." In *La enseñanza en la Edad Media: X semana de estudios medievales (Nájera 1999)*, ed. José Ignacio De La Iglesia Duarte, 61–96. Logroño: Instituto de Estudios Riojanos, 2000.

—. *Maestros, escuelas y libros: El universo cultural de las catedrales en la Castilla medieval*. Madrid: Editorial Dykinson, 2004.

Guillaumin, Jean-Yves. "Boethius's *De institutione arithmetica* and Its Influence on Posterity." In *A Companion to Boethius in the Middle Ages*, ed. Noel H. Kaylor and Philip E. Philipps, 135–61. Leiden: Brill, 2012.

Gutas, Dimitri. *Avicenna and the Aristotelian Tradition: Introduction to Reading Avicenna's Philosophical Works*. Leiden: Brill, 1988.

—. *Greek Thought, Arabic Culture: The Graeco-Arabic Translation Movement in Baghdad and Early ʿAbbāsid Society (2nd–4th / 8th–10th Centuries)*. London: Routledge, 1998.

Gutman, Oliver. "On the Fringes of the Corpus Aristotelicum: The Pseudo-Avicenna *Liber celi et mundi*." *Early Science and Medicine* 2 (1997): 109–28.

Guttmann, Julius. *Philosophies of Judaism*. New York: Holt, Rinehart and Winston, 1966.

Gutwirth, Elazar. "L'accueil fait a Abraham Ibn Daud dans l'Europe de la Renaissance." In *Tolède et Jérusalem: Tentative de symbiose entre les cultures espagnole et judaïque*, ed. Shlomo Giora Shoham and Francis Rosenstiel, 97–110. Lausanne: L'Âge d'Homme, 1992.

Hackett, Jeremiah. "Roger Bacon on the Classification of the Sciences." In *Roger Bacon and the Sciences: Commemorative Essays*, ed. Jeremiah Hackett, 49–65. Leiden: Brill, 1997.

Halleaux, Robert. "The Reception of Arabic Alchemy in the West." In *Encyclopedia of the History of Arabic Sciences*, ed. Roshdi Rashed, 3: 886–902. London: Routledge, 1996.

Hamesse, Jacqueline. "Un nouveau glossaire des néologismes du latin philosophique." In *Aux origines du lexique philosophique européen: L'influence de la latinitas, actes du colloque international (Rome, 23–25 mai 1996)*, ed. Jacqueline Hamesse, 237–54. Louvain-la-Neuve: FIDEM, 1997.

Hanley, Thomas. "St. Thomas' Use of Al-Ghazali's 'Maqasid al-Falasifa.'" *Mediaeval Studies* 44 (1982): 243–70.

Häring, Nikolaus. "Chartres and Paris Revisited." In *Essays in Honour of Anton Charles Pegis*, ed. Reginald O'Donnell, 268–329. Toronto: Pontifical Institute of Mediaeval Studies, 1974.

—. "The Creation and Creator of the World According to Thierry of Chartres and Clarenbaldus of Arras." *Archives d'histoire doctrinale et littéraire du Moyen Âge* 30 (1955): 137–216.

—. "Thierry of Chartres and Dominicus Gundissalinus." *Mediaeval Studies* 26 (1964): 271–86.

Harvey, Steven. "Avicenna's Influence on Jewish Thought: Some Reflections." In *Avicenna and His Legacy: A Golden Age of Science and Philosophy*, ed. Yitzhak Tzvi Langermann, 327–40. Turnhout: Brepols, 2009.

—. "Philosophies juive et musulmane: Similitudes et différences." In *Histoire des relations entre juifs et musulmans des origines à nos jours*, ed. Abdelwahab Meddeb and Benjamin Stora, 737–57. Paris: Albin Michel, 2013.

—. "Shem-Tov Falaquera, a Paragon of an Epigone, and the Epigone's Importance for the Study of Jewish Intellectual History." *Studia Rosenthaliana* 40 (2007–08), 61–74.

Harvey, Warren Z. "Aspects of Jewish Philosophy in Medieval Catalonia." In *Mossé ben Nahman i el seu temps: Simposi commemoratiu del vuitè centenari del seu naixement 1194–1994*, ed. Joan Boadas i Raset and Sílvia Planas Marcé, 141–57. Girona: Ajuntament de Girona, 1994.

—. "Filosofía y poesía en Ibn Gabirol: Revisión del Neoplatonismo." *Anuario filosófico* 2 (2000): 491–504.

Haskins, Charles H. *Michael Scot and Fredrick II*. Brussels: Weissenbruch, 1921.

—. *Studies in the History of Medieval Science*. Cambridge: Cambridge University Press, 1924.

Hasse, Dag Nikolaus. *Avicenna's De Anima in the Latin West: The Formation of a Peripatetic Philosophy of the Soul 1160–1300*. London: The Warburg Institute, 2000.

—. "Avicenna's 'Giver of Forms' in Latin Philosophy, Especially in the Works of Albertus Magnus." In *The Arabic, Hebrew and Latin Reception of Avicenna's Metaphysics*, ed. Dag N. Hasse and Amos Bertolacci, 225–50. Berlin: De Gruyter, 2012.

—. "The Early Albertus Magnus and His Arabic Sources on the Theory of the Soul." *Vivarium* 46 (2008): 232–52.

296 | *Bibliography*

—. "Spontaneous Generation and the Ontology of Forms in Greek, Arabic, and Medieval Latin Sources." In *Classical Arabic Philosophy: Sources and Reception*, ed. Peter Adamson, 150–75. London: The Warburg Institute, 2007.

Hasse, Dag Nikolaus, and Andreas Büttner. "Notes on Anonymous Twelfth-Century Translations of Philosophical Texts from Arabic into Latin on the Iberian Peninsula." In *The Arabic, Hebrew, and Latin Reception of Avicenna's Physics and Cosmology*, ed. Dag Nikolaus Hasse and Amos Bertolacci, 313–69. Berlin: De Gruyter, 2018.

Hernández, Francisco J. *Los Cartularios de Toledo: Catálogo Documental*. Madrid: Fundación Ramón Areces, 1985.

Hicks, Andrew. *Composing the World: Harmony in the Medieval Platonic Cosmos*. Oxford: Oxford University Press, 2017.

Hoenen, Maarten F.M. and Lodi Nauta, eds. *Boethius in the Middle Ages: Latin and Vernacular Traditions of the* Consolatio philosophiae. Leiden: Brill, 1997.

Hoenig, Christina. "Calcidius' Platonic Method: On *syllogismus, compositio* and *resolutio.*" Paper discussed at Notre Dame University on 27 March 2015.

—. *Plato's* Timaeus *and the Latin Tradition*. Cambridge: Cambridge University Press, 2018.

Hudry, Françoise. "La traduction latine de la *Logica Avicennae* et son auteur." *Documenti e Studi sulla Tradizione Filosofica Medievale* 28 (2017): 1–28.

Hughues, Barnabas B. *Robert of Chester's Latin Translation of Al-Khwarizmi's* Al-Jabr. Stuttgart: Perfect Paperback, 1989.

Hugonnard-Roche, Henri. "La classification des sciences de Gundissalinus et l'influence d'Avicenne." In *Études sur Avicenne*, ed. Jean Jolivet and Roshdi Rashed, 41–75. Paris: Vrin, 1984.

—. "La tradition syro-arabe et la formation du vocabulaire philosophique latin." In *Aux origines du lexique philosophique européen: L'influence de la latinitas, actes du colloque international (Rome, 23–25 mai 1996)*, ed. Jacqueline Hamesse, 59–80. Louvain-la-Neuve: FIDEM, 1997.

Huici Miranda, Ambrosio. *Historia política del imperio almohade*. Tetuán: Universidad de Granada, 1956.

Hunt, Richard W. "The Introduction to the 'Artes' in the Twelfth Century." In *Studia mediaevalia in honorem admodum Reverendi Patris Raymundi Josephi Martin*, 85–112. Bruges: De Tempel, 1948.

Husik, Isaac. *A History of Mediaeval Philosophy*. New York: Dover Publications, 2002.

Hyman, Arthur. "Aristotle's 'First Matter' and Avicenna's and Averroes' 'Corporeal Form.'" In *Essays in Medieval Jewish and Islamic Philosophy*, ed. Arthur Hyman, 335–406. New York: Ktav, 1977.

Inan, Muhammad Abd Allah. *The Andalusian Petty Kingdoms: From Their Rise to the Almoravide Conquest*. Cairo: al-Khangi, 1970.

Ingarao, Alessandra. "Lo *status quaestionis* sulla paternità del *De immortalite animae* attribuito a Domingo Gundisalvi (Toledo 1170 ca. – Parigi 1228 ca.)." In *Enosis kai filia: Unione e amicizia: omaggio a Francesco Romano*, ed. Maria Barbanti, Giovanna Giardina, and Paolo Manganaro, 557–68. Catania: CUECM, 2002.

Jacquart, Danielle. "Aristotelian Thought in Salerno." In *A History of Twelfth-Century Western Philosophy*, ed. Peter Dronke, 407–28. Cambridge: Cambridge University Press, 1988.

—. "L'école des traducteurs." In *Tolède, XIIe–XIIIe: Musulmans, chrétiens et juifs: Le savoir et la tolérance*, ed. Louis Cardaillac, 68–74. Paris: Autrement, 1991.

—. "Le latin des sciences: Quelques réflexions." In *Les historiens et le latin médiéval*, ed. Monique Goullet and Michel Parisse, 237–44. Paris: Vrin, 2001.

—. "Principales étapes dans la transmission des textes de médecine (XIe–XIVe siècle)." In *Rencontres de cultures dans la philosophie médiévale: Traductions et traducteurs de l'antiquité tardive au XIVe siècle: Actes du Colloque internationale de Cassino, 15–17 juin 1989*, ed. Jacqueline Hamesse and Marta Fattori, 251–71. Louvain-la-Neuve: Université Catholique de Louvain, 1990.

—. "Quelques réflexions sur la traduction du 'Kitâb al-Mansûrî' de Rhazès par Gérard de Crémone." In *Actas XXVII Congreso Internacional de la Medicina*, 264–66. Barcelona: Acadèmia de Ciències Mèdiques de Catalunya i Balears, 1981.

Jalbert, Guy. "Le nécessaire et le possible dans la philosophie d'Avicenne." *Revue de l'Université d'Ottawa* 30 (1960): 89–101.

Janos, Damien. "Moving the Orbs: Astronomy, Physics, and Metaphysics, and the Problem of Celestial Motion According to Ibn Sina." *Arabic Sciences and Philosophy* 21 (2011): 165–214.

Janssens, Jules. "Al-Ghazali and His Use of Avicennian Texts." In *Problems in Arabic Philosophy*, ed. Miklós Maróth, 37–49. Piliscaba: Klaus Schwarz, 2003.

—. "Al-Ghazzālī's *Tahāfut*: Is It Really a Rejection of Ibn Sīnā's Philosophy?" *Journal of Islamic Studies* 12 (2001): 1–17.

—. "L'Avicenne latin: Particularités d'une traduction." In *Avicenna and His Heritage: Acts of the International Colloquium Leuven – Louvain-la-Neuve, September 8 – September 11, 1999*, ed. Jules Janssens and Daniël De Smet, 113–29. Leuven: Leuven University Press, 2002.

—. "Creation and Emanation in Ibn Sīnā." *Documenti e Studi sulla Tradizione Filosofica Medievale* 8 (1997): 455–77.

—. "Le *Dânesh-Nâmeh* d'Ibn Sînâ: Un text à revoir?" *Bulletin de Philosophie Médiévale* 28 (1986): 163–77.

—. "Le *De divisione philosophiae* de Gundissalinus: Quelques remarques préliminaires à une édition critique." In *De l'antiquité tardive au Moyen Âge: Études de logique aristotélicienne et de philosophie grecque, syriaque, arabe et latine offertes à Henri Hugonnard-Roche*, ed. Elisa Coda and Cecilia Martini Bonadeo, 559–70. Paris: Vrin, 2014.

—. "Éléments avicenniens dans le livre *al-Maqṣad* d'al-Ghazālī." *Miscellanies of the Dominican Institute for Oriental Studies* 30 (2014): 91–103.

—. *Ibn Sina and His Influence on the Arabic and Latin World*. Burlington: Ashgate, 2006.

—. "Ibn Sīnā on Substance in Chapter Two of the *Maqūlāt* (*Categories*) of the Shifā.'" In *More modoque: Die Wurzeln des europäischen Kultur und deren Rezeption im Orient und Okzident. Festschrift für Miklós Maróth zum siebzigsten Geburtstag*, ed. Pal Fodor

298 | Bibliography

et al., 353–60. Budapest: Forschungszentrum für Humanwissenschaften der Ungarischen Akademie der Wissenschaften, 2013.

—. "The Latin Translation of the *Physics*: A Useful Source for the Critical Edition of the Arabic Text?" *Oriens* 40 (2012): 515–28.

—. "The *Liber primus naturalium*, i.e. the *Physics* of the Avicenna Latinus." *Documenti e Studi sulla Tradizione Filosofica Medievale* 28 (2017): 219–38.

—. "The *Physics* of the Avicenna Latinus and Its Significance for the Reception of Aristotle's Physics in the Latin West." In *The Letter before the Spirit: The Importance of Text Editions for the Study of the Reception of Aristotle*, ed. Aafke M.I. van Oppenraay, 311–30. Leiden: Brill, 2012.

—. "The Reception of Avicenna's *Physics* in the Latin Middle Ages." In *O Ye Gentlemen: Arabic Studies on Science and Literary Culture in Honour of Remke Kruk*, ed. Arnoud Vrolijk and Jan P. Hogendijk, 55–64. Leiden: Brill, 2007.

Jeauneau, Édouard. "Deux rédactions des gloses de Guillaume de Conches sur Priscien." *Recherches de théologie ancienne et médiévale* 27 (1960): 212–47.

—. "Gloses sur le *Timée* et Commentaire du *Timée* dans deux manuscrits du Vatican." *Revue des études augustiniennes* 8 (1962): 365–73.

—. "La lecture des auteurs classiques à l'École de Chartres durant la première moitié du XIIe siècle." In *Classical Influences on European Culture: A.D. 1500–1700*, ed. Robert R. Bolgar, 95–102. Cambridge: Cambridge University Press, 1971.

—. "Mathématiques et Trinité chez Thierry de Chartres." In *Die Metaphysik im Mittelalter, ihr Ursprung und ihre Bedeutung*, ed. Paul Wilpert, 289–95. Berlin: De Gruyter, 1963.

—. "Note sur l'Ecole de Chartres." *Studi medievali* 5 (1964): 821–65.

—. "Un représentant du platonisme au XIIe siècle: Maître Thierry de Chartres." *Mémoires de la Société archéologique d'Eure-et-Loire* 10 (1954–7): 171–75.

—. "Simples notes sur la cosmogonie de Thierry de Chartres." *Sophia* 23 (1955): 172–83.

—. "L'usage de la notion d'*integumentum* à travers les *Gloses* de Guillaume de Conches." *Archives d'histoire doctrinale et littéraire du Moyen Âge* 24 (1957): 127–92.

Jerez Riesco, José Luis. "Tolerancia e intolerancia en el Toledo medieval." *Revista del Instituto Egipcio de Estudios Islámicos en Madrid* 26 (1993): 91–101.

Johansen, Thomas Kjeller. *Plato's Natural Philosophy: A Study of the Timaeus-Critias.* Cambridge: Cambridge University Press, 2004.

Jolivet, Jean. "The Arabic Inheritance." In *A History of Twelfth-Century Western Philosophy*, ed. Peter Dronke, 113–48. Cambridge: Cambridge University Press, 1988.

—. "Aux origines de l'ontologie d'Ibn Sina." In *Études sur Avicenne*, ed. Jean Jolivet and Roshdi Rashed, 221–37. Paris: Vrin, 1984.

—. "Etapes dans l'histoire de l'intellect agent." In *Perspectives arabes et médiévales sur la tradition scientifique et philosophique grecque: Actes du colloque de la SIHSPAI (Société internationale d'histoire des sciences et de la philosophie arabes et islamiques), Paris, 31 mars – 3 avril 1993*, ed. Ahmed Hasnawi and Abdelali Elamrani Jamal, 569–82. Leuven: Peeters, 1997.

—. "Intellect et intelligence: Note sur la tradition arabo-latine des XIIe et XIIIe siècles." In *Mélanges offerts a Henry Corbin*, ed. Seyyed Hossein Nasr, 681–702. Tehran: Institute of Islamic Studies, 1977.

—. "Philosophie au XIIe siècle latin: L'héritage arabe." In *Philosophié médiévale arabe et latine*, ed. Jean Jolivet, 47–77. Paris: Vrin, 1995.

—. "Le vocabulaire de l'être et de la création dans la *Philosophia Prima* de l'Avicenna latinus." In *L'élaboration du vocabulaire philosophique au Moyen Âge*, ed. Jacqueline Hamesse and Carlos Steel, 35–49. Turnhout: Brepols, 2000.

Jourdain, Amable. *Recherches critiques sur l'âge et l'origine des traductions latines d'Aristote et sur des commentaires grecs ou arabes employés par les docteurs scolastiques*. Paris: Joubert, 1843.

Kantorowicz, Ernst H. "Plato in the Middle Ages." *The Philosophical Review* 51 (1942): 312–23.

Kaufmann, David. *Studien über Salomon Ibn Gabirol*. Budapest: Alkalay, 1899.

Kijewska, Agnieszka. "Mathematics as a Preparation for Theology: Boethius, Eriugena, Thierry of Chartres." In *Boèce, ou La chaîne des savoirs: Actes du colloque international de la Fondation Singer-Polignac Paris, 8–12 juin 1999*, ed. Alain Galonnier, 625–47. Louvain: Peeters, 2003.

King, Edward B. and Jacqueline T. Schaefer. *Saint Augustine and His Influence in the Middle Ages*. Sewanee: The Press of the University of the South, 1988.

Kinoshita, Noburu. *El pensamento filosófico de Domingo Gundisalvo*. Salamanca: Universidad Pontificia de Salamanca, 1988.

König-Pralong, Catherine. *Avènement de l'aristotélisme en terre chrétienne*. Paris: Vrin, 2005.

Krakowski, Eve. "On the Literary Character of Abraham Ibn Daud's 'Sefer ha-Qabbalah.'" *European Journal of Jewish Studies* 1 (2007): 219–47.

Krause, Katja. "Albert the Great on Animal and Human Origin in His Early Works." *Lo sguardo: Rivista di filosofia* 18 (2015): 205–32.

Kristeller, Paul O. "The School of Salerno." *Bulletin of the History of Medicine* 17 (1945): 138–92.

Kritzeck, James. *Peter the Venerable and Islam*. Princeton: Princeton University Press, 1964.

Kunitzsch, Paul. "Translation from Arabic (Astronomy/Astrology): The Formation of Terminology." In *La création verbale en latin médiéval: Word Creation in Medieval Latin*, ed. Anne Grondeux and François Dolbeau, 161–68. Brussels: Union Académique Internationale, 2005.

Kutleša, Stipe. "Croatian Philosophers I: Hermann of Dalmatia (1110–1154)." *Prolegomena: Journal of Philosophy* 3 (2004): 57–71.

Labbé, Philippe and Gabriel Cossart. *Sacrosancta Concilia ad regiam editionem exacta*. Venice: Baptistamet Coleti, 1730.

Ladero Quesada, Miguel Ángel. *La formación medieval de España: Territorios, regiones, reinos*. Madrid: Alianza Editorial, 2004.

Lammer, Andreas. "Defining Nature: From Aristotle to Philoponus to Avicenna." In

300 | Bibliography

Aristotle and the Arabic Tradition, ed. Ahmed Alwishah and Josh Hayes, 121–42. Cambridge: Cambridge University Press, 2015.

—. *The Elements of Avicenna's Physics: Greek Sources and Arabic Innovations*. Berlin: DeGruyter, 2018.

Lampe, Kurt. "A Twelfth-Century Text on the Number Nine and Divine Creation: A New Interpretation of Boethian Cosmology?" *Mediaeval Studies* 67 (2005): 1–26.

Lapidus, Ira. *A History of Islamic Societies*. Cambridge: Cambridge University Press, 2014.

Laumakis, John A. "Aquinas' Misinterpretation of Avicebron on the Activity of Corporeal Substances: *Fons Vitae* II, 9 and 10." *The Modern Schoolman* 81 (2004): 135–49.

—. "Avicebron (Ibn Gabirol): Creation ex Nihilo." *The Modern Schoolman* 79 (2001): 41–55.

—. "Weisheipl's Interpretation of Avicebron's Doctrine of the Divine Will." *American Catholic Philosophical Quarterly* 77 (2003): 35–55.

Lejbowicz, Max. "Le choc des traductions arabo-latines du XIIe siècle et ses conséquences dans la spécialisation sémantique d'astrologia et astronomia: Dominicus Gundissalinus et la *sciencia iudicandi*." In *Transfert de vocabulaire dans les sciences*, ed. Martine Groult, Pierre Louis, and Jacques Roger, 213–75. Paris: Éditions du CNRS, 1988.

—. "Cosmogenèse, traditions culturelles et innovations (sur les sections 18–21 du *Tractatus de sex dierum operibus* de Thierry de Chartres)." In *Langage, sciences, philosophie au XIIe siècle: Actes de la table ronde internationale organisée les 25 et 26 mars 1998 par le Centre d'histoire des sciences et des philosophies arabes et médiévales (UPRESA 7062, CNRS/Paris VII/EPHE)*, ed. Joël Biard, 39–59. Paris: Vrin, 1999.

Lemay, Richard. "L'authenticité de la préface de Robert de Chester à sa traduction du Morienus (1144)." *Chrysopoeia* 4 (1991): 3–32.

—. "Science and Theology at Chartres: The Case of the Supracelestial Waters." *The British Journal for the History of Science* 10 (1977): 226–36.

Lértora Mendoza, Celina. "El concepto y la clasificación de la ciencia en el medioevo (ss. VI–XV)." *Veritas* 43 (1998): 497–512.

Lizzini, Olga. *Avicenna*. Rome: Carocci, 2012.

—. *Fluxus (fayd). Indagine sui fondamenti della metafisica e della fisica di Avicenna*. Bari: Edizioni di Pagina, 2011.

—. "Il nulla, l'inesistente, la cosa: Note intorno alla terminologia e alla dottrina del nulla nel pensiero islamico." In *Discussioni sul nulla tra Medioevo ed Età Moderna*, ed. Massimiliano Lenzi and Alfonso Maierù, 63–103. Florence: Olschki, 2009.

—. "Occasionalismo e causalità filosofica: La discussione della causalità in al-Ghazali." *Quaestio* 2 (2002): 155–83.

—. "The Relation Between Form and Matter: Some Brief Observations on the 'Homology Argument' (*Ilahiyat*, II.4) and the Deduction of Fluxus." In *Interpreting Avicenna: Science and Philosophy in Medieval Islam*, ed. Jon McGinnis, 175–85. Paris: Brill, 2004.

—. "*Wugud-Mawgud*/Existence-Existent in Avicenna: A Key Ontological Notion of Arabic Philosophy." *Quaestio* 3 (2003): 111–38.

Llavero Ruiz, Eloísa. "Panorama cultural de Al-Andalus según Abū l-Qāsim Ṣāʿid b.

Aḥmad, cadí de Toledo." *Boletín de la Asociación Española de Orientalistas* 23 (1987): 79–100.

Loewe, Raphael. *Ibn Gabirol*. London: Peter Halban, 1989.

Loewenthal, Abraham. *Pseudo-Aristoteles über die Seele*. Berlin: Mayer & Müller, 1891.

Lorch, Richard. "The Treatise on the Astrolabe by Rudolf of Bruges." In *Between Demonstration and Imagination: Essays in the History of Science and Philosophy Presented to John D. North*, ed. Lodi Nauta and Arjo J. Vanderjagt, 55–100. Leiden: Brill, 1999.

Lottin, Odon. "La composition hylémorphique des substances spirituelles: Les débuts de la controverse." *Revue néo-scolastique de philosophie* 34 (1932): 21–41.

Luscombe, David. "La création du monde chez Thierry de Chartres." In *Vie spéculative, vie méditative et travail manuel à Chartres: Actes du colloque international des 4 et 5 juillet 1998*, 79–91. Chartres: Association des Amis du Centre Médiéval Européen de Chartres (AACMEC), 1998.

Lynch, Hannah. *Toledo: The Story of an Old Spanish Capital*. London: Dent, 1898.

Maccagnolo, Enzo. "David of Dinant: Aristotelianism in Paris." In *A History of Twelfth-Century Western Philosophy*, ed. Peter Dronke, 429–42. Cambridge: Cambridge University Press, 1988.

—. *Il divino e il megacosmo: Testi filosofici e scientifici della scuola di Chartres*. Milan: Rusconi, 1980.

—. "Il Platonismo nel XII secolo: Teodorico di Chartres." *Rivista di Filosofia Neo-Scolastica* 73 (1981): 283–99.

—. *"Rerum universitas": Saggio sulla filosofia di Teodorico di Chartres*. Florence: Le Monnier, 1976.

MacDonald, Scott. "Boethius's Claim That All Substances Are Good." *Archiv für Geschichte der Philosophie* 70 (1988): 245–79.

Maierù, Alfonso. "Saperi scientifici e antropologia: L'apporto della cultura araba." In *Il secolo XII: La "renovatio" dell'Europa cristiana*, ed. Giles Constable, 423–59. Bologna: Il Mulino, 2003.

Mandonnet, Pierre. *Siger de Brabant et l'averroisme latin au XIIIe siècle*. Louvain: Institut Supérieur de Philosophie de l'Université de Louvain, 1900.

Mansilla, Demetrio. *Catálogo documental del archivo catedral de Burgos (804–1416)*. Madrid: CSIC, 1971.

—. "La documentación pontificia del archivo de la catedral de Burgos." *Hispania Sacra* 1 (1948): 141–62 and 427–38.

Mantas-España, Pedro. "Una aproximación al sentido de la 'Filosofía' en el 'Renacimiento del s. XII.'" *Revista Española de Filosofía Medieval* 11 (2008): 69–74.

—. "El diálogo poético del de 'Eodem et Diverso' de Adelardo de Bath: Un elogio al conocimiento en el renacimiento del siglo XII." *Alfinge* 8 (1997): 177–87.

—. "Interpreting the New Sciences: Beyond the Completion of the Traditional Liberal Arts Curriculum." In *Appropriation, Interpretation and Criticism: Philosophical and Theological Exchanges Between the Arabic, Hebrew and Latin Intellectual Traditions*, ed. Alexander Fidora and Nicola Polloni, 51–91. Barcelona: FIDEM, 2017.

—. "El 'realismo' de principios del s. XII y el 'eclecticismo' platónico-aristotélico." In

302 | Bibliography

Method and Order in Renaissance Philosophy of Nature, ed. Daniel Di Liscia, Eckhard Kessler, and Charlotte Methuen, 23–51. Aldershot: Ashgate, 1997.

Marcos Cobaleda, María. *Los almorávides: Arquitectura de un imperio*. Granada: Editorial Universidad de Granada, 2015.

Marenbon, John. *Aristotelian Logic, Platonism, and the Context of Early Medieval Philosophy in the West*. Aldershot: Ashgate, 2000.

—. *Boethius*. New York: Oxford University Press, 2002.

—, ed. *The Cambridge Companion to Boethius*. Cambridge: Cambridge University Press, 2009.

—. "Divine Prescience and Contingency in Boethius's *Consolation of Philosophy*." *Rivista di storia della filosofia* 68 (2013): 9–19.

—. "Rationality and Happiness: Interpreting Boethius's *Consolation of Philosophy*." In *Rationality and Happiness: From the Ancients to the Early Medievals*, ed. Jiyuan Yu and Jorge J.E. Gracia, 175–97. Rochester: University of Rochester Press, 2003.

Marmura, Michael E. "Avicenna on Primary Concepts in the Metaphysics of His *al-Shifa*." In *Logos Islamikos: Studia islamica in honorem Georgii Michaelis Wickens*, ed. Roger Savory and Dionisius Agius, 219–39. Toronto: Pontifical Institute of Mediaeval Studies, 1984.

—. "Avicenna's Proof from Contingency in the Metaphysics of His *al-Shifa*." *Mediaeval Studies* 42 (1980): 337–52.

—. "Some Questions Regarding Avicenna's Theory of the Temporal Origination of the Human Rational Soul." *Arabic Sciences and Philosophy* 18 (2008): 121–38.

Marrone, Steven P. "From Gundisalvus to Bonaventure: Intellect and Intelligences in the Late Twelfth and Early Thirteenth Centuries." In *Intellect et imagination dans la philosophie médiévale: Actes du XIe Congrès international de philosophie médiévale de la Société Internationale pour l'Étude de la Philosophie Médiévale (SIEPM)*, ed. Maria Cândida Da Costa Reis Monteiro Pacheco and José F. Meirinhos, 1071–81. Turnhout: Brepols, 2006.

Martello, Concetto. *Platone a Chartres*. Palermo: Officina di Studi Medievali, 2011.

Martin, Raymond M. "L'immortalité de l'âme d'après Robert de Melun." *Revue néoscolastique de philosophie* 41 (1934): 128–45.

Martínez Gázquez, José. *La ignorancia y negligencia de los latinos ante la riqueza de los estudios árabes*. Barcelona: Real Academia de Buenas Letras de Barcelona, 2007.

Martínez Gázquez, José, and Anna Maranini. "La *recensio* única del *De differentia inter spiritum et animam* de Costa Ben Luca." *Faventia* 19/2 (1997): 115–29.

Martinez-Gros, Gabriel. "La clôture du temps chez le cadi Ṣā'id, une conception implicite de l'histoire." *Revue de l'Occident musulman et de la Méditerranée* 40 (1985): 147–53.

Masnovo, Amato. *Da Guglielmo d'Auvergne a san Tommaso d'Aquino*. Milan: Vita e pensiero, 1945–46.

Mavroudi, Maria. "Translations from Greek into Latin and Arabic during the Middle Ages: Searching for the Classical Tradition." *Speculum* 90 (2015): 28–59.

McGinnis, Jon. *Avicenna*. Oxford: Oxford University Press, 2010.

—. "Avicenna's Natural Philosophy." In *Interpreting Avicenna: Critical Essays*, ed. Peter Adamson, 71–90. Cambridge: Cambridge University Press, 2013.

—. "The Eternity of the World: Proofs and Problems in Aristotle, Avicenna and Aquinas." *American Catholic Philosophical Quarterly* 88 (2014): 271–88.

—. *Interpreting Avicenna: Science and Philosophy in Medieval Islam*. Paris: Brill, 2004.

—. "Making Something of Nothing: Privation, Possibility and Potential in Avicenna and Aquinas." *The Thomist* 76 (2012): 1–25.

—. "Natural Knowledge in the Arabic Middle Ages." In *Wrestling with Nature: From Omens to Science*, ed. Peter Harrison, Ronald L. Numbers, and Michael H. Shank, 59–82. Chicago: University of Chicago Press, 2011.

—. "New Light on Avicenna: Optics and Its Role in Avicennan Theories of Vision, Cognition and Emanation." In *Philosophical Psychology in Arabic Thought and the Latin Aristotelianism of the Thirteenth Century*, ed. Luis Xavier López-Farjeat and Jörg Alejandro Tellkamp, 41–47. Paris: Vrin, 2013.

—. "A Penetrating Question in the History of Ideas: Space, Dimensionality and Interpenetration in the Thought of Avicenna." *Arabic Sciences and Philosophy* 16 (2006): 47–69.

—. "Pointers, Guides, Founts and Gifts: The Reception of Avicennan Physics in the East." *Oriens* 41 (2013): 433–56.

—. "Scientific Methodologies in Medieval Islam: Induction and Experimentation in the Philosophy of Ibn Sina." *Journal of the History of Philosophy* 41 (2003): 307–27.

Menéndez Pelayo, Marcelino. *La historia de los heterodoxos españoles*. Madrid: Librería católica de San José, 1880–82.

Micaelli, Claudio. "Teologia e filosofia nel *Contra Eutychen et Nestorium* di Boezio." In *Atti del congresso internazionale di studi boeziani (Pavia, 5–8 ottobre 1980)*, ed. Luca Obertello, 177–99. Rome: Editrice Herder, 1981.

Mičaninová, Maria. "The Synthetic Thinking of Solomon Ibn Gabirol." *Studia Judaica* 11 (2008): 215–31.

Miccoli, Lucia. "Le arti meccaniche nelle classificazioni delle scienze di Ugo di San Vittore e Domenico Gundisalvi." *Annali della Facoltà di lettere e filosofia dell'Università di Bari* 24 (1981): 73–101.

Michot, Jean R. *La destinée de l'homme selon Avicenne: Le retour à Dieu (ma'ad) et l'imagination*. Louvain: Peeters, 1986.

Millás Vallicrosa, Josep María. *Las traducciones orientales en los manuscritos de la Biblioteca Catedral de Toledo*. Madrid: CSIC, 1942.

Minio-Paluello, Lorenzo. "Iacobus Veneticus Grecus: Canonist and Translator of Aristotle." *Traditio* 8 (1952): 265–304.

—. "Les traductions et les commentaires aristotéliciens de Boèce." *Studia Patristica* 2 (1973): 356–65.

Minnema, Anthony H. "Algazel Latinus: The Audience of the *Summa Theoricae Philosophiae*, 1150–1600." *Traditio* 69 (2014): 153–215.

—. "A Hadith Condemned at Paris: Reactions to the Power of Impression in the

304 | Bibliography

Latin Translation of Al-Ghazali's *Maqasid al-Falasifa.*" *Mediterranea* 2 (2017): 145–62.

Minnis, Alastair J., ed. *The Medieval Boethius: Studies in the Vernacular Translations of* De Consolatione Philosophiae. Cambridge: Cambridge University Press, 1987.

Molénat, Jean Pierre. "Mudéjars et mozarabes à Tolède du XIIe au XVe siècle." *Revue du monde musulman et de la Méditerranée* 63–64 (1992): 143–53.

Moreschini, Claudio. "Boezio e la tradizione del Neoplatonismo latino." In *Atti del congresso internazionale di studi boeziani (Pavia, 5–8 ottobre 1980)*, ed. Luca Obertello, 297–309. Rome: Editrice Herder, 1981.

—. *Storia dell'ermetismo cristiano*. Brescia: Morcelliana, 2000.

Nagel, Tilman. "Le Mahdisme d'Ibn Tûmart et d'Ibn Qasî: Une analyse phénoménologique." *Revue des mondes Musulmans et de la Méditerranée* 91–94 (2000): 125–36.

Nauta, Lodi. "The *Consolation*: The Latin Commentary Tradition, 800–1700." In *The Cambridge Companion to Boethius*, ed. John Marenbon, 255–78. Cambridge: Cambridge University Press, 2009.

Nédoncelle, Maurice. "*Prosopon* et *persona* dans l'antiquité classique: Bilan linguistique." *Revue des sciences religieuses* 22 (1948): 277–99.

Newell, John. "Rationalism at the School of Chartres." *Vivarium* 21 (1983): 108–26.

Obertello, Luca. "L'universo boeziano." In *Atti del congresso internazionale di studi boeziani (Pavia, 5–8 ottobre 1980)*, ed. Luca Obertello, 59–70. Rome: Editrice Herder, 1981.

Olstein, Diego Adrián. *La era mozárabe: Los mozárabes de Toledo (siglos XII y XIII) en la historiografía, las fuentes y la historia*. Salamanca: Universidad de Salamanca, 2006.

O'Reilly, Francisco. *Avicena y la propuesta de una antropología aristotélico-platónica*. Pamplona: Cuadernos de Anuario Filosófico, 2010.

Orlandis, José. *La Iglesia antigua y medieval*. Madrid: Palabra, 1974.

Oro Hershtein, Lucas. "Saadia Gaón como integrante de la familia doctrinal de Ibn Gabirol." In *Fuentes del pensamiento medieval: Continuidad y divergencias*, ed. Juan José Herrera, 355–69. San Miguel de Tucumán: UNSTA, 2012.

—. "Singularidad ontológica y antropológica en *Fons Vitae* de Ibn Gabirol." *Em curso* 1 (2014): 52–62.

Ovitt, George. "The Status of the Mechanical Arts in Medieval Classifications of Learning." *Viator* 14 (1983): 89–105.

Panti, Cecilia. *Moti, virtù e motori celesti nella cosmologia di Roberto Grossatesta: Studio ed edizione dei trattati 'De sphera,' 'De cometis,' 'De motu supercelestium.'* Florence: SISMEL, 2001.

Pasnau, Robert. *Metaphysical Themes 1274–1671*. Oxford: Oxford University Press, 2011.

Pastor García, Juan Tomás. "Domingo Gundisalvo, el arcediano segoviano." In *La filosofía española en Castilla y León: De los orígines al siglo de oro*, ed. Maximiliano Fartos Martínez and Lorenzo Velázquez Campo, 39–55. Valladolid: Universidad de Valladolid, 1997.

Patterson, Richard. *Image and Reality in Plato's Metaphysics*. Indianapolis: Hackett Publishing, 1985.

Pattin, Adriaan. "Autour du 'Liber de Causis.' Quelques réflexions sur la récente littérature." *Freiburger Zeitschrift für Philosophie und Theologie* 41 (1994): 354–88.
—. "Le *Liber de Causis.*" *Tijdschrift voor Filosofie* 28 (1966): 90–203.
Pereira, Michela. "Cosmologie alchemiche." In *Cosmogonie e cosmologie nel medioevo: Atti del convegno della Società Italiana per lo Studio del Pensiero Medievale (SISPM), Catania, 22–24 settembre 2006*, ed. Concetto Martello, Chiara Militello, and Andrea Vella, 363–410. Turnhout: Brepols, 2008.
—. *La filosofia nel Medioevo*. Rome: Carocci, 2008.
—. "Heavens on Earth: From the *Tabula Smaragdina* to the Alchemical Fifth Essence." *Early Science and Medicine* 5 (2000): 131–44.
—. "Remarks on *materia naturalis*." In *Roger Bacon's* Communia Naturalium*: A Thirteenth-Century Philosopher's Workshop*, ed. Paola Bernardini and Anna Rodolfi, 103–38. Florence: SISMEL, 2014.
Pérez-Estévez, Antonio. *La materia, de Avicena a la escuela franciscana*. Maracaibo: Ediluz, 1998.
—. "Substantiality of Prime Matter in Averroes." *The Modern Schoolman* 78 (2000): 53–70.
Pérez Rodríguez, Francisco Javier. *La Iglesia de Santiago de Compostela en la Edad Media: El cabildo catredalicio (1100–1400)*. Santiago de Compostela: Xunta de Galicia, 1996.
Pergola, Ruggiero. "*Ex arabico in latinum*: Traduzioni scientifiche e traduttori nell'occidente medievale." *Studi di Glottodidattica* 3 (2009): 74–105.
Perl, Eric D. "The Demiurge and the Forms: A Return to the Ancient Interpretation of Plato's *Timaeus.*" *Ancient Philosophy* 18 (1998): 81–92.
Perler, Dominik. *Ancient and Medieval Theories of Intentionality*. Leiden: Brill, 2001.
—, ed. *The Faculties: A History*. Oxford: Oxford University Press, 2015.
—. "Why is the Sheep Afraid of the Wolf? Medieval Debates of Animal Passions." In *Emotion and Cognitive Life in Medieval and Early Modern Philosophy*, ed. Martin Pickavé and Lisa Shapiro, 32–52. Oxford: Oxford University Press, 2012.
Pessin, Sarah. "Chains, Trees, and the Spirit-to-Body Boundary: Substance, Spiritual Matter, and the Principle of Matter as Higher Cause in Ibn Gabirol." In *Solomon Ibn Gabirol's Philosophy and Its Impact in the Middle Ages,* ed. Nicola Polloni, Marienza Benedetto, and Federico Dal Bo, forthcoming.
—. "Ibn Gabirol's Emanationism: On the Plotinian (v. Augustinian) Theology of 'Divine Irāda.'" In *Appropriation, Interpretation and Criticism: Philosophical and Theological Exchanges Between the Arabic, Hebrew and Latin Intellectual Traditions*, ed. Alexander Fidora and Nicola Polloni, 1–18. Barcelona: FIDEM, 2017.
—. *Ibn Gabirol's Theology of Desire: Matter and Method in Jewish Medieval Neoplatonism.* Cambridge: Cambridge University Press, 2013.
—. "Jewish Neoplatonism: Being above Being and Divine Emanation in Solomon Ibn Gabirol and Isaac Israeli." In *The Cambridge Companion to Medieval Jewish Philosophy*, ed. Daniel H. Frank and Oliver Leaman, 91–110. Cambridge: Cambridge University Press, 2003.
—. "The Manifest Image: Revealing the Hidden in Halevi, Saadya and Gabirol." In *History of Platonism: Plato Redivivus*, ed. John F. Finamore and Robert M. Berchman, 253–70. New Orleans: University Press of the South, 2005.

306 | Bibliography

—. "Matter, Form and the Corporeal World." In *The Cambridge History of Jewish Philosophy: From Antiquity to the Seventeenth Century*, ed. Tamar Rudavsky and Steven Nadler, 269–301. Cambridge: Cambridge University Press, 2009.

Pines, Shlomo. "Sefer 'Arugat ha-Bosem: Ha-Qeta'im mi-tokh Sefer *Meqor Hayyim*." *Tarbiz* 27 (1958): 218–33.

Pizzamiglio, Pierluigi. *Gerardo da Cremona*. Cremona: Libreria del Convegno, 1992.

Plessner, Martin. "The Place of the *Turba Philosophorum* in the Development of Alchemy." *Isis* 45 (1954): 331–38.

—. "The *Turba Philosophorum*, a Preliminary Report on Three Cambridge Manuscripts." *Ambix* 7 (1959): 159–63.

Poirel, Dominique. "Physique et théologie: Une querelle entre Guillaume de Conches et Hugues de Saint-Victor à propos du chaos originel." In *Guillaume de Conches: Philosophie et science au XII siècle*, ed. Barbara Obrist and Irene Caiazzo, 289–327. Florence: SISMEL, 2011.

Polloni, Nicola. "L'acqua che si trasforma in pietra: Gundissalinus e Avicenna sulla generazione dei metalli." In *Vedere nell'ombra: Studi su natura, spiritualità e scienze operative offerti a Michela Pereira*, ed. Cecilia Panti and Nicola Polloni, 103–19. Florence: SISMEL, 2018.

—. "Aristotle in Toledo: Gundissalinus, the Arabs, and Gerard of Cremona's Translations." In *'Ex Oriente Lux': Translating Words, Scripts and Styles in the Medieval Mediterranean World*, ed. Charles Burnett and Pedro Mantas España, 147–85. Córdoba: UCO Press, 2016.

—. "Il *De processione mundi* di Gundissalinus: Prospettive per un'analisi genetico-dottrinale." *Annali di Studi Umanistici* 1 (2013): 25–38.

—. *Domingo Gundisalvo: Una introducción*. Madrid: Editorial Sindéresis, 2017.

—. "Dominicus Gundissalinus's *On Unity and the One*." In *Medieval Philosophy and the Jewish, Islamic, and Christian Traditions: Essays in Honor of Richard Taylor*, ed. Luis Xavier López Farjeat, Katja Krause, and Nicholas Oschman, forthcoming.

—. "Elementi per una biografia di Dominicus Gundisalvi." *Archives d'histoire doctrinale et littéraire du Moyen Âge* 82 (2015): 7–22.

—. "Gundissalinus and Avicenna: Some Remarks on an Intricate Philosophical Connection." *Documenti e Studi sulla Tradizione Filosofica Medievale* 28 (2017): 515–52.

—. "Gundissalinus on Necessary Being: Textual and Doctrinal Alterations in the Exposition of Avicenna's *Metaphysics*." *Arabic Sciences and Philosophy* 26 (2016): 129–60.

—. "Gundissalinus on the Angelic Creation of the Human Soul: A Peculiar Example of Philosophical Appropriation." *Oriens* 47 (2019): 313–47.

—. "Gundissalinus's Application of al-Fārābī's Metaphysical Programme: A Case of Epistemological Transfer." *Mediterranea: International Journal on the Transfer of Knowledge* 1 (2016): 69–106.

—. "Misinterpreting Ibn Gabirol? Questions, Doubts, and Remarks on the Latin Translation of the Font of Life." In *Solomon Ibn Gabirol's Philosophy and Its Impact in the Middle Ages*, ed. Nicola Polloni, Marienza Benedetto, and Federico Dal Bo, forthcoming.

—. "'Natura vero assimilatur quaternario': Numerologia e neoplatonismo nel *De processione mundi* di Dominicus Gundissalinus." In *De Natura: La naturaleza en la Edad Media*, ed. José Luis Fuertes Herreros and Ángel Poncela González, 2: 679–88. Ribeirão: Húmus, 2015.

—. "Nature, Souls, and Numbers: Remarks on a Medieval Gloss on Gundissalinus's *De processione mundi*." In *Causality and Resemblance: Medieval Approaches to the Explanation of Nature*, ed. María Jesús Soto Bruna, 75–87. Hildesheim: OLMS, 2018.

—. "Thierry of Chartres and Gundissalinus on Spiritual Substance: The Problem of Hylomorphic Composition." *Bulletin de philosophie médiévale* 57 (2015): 35–57.

—. "Toledan Ontologies: Gundissalinus, Ibn Daud, and the Problems of Gabirolian Hylomorphism." In *Appropriation, Interpretation and Criticism: Philosophical and Theological Exchanges between the Arabic, Hebrew and Latin Intellectual Traditions*, ed. Alexander Fidora and Nicola Polloni, 19–49. Barcelona: FIDEM, 2017.

—. "The Toledan Translation Movement and Gundissalinus: Some Remarks on His Activity and Presence in Castile." In *A Companion to Medieval Toledo: Reconsidering the Canons*, ed. Yasmine Beale-Rivaya and Jason Busic, 263–80. Leiden: Brill, 2018.

Puig Montada, Josep. "The Transmission and Reception of Arabic Philosophy in Christian Spain." In *The Introduction of Arabic Philosophy into Europe*, ed. Charles E. Butterworth and Blake Andrée Kessel, 7–30. Leiden: Brill, 1994.

Quain, Edwin A. "The Medieval *accessus ad auctores*." *Traditio* 3 (1945): 215–64.

Ramón Guerrero, Rafael. "Sobre el uno y la unidad en la filosofía árabe: Apunte historiográfico." In *Metafísica y antropología en el siglo XII*, ed. María Jesús Soto Bruna, 69–80. Pamplona: EUNSA, 2005.

Renan, Ernest. *Averroès et l'averroïsme: Essai historique*. Paris: Calmann Lévy, 1861.

Renzi, Stanislao. "La fondazione radicale dell'essere possibile nell'Avicenna Latino." *Aquinas* 9 (1966): 294–313; and 10 (1967): 153–69.

Retucci, Fiorella. "The *Sapientiale* of Thomas of York, OFM: The Fortunes and Misfortunes of a Critical Edition." *Bulletin de philosophie médiévale* 52 (2010): 133–59.

Ribémont, Bernard. *La "Renaissance" du XIIe siècle et l'encyclopédisme*. Paris: Honoré Champion, 2002.

Richter-Bernburg, Lutz. "Ṣāʿid, the Toledan Tables, and Andalusī Science." In *From Deferent to Equant: A Volume of Studies in the History of Science in the Ancient and Medieval Near East in Honor of E.S. Kennedy*, ed. David King and George Saliba, 373–401. New York: New York Academy of Science, 1987.

Ricklin, Thomas. "Calcidius bei Bernhard von Chartres und Wilhelm von Conches." *Archives d'histoire doctrinale et littéraire du Moyen Âge* 67 (2000): 119–41.

Riesenhuber, Klaus. "Arithmetic and the Metaphysics of Unity in Thierry of Chartres: On the Philosophy of Nature and Theology in the Twelfth Century." In *Nature in Medieval Thought: Some Approaches East and West*, ed. Chūmaru Koyama, 43–73. Leiden: Brill, 2000.

Rivera Recio, Juan Francisco. *Los arzobispos de Toledo en la baja Edad Media (s. XII–XV)*. Toledo: Diputación Provincial de Toledo, 1969.

308 | Bibliography

—. *La Iglesia de Toledo en el siglo XII (1086–1208)*. Rome: Iglesia Nacional Española, 1966.

—. "Nuevos datos sobre los traductores Gundisalvo y Juan Hispano." *Al-Andalus* 31 (1966): 267–80.

Robinson, Maureen. "The Heritage of Medieval Errors in the Latin Manuscripts of Johannes Hispalensis." *Al-Qantara* 28 (2007): 41–71.

—. "The History and Myths Surrounding Johannes Hispalensis." *Bulletin of Hispanic Studies* 80 (2003): 443–70.

Rodolfi, Anna. "*Dicitur materia propriissime et strictissime*: Roger Bacon and the Ontological Status of Matter." In *Roger Bacon's* Communia Naturalium*: A Thirteenth-century Philosopher's Workshop*, ed. Paola Bernardini and Anna Rodolfi, 83–102. Florence: SISMEL, 2014.

—. "L'idea di materia in Dio: Essenza ed esistenza della materia nel dibattito teologico nella seconda metà del XIII secolo." *Quaestio* 7 (2007): 317–37.

—. "Interpretazioni dell'ilemorfismo universale nella scuola francescana: Bonaventura, Bacone, Olivi." *Rivista di Filosofia Neo-Scolastica* 4 (2010): 569–90.

Rose, Valentin. "Ptolemaeus und die Schule von Toledo." *Hermes* 8 (1874): 327–49.

Roth, Norman. "Forgery and Abrogation of the Torah: A Theme in Muslim and Christian Polemic in Spain." *Proceedings of the American Academy for Jewish Research* 54 (1987): 203–36.

Rouse, Richard H. "Manuscripts Belonging to Richard de Fournival." *Revue d'histoire des textes* 3 (1973): 253–69.

Rucquoi, Adeline. "Gundisalvus ou Dominicus Gundisalvi?" *Bulletin de philosophie médiévale* 41 (1999): 85–106.

—. "Littérature scientifique aux frontières du Moyen Âge hispanique: Textes en traduction." *Euphrosyne* 27 (2009): 193–210.

Rudavksy, Tamar M. "Conflicting Motifs: Ibn Gabirol on Matter and Evil." *The New Scholasticism* 52 (1978): 54–71.

Saliba, George. "Avicenna's *Shifa* (*Sufficientia*): In Defense of Medieval Latin Translators." *Der Islam* 94 (2017): 423–33.

Salman, Dominique. "Algazel et les latins." *Archives d'histoire doctrinale et littéraire du Moyen Âge* 10 (1935): 103–27.

Samsó, Julio. *Islamic Astronomy and Medieval Spain*. Aldershot: Variorum, 1994.

Sangrador Gil, José. "The Translators of the Period of D. Raymundo: Their Personalities and Translations (1125–1187)." In *Rencontres de cultures dans la philosophie médiévale: Traductions et traducteurs de l'Antiquité tardive au XIVe siècle*, ed. Jacqueline Hamesse and Marta Fattori, 109–19. Louvain-la-Neuve: Université catholique de Louvain, 1990.

Sanrayana, J.I. "Sobre la inmaterialidad de las sustancias espirituales (Santo Tomás versus Avicebrón)." *Rivista de filosofia neoscolastica* 70 (1978): 63–97.

Sattler, Barbara. "A Likely Account of Necessity, Plato's Receptacle as a Physical and Metaphysical Basis of Space." *Journal of the History of Philosophy* 50 (2012): 159–95.

Schlanger, Jacques. "Le maître et le disciple du *Fons Vitae*." *Revue des études juives* 127 (1968): 393–97.

—. *La philosophie de Salomon Ibn Gabirol: Étude d'un néoplatonisme*. Leiden: Brill, 1968.

Schlapkohl, Corinna. *Persona est naturae rationabilis individua substantia: Boethius und die Debatte über der Personbegriff*. Marburg: Elwert, 1999.

—. "Sur le role du 'tout' dans la creation selon Ibn Gabirol." *Revue des études juives* 124 (1965): 125–35.

Schneider, Jakob H.J. "Philosophy and Theology in the Islamic Culture: Al-Farabi's *De scientiis*." *Philosophy Study* 1 (2011): 41–51.

Schrimpf, Gangolf. *Die Axiomenschrift des Boethius (De Hebdomadibus) als philosophisches Lehrbuch des Mittelalters*. Leiden: Brill, 1966.

Schwartz, Yossef. "The Medieval Hebrew Translations of Dominicus Gundissalinus." In *Latin-into-Hebrew: Texts and Studies*, ed. Alexander Fidora, Harvey Hames, and Yossef Schwartz, 2: 19–45. 2 vols. Leiden: Brill, 2013.

Sesiano, Jacques. "Un recueil du XIIIème siècle de problèmes mathématiques." *Sciamus: Sources and Commentaries in Exact Sciences* 1 (2000): 71–132.

Shihadeh, Ayman. "Avicenna's Corporeal Form and Proof of Prime Matter in Twelfth-Century Critical Philosophy: Abu l-Barakat, al-Ma'sudi and al-Razi." *Oriens* 42 (2014): 364–96.

—. "New Light on the Reception of al-Ghazâlî's *Doctrines of the Philosophers (Maqâsid al-Falâsifa)*." In *In the Age of Averroes: Arabic Philosophy in the Sixth/Twelfth Century*, ed. Peter Adamson, 77–92. London: Warburg Institute, 2011.

Silverstein, Theodore. "Daniel of Morley, English Cosmogonist and Student of Arabic Science." *Mediaeval Studies* 10 (1948): 179–96.

—. "*Elementatum*: Its Appearance among the Twelfth-Century Cosmogonist." *Mediaeval Studies* 16 (1954): 156–62.

Simonet, Francisco Javier. *Historia de los mozárabes de España*. Madrid: Turner, 1983.

Sirat, Colette. *A History of Jewish Philosophy in the Middle Ages*. Cambridge: Cambridge University Press, 1985.

—. "Juda ben Salomon ha-Cohen." *Italia* 1/2 (1978): 39–61.

Smith, Gerard. "Avicenna and the Possibles." *The New Scholasticism* 17 (1943): 340–57.

Solère, Jean Luc. "Cercles, sphères et hebdomades: L'art platonicien d'écrire chez Boèce et Proclus." In *Boèce ou la chaîne des savoirs: Actes du colloque international de la Fondation Singer-Polignac Paris, 8–12 juin 1999*, ed. Alain Galonnier, 55–110. Leuven: Peeters, 2003.

Somfai, Anna. "Calcidius' 'Commentary' on Plato's 'Timaeus' and Its Place in the Commentary Tradition: The Concept of 'Analogia' in Text and Diagrams." *Bulletin of the Institute of Classical Studies* Supplement 83.1 (2004): 203–20.

—. "The Eleventh-Century Shift in the Reception of Plato's *Timaeus* and Calcidius's Commentary." *Journal of the Warburg and Courtauld Intitutes* 65 (2002): 1–21.

Sorabji, Richard. *Matter, Space and Motion: Theories in Antiquity and Their Sequel*. London: Duckworth, 1988.

310 | *Bibliography*

—. *Time, Creation and the Continuum.* Ithaca: Cornell University Press, 1983.

Soto Bruna, María Jesús. "La 'causalidad del uno' en Domingo Gundisalvo." *Revista Española de Filosofía Medieval* 21 (2014).

—. "El concepto de naturaleza como unidad causal en D. Gundissalinus." In *De Natura: La naturaleza en la Edad Media,* ed. José Luis Fuertes Herreros and Ángel Poncela González, 2: 851–58. Ribeirão: Húmus, 2015.

—. "La *lux intelligentiae agentis* en el pensamiento de Domingo Gundisalvo." *Revista Española de Filosofía Medieval* 10 (2003): 335–43.

Southern, Richard W. *Scholastic Humanism and the Unification of Europe.* Oxford: Blackwell, 1995.

Spade, Paul Vincent. "Boethius Against Universals: The Arguments in the Second Commentary on Porphyry." Unpublished. Available at http://www.pvspade.com /Logic/index.html.

—. *Five Texts on the Mediaeval Problem of Universals: Porphyry, Boethius, Abelard, Duns Scotus, Ockham.* Indianapolis: Hackett, 1994.

Speer, Andreas. "The Discovery of Nature: The Contribution of the Chartrians to Twelfth-Century Attempts to Found a *Scientia Naturalis.*" *Traditio* 52 (1997): 135–51.

Stiefel, Tina. *The Intellectual Revolution in Twelfth-Century Europe.* New York: Croom Helm, 1985.

Straface, Antonella. *L'origine del mondo nel pensiero islamico dei secc. X–XI.* Naples: Istituto Universitario Orientale, 1996.

Strobino, Riccardo. "Avicenna's *Kitab al-Burhan,* II.7 and Its Latin Translation by Gundissalinus: Content and Text." *Documenti e Studi sulla Tradizione Filosofica Medievale* 28 (2017): 105–47.

Stroumsa, Sarah. "Al-Fārābī and Maimonides on Medicine as a Science." *Arabic Sciences and Philosophy* 3 (1993): 235–49.

Szilágyi, Krisztina. "Ibn Daud and Avendauth? Notes on a Lost Manuscript and a Forgotten Book." *Aleph* 16 (2016): 10–31.

Taylor, Richard C. "A Critical Analysis of the Structure of the *Kalam fi mahd al-khair* (*Liber de causis*)." In *Neoplatonism and Islamic Thought,* ed. Parviz Morewedge, 11–40. Albany: SUNY Press, 1992.

—. "Faith and Reason, Religion and Philosophy: Four Views from Medieval Islam and Christianity." In *Philosophy and the God of Abraham,* ed. R. James Long, 217–33. Toronto: Pontifical Institute of Mediaeval Studies, 1991.

—. "St. Thomas and the *Liber de causis* on the Hylomorphic Composition of Separate Substances." *Mediaeval Studies* 41 (1979): 506–13.

Teicher, Jacob. "Gundissalino e l'agostinismo avicennizzante." *Rivista di filosofia Neo-Scolastica* 26 (1934): 252–58.

Thorndike, Lynn. *History of Magic and Experimental Science.* New York: Macmillan, 1929–1934.

—. *Michael Scot.* London: Nelson, 1965.

—. *University Records and Life in the Middle Ages.* New York: Columbia University Press, 1944.

Torija Rodríguez, Enrique. "La Iglesia de Toledo en la Edad Media: Organización institucional y formas de vida religiosa. Estado de la cuestión: archivos y descripción de manuscritos." *Hispania Sacra* 69 (2017): 31–47.

Travaglia, Pinella. *Una cosmologia ermetica: Il* Kitab sirr al-haliqua / De secretis naturae. Naples: Liguori Editore, 2001.

Troncarelli, Fabio. *Boethiana aetas: Modelli grafici e fortuna manoscritta della "Consolatio Philosophiae" tra IX e XII secolo.* Alessandria: Edizioni dell'Orso, 1987.

—. *Tradizioni perdute: La "Consolatio Philosophiae" nell'Alto Medioevo.* Padua: Antenore, 1981.

Trouillard, Jean. "Les degrés du ποιεῖν chez Proclos." *Dionysius* 1 (1977): 69–84.

—. "La genèse de l'hylémorphisme selon Proclos." *Dialogue: Revue Canadienne de Philosophie* 6 (1967–1968): 1–17.

—. "Le 'Parménide' de Platon et son interprétation néoplatonicienne." *Revue de Théologie et de Philosophie* 23 (1973): 83–100.

Tummers, Paul M.J. "Some Notes on the Geometry Chapter of Dominicus Gundissalinus." *Archives internationales d'histoire des sciences* 34 (1984): 19–24.

Van Steenberghen, Fernand. *Aristotle in the West.* Louvain: Nauwelaerts, 1955.

—. "L'organisation des études au Moyen Âge et ses répercussions sur le mouvement philosophique." *Revue philosophique de Louvain* 52 (1954): 572–92.

—. *The Philosophical Movement in the Thirteenth Century.* Edinburgh: Nelson, 1955.

—. *La philosophie au XIIIe siècle.* Louvain: Institut supérieur de philosophie, 1966.

Van Winden, Jacob. *Calcidius on Matter: His Doctrine and Sources.* Leiden: Brill, 1959.

Vegas González, Serafín. "La aportación de la Escuela de traductores de Toledo a la reconstitución de la metafísica en el siglo XII." In *Metafísica y antropología en el siglo XII,* ed. María Jesús Soto Bruna, 35–68. Pamplona: EUNSA, 2005.

—. *La Escuela de Traductores de Toledo en la historia del pensamiento.* Toledo: Ayuntamiento de Toledo, 1998.

—. "Significado histórico y significación filosófica en la revisión de los planteamientos concernientes a la Escuela de traductores de Toledo." *Revista Española de Filosofía Medieval* 13 (2005): 109–34.

Velazco Bayón, Balbino. *Colección documental de Cuéllar (943–1492).* Cuéllar: Ayuntamiento de Cuéllar, 2010.

Vicaire, Marie-Hubert. "Les Porrétaines et l'avicennisme avant 1215." *Revue des sciences philosophiques et théologiques* 26 (1937): 449–82.

Villar García, Luís Miguel. *Documentación medieval de la Catedral de Segovia (1115–1300).* Salamanca: Universidad de Salamanca, 1990.

Wasserstein, David J. "Langues et frontières entre juifs et musulmans en al-Andalus." In *Judíos y musulmanes en al-Andalus y el Magreb: Contactos intelectuales,* ed. Maribel Fierro, 1–11. Madrid: Casa de Velázquez, 2002.

Weijers, Olga. "L'appellation des disciplines dans les classifications des sciences aux XIIe et XIIIe siècles." *Archivum Latinitatis Medii Aevi* 46–47 (1986–87): 39–64.

Weisheipl, James A. "Albertus Magnus and Universal Hylomorphism: Avicebron. A Note on Thirteenth-Century Augustinianism." In *Albert the Great: Commemorative Essays*, ed. Francis Joseph Kovach, Robert W. Shahan, 239–60. Norman: University of Oklahoma Press, 1980.

—. "Classification of the Sciences in Medieval Thought." *Mediaeval Studies* 27 (1965): 54–90.

Wetherbee, Winthrop. "The Consolation and Medieval Literature." In *The Cambridge Companion to Boethius*, ed. John Marenbon, 279–302. Cambridge: Cambridge University Press, 2009.

—. "Philosophy, Cosmology and the Twelfth-Century Renaissance." In *A History of Twelfth-Century Western Philosophy*, ed. Peter Dronke, 21–53. Cambridge: Cambridge University Press, 1988.

Wisnovsky, Robert. *Avicenna's Metaphysics in Context*. Ithaca: Cornell University Press, 2003.

—. "Final and Efficient Causality in Avicenna's Cosmology and Theology." *Quaestio* 2 (2002): 97–123.

Wolfson, Harry A. "The Jewish Kalam." *The Jewish Quarterly Review* 57 (1967): 544–73.

Yaqub, Aladdin M. "Al-Gazali's Philosophers on the Divine Unity." *Arabic Sciences and Philosophy* 20 (2010): 281–306.

Zalta, Edward N. "Essence and Modality." *Mind* 115 (2006): 659–93.

Zimmermann, Albert. "Les divers sens du terme 'compositio' chez Thomas d'Aquin." In *Aux origines du lexique philosophique européen: L'influence de la latinitas, actes du colloque international (Rome, 23–25 mai 1996)*, ed. Jacqueline Hamesse, 221–36. Louvain-la-Neuve: FIDEM, 1997.

Zonta, Mauro. "Avicenna's Metaphysics in the Medieval Hebrew Philosophical Tradition." In *The Arabic, Hebrew and Latin Reception of Avicenna's Metaphysics*, ed. Dag N. Hasse and Amos Bertolacci, 153–58. Berlin: De Gruyter, 2012.

—. "La creazione dal nulla nella filosofia ebraica medievale in terra d'Islam." In *Discussioni sul nulla tra Medioevo ed Età Moderna*, ed. Alfonso Maierù and Massimiliano Lenzi, 53–62. Florence: Olschki, 2009.

—. "La *divisio scientiarum* presso al-Farabi." In *La divisione della filosofia e le sue ragioni: Lettura di testi medievali (VI–XIII secolo)*, ed. Giulio D'Onofrio, 65–78. Cava de' Tirreni: Avagliano, 2011.

—. *La filosofia ebraica medievale: Storia e testi*. Rome: Laterza, 2002.

Index

Abelard, Peter 104
act: *see* being: actual
Albert the Great: *De homine* 226n, 267
alchemy 4, 54
Alexander of Aphrodisias 18
Alexander of Hales 267
al-Farabi 8, 18n, 28, 29, 48, 52, 54, 59–61,
226, 231, 233, 246n
pseudo-al-Farabi: *De ortu scientiarum* 28,
54
al-Farghani 8
Alfonso VI of Castile 3
al-Ghazali: *Summa theoricae philosophiae*
5, 18, 48, 143, 210, 226, 230n, 231,
240–44, 253, 266, 269n, 270
al-Khwarizmi: *al-Jabr* 26
al-Kindi 8, 77n, 48
Allard, Baudoin 23
Almohads (Islamic dynasty) 5–7
Almoravids (Islamic dynasty) 3–5
al-Mu'min 5
Alonso Alonso, Manuel 29, 87n, 121
Alphanus of Salerno 2
al-Zarqali 6
Amaury of Bène 269
angels 22, 33, 41, 42, 50n, 70, 71, 74, 83,
98, 113, 116, 123, 133n, 140, 142, 143,
178, 180, 181, 184, 185, 205, 219,
226n, 227, 228, 260, 264, 265; angelic
creation of the soul: *see* soul. *See also*
giver of forms
animals 22, 45, 54, 133, 137, 139

Anzulewicz, Henryk 267
Apollonius of Thiana 129n
Aristotle 1, 3, 8, 18, 28, 38, 47n, 53, 55,
58n, 60, 78, 80, 84, 87, 88n, 110, 112,
125, 157, 211n, 221, 246n, 249, 251,
253, 269, 270, 271
–, works: *Categories* 87, 153; *De animalibus* 53; *Metaphysics* 269; *Meteorology*
8, 55n; *On Generation and Corruption*
8, 53, 55n; *On the Heavens* 8, 53, 55n;
On the Soul 54; *Physics* 8, 53, 246n,
269; *Posterior Analytics* 8, 58n
pseudo-Aristotle: *De causis et proprietatum elementorum* 8; *De impressionibus
superioribus* 53; *De mineris* 53; *De vegetabilibus* 53; *Liber de causis* 8
arithmetic: *see* mathematics
Augustine 1, 42, 95, 112, 172
Averroes 18
Avicenna 9, 15, 16, 17, 18, 21, 29, 38, 40,
42, 43, 44, 46, 47, 48, 49, 50, 51, 52n,
54, 55, 60, 61, 68, 77, 79, 84, 125, 128,
135, 141, 142, 143, 177, 180n, 181,
189, 190, 199, 200, 208, 209, 210–27,
230, 231, 232–42, 244–53, 258–62,
263, 264, 265, 266, 267, 269n, 270;
cosmology 217–21; ontology 210–17,
221–25, 244–53; psychology 38, 39,
43, 44, 46, 47; theory of subordination
50–52
–, works: *De anima* 16, 17, 21, 29, 37n,
38, 47; *De causis et principiis natural-*

314 | Index

ium 244; *De diluviis* 18n; *De generatione et corruptione* 251; *De universalibus* 18n; *De viribus cordis* 18n; *Kitab al
Burhan (De convenientia et differentia
scientiarum)* 18n, 29, 51; *Liber de
philosophia prima* 9, 18n, 29, 211, 214,
215, 232, 233, 235, 236, 237, 238, 239,
241, 262; *Liber sufficientiae / Kitab aš-
Šifa* 16, 17, 211, 225, 241n
pseudo-Avicenna: *Liber celi et mundi* 18n,
210

Bacon, Francis 271
Bacon, Roger 251; *Questions on Aristotle's
Physics* 268
Bakhouche, Béatrice 90
Banu Hud (Islamic dynasty) 7
being: actual 30, 31, 46, 49, 62, 66, 67,
68n, 70n, 83, 85, 99, 114, 149, 150,
153, 154, 157–60, 166, 167, 194–203,
206, 212, 230, 238–44, 252, 253, 254,
257, 263, 264; as such 84, 85, 237,
239; celestial 22, 33, 41, 42, 50n, 70,
71, 74, 83, 98, 112, 113, 116, 123–25,
128, 132, 133n, 140, 142, 143, 178,
180, 181, 184, 185, 205, 218–22, 228,
247, 260, 264, 265 (*see also* angels;
celestial spheres); corporeal 22, 30,
31, 34, 39, 41, 59, 68, 72–75, 81, 84,
91, 94, 98, 111–15, 117, 127, 130, 131,
137, 138, 139, 140, 147, 150, 151–55,
157, 162n, 163, 165, 169, 170, 173,
176, 180, 184–86, 205–8, 219, 220,
221, 224, 225, 228–31, 238, 241–45,
247, 258, 259; eternal 40, 63, 69, 90,
91, 92, 93, 94, 101, 102, 104, 160, 192,
214–17, 219, 257, 269 (*see also* God);
formal 67, 68n, 70, 80, 84, 195–97,
204, 240, 242, 243, 253, 263, 264;
material 67, 69, 195–97, 240, 243,
263, 264; necessary: *see* modal ontology; perpetual 33, 70, 75n, 98, 141,
142, 158, 169, 172, 227, 251 (*see also*

angels; celestial spheres); possible: *see*
modal ontology; potential 41, 46, 66,
68, 69, 83, 157–60, 167, 194–203, 223,
229, 238–45, 253, 263, 264; spiritual
22, 30, 31, 39, 40, 42, 60n, 73–75, 83,
84, 91, 94, 95, 98, 100, 105, 112, 127,
130n, 131, 137–40, 142n, 147, 151–
55, 161–63, 169, 172, 177, 180, 182–
87, 205–8, 219, 220, 226n, 227, 228–
31, 238, 242–44, 249, 251, 258, 265,
270; transient 93, 133, 169, 227 (*see
also* corruption)
Bernard of Clairvaux 105
Bertolacci, Amos 15, 16, 270
Bible 46n, 56, 63, 110, 113, 116, 121, 124,
226n; *Genesis* 113, 124; *Letter to the
Romans* 55, 190n
Boethius ix, 1, 21n, 25, 30, 48, 49, 57n,
60, 77–88, 99, 100, 106, 107, 115, 143,
167, 267; *Contra Eutychen et Nestorium*
80, 81n; *De consolatione philosophiae*
78, 79; *De hebdomadibus* 81, 84; *De
Trinitate* 57n, 78, 80, 81
Bülow, Georg 22–24, 268
Burnett, Charles 7, 10n, 12, 13, 15, 17,
24, 25, 131n, 133, 141

Caiazzo, Irene 269
Calcidius 1, 58n, 77, 83, 88–100, 107,
143, 150n, 190n, 197, 268, 271
cause: accidental cause 43, 71; first cause
34, 52, 59–62, 64, 65, 70, 71, 78, 79,
85, 99, 140, 141, 191, 204, 207, 211,
212, 215n, 217, 227, 235–37, 239; secondary causes 57, 70, 132, 142, 205,
260
celestial intelligences: *see* angels
celestial spheres 33, 70, 71, 132, 140, 142,
143, 205, 217, 219, 220, 222, 228n,
229, 247, 260
chaos 12, 13, 64, 77, 89, 91, 92, 95, 101,
110–28
Cicero 1n, 11, 48, 88n

compositio et resolutio (epistemic strategy) 58, 95–99, 106, 107, 150n, 190n, 197

composition (first and secondary) 70–72, 120, 140, 141, 143, 250

Constantine the African 2, 103

corruption 21, 33, 53, 60, 72, 84, 97, 98, 107, 133, 140, 142, 169, 170, 172, 219–21, 250, 251, 260

cosmic institution: *see* creation

creation 31, 40, 52, 55, 56, 57, 63, 64, 66, 69–72, 75, 76, 83, 92, 98, 101–3, 107–15, 119–21, 122–24, 126, 131–33, 136, 139, 140, 142, 143, 149, 150, 159, 161, 162, 178, 179, 180, 182–84, 201, 205, 207, 208, 217, 227, 228, 249, 263, 270

Daniel of Morley 13

David of Dinant 269–71

Demiurge 64, 89, 91, 92, 111, 114, 120

disposition (first and secondary) 57, 111, 130–33, 136

duality 12, 40, 44, 54, 62–66, 68, 81–86, 105, 134, 154, 155, 159, 165, 168, 176, 177, 182, 193, 194, 197, 201–9, 212–20, 227–30, 234, 236, 237–39, 241–44, 247, 249, 258, 263–66; compositional duality 82, 83, 204, 220, 258, 263, 264; dynamic duality 204, 239, 264; hylomorphic duality 68, 154, 168, 176, 230; modal duality 204, 209, 219, 220, 237, 238, 264, 265

Dutton, Paul 105

elements (physical constituents) 39, 53, 57, 59, 70–72, 74–76, 89, 90, 95, 103n, 104, 112–28, 130–32, 137, 140, 142, 143, 151, 152, 159, 205, 218n, 229, 231, 260; elemental transmutation 72, 89, 229; *elementata* (elemental aggregates) 39, 72, 74, 123, 124, 126, 127, 130n, 140; ordering of elements 89, 110–28, 129–32

epistemology 28, 29, 87n, 98, 210, 261

essence 31, 35, 51, 52, 60, 80, 81n, 84, 109, 111, 120, 131, 132, 137, 138, 142n, 147n, 150, 156, 157, 159, 160, 179, 190n, 192, 193, 208, 211, 212, 214, 215, 218n, 227–29, 236, 237, 247, 253–57; essence as different from existence 211–14, 236, 237

Euclid 8

Fernández Conde, Francisco 7

Fidora, Alexander 12, 13, 48n, 49, 51, 78, 87, 100, 122, 127, 128

form: dependence on matter 31–33, 81, 129, 130, 136, 137, 147n, 149–55, 165, 193, 194, 198, 199, 202, 257, 263; formal cluster 206, 249, 250, 264; of corporeity 73, 84, 151, 152, 162, 205, 225, 231, 247, 248, 250, 251, 255; of spirituality 73, 184, 248; of substantiality 73, 249, 258; of unity: *see* unity; plurality of forms 74, 83, 130, 145n, 161, 162, 165, 177, 184, 206, 246–50, 264

Fredborg, Karin 12

Freudenthal, Gad 27, 259

Galen 8

Galippus 8

Geminus of Rhodes 8

generation 33, 43, 60, 70, 71, 72, 76, 84, 90, 102, 119, 131–33, 139–43, 219–21, 225, 250, 251, 260

genus 39, 53, 86, 129, 131n, 146, 149, 150, 151, 153–55, 157, 161, 183, 186–89, 193, 196–98, 200, 204, 208, 215, 234, 237, 239, 250, 251, 264, 265; *genus generalissimus* 146, 153, 161, 187, 189

Geoffrey of Aspall: *Questions on Aristotle's Physics* 269

Gerard de Abbatis 23, 24

Gerard of Cremona 7, 8, 9, 14, 28, 55n, 246n

316 | *Index*

giver of forms (*dator formarum*) 218, 221, 222, 224, 228, 229, 247, 260

God: Christ 42, 181; creator 33, 36, 40, 55, 56, 61–66, 73, 79, 83, 97, 101, 108, 118, 138, 168, 169, 175, 177, 178, 201, 202, 233, 237; divine essence 60, 84, 157, 160, 192, 212, 227; divine ideas 81, 89, 90, 91, 92, 93, 96, 97, 129, 145n; divine mind 81, 83, 92, 93, 94, 130; divine will 63, 70, 83, 103, 104, 109, 132, 147n, 157, 158, 161, 192, 207, 208, 228, 235n; first cause: *see* cause; *invisibilia Dei* 55–59, 63, 98, 99, 108, 263; Necessary Existent 61–64, 66, 135, 209, 212–16, 218, 224, 227, 232–37, 239–41, 263, 266; Trinity 63, 64, 77, 78, 80, 101–10, 235n. *See also* Demiurge

pseudo-Grosseteste: *Summa philosophiae* 269

Gundissalinus: biography 9–19; medieval reception 268–70; psychology 37–47, 177–89; theory of knowledge 47–54; translating activity 15–19; uncertain authorship 20–29; variants of the name 9, 10

Häring, Nikolaus 11, 12

Hasse, Dag Nikolaus 18n, 267

Hermann of Carinthia 4, 12, 70, 77, 93, 128–43, 189, 190, 197, 207, 228n, 265

Hermetic tradition 4. *See also* alchemy

Hugh of Santalla 4

Hugh of St Victor: *De sacramentis* 13, 110–16, 118, 121, 122, 124, 127

Hugonnard-Roche, Henri 47, 49

Hunt, Richard 12

hylomorphism, universal hylomorphism 19, 22, 31, 36, 39, 50, 55, 60n, 66, 83, 94, 98, 100, 122, 127, 136, 145n, 147, 149, 154, 162, 167, 177, 182, 184, 190, 205, 230, 232n, 237, 239n, 240, 243, 244, 249, 261, 262, 265, 267; analytical

reading of 146, 153, 154, 155, 183, 187, 189, 193, 197, 208; compositional reading of 146, 152, 153, 154, 155, 162, 183, 189, 193, 196, 197, 208, 238; functional reading of 146, 155, 189, 195, 197, 198, 205, 206, 208, 242; matter and form as composing elements 146, 152, 153, 154, 155, 194, 197, 198, 263, 264, 266; matter and form as functional aspects 155, 194, 198, 248, 266; reciprocal functionality of matter and form 147, 155, 186. *See also* form; matter

hypostases 34, 70, 146, 147, 149, 153, 158, 159, 161, 163, 175–77, 180–86, 189, 194, 205, 208

Ibn Daud, Abraham 7, 15–17, 27, 87n, 142, 157, 210, 225–32, 239, 240, 243, 244, 253–62, 266; *Physics* (colophon) 226n

Ibn Gabirol, Solomon 18, 21, 30, 38, 39, 41, 42, 55, 63, 70, 77, 79, 94, 95n, 106, 107n, 109, 110, 124, 127, 128, 135, 136, 143, 144–209, 226, 230, 231, 232n, 238, 239, 240, 242–44, 249, 253, 254–59, 261, 262, 265, 266; cosmology 161–65; Ibn Daud's criticism of 253–59; interpretative problems 144–47; metaphysics 147–61; voluntarism 157, 158. *See also* hylomorphism

Ibn Tumart 5

Ikhwan as-Safa (Brethren of Purity) 18n, 48

Ingarao, Alessandra 23, 24

Isaac Israeli 8, 18n, 48

Isidore of Seville 48, 87

James of Venice 3

Jean de la Rochelle 24

Johannes Hispanus (John of Spain) ix, 15, 17, 25, 26, 144, 145, 210n; *Liber alchorismi de pratica arismetice* 26

Index | 317

John Blund 267
John of Castelmoron, John II (bishop of Segovia and archbishop of Toledo) ix, 15–17
John of Seville (Johannes Hispalensis atque Limiensis) 4
Jolivet, Jean 29, 47

Lammer, Andreas 247, 248
Liber mahamelet 24–27
light 34, 35, 42, 46, 73, 90, 106, 109, 113, 150, 163, 170–74, 192n, 204
Lizzini, Olga 220n, 222n
Loewenthal, Abraham 22

Macrobius: *Commentarius in somnium Scipionis* 1, 88
Maimonides ix, 5, 18
Martianus Capella: *De nuptiis Philologiae et Mercurii* 1, 88
Masnovo, Antonio 22, 23
mathematics 8, 24, 25, 26, 27, 28, 49, 52, 57, 58, 78, 101, 106, 131, 211; numerological series 63, 75, 105, 203n, 207n
matter: corpulence of 34, 163, 170–73; creation of 64, 65, 73–75, 98, 104, 107–9, 160; dependence on form 32, 33, 66–68, 81, 83, 93, 94, 223–24, 129, 130, 136, 137, 147n, 149–55, 165, 192, 193, 194, 198, 199, 202, 222–25, 229, 230, 252, 257, 263; dependence on unity 31–33, 201, 203, 204; eternity of 63, 69, 70, 160, 197; multiplication of 167; as principle of alterity 65, 105, 201; universal hylomorphism: *see* hylomorphism. *See also* form; unity
Mauritius Hispanus 270
Menéndez y Pelayo, Marcelino 54n
metaphysics (discipline) 29, 49–52, 54, 55, 57–59, 87, 110, 148n, 165, 167, 197, 210, 211, 218, 220n, 225, 226n, 239n, 261, 264, 265, 266, 270, 271; metaphysical procedure (epistemic

strategy) 52, 56, 59, 60n, 61, 64, 76, 233
modal ontology (necessary/possible existence) 61–64, 66, 69, 135, 209, 212–18, 220, 221, 224, 228–44, 261, 263, 264, 266
Morienus Latinus: *Liber de compositione alchemiae* 4n
movement 37, 44, 49, 53, 54, 59, 60, 61, 71, 72, 85, 91, 117, 125, 129, 132, 133, 142n, 155, 168, 211n, 216, 217, 219n, 222, 229, 231, 238, 264

natural philosophy (discipline) 27, 49, 52, 53, 54, 57, 58, 59, 72n, 78, 110, 210, 211n, 251, 265, 269, 271
natural science: *see* natural philosophy
Nemesius: *De natura hominis* 103
Nicholas of Cusa 101, 267

Ovid: *Metamorphoses* 118, 119, 121, 128

Panti, Cecilia 228n
Perler, Dominik 147n
Pessin, Sarah 144, 145, 155n
Peter Lombard: *Sentences* 13, 112–15, 122, 124, 127, 181, 182
Peter of Corbeil 269
Petrus Helias 12
physics (discipline): *see* natural philosophy
Plato 1, 38, 64, 80, 83, 88, 92, 93, 95, 103, 110, 112, 113, 115, 125, 128, 130, 191, 228, 271; *Timaeus* 1, 88–92, 95, 100, 103, 110, 113, 116, 124, 128, 130, 136
Plato of Tivoli 4
Poirel, Dominique 116
Porphyry 186, 187, 189, 205; tree of 25, 74, 94, 133n, 137–39, 178, 184, 186, 205, 206, 249; *Isagoge* 78, 86, 184, 259
potency: *see* being: potential
psychology (discipline) 29, 39, 47, 208, 210, 261

318 | *Index*

Ptolemy: *Almagest* 8

Qusta Ibn Luqa: *De differentia spiritus et animae* 4, 38

Reed Gold, Rosie 154n
Richard de Fournival 23, 24
Rivera Recio, Juan Francisco 15
Robert of Chester 4, 26
Robert of Ketton 4
Robert of Melun 24
Rose, Valentin 8

Sa'id Andalusi 6
Sesiano, Jacques 26
Shem Tob Ibn Falaquera 144
soul: angelic creation of 41, 42, 179–84; definitions of 38; faculties of 43–47; immortality of 21–23, 37, 43; psychological hylomorphism 37–43, 177–89
species 33, 39, 44, 46, 51, 53, 54, 70, 71, 73, 74, 75n, 86, 94, 113, 129, 131n, 132, 133, 138, 141, 146, 149–51, 153–55, 163, 169, 172, 173, 183–89, 193, 196, 198, 200, 204, 206, 208, 220n, 222, 234, 237, 239, 247, 249–51, 264
Szilágyi, Krizstina 226

Teske, Roland 23
Themistius: *Paraphrase of Aristotle's De anima* 47n
Theodosius 8
Thierry of Chartres 11, 12, 13, 48, 77, 99–103, 105, 106, 107, 109, 115, 190n,
265; *Commentum super Boethii librum de Trinitate* 99; *Glosa super Boethii librum* 115; *Tractatus de sex dierum operibus* 106
Thomas Aquinas 30, 74, 267
Thomas of York: *Sapientiale* 268
traducianism 42, 43. *See also* soul
translations 1–19, 144–47, 210, 211n, 225, 266, 269–71; Arabic-into-Latin 1–9, 14–19; Greek-into-Latin 2, 3; translation movement 4, 26

unity: compositional 31, 68, 69, 149, 150, 154, 177, 189, 194, 249; form of 32, 68, 72, 73, 74, 83, 85, 107, 159, 161, 166–72, 183, 200, 201, 203, 205, 206, 249, 252; function of 159, 160, 166, 206, 252, 253, 263; metaphysical 31, 100, 159, 165, 177, 200, 236; thirdness of compositional unity 149, 154, 189, 194, 249

Van Winden, Jacob 94
Vlasschaert, Anne-Marie 24, 25

William of Auvergne 22–24
William of Conches 11, 12, 13, 48, 72n, 77, 100, 103, 104, 105, 110, 115–19, 122, 125, 126, 127, 128, 130n, 265; *Dragmaticon philosophiae* 115, 118, 119; *Glosae super Boetium* 103, 104, 115; *Glosae super Platonem* 103, 104, 115, 125, 128; *Philosophia mundi* 103
William of Saint Thierry 104, 105